FAIRS AND FESTIVALS OF INDIA

FAIRS AND FESTIVALS OF INDIA

(In 6 Volumes)

(Vol. 1)

(Major Festivals of India)

by
DR. KRISHAN GOPAL

Edited by
M.P. BEZBARUAH

Photographs
Phal S. Girota

GYAN

GYAN PUBLISHING HOUSE
New Delhi - 110002

Fairs and Festivals of India
(Culture, Religion, Sociology)

Rs. 15000

ISBN: 81-212-0589-1 (Set)
ISBN: 81-212-0814-9 (Vol. 1)

Published in 2010 in India by
Gyan Publishing House
23, Main Ansari Road, Darya Ganj
New Delhi - 110002
Phones : 23282060, 23261060
Fax : 91-11- 23285914
e-mail : books@gyanbooks.com
gyanbook@vsnl.com
website : gyanbooks.com

Laser Typesetting: Graphic Print, Delhi
Printed at :Young Art Press, Delhi

Contents

Preface 9
Acknowledgements 11
Introduction 17
Major Festivals of India 37
Hindu Festivals 39
Sindhi Festivals 99
Nav-Buddhists Festivals 105
Jain Festivals 107
Muslim Festivals 117
Christian Festivals 131
Parsi (Zoroastrian) Festivals 139
Jewish Festivals 147
National Festivals 155
Alphabetical Index of Fairs and Festivals Vols. 1 to 6 159

List of Colour Photographs

Celebration of Diwali with fire Crackers.

Played with colorful abandon, Holi is a day of revelry, gaiety and reconciliation.

Dussehra celebrates the victory of good over evil as depicted by the battle between Lord Rama and King Ravana of Lanka. During ten days celebration of events of the battle are re-enacted culminating of the final day with the burning the effigies of Ravana, Kumbhakaran and Meghnad.

Bejeweled idol of Durga during Durga Puja Celebration.

Status of Ganesh are immersed in water Ganesh Chaturthi Celebration.

Baisakhi Celebration at Harminder Saheb, Golden Temple, Amritsar, Punjab.

The religious Procession is of ritual significance to the Sikhs on Gurpurb.

The festival of Id brings out all Muslims participating in feasting, visiting merry-making and embracing one another Id Milan.

Thousands of devotees Pray *Namaj* in Unison at Jama Masjid in Delhi during Id.

Mahavira, the last and the most significant Tirthankara of the Jains, Mahavira Jayanti.

Hundreds of thousands of devotees make the arduous climb to Jain temple at Palitana, Gujarat.

Santa Claus with children, Christmas.

Christmas celebrations take on a distinctly Indian flavour in mood, dress and food.

Parsi celebrate New Year Days, Novroj.

Republic Day celebration at Rajpath, New Delhi.

Preface

India is being a huge sub-continent is well-known for its charm and beauty having deep roots in its diversity. Culturally, the Indian nation's, contribution is fairly rich not only in Asia, but all over the world.

This vast nation is known for its pompous and most colourful festivals and in this regard our national calendar is heavily dotted with numerous fairs and festivals. It depicts our societal progress and prosperity in several ways.

Virtually, each city, town and village celebrates its fair with much pomp and show in which men, women, young boys and girls participate in large numbers. Being a social gathering, normally and annual feature, the people are clad in colourful costumes and their festivities mark a remarkable phenomenon. It thus depicts a 'colourful and wonderful world' in several regions of the Indian sub-continent, from North to South, West to East, North-Eastern region and Central India. The set, consisting of five comprehensive volumes, covers all the twenty-eight states and seven Union Territories.

The first volume covers the origin and history of fairs and festivals, their observance and impact on social and culture life of peoples, and major festivals of India, which have been classified under the various religious grouping namely Hindu Festivals. It also includes an alphabetical index of all the fairs and festivals enlisted in all the five volumes, indicating the volumes number and page. Sikh Festivals, Nav-Buddhist Festivals, Jain Festivals, Muslim Festivals, Christian Festivals and National Festivals.

The second volume covers several fairs and festivals of Andhra Pradesh, arranged alphabetically and followed in the same pattern by Karnataka indeed an effort has been made to take up details of numerous fairs and festivals of this region. Their complete identity with our religion makes us feel for national unity and integrity. This fact greatly strengthens the bonds of oneness and generates the spirit of spontaneous support to each other.

The third volume depicts the history and celebration of fairs and festivals in the Christian-dominated state of Kerala, Andaman and Nicobar Islands and Lakshadweep Islands. Several Hindu festivals are celebrated with much fervour. It is followed by Tamil Nadu and Pondicherry. Again the pattern of alphabetical order has been followed and the element of comprehensiveness have been maintained.

The fourth volume has a fairly large spectrum covering several states of North India. Mostly dominated by Hindu community, even minority communities; fairs and festivals have been meticulously taken up. The states covered in this volume are Himachal Pradesh, Haryana, Jammu and Kashmir, Punjab, Rajasthan, Uttar Pradesh, Uttaranchal, Chandigarh and Delhi. Their celebrations clearly depict the ardent faith of the people in numerous gods, saints, fakirs, temples, mosques, gurdwaras, dargahs and churches. The celebrations have deep involvement of millions of people.

The fifth volume depicts in a comprehensive way about the description of fairs and festivals in the western regions of India, including Gujarat and Maharashtra, Madhya Pradesh, Chhattisgarh, and the Union Territories, well-weaved into small and big festivals and fairs, the major states of Gujarat and Maharashtra give us details well-arranged alphabetically, Besides the regions of western coast including Goa, Dadra and Nagar Haveli, Daman and Diu, all Union Territories, Mostly inhabited by Christian communities as well as Hindus, Muslims, Parsis and Tribals have been comprehensively dealt with indeed the micro study of this region has afforded an academic colour to the whole write up. Undoubtedly these fairs and festivals attract a large gathering from the neighbouring villages and town. This crowd is from a few thousands to a few lakhs, depending upon the significance of the celebration. Men, women and children are seen in their joyful mood with several kinds of decorations of new clothes and costumes. The large scale of shopping centres do attract the customers on a account of the easy, neat and clean availability of eatables. Joy rides and numerous kind of other material dance, drama and music are the common features which the villages like very much and participate in various functions. It appears quite a joyful and hilarious scene, which normally consists of a day or a few days.

The sixth volume has main thrust on East and North-East of the Indian Sub-continent. An effort has been made to cover up numerous major and other small fairs and festivals along with their history, social and religious fervour in their celebration by 8 millions of people. It has been felt that each and every community gives much importance to its fair and festival and participates in it with much pomp and show. Mostly these are annual features and may last for a day or a few days. The states covered in this volume are Assam, Orissa, West Bengal, Bihar, Arunachal Pradesh, Jharkhand, Manipur, Meghalaya, Mizoram, Nagaland, Sikkim and Tripura.

Undoubtedly these five volumes contain numerous facts and figures which have deep bearing on socio-economic, cultural and educational life of the people. Indeed such an attempt in a comprehensive way has never been taken up by any scholar earlier. The academic value of these volumes is greatly enhanced with the meticulous inclusion of significant details of numerous fairs and festivals where the attendance is spontaneous and out of love, respect and unique honour for the deity or the god or goddess. This kind of majestic and religious atmosphere generates a new spirit of unity and national integration between high and low and enhances and spirit of brotherhood. Indeed the social aspect is strengthened and it definitely gives a new twist to the emergence of the future generation. In other words, such a social style enhances the prestige of the society. Therefore, its usefulness is enhanced for social scientists, religious institutes, teachers, research scholars and students in India and abroad.

Krishan Gopal

M.P. Bezbaruah

Acknowledgements

For the compilation of these comprehensive six volumes of Fair and Festivals of India. I have used the relevant material from several institutions of higher learning which have afforded me their academic support during my researches. I feel much beholden to them. I feel much indebted to them as the facts and figures gathered from the writings of eminent authors enabled me to fill up several gaps in these volumes. Besides, I have taken advantage of the material from the printed sources of eminent authors and institutions. Notable among those are listed below:

Abbott J. *Indian ritual and belief: The keys of power*, New Delhi: Manohar Publishers and Distributors, 2000, 560 p.

Anderson, Leona M. *Vasantotsava: The Spring Festivals of India: Texts and Traditions*, New Delhi: D.K. Printworld, 1993, 254 p.

Anderson, Mary M. *Festivals of Nepal*, London: George Allen & Unwin, 1971, 288 p.

Bahadur, Om Lata. *The book of Hindu Festivals and Ceremonies*, New Delhi, UBS Publishers Distributors, 1996. 177 p.

Barua, Benu Prasad, Buddhist Festivals and rituals, *Man in India*, 79 (1-2), 1999 (Jan.-June): 77-87.

Behuria, Ashok K. Unfolding culture of introlerance: A tale of two festivals, *Journal of Peace Studies*, 8(1), 2001 (Jan.-Feb.): 55-62.

Bentley, A. *Fairs and Festivals in Bengal*, Calcutta: The Bengal Secretariat Book Depot, 1921, 79 p.

Bhattacharya, N. N., *Ancient Indian Rituals and their Social Contents*, New Delhi: Manohar Publications, 1996, 305 p.

Bindley, A. H. *Sikhs: Their Origin, History, Religion, Customs, Fairs and Festivals*. New Delhi: Sumit, 1984, 152 p.

Buck, C.H. *Faiths, Fairs and Festivals of India*, Calcutta: Thacker, Spink, 1917, ix, 262 p.

Cannadiane, David, (Ed.) *Rituals of Royalty: Power and Ceremonial in Traditional Societies*. Cambridge: Cambridge University Press, 1987, 351 p.

Census of India, 1961, Vol. 7, *Fairs and Festivals*, Delhi: Manager of Publications.

Chatterjee, Chanchal Kumar, *Studies in the Rites and Rituals of Hindu Marriage in Ancient India*, Calcutta: Sanskrit Pustak, 1978, 372 p.

Chaudhuri, Buddhadb, (Ed.), *Religion, Rituals and Festivals*, New Delhi: Inter-India Publications, 1992, 262 p.

David, Robin, *Fairs and Festivals of Indian Tribes*, New Delhi, Discovery Publishing House, 2003, 233 p.

Deep, Dhruba K. *Nepal Festivals: With Some Articles Enquiring into Nepalese Arts, Religion and Culture*, 2nd ed, Kathmandu: Ratan Pustak, 1982, 128 p.

Festivals of India, Delhi: Pub. Division, Minister of Information and Broadcasting, India, 1960.

Fuller; C. J., Vinayaka Chaturthi, Festival and Hindutva in Tamil Nadu, *Economic and Political Weekly*, 36(19), 2001 (12-18 May): 1607-16.

Gonda, J. *Vedic ritural: the non-solemn rithes*, Leiden: E.J. Brill, 1980, xiv, 516 p.

Gupta, Shakti M., *Festivals, Fairs and Fasts of India*, Delhi, Clarion Books, 1991, 228 p.

Guss, David M., *The Festive State: race, ethnicity, and nationalism as cultural performance*. Berkeley: University of California Press, 2001., 239 p.

Hanchett, Suzanne, *Coloured rice: symbolic structure in Hindu family festivals* with contributions by Stanley Regelson. Delhi : Hindustan Pub. Corp., 1988. 335 p.

India Perspectives. Published by External Publicity Division, Ministry of External Affairs. Govt. of India, New Delhi.

Indrama: The Magazine of India, Published by Sita World Travel (India), Ltd.

Janaki S.S., Shiva temple and temple rituals, Madras: Kuppuswami Sastri Research Institute, 1988, 208 p.

Jetwings, Published by Jet Airways, Bombay.

Kani, Takhe, (Comp). Agricultural festivals of Arunachal Pradesh/ compiled by Takhe Kani—Ittanagar: IPACL, 1995. 128 p.

Karmarkar, A.P. *The religions of India*, Lonavala: Mira Publishing House, 1950, 327 p.

Lee, Kwangsu *Buddhist ideas and rituals in early India and Korea*, New Delhi : Manohar Publishers & Distributors, 1998. 196 p.

Maity P.K. *Human fertility cults and rituals of Bengal: a comparative study*, New Delhi: Abhinav Publications, 1989. 216 p.

Marglin, Fredirique Apffel. *Wives of the God-king: The rituals of the devadasis of Puri*, Delhi: Oxford University Press, 1989, 388 p.

Mathewson, Kent Cultural landscapes and ecologya Foraging/farming, food, festivities. *Progress in Human Geography*, 24(3), 2000 (Sep.): 457-74.

Niyogi, Tushar K. Sacred bath ceremony and myth-ritual complex at Gangasagar *Journal of the Anthropological Survey of India*, 47(1), 1998 (Mar.): 25-47.

Oki, Morihiro. *India: Fairs and festivals*, New Delhi: Bookwise, 1989. 160 p.

Oman, John Campbell. *The Brahmans, theists and Muslims of India: studies of Goddess-worship in Bengal, caste, Brahmaisma and social reforms, with descriptive sketched of curious festivals, ceremonies, and faquirs* 2nd ed., Delhi: Heritage Publishers, 1973. 341 p.

Oster, Akos. The play of the Gods: locality, ideology, structure, and time in the festivals of a Bengali town, Chicago: University of Chicago Press, 1980. 241 p.

Pandit, M. Amin. *Festivals of Kashmir, Srinagar*. Gulsan Publishers, 1997. 116 p.

Parratt, Saroj Nalini, *The religion of Manipur: Beliefs, rituals and historical develoment*, Calcutta: Firma KLM, 1980, 218 p.

Patnaik, Dhirendranath *Festivals of Orissa*, Bhubaneshwar, Orissa Sahitya Academi, 1982, 80 p.

Pathak, Avijit. Durga puja as mass cultural consumption: Changing character of religious festivals, *Mainstream*, 36(49), Nov. 28, 1998: 11

Ram Gopal, *India Vedic Kalpasutras*, Delhi: National Publishing House, 1959, 504 p.

Richardson, Hugh, *Ceremonies of the Lhasa Year*. London : Serindia Publications, 1993. 133 p.

Sanon, Arun. *Festive India*. New Delhi, Frank Bros. 1987, 125 p.

Saraswati, Baidyanath *Brahmanic ritual traditions in the crucible of time*, Simla: Indian Institute of Advanced Study, 1977. 299 p.

Sarkar, Benoy Kumar. The folk-element in Hindu culture : a contribution to socio-religious studies in Hindu folk-institutions, New Delhi, Orient Books Reprint Corporation, 1972. 312 p.

Sharma, T.R. *Studies in the sectarian Upanisads: metaphysics, ethics and rituals*, Varanasi: Indological Book House, 1972. 184 p.

Shastri, Dakshina Ranjan. *Origin and development of the rituals of ancestor worship in India*. Calcutta: Bookland., 1963. 399 p.

Shastri, Dakshina Ranjan, Origin Development of the rituals of ancestor worship in India, Calcutta: Bookland, 1963, 399 p.

Singh, K.S. (Ed.), *Peoples of India: Series*. Anthropological Society of India: Gazeteers of India, Delhi, Manager of Publications.

Singh, S.B., *Fairs and festivals in rural India*: A geospatial study of belief systems. Varanasi: Tara Book Agency 1989. 142 p.

Sivananda (Swami), *All about Hinduism*, Rishikesh: Sivananda Publication League, 1947. 270 p.

Smith, Brian K. *Reflection on resemblance, ritual, and religion*, New York: Oxford University Press, 1989. 265 p.

Swagat, Published by Indian Airlines, New Delhi.

Tarlekar, G.H., *Vedic music and its application in rituals*, Delhi : Dharam Hinduja International Centre of India Research, 1995, 71 p.

Thomas, P., *Epics, myths and legends of India: A comprehensive survey of the sacred lore of the Hindus, Buddhists and Jains*, Bombay: D.B. Taraporevala Sons & Co., 1973.

Thomas, P., *Festivals and holidays of India*. Bombay: D. B. Taraporevala, 1971. 155 p.

Wilkins, W.J., *Modern Hindusim : An account of the religion and life of the Hindus in Northern India* —2nd ed., Calcutta : Rupa and Co., 1975. 423 p.

Williams, Monier, *Religious thought and life in India: Vedism, Brahminism and Hinduism*. New Delhi: Oriental Books Reprint Corporation, 1974, 520 p.

INTRODUCTION

FESTIVALS

Festival is a day or time of religious or other celebration, marked by feasting, ceremonies or other observances-means a periodic commemoration or celebration.[1] It is a day or season for rejoicing or merry-making, public celebration, or series of performances of music, ballet, drama etc. given periodically.[2] Festivals are intended to promote a flourishing of nature, and fertility in humans beings. Their desire to share his pleasures with his fellow beings by rejoicing in common is at the root of all festivals, either primitive or modern, religious or secular, social or political. The origin of all festivals in the world has been primarily social. For the primitive man it supplied an occasion for expressing his joy at the occurrence of some event which he thought was unusual and for which he desired to share his pleasure with his fellowmen. This might be some striking phenomenon of nature, movement of the sun, the moon and the earth, change of seasons as at the time of winter and summer solstices, the advent of spring, the coming of rains, reaping of bumper harvest or a sense of fear, awe or amazement at the activity of nature. These were events which came to be celebrated as festivals. The mode of and occasions for celebration, however, changed with the progress of civilisation and transition from primitive to agricultural economy. Celebrations which had their origin in the veneration of supernatural powers came to be replaced in course of time by seasonal festivities. The two harvest festivals or summer and winter solstices continue today even in the West as remnants of agricultural civilisation, wherein the primitive participation by a social group is replaced by a celebration in which the entire community joins. The forms of ritual and observance also undergo changes in conformity with the civilisation and culture of society. Primitive forms of celebration give way to revelry and merriment when the usual social restrictions disappear and pleasure is indulged in for the sake of pleasure. The collective or mass celebration takes a different turn. Pomp and pageantry take the place of ritualistic observances which degenerate into license and liberty, the State and the religion intervening every now and then to introduce austerity and restrictions of a social and moral character. Thus, "the extreme license and orgiastic character of festivals directly derived from primitive ritual were from an early date subjected to moderating regulations on the part of religious and political authorities. The drunkenness and disorder which characterised the Jewish harvest festival of *chag hasuccoth*, the Feast of Tabernacles, called forth ....the individual in regulated expressions of sentiments which he may not always truly share."[3]

While the primitive festivals derive their origin in collective rituals primarily designed as magical operations to influence supernatural agencies, the vestiges of these rituals still continue even in some of the festivals, which are purely religious as seen from the observance of fast, abstinence and penance on certain specified days. As time went by, the festivals got simplified with the added element of pleasure and rejoicing and occasions for manifestation of joy and merriment with which they became later associated. Thus "festivals originally intended to promote the activity of nature by sympathetic exertion on the part of the participants have tended to be valued for their own sakes as dances, athletic contests and sports. The vestments, disguises and ritual symbols, which at first possessed a functional magical significance, have given rise to pomp, decoration, ceremonial and display that are enjoyed on their own account."[4] Festivals symbolise people's cultural, social and religious aspirations which, besides helping them to lead a fuller and better life, also remove its monotony by providing physical diversion and mental recreation.

Festivals in India

India is known for the diversity and colour of her festivals, whether religious, seasonal or secular. Practically every religion in the world is professed and practised in Indian sub-continent. Having a variegated landscape, yet India is a single country, and the fairs and festivals being unit to the variety of her traditions. There may be different ways of celebrating these festivals, but the basic form of the festivity or the belief behind their origin and traditions are the same. Though festivals of all religions are celebrated in India, it is Hindu festivals that dominate since the majority of the people are Hindus.

Festivals in India are quite unique in their import and observance and have a much deeper significance. Festivals are those special days, periods of time and seasons which are so designed as to ensure individual happiness by practising religion commingled with social joy and domestic happiness. All festivals, to which fairs are not infrequently attached, are mostly religious in their origin, and primarily aim at acquiring spiritual bliss, heavenly merit, and self-realisation as the ultimate goal of existence by being in tune with the Infinite. Most of the festivals are associated with fasting and practice of penance and austerity which help keeping body and mind pure and free from attachment to worldly objects, by putting the individual in a proper frame of mind to look within himself for self-introspection. It is, therefore, but natural that the festivals which have placed before the people such a noble objective, should have evolved a mode of observance all its own. Hindu festivals have thus become a way of life—plain living and high thinking, designed to promote physical well-being, mental peace and spiritual elevation. This ideal the people were enabled to translate into action through the medium of various fairs and festivals celebrated during the year. Though they marked occasions for joy and rejoicing, it was not the earthly joy alone in which people revelled. They rejoiced in the glory of God by observing fast, practising penance and austerity, reading holy scriptures, visiting temples and participating in the rituals and ceremonies organised on these occasions. It was this way of life which the Hindu festivals have preached and the people have practised throughout the ages. The festivals thus became a mode of living which helped people rise higher in the moral and spiritual scale. They laid down definite standards of conduct and propriety. Their practice had no element of compulsion but a universal appeal, because of their innate simplicity and nobility of purpose. The various directives commanded spontaneous observance as people sincerely believed that they were a means to attain happiness not only in this but also in the world to come. The institution of fairs and festivals enjoining as it did self-discipline and austerity also provided innocent joy and pleasures which made life happy and worth living and facilitated the onward march of the individual and society towards a nobler and fuller existence. The mass gathering at the temple, where some *mahapuja* or special religious rituals were performed, inculcated a sense of fellow-feeling, unity and brotherhood, and the ceremonies performed with some pomp and display provided the people with necessary element of joy and exultation. Festivals in India are thus days of special significance, different from ordinary days, designed to serve a specific purpose. They help preserve certain aspects of the country's civilization and culture, promote social unity and mutual cooperation. Fairs and festivals thus became the embodiment of the cultural unity of the Indian people throughout the length and breadth of the country, a token of their oneness, inspired by the same ideals and objectives of life. Though living in different parts and speaking different languages, there was this thread of fundamental unity which pervaded the life of the people actuated by community of ideals and aspirations.

Indian festivals thus have a universal appeal, a common purpose and a special meaning. To an Indian, wherever he is, be it in the north, south, east or west, festivals are days of special significance different from ordinary ones, designed to serve a special purpose. While preserving certain aspects

Bejeweled Idol of Durga during **Durga Puja** celebration.

Statues of Ganesh are immersed in water **Ganesh Chaturthi** celebration

Baisakhi celebration at Harimander Saheb, Golden Temple, Amritsar, Punjab.

The religious procession is of ritual significance to the Sikhs on **Gurupurb**.

Celebration of **Diwali** with fire Crackers.

Played with colourful abandon, **Holi** is a day of revelry, gaiety and reconciliation.

Dussehra celebrates the victory of good over evil as depicted by the battle between Lord Rama and King Ravana of Lanka. During ten days celebration of events of the battle are re-enacted culminating of the final day with the burning the effigies of Ravana, Kumbhkaran and Meghnad.

Santa Claus with children, **Christmas**.

Christmas celebration take on a distinctly Indian flavour in mood, dress and food.

Parsi celebration New Year Days, **Novroj**.

Republic Day celebration at Rajpath, New Delhi.

The festival of **Id** brings out all Muslims participating in feasting, visiting, merry-making and embracing one another **Id** milan.

Thousands of devotees pray ***Namaj*** in Unision at Jama Mashid in Delhi during **Id**.

Mahavira, the last and the most significant Tirthankara of the Jains, **Mahavira Jayanti**.

Hundreds of thousands of devotees make the arduous climb to **Jain Temple** at Palitana, Gujarat

of his civilisation and culture, they promoted social unity, fellow-feeling, mutual help and cooperation, and provided withal innocent means of enjoyment and recreation, at the same time emphasising the moral and spiritual values of human existence, by self-discipline and austerity. There is a fundamental difference in the observance of festivals in India and other countries where festivals generally mean feasting. Not so in India, where the nature of festivals being essentially religious, they mean fasts first and festivity afterwards. For, it is the common belief of the people that fasting and practice of austerity and penance, coupled with specified religious observances and visit to the temple or some sacred site, help bring about in a person the necessary mental frame required for self-introspection. As will be seen later, the mode of celebration was so designed as to lay down certain standards of conduct and propriety, which were spontaneously practised by every individual. This spirit of celebration pervaded the entire length and breadth of the country. Small wonder, therefore, that most of the festivals celebrated in India are common to all parts of the country and sections of society. Makara Sankranti, Holi or Spring Festival, Navratri or Durga Puja, Divali and New Year are all celebrated in every home in the same spirit, in the same manner, on the same day and with the same joy and rejoicing. Festivals are thus the embodiment of the cultural and religious unity of the Indian people, a symbol of their oneness, inspired by the same ideals and objectives of life. Though living in different climates and different regions and speaking different languages, there is this fundamental unity—unity of ideals, community of aims and aspirations, which runs through the life of the people of this land. Festivals thus become occasions for joint action for a common objective, which at times combines physical activity with emotional excitement and spiritual exultation.

Festivals and their Social Character

Festivals are usually associated with seasons, phases of the moon, movement of planets and constellations, agricultural operations or harvest seasons, birth of great men—deemed incarnations of God, prophets or saviours of humanity, anniversaries of eras current in a region, i.e., new years, etc. Festivals are observed also in honour of the dead. There are certain festivals, however, which are prescribed by religion, enjoined by society and ordained by the individual himself. These are social occasions like marriage, sacred thread ceremony, birth of a child and religious observances such as Satyanarayan Puja and certain *yajnas* or sacrifices like Gayatri Purashcharan, Navchandi, Shatachandi, Maharudra, Vishnuyag, and others performed to earn religious merit and at times to ensure world peace. In modern days, some new festivals like the Independence Day and the Republic Day are also coming into being. There are many others as well, organised either by the State or by some public bodies, such as cultural festival, Youth Festivals Music Festivals, Ras and Garba Festival, Van Mahotsav, Natya Mahotsav, Sports Games, etc., and a host of others such as Book Fairs, Anand Mela, etc., which have enlisted scant enthusiasm on the part of the people at large and participation by only a few officially concerned with the celebrations.

When festivals changed their social character and came under the influence of religion, fast or miss a meal or avoidance of a particular item of food became an invariable concomitant of their observance and celebration all the world over. The *ekadashi* and other fasts of the Hindus, the *Paryushana* of the Jains, the *rozas* of the Muslims and the avoidance of meat during certain periods and fasting on specified days advised by Christianity and Zoroastrianism all fulfil the same purpose of purifying the mind by curbing the senses of the flesh. Fast and practice of penance and austerity are such as only a few can practice, and a fewer still can observe with proper understanding and consistency. Bearing this psychological aspect in mind, the festivals in India had from the very start been so moulded by the great thinkers of this country that they came to be recognised as an essential part of human existence. What were originally social in character became in course of time essentially religious in practice. Fundamental principles of health and hygiene were so tactfully interwoven under the guise of religion that the people automatically practised them and derived the benefits accruing from them. Even the cereals, other grains and fruits, while emphasising their importance as the agricultural produce raised during the period when they are prescribed to be taken, also denote their intimate connection with the health of the individual. *Til* is advised to be taken on Makara Sankranti day during winter when taking of oily substances is good for body-building; parched gram and *jowar* taken at the time of the Holi festival are equally essential at the junction of two seasons; use of juice of *nim* leaves on Gudi Padva is likewise helpful in keeping fever away; and rice with milk taken at the time of Sharad Purnima kept in the open moonlight are popularly credited with the properties of curing many a disease to which an individual is prone particularly during autumn. Taking of *jambu* fruits and sprouted pulses, which contain vitamin B, is also health-giving. All such practices which ostentatiously have some religious significance are in effect instrumental in preserving health and keeping up bodily vigour. The faith of the people in these practices declined as education spread and people began to think for themselves. Instead of missing a meal or fasting, sweets, fruits and certain items of non-cereal diet heavier and richer than normal food were substituted for fasting. People ate more on these days than on the ordinary ones. It was because of this unhealthy tendency on the part of the people in the observance of fast that Gandhiji stressed that the purificatory fast advised by him should be a complete fast for 24 hours commencing from the previous evening and lasting till the next when nothing except water should be taken.

Types of Festivals

All traditional or conventional festivals can be divided into two broad categories, viz., (i) purely religious and (ii) socio-religious, to which a third category can now be added in the form of national festivals. Its further classification according to occasion or event would be :

(a) Seasonal

(b) Birth anniversary of incarnations of God, prophets, masters, religious preceptors, etc.

(c) Events or objects of religious significance

(i) Religious occasions

(ii) Propitiation of some deity or element of nature

(iii) Practice of penance and austerity and performance of *yajnas* (a) to earn religion merit or (b) to achieve a cherished desire

(d) Commencement of different eras

(e) National festivals

(f) Domestic festivals and social events

(g) Miscellaneous

(a) *Seasonal Festivals.* Among the various festivals celebrated in India, the most ancient are those associated with seasons. The appearance of certain phenomena of nature has had special significance for man since time immemorial. The two solstices or the crossing of the sun into the constellation of Makara and Karka represent two outstanding natural events or astronomical phenomena called *Uttarayana* and *Dakshinayana* marking two distinct periods of the year—each of six months having distinct physical characteristics. *Uttarayana* is the period of longer days and shorter nights, the victory of light over darkness, when everything assumes a new shape and a new look. It was in anticipation of this period of *Uttarayana* that Bhishma put off his death while lying on the bed of arrows. Every object, animate or inanimate, creates its own atmosphere and exercises its influence on its surroundings. Seasons have their own individuality and imperceptible impact on all living beings. Morn, noon, even tide and night each creates its own atmosphere and radiates an influence all its own. The variation in seasons, winter, summer and monsoon is marked by a corresponding change in the spirit and behaviour of the individual. Most of the festivals associated with rejoicing and merrymaking take place in the fair weather, when the days are long and bright. Festivals like Makara Sankranti, Vasant Panchami, Holi, Dolotsav, Navratri, Divali, etc. are celebrated during such periods. The period of *Dakshinayana*, monsoon in particular, is generally avoided as it means rains, shorter days and dull and cloudy weather all of which are the antithesis of festive mood and favour austerity, fasting and penance. This also is the period when free movement from one place to another is not possible, more so in days when modern means of transport and communications were unknown. It is during this period that sages, saints and others belonging to the holy order have been ordained to observe *chaturmas* and confine themselves to one place, preaching and practising a life of intense devotion and austerity. A number of days is earmarked for fasting, and there were many who took only one meal during the entire period of *chaturmas*. These were practices introduced with a view to promote health and hygiene in the rainy season, when much outside activity is not possible and the digestive power is normally at a low ebb. It was for this reason also that all personal or domestic festivals and social functions like marriage, etc., were prohibited during this period, while religious observances such as Gauri Vrata, Kajali, Vat-Savitri Vrata, Ekadashi, Bol Choth, Rishi panchami, Paryushana were propularised and practised. But immediately the rainy season was over, the period of rejoicing reappeared with Navratri or Durga Puja, Sharadutsav, followed by Divali and Dev Divali, when people could think of merriment and enjoy under an open and clear sky resplendent with shining starts. The influence of seasons has thus been a unique factor in the celebration of festivals all the world over, as can be seen from the similarity of festivals celebrated in other countries. For, the various peoples, races and nations of the world of whatever religious denomination have been actuated by the same motive and inspired by the same event in the celebration of festivals some of which have been celebrated more or less on the same days. The Holi or the Spring Festival resembles the Roman Saturnalia, May Day of the present times and the rites performed by the Zoroastrians on the Water Day. Makara sankranti of the Hindus was the Kite Day of the Chinese. Thadingyat, the festival celebrated by the Burmese on full-moon day in October, is akin to Sharadutsav and Divali of India. "The procession of the seasons (with their relevance to sowing and reaping of crops, the mating of animals, hunting, and all that was essential to the economy of our forefathers) is the most common and obvious basis of regular festivals. Divinities such as the Sun and the Moon and the fertile Mother Earth were, and still are, propitiated by seasonal celebrations; and to a lesser extent many planets and constellations share these honours for similar reasons."[5]

(b) *Birth Anniversaries.* Festivals in honour of the great who lived and worked for the welfare of humanity is the commonest and most popular form of celebrations. Birth anniversaries of incarnations of God, such as Rama and Krishna, of prophets like Buddha, Mahavir, Mohammed, Christ and Zoroaster, of religious masters like Shankaracharya and Vallabhacharya, and of great personages like Mahatma Gandhi, Ramakrishna Paramahansa, Swami Vivekanand, etc., are all examples of this kind, when people pay their homage to their departed heroes.

(c) *Religious Festivals.* Among religious events with spiritual significance celebrated as festivals may be counted Mahashivratri, the great night, and Navratri or the Festival of Nine Nights dedicated to the Goddess Durga who freed gods from the tyranny and oppression of Mahishasur. Festivals celebrated to propitiate serpents on Nag Panchami day or for worship of plants and trees which are benefactors of humanity as of *tulsi* or basil plant in Tulsi Vivah, of banyan tree on Vat-Savitri day and of *shami* or *Prosopis spicigera* on Dassera day are not uncommon. There are certain festivals, however, which are observed solely by way of penance and austerity. These are Rishi Panchami, Paryushana, Ekadashi, etc. But there are others like Gauri Vrata, Kajali, Vat-Savitri Vrata, which are performed by unmarried girls and married women for being blessed with the good fortune of having a good husband and *akhand saubhagya* or unbroken marital bliss.

(d) *New Year's Day.* There are several eras according to the various calendars, the commencement of which has come to be celebrated as New Years; we have the Vikram era, Shaka or Shalivahan era, Hijri era and Christian era, and a number of others of national as well as regional importance associated either with certain outstanding events or personages or connected with some period of economic or official activity, all of which have become occasions for celebration.

(e) *National Festivals.* Some modern festivals which are recently coming into being are designed to commemorate certain events of special significance in the life of the nation, such as the Independence Day and the Republic Day, the former when this country attained freedom from foreign bondage, and the latter when the people of this land established themselves into a Sovereign Democratic Republic under the Constitution framed by the representatives of the people. Cultural and youth festivals are organised at national level as national festivals.

(f) *Domestic Festivals.* In addition to various types of festivals seen above, there are many more of a domestic nature, celebrated in the family or household or circle of relatives and friends and still others celebrated by members of a community or common religious denomination, e.g., birthday, marriage, Satyanarayan Puja, religious sacrifices or *yajnas*, etc.

Of all the numerous festivals that are being observed in this country and classified as above, the most common, the most important and the most popular among the people are the Divali and Holi festivals, followed by Navratri or the Festival of nine Nights. These are the festivals which are spontaneous in their observation and distinguished by a spirit of gay revelry and even fun and mischief, as at the time of Holi or the Spring Festival. People do require occasions when they may enjoy at times at the expense of others. Such festivals are not uncommon in other countries where festivals such as Fools' Festival are celebrated practically in the same spirit. But on the whole festivals which are celebrated in India are essentially religious, emphasising a certain way of life, though not without mass enjoyment and merrymaking.

(g) *Miscellaneous.* A large number of local festivals in honour of local deities, saints, etc., as well as social and domestic functions, will fall under this category.

Changing Festivals and People's Attitudes

Religion which was once the means of inspiring people into a certain way of life, dedicated to plain living and high thinking, in course of time became instrumental in bringing about its gradual decay. For, with the spread of education, the rituals and ceremonials lost their former glamour and people began to lose faith and interest in the traditional mode of observance, which naturally fell into neglect when the original spirit of celebration was lost sight of. The festive occasions which once attracted large gatherings and inspired people with unbounded enthusiasm have now become a thing of the past. And the new ones which are coming up have failed to evoke that response and spontaneity which the traditional ones even now do. Since festivals play an important role in the social and cultural life of the people and bring together on a common plane various sections of society for a common purpose and community enjoyment, it is essential to reorganise them in such a way that they suit modern conditions of life. What is necessary is not the creation of new festivals but finding out a novel mode of celebration which would appeal to the popular mind. They must be so renovated as to promote communal harmony and national unity and at the same time provide cultural entertainment. Efforts which are being made these days to create new festivals unrelated to any event or occasion in the life of the people such as the Drama Festival or the Music Festival have failed to enlist popular support. For, the popular mind has been accustomed to associate festivals with specific religious or social events or occasions. Anything which is different is unacceptable. Another defect in these new festivals is that they have no mass appeal, as they are confined to the selected few or the invites who alone can participate in such celebrations. Any festival to be popular must have mass appeal and mass interest. It should aim as much at the participation of the common man as of the elite. Unless this defect in the observance and celebration of the new festivals is remedied, there is no hope for any festival achieving any substantial measure of success. In that way, the only new festival which has found a place in the heart of the people and appealed to their sentiments is the celebration of the Republic Day, wherein all participate on an equal footing.

FAIRS

The word "fair" is defined as a periodical gathering of people away from the normal place of residence, often with entertainments. The real meaning of the word 'Fair' is amply and truly conveyed by its vernacular term *mela* which means a gathering of people. This gathering has been actuated by different motives in different parts of the world, though it had more or less the same origin everywhere. The institution of fairs developed on two separate lines in the East and the West. In Europe it started and grew as a commercial gathering with a view "to centralise supply and demand of merchandise at a particular place and a particular time."[6] In India, however, the purpose was purely religious. It was an essential adjunct to some religious festival, celebrated either locally or regionally. At times such fairs assumed national importance also, when pilgrims from all parts of the country gathered together at a holy place on a particular day as on the occasion of the Kumbha Fair at Hardwar, Prayag now called Allahabad, Nasik and Ujjan.

The fairs of the West were quite different from those held in India in that though religious in origin, they came to be organised as boundary markets held at neutral sites, first, in or near the temples on the occasion of some religious feasts, but later solely for the purpose of trade and commerce. Among the Romans these fairs were connected with some of the 'Annual Feasts', where large gathering participated on the Aventine Hill near the Temple of Voltuna in Etruria in the holy grove of Feronia. These fairs were different from the weekly markets which were usually held for the sale of cattle. They offered special facilities for trading and received the protection of the Church as well as of the kings, who had in the holding of the fairs a source of financial gain which they derived from some of the levies and fines collected by tribunals specially instituted for the purpose of settling trade disputes. The safety of person and property was guaranteed during the period of the fairs and certain concessions were granted to traders participating in these gatherings. Foreigners as well as local merchants were treated on par and allowed to carry on retail transactions which were otherwise forbidden. Traders participating in the fairs were not liable for offences committed elsewhere by their countrymen. The facility of a special court to decide trade offences on spot was an added advantage. The result of the varied concessions and facilities which were thus offered on the occasion of fairs was that some of the greatest and noted fairs came into existence at markets visited by caravans of merchants, which timed their arrival in such a way as to reach that place on the occasion of some religious feast. As time passed, some of these fairs grew into size and importance. Among the most popular and important may be mentioned the Fair of Champagne, the Antwerp Fair, the Geneva Fair and many others which came into being during the 17th and 18th centuries. The institution of fairs thus gradually developed into a purely economic institution and later evolved itself into a distinct pattern with the improvement in transport and communications. As a result of the introduction of free trade and removal of former restrictions, some of the well-known wholesale fairs of national and international importance came into existence, the principal among them being those held at Stourbridge and Bristol in England, at Beaucaire, Bordeaux, Rouen, and Lyons in France, at Leipsic, Frankfort on the Main, Frankfort-on-Oder and Bozen in Germany, at Novi and Senigaglia and later the fair of Nizhni Novgorod in Russia. With the advent of scientific and technological developments and modern means of communications, the fairs took up an entirely new form, wherein their former importance and utility of offering credit and exchange facilities were replaced by such modern business institutions as stock exchanges, banks, clearing houses and post offices. There was no actual flow of merchandise as business could be transacted on the basis of samples shown at the fairs, which were now in the nature of expositions or exhibitions, displaying manufactured goods, where advertisement and publicity were mainly resorted to promote and popularise various articles manufactured in the country holding it as well as in others participating in it. What were originally religious or pleasure fairs, in course of time developed into commercial fairs entirely economic in their character and dealings. The term fair thus acquired quite a new connotation and importance in the beginning of the nineteenth century, when it took the form of exhibitions.

In India the traditional fairs held do not seem to have ever gained any economic importance as in the West where traders from various parts of Europe gathered together for carrying out large-scale commercial transactions. The reason is not far to seek. The fairs held in India have retained throughout their religious character, associated as they have always been with religious gatherings and festivals to which fairs have merely been a side-show, and what was sold at fairs was only consumer goods and articles of religious worship. In the economy of the country then existing, people had few wants and needed very little comforts, which were satisfied by the weekly markets held at various towns in the country, making any wholesale trade at gatherings in distant places absolutely unnecessary. The food the people required they got from the soil they tilled, their clothing they obtained from the cloth woven by them or by the village weaver, and their utensils which were mainly earthen, they procured from the local potter. Any other articles which they required could be obtained at some of the local fairs, which the consumers themselves visited. The larger fairs, however, like those held at Hardwar or Prayag, did afford an opportunity of purchasing some of the articles of artistic value which the pilgrims brought home as a momento of their pilgrimage.Thus, the essentially religious type of fairs on the one hand and the economic structure prevalent in former times on the other offered no scope whatever for the development of fairs as a purely commercial institution as it did in most of the European countries. The wares, mostly consumer goods, marketed at the fairs did not involve any large scale transactions but catered to the needs of the visiting public. This character of fairs where trading is retail rather than wholesale and where consumer goods only are sold and purchased by the consumers themselves, persists even to this day. In most of the present-day fairs, articles of food, sweets and household needs like utensils, footwear, ornaments made of silver and other inferior metals, earthen pots, clothing, toys, bangles, etc., are the main items offered for sale, though a few stalls displaying posters of modern methods of agriculture and extension and exhibiting improved implements and seeds are the latest addition. In contrast to the traditional fairs which are still in vogue without any change or innovation, fairs of modern complexion have recently come into being, as can be seen from the various agricultural and industrial fairs and exhibitions organised after Independence to demonstrate the progress made by the country in the field of scientific and technological development in the wake of successful working of Five Year Plans.

Fairs are not easy to distinguish from festivals. They are both; they are synonymous with festivals. In India every fair is generally associated with some festival or another, but every festival is not an occasion for a fair. There are certain festivals which are observed and celebrated at home and others which are celebrated outside and away from home. The latter naturally assume the form of fairs, the character of which is determined by the place, occasion and time of celebration.

The institution of fairs and festivals as it has developed in India has been quite unique and bears testimony to the native genius of the people. It has an aspect which is both social and religious, and has as its sole aim, the realisation of higher and fuller life through the medium of pilgrimage undertaken to earn religious merit. All great fairs are held at some important centres of pilgrimage where millions of pilgrims gather together at such places as Hardwar, Prayag, Benares, Jagannathpuri, Dwarka, Rameshwaram, Gangasagar and numerous others, where the pilgrim becomes attuned to nature and forgets for the time being his worldly attachments and worries. His sole objective in travelling such a long distance is a bath in the holy river, which he believes purifies not only his body but also his mind and brings salvation to his soul. It gives him an opportunity to fulfil his longing for the *darshan* of his cherished deity and listen to the religious discourses from the sages and saints coming to the fair. In ancient days these fairs had great educational value. The visitors came to learn through the medium of these fairs the geography of their country, the history of its people, their social customs, their languages, ways of life and cultivated the spirit of sufferance and renunciation, which such journey then entailed. People gathered together from different parts of the country with one common purpose. Though unknown to each other and speaking a different language, they were united in thought and deed by community of ideals and aspirations. It is these fairs which have helped in no small measure in keeping the cultural and religious unity of this country intact through ages.

Location for Fairs and Festivals

The location or place where fairs and festivals are held has been varied, dependent on the occasion, time and mode of celebration. All fairs on any description are usually held at some place of religious significance. They have either been the precincts of some temple, outside the town or village, where people would meet and gather freely on equal status, on the bank of some holy river such as the Ganges, the Yamuna, the Narmada, the Gangasagar or in the alternative some seashore or lake or at times near the site of some sacred mountain, such as Girnar, Shatrunjay, etc. Behind the location and selection of site of all such fairs and festivals lies the lure of nature which always has profound influence and fascination on mankind, either primitive or modern. Of all such places, preference for the banks of rivers and ocean, lakes and waterfalls has been marked. The serene calmness and celubrious effect of their waters in ensuring mental peace and physical purification have worked as a potent factor in the selection of sites of some of the most important of fairs and festivals held in India.

Rivers have played a very important role not only in the life of the people of this land but of others as well. In Egypt, the annual rising of the Nile was from the earliest times an occasion for great festivity. All the great centres of pilgrimage and early settlements of man have been located on the banks of rivers, the Nile, the Tigris, the Euphrates, etc. The entire Aryan civilisation is interlinked with rivers. The Ganges and the Yamuna are so many currents of Aryan civilisation and culture. Veneration for rivers on the part of the primitive man born either from the sense of mute amazement and seemingly unconquerable forces of Nature or from the sense of gratefulness towards Lok-Mata, the mother of the people, has been unparalleled. Its bounty in securing freedom from thirst, hunger and famine are no less important today than yesterday. The large dams which are being constructed nowadays bear ample testimony to their immense usefulness to mankind even in modern times. Rivers mean waters which provide means of communications, facilitate trade and commerce and accelerate the pace of human progress through the supply of motive power they generate. In short they are a boon to the individual and society; they ensure human happiness, help human habitation, sustain human life and carry forward the torch of human culture and civilisation. Waters of the holy rives are indispensable on various social and religious occasions, at the time when the idol of the God is installed, at the time when a monarch was enthroned at the time when religious sacrifices or *yajnas* are performed, at the time a soul departs for heaven, and even thereafter when the last bodily remains are immersed in the holy rivers for the salvation of the soul from the bondage of flesh. The remains of the Father of the Nation were carried for immersion in the rivers and oceans in all parts of the country. It is, therefore, but natural that the river should have unique fascination for the people of this land which purifies the body, gives peace and innocent joy to the mind and promotes human progress and prosperity in all its varied aspects. So, rivers and mountains have had a special attraction for the people of India who have appropriately chosen them as suitable places for the holding of fairs. Their influence is so to say magnetic. People have liked the waters of rivers, holy places on their banks and the quiet beauty of their surroundings which receive a worried mind and bestow mental peace.

The Kumbha and Ardha-Kumbha Melas at Ujjain, Nasik, Allahabad and Hardwar are occasions when thousands of people from all over the country go long distances with the sole purpose of having a dip in the holy river and attaining salvation from worldly worries. One wonders why people so willingly suffered in the past the privations of such arduous journeys, when the modern modes of quick transport were not available and travelling on foot or horseback or by bullock-cart in times which were insecure entailed risk to life and property while going from one end of this vast sub-continent to another. It will not be difficult to understand the reason at the back of this attraction, if one considers the influence the very sight of these rivers produces on the human mind. At Hardwar or Rishikesh, standing on the bank of the Ganges, one completely forgets oneself in the natural beauty that surrounds him. The peace of mind and relief from tension and worries of life which these places bring about put man into the proper frame of mind for meditation, and enable him to be in tune with the Infinite. The praises and the eulogies showered in various *stotras* dedicated to some of the holy rivers as in *Ganga, Lahari*, *Narmadashtak*, *Yamunashtak*, written by no less a master than Adya Shankaracharya, are the outpourings of heart which express human gratitude for what the rivers have done for the progress and happiness of mankind. It is, therefore, but natural that their banks should have become centres of pilgrimages which people visit with great devotion, veneration and love.

Some new centre of pilgrimages are also coming into existence in modern times side by side with those of ancient time. The attraction of both the new and the old lies in the contribution they have made to make the life of the people of this country happy, and helped their march towards progress by raising them higher in the social and economic scale. Though both of them have thus served the same purpose, the pilgrim centres of yore did something more. They gave peace and contentment which are so very essential for a healthy existence, but utterly lacking in these days of economic stress.

Time of Celebration of Fairs and Festivals

The most important natural phenomena which have influenced the people in the observance of fairs and festivals are connected with the changes in season, planetary movements and phases of the moon. The Hindu almanac takes account of all these in fixing dates of festivals and mode of their celebration. It is, however, significant to note that all of them are so arranged as not to interfere with the basic agricultural economy of the country. The two principal calendars which are current in the greater part of the country, viz., (i) the Vikram era, and (ii) the Shaka era are also based on this fundamental fact. While the first begins with the month of Kartik, i.e., October/November, and coincides with the end of monsoon season and harvesting of *kharif* crop, the other marks the end of the *rabi* season and falls in Chaitra, i.e., March/April. The commencement of the new and close of the preceding year is the time for stock-taking and working out the balance-sheet for the year that has gone by. Since the entire economy of India is for the most part agrarian, the periods when people have some money to spend are the periods when the crop is harvested. It is, therefore, but natural that these two eras should start at these two distinct periods of time, when people can direct their energies to the celebration of festivals, and have the money they require for rejoicing from the sale proceeds of their produce. Of the two harvest seasons—*kharif* and *rabi*—the former is the principal one, when the major part of the agricultural produce is raised. It is, therefore, the period when the most popular festival, the Divali, coinciding with the conclusion of the *kharif* season is celebrated during the last days of Ashvin (October).

The congregations at fairs are mainly dependent upon the period when they are held. Generally speaking, those periods when climate is favourable, agricultural operations are scarce and people have leisure to go out, are the occasions when larger fairs are held. Such periods usually fall between the first six months of the year, Kartik to Chaitra, i.e., October/November to March/April, when the two greatest of fairs, i.e., Kartik Purnima and Mahashivratri or those connected with Holi are held. After Chaitra, Vaishakh (April/May) begins with Akshaya Tritiya, when the entire countryside is engaged in pre-monsoon farming operations which continue till the close of the rainy season, i.e., Bhadrapad or September. During this period large congregations are avoided and whatever the fairs and festivals held are confined to local places only. As will be seen presently the various tables which have been compiled from the special schedules amply bear out these observations.

The arrangement of fairs and festivals is also practical in its approach in that it takes into account the time of the season and the mood of the people to enjoy. In this way, Divali, Holi and Navratri festivals which have assumed the greatest importance in the life of the people of India are celebrated after the rains disappear and the main agricultural season is over. Navratri, Sharadutsav and Divali 'the autumn festival are celebrated in Ashvin (October) at a time when the atmosphere is calm, peaceful and lovely with greenery all-round, the climate is bracing and the people comparatively free to devote themselves to pleasure and enjoyment, and mingle with their fellowmen. Likewise, Vasant Panchami and Holi (February-March) are the spring festivals which mark the conclusion of the *rabi* season, another harvest season, when the nature is again in full bloom and the people are in a natural mood to enjoy. These also are the occasions which are either preceded or followed by many of the important fairs. Thus the occasion and time chosen for fairs are such as enable the people to camp in the open without any discomfort. The climate is temperate, neither cold nor hot. After the rains the nature is at its best. Springs and rivers are overflowing with water. The sky is clear and the nights are bright. The places selected are such where water is plentiful and space ample.

Phases of the moon have influenced the celebration of Hindu festivals to a very large extent, the most important among them being those held on *purnima* or full-moon day and *amavasya* or new-moon day. Among *purnima* fairs those held on Kartik Purnima day and Holi are the most important, whereas among fairs held on *amavasya* or new-moon day, those which take place on Mahashivratri and *amavasya* of Shravan attract the largest number of visitors.

The periods which appear to be the most convenient from the point of view of holding fairs are August to November and February to April. These periods mark the end of two agricultural seasons when the countryside is free from major field operations and can move away from home for some diversion. Though the months of Shravan and Bhadrapad have the largest number of fairs to their credit, they are mainly in the nature of visits to temples in or near the village/towns and are purely local in character. If these two months are excepted, the largest congregations take place during the fair season and particularly in the months of October-November and February-March when Kartik Purnima, Mahashivratri and Holi fairs are held. Conversely the months, when the holding of fairs is avoided are May to June and December-January, when the agriculturists are busy preparing their fields for sowing or thrashing of crops already gathered in the *khalians*. It is obvious that large fairs take place only after the crops are harvested and the people have ready cash on hand.

Participations in Fairs and Festivals

The participants at the various fairs are drawn from the urban and rural strata of society. The urbanite is incapable of throwing himself heart and soul into the spirit of the fair which he considers only as some demonstration which he does not have a chance to see in his urban surroundings. But, for those coming from rural areas, the fairs have a special meaning. These gatherings apart from their religious significance transform themselves into real harvest and seasonal festivals, coming as they do on the conclusion of *kharif* or *rabi* crops. The very journey from their place of residence by various modes of transport is exciting. Numerous camps, which rise overnight at the banks of rivers under an open and clear sky resplendent with stars, present a delightful appearance. The folk-dramas which are the salient features of these congregations—the *duhas*, *ras* and *garba*—lend charm to the atmosphere of the fair by providing entertainment which makes them completely forget themselves. The money they have on hand after harvesting at the same time enables them to meet their requirements for the coming year. People from distant parts gather together at the fair where they can meet their relatives at least once in a year and learn about their welfare. All these provide attraction for the village people to which they look forward with pleasure and delight. It is, therefore, but natural that the participants at the fair should come mostly from villages and consist of the peasantry, who are in such dire need of recreation after a hard and strenuous life on the field. On the other hand, the townsman has a variety of attractions at his door. The former religious aspect is on the wane, he has little faith either in the dip in the waters of the holy rivers or in the *darshan* of the deity; nor has he any fascination for the entertainments at the fair. Busy as he is with his hackneyed life he can spare little time for staying out some nights in the company of friends and relatives. Much less has he the capacity for putting up with the inconveniences it entails. In fine, the present day fairs are the fairs only of the masses who still have retained their original zest and capacity for enjoyment.

The attendance at various fairs is not always confined to the particular community worshipping the deity. While the religious aspect of the fair like ceremonies, *puja*, *prasad*, etc., is generally confined to that community, all the sections of the public take part in the fair for recreation or trade. But this is not all. In some instances persons venerate the deities of other communities and creeds also. Keeping *manatas* of Muslim *pirs* is not an uncommon phenomenon especially among the low class Hindus. Famous *dargahs* also attract many Hindu pilgrims.

It is noteworthy that the Persian word *pir* has been adopted in certain areas like Rajasthan, Uttar Pradesh, Maharashtra, Madhya Pradesh, Andhra Pradesh and Karnataka etc. for the religious saints among Hindus and is taken to mean a *mahant*, *gadipati* or saint. Ramdev Pir is a well-known instance to the point.

Instances have also come to notice where Muslim priests officiate at some of the Hindu temples. Adoption of the Hindu costume and practice by Parsis is well-known. This was more or less influenced by historical factors. Yet, while keeping their religion a very exclusive affair, some of them have been known to keep *manatas* and entertain belief in cures by miracles ascribed to deities and holy personages of other faiths revealing the tendency of the followers of one religion to revere deities of another religion also.

Yatras/Jatras

A noteworthy feature of pilgrimage to important shrines is that a large number of devotees form themselves into groups of different religious places called *yatras* and visit them on specific occasions. The institution of *yatras* started when times were insecure and long journeys involved hazards to life and property. People, therefore, thought it advisable to move in groups or numbers. It thus took the form of a cooperative undertaking wherein expenses were shared by the participants. Devotional songs are sung on way and the devotees take household deities with them for worship *en route*. Such *yatras* are still taken out but the former mode of transport has disappeared and quicker means like special rail coaches or buses used instead.

Retrospect

The fairs and festivals as they are observed in this country are a unique institution which characterises the march of human civilisation and culture in this vast sub-continent. Essentially religious in nature, they are also equally associated with the social and domestic life of the individual and society at all levels. They prescribe a higher way of life, which ensures physical well-being and mental peace with a promise for spiritual bliss. The bath in the waters of the holy rivers Ganga, Yamuna or Godavari at the bathing festivals at Hardwar, Allahabad or Nasik may not absolve a person from sins committed and give a permit for starting once again on the old path, but it will certainly purify the body and mind and prepare him for a way of life, which if practised, would absolve him from sins. The *darshan* of the deity and the fervent zeal with which the pilgrim is inspired at these centres of pilgrimage would certainly make him look within himself. With a view to appreciate the usefulness and role of fairs and festivals in the life of the people of India, the real significance of the various symbols and the hidden meaning underlying the legends with which they are associated should be properly understood. For, symbols are the very essence of Hindu theology, which garb some of the supreme truths of Hindu religion and philosophy. They give form and life to the various sentiments and ideals which have inspired and guided the people of this country. That is not all. They have also enabled them to grapple with the elements of nature, and march towards civilisation with courage and fortitude. They have given them contentment, joy and music of life without ignoring its higher values.

The dual aspects of festivals, viz., (i) religious and (ii) social, are so beautifully intermixed that the one is inseparable from the other. In its religious aspect it has been appropriately called *vrata*. In its social aspect it is *parva*. *Vrata* requires austerity penance and observances, which purify body and mind. *Parva* gives the zest of living cheers the man, gives him diversion, innocent joy and pleasure and makes his life worth living. Both these aspects of celebration are blended together in the Indian fairs and festivals in a way which no other nation in the world has perhaps succeeded in doing. In fairs it is the social and cultural aspect which is uppermost, but in the celebration of most of the festivals with the exception of two major festivals Holi and Dipavali it is the religious aspect that generally predominates. Though fairs are not without their religious aspect, the festivals are also not without their social aspect. Both have immense social and cultural value, emphasising as they do, the unity and oneness of the Indian people through ages and throughout the length and breadth of this land. The profound faith and devotion of masses in their observance is something which is really inspiring. The enthusiasm and spontaneity with which Holi, Divali, Durga Puja, Dassera, Paryushana, Id or Christmas are celebrated in every home evidence the social and cultural impact they have in keeping alight the torch of civilisation and welding together the various elements of society into a single whole by injecting new power, new energy, new life, year after year.

Fairs are so many centres of pilgrimage. They offer opportunity not only for a dip in the holy river or for *darshan* of the cherished deity but also for enjoying the scenic beauty and loveliness of nature. They have an influence all their own. Fairs and festivals make one forget for the time being all the worldly worries and concourse of life. They hold out to the people a message which is handed down from generation to generation in the form of various symbols, legends and practices, which are voluntarily practised to derive the benefit accruing therefrom.

The association of fairs and festivals with the procession of seasons is a unique feature of the fairs and festivals in India. It is for this reason that they are closely interlinked with the calendar which computes with meticulous care the date and time appointed for the observance of each of them. The *sankrantis*, solstices, equinoxes and the appearance of the numerous astronomical and natural phenomena indicate the days and time auspicious as well as inauspicious for their observance and celebration. They regulate the very routine of their life from morning to night. Day and time auspicious for starting on a journey, celebration of marriage, giving of sacred thread, starting a business, sending a child to school and all the varied activities of day-to-day life are regulated according to the Hindu religious calendar. The innate connection between a season and climate on the one hand and human mind and body on the other as affecting the mood and the well-being of the people is unmistakable. It is for this reason that the rainy season is avoided not only for the celebration of festivals and holding of fairs but also for all social functions and occasions. Excessive heat and cold are likewise avoided, and days with temperate climate preferred for various celebrations in which people indulge. During the rainy season or *chaturmas* which follows the summer solstic, when the climate is dull and has a depressing effect on body and mind, travelling is avoided and austere living enjoined to preserve physical and mental health. For, people can be in good cheer only if they are in a position to take delight in their surroundings. One does not like to mix with others when nature is against merry-making and the mood and the spirit of the people offend against enjoyment in any form. It is this basic psychological fact coupled with the agrarian nature of its economy which has governed the holding of fairs and celebration of festivals in India and which should also determine the celebration of any new festival which may be introduced in future, if it is to enlist any public support and acceptance.

All fairs of olden times persist more or less in the same fashion, though certain welcome innovations are being introduced these days. Rather than being mere occasions for merriment and some religious observance, they are assuming importance as useful media of popular education. The various stalls which are nowadays put up also include those by Government, semi-Government and social agencies, which aim at educating the public in a variety of ways. Improved implements of farming, seed and manure, progress made in the various fields of development in the wake of successive Five Year Plans, advantages of prohibition, cleanliness and health and a number of other items of public welfare are exhibited at the stalls set up for the purpose. Means to increase production and minimise labour are also displayed by actual demonstration to improve the economic condition of the agriculturist, technologist, industrialist and the artisan.

Celebration of Fairs and Festivals through Calendar

The various cultures that flourished in the past evolved their own systems of reckoning time whereby their religious, social and economic activities were regulated. The appearance and reappearance of certain natural events and astronomical phenomena such as the advent of spring, summer, rains, the movement of the sun and moon, stars and planets, the occurrence of winter and the summer solstices, or equinoxes, etc., marked the occasions for the celebration of various festivals by different peoples at different times.

The primitive man observed the recurrences of seasons and certain familiar events of nature in a particular sequence and arrived at his computation of the order in which the cycle of seasons appeared. He adopted the solar year by reckoning the days from one solstice to another or from one equinox to another, with reference to the heliacal risings or settings of some conspicuous star, such as Sirius,

Rigel, Antares or the Pleiades, in the eastern horizon immediately before sunrise, after it was invisible owing to its nearness to the Sun. As the knowledge of man advanced, a systematic and scientific study of the movement of heavenly bodies was made to fix time for the celebration of festivals, observance of fasts and feasts and performance of religious ceremonies, giving birth to various methods of time reckoning or calendars.

All calendars have adopted the practice of indicating time in terms of movement of the earth, the sun and the moon and agree in measuring time by the year, months, and days, though their duration varies according as the cycle by which they are computed is solar or lunar. The commencement of each of them also varies, dependent as it is on the purpose, occasion or some epoch-making event which was instrumental in bringing it into being. A calendar may be based either on the solar or lunar cycle, mark the beginning of seasons, solstices or equinoxes, and commemorate birthdays of prophets or the incarnations of God, such epoch-making events as victory over alien rulers, the commencement of some ruling dynasty, etc. It may be dated from any day since the creation of the world and carried till its dissolution.

The astronomical year, based as it is on the movement of the celestical bodies, is one which is in accord with nature. It is either solar or lunar, or a combination of both when it is called luni-solar.

(i) *Solar Year.* A solar year represents the time taken by the earth while revolving in its orbit around the sun, going through a point of the ecliptic, i.e., solstice or equinox to which it returns after completing its journey in heaven. The solar year thus consists of 365 days, 5 hours, 48 minutes and 46 seconds. The Gregorian calendar of the Christian era being solar, maintains the closest correspondence between the year and the seasons.

(ii) *Lunar Year.* The lunar year consists of 12 lunar months or lunations. Each lunation is the synodic month as measurerd by the period falling between two successive full-moons or new-moons which mark the two successive conjunctions of the moon with the sun. Since a lunar month varies from 29.26 to 29.80 days, it gives a period of 354 days, short of 11 days to the solar year. As will be seen later, this period came to be accounted for by an intercalation or suppression, to make the lunar year conform to the solar. This contrivance was deemed necessary to ensure that the natural events and cycle of seasons which occurred in particular months were not upset by falling into different months, owing to this difference between the solar and lunar years. The Muslim calendar of the Hijri era is entirely lunar. Since it does not make any adjustment with the solar cycle, there is no coordination between the months and seasons.

(iii) *Luni-solar Year.* In the luni-solar year, the year is calculated by the solar cycle and the months by lunar divisions or lunations, as in the Hindu calendar, the adjustment between the two being brought about by intercalation and suppression of days and months.

(iv) *Civil Year.* The civil year based on Christian era which is nowadays followed practically all the world over for civil purposes is also a solar year, but differs from the astronomical solar year of 365 days, 5 hours, 48 minutes and 46 seconds, as against 365 days given by the Civil year. This difference has been removed by intercalation or having an additional day in the month of February every four years called a leap-year.

CALENDARS IN INDIA

Varied systems of time reckoning have come into vogue at different periods of history to mark the commencement of new years. These are either solar, lunar or luni-solar. The various eras they represent will be referred to later. But the two most important that are followed in one or the other part of the country are (i) Vikrama and (ii) Shalivahan eras based on the Hindu system of time reckoning called *panchanga* or calendar.[7]

(i) *Hindu Calendar.* Early Aryans had taken meticulous care to evolve a very detailed and comprehensive system of measuring time based on minute observation of astronomical phenomena, such as movement of stars, planets, the sun, the moon and the earth. The science was brought to perfection by systematic study at observatories at the ancient universities of Taxila, Mathura, Kashi, Ujjain, Jaipur and other places whereby the movement of celestial bodies was forecast with a high degree of accuracy and precision. As mentioned earlier that there are solar or lunar years, likewise there are solar or lunar months as well as solar or lunar days according to the system of time reckoning followed. Just as there are the days and years of men, there are also years of gods called divine years—each day of the divine year being equivalent to one solar year. The solar year is divided into two halves. The first six months of *Uttarayana* from Makara Sankranti to Karka Sankranti—Paush (January) to Ashadh (June)—is god's day and the *Dakshinayana*, i.e., July-December god's night. One solar year thus equals one day and night of the gods, while one month or 30 days of gods equal 30 solar years and 1 year or 12 months of gods equal 360 solar years.

(ii) *Vikram Era.* The Vikram era is said to have been established by King Vikramaditya of Ujjain to commemorate his victory over the Shakas who invaded India from the north about 57 B.C. Historians and scholars, however, differ as to the origin of this era, who believe that there was no king Vikramaditya by name earlier than 842 A.D. Some authorities are of the view that what is called Vikram era was originally started in 58 B.C. in the reign of Kanishka, the Kushan emperor, and later adopted by the Malava people, when it came to be named Vikram era. Another authority traces Vikram's reign to the year 58 B.C. itself and associates Vikram era with the defeat of Shaka king Nahapana by Vikramaditya of Ujjain in 58 B.C.

(iii) *Shake Era.* This era was started by King Shalivahan in 78 A.D. It was also called Shaka era, as it is to this tribe that Shalivahan belonged. According to a legend, a potter's son, Shalivahan by name, made an army of clay, put life into it, and defeated the Shakas with its aid—an incident which came to be commemorated as the Shaka era of King Shalivahan. It is both solar and lunar, and started by some king Shalivahan who was either Shaka himself or conquered Shakas.

Both Vikrama and Shaka eras have the same months, though commencing at different periods. The Vikram era for the most part starts from the month of Kartik, when it is called *Kartikadi.* But it is *Chaitradi* or *Ashadhadi* as well, when it starts after full-moon of Chaitra as in Rajputana or from Ashadh Sud I as in Kathiawar or Saurashtra. The Shaka or Shalivahan era commences from Chaitra. The Shalivahan Shaka commences from what is popularly known as Gudi Padvo, when it is lunar *Chaitradi.* But the Shaka era of the Indian Calendar is solar *Chaitradi* beginning on March 21 or 22 which is the first day of the entry of the sun into the sidereal sign Mesha (Aries) of the zodiac at the vernal equinox. "The first civil day of the Chaitradi year is the day after the new-moon conjunction which occurs next after the entrance of the sun into Mina, and it now falls from about March 13 to about April 11; the first civil day of the Kartikadi year is the first day after the new-moon conjunction which occurs next after the entrance of the sun into Tula, and it now falls from about October 17 to about November 15."

(iv) *Panchanga.* The Hindu calendar is called *panchanga*, as it takes account of *panch*, i.e., five *angas*, i.e. limbs, viz., year, month, fortnight, *tithi* and *ghatika* or alternatively, *tithi*, *vara*, *nakshatra*, *yoga* and *karana*, which are the five sections usually noted in all traditional calendars.

(v) *The Year.* All the nations divide their year into 12 months. The synodic revolution of the moon takes place in about 29.5 days, giving a period of 354 days for 12 lunations and a difference of 11.25 days between the solar and lunar years. This difference the various calendars have tried to adjust according to their convenience and needs to commence the lunar year according to the solar. Otherwise, there would be great disharmony between the seasons and the months in which they would ordinarily fall according to the lunar calendar. The Aryans measured time both according to the sun and the moon, viz., (i) the time taken by the sun to complete its apparent journey through the heaven while passing through 12 signs of the zodiac (365.25 days) and (ii) the time taken by the 12 lunations of the moon—354 days. "The two systems were united into one, the present luni-solar or Samvatsara year, about 1181 B.C. The first day of the solar year is the day of the entry of the sun into the zodiacal sign Mesha (Aries) at the Vernal equinox, and the actual beginning of the civil and religious year is, in general, dated from the new-moon immediately preceding that day. The old Vikrama-samvat year began with the autumn equinox."

(vi) *Months.* In the Hindu calendar, the year is divided into 12 months of varying sizes, as determined by a *sankranti* or entrance of the sun into sidereal signs of the Zodiac which also are 12 in number. Though it is the earth which moves round the sun, it appears that it is the sun which change place every month. The 12 places, through which the sun passes during a year, are named are groups of stars called *rashis*. The ecliptic is divided into 27—according to some 28—*nakshtras* or constellations, grouped into twelve *rashis* mansions. The *Nakshatras* being unequal in size do not have the same number of stars, some having even one or two and others many more, e.g., Shatabhishak conventionally said to have 100 but which really has one, Revati 32, Mula 11 and Ardra Chitra, and Swati having one only. Each *rashi* in turn consists of two to three *nakshatras*, some of which appear on the full-moon day of the month and the lunar month is known by that constellation in which the full-moon appear. As for example, when the full-moon day is in the constellation Chitra, the month is known as Chaitra when it is in Kartika, it is known as Kartik; when it is in Mrigashirsha, Margashirsh, and so on.

Solar	*Lunar*	*Nakshatra*
1. Mesha (Aries)	Chaitra	14th Chaitra 15th Swati
2. Vrishabha (Taurus)	Vaisakha	16th Vishakha 17th Anuradha
3. Mithuna (Gemini)	Jyeshtha	18th Jyeshtha 19th Mula
4. Karka (Cancer)	Ashadha	20th Purva Ashadha 21st Uttara Ashadha and (Abhijit) (Balance)
5. Simha (Leo)	Sravana	(Abhijit) 22nd Sravana 23rd Dhanishtha
6. Kanya (Virgo)	Bhadrapada	24th Satataraka 25th Purvabhadrapada 26th Uttarabhadrapada
7. Tula (Libra)	Asvina	27th Revati 1st Ashvini 2nd Bharuni
8. Vrischika (Scorpio)	Kartika	3rd Kritika 4th Rohini
9. Dhanu (Sagittarius)	Margasirsha	5th Mrigasiras 6th Ardra
10. Makara (Capri-cornus.)	Pausha	7th Punarvasu 8th Pushya
11. Kumbha (Aquarius)	Magh	9th Aslesha 10th Magha
12. Mina (Pisces)	Phalguna	11th Purva Phalguni 12thUttara Phalguni 13th Hasta"[8]

The solar months are 12 in number and bear the names of the twelve signs of the zodiac called *rashis* or mansions by which they are also known in some parts of India. The 12 *rashis* are Mesha, the Ram (Aries); Vrishabham, the Bull (Taurus); Mithuna, the Pair, the Twins (Gemini); Karka, Karkata, Karkataka, the Crab (Cancer); Simha, the Lion (Leo); Kanya, the Maiden (Virgo); Tula, the Scales (Libra); Vrischika, the Scorpion (Scorpio); Dhanus, the Bow (Sagittarisu); Makara, the Sea-monster (Capricornus); Kumbha, the Water-pot (Aquarius); Mina, the Fish (Pisces). The names of the lunar months corresponding to these signs are given below along with the names by which they are generally known in India; viz. Chaitra, Vaishakh, Jyeshtha (Jeth), Ashadh, Shravan, Bhadrapad (Bhadarvo), Ashvin or Ashvayuja (Asoj), Kartik (Kartak), Margashirsh (Magshar), Paush, (Posh), Magha (Mah), and Phalgun (Fagan).

Of the two series of months described above, it is the lunar or moon-months which are followed in the greater part of the country, and common to both the eras, viz., Vikram and Shaka or Shalivahan. But these were not the names prevalent in olden times, when names such as Madhu (Chaitra), Madhava (Vaishakh), Shukra (Jyeshtha), Shuchi (Ashadh), Nabhas (Shravan), Nabhasya (Bhadrapad), Isha (Ashvin), Urja (Kartik), Saha (Margashirsh), Sahasya (Paush), Tapas (Magh) and Tapasya (Phalgun) were current according to the solar year.

The lunar month ends either with newmoon (*amavasya*) or full-moon (*purnima*). There are two methods in vogue for the commencement of the months. They are either *amasanta* or *purnimanta,* that is to say, they commence either with the bright or dark fortnight, on the day following either the new-moon or the full-moon[9].

Adhik Masa or Intercalary Month

The time the moon takes to rotate round the earth is called a lunar month. It takes 354 days to complete 12 lunations at the rate of 29.5 days per lunation or lunar month. But the earth completes its movement round the sun, within 365 days, 5 hours, 48 minutes and 46 seconds. There is thus a difference of about 11 days between the solar and lunar year, which is adjusted by introducing an intercalary month every 2.5 years, to adjust the lunar to the solar years. It is this additional or extra month which is called intercalary month or *adhik masa*. The sun passes from one *rashi* to another every month. The apparent motion of the sun not being uniform, the time taken by the sun to pass through different *rashis* is not always the same. This entry of the sun into a zodiacal sign is called a *sankraman* or *sankranti*, which occurs every month. There are 12 such *sankramans* during a year. It, however, so happens sometimes that the sun does not pass through any of the *rashis* during one of the lunar months, and consecutive two new-moon days intervene between one *sankranti* and another, when the *adhik masa* or intercalary month is introduced. In other words intercalary month is that month during which there is no *suryasankranti*. Conversely, the month during which there are two *surya-sankrantis* is called *kshaya masa* or suppressed month, which comes once in 141 years. When this phenomenon occurs the first of the two lunar months is expunged from the calendar and is called *kshaya* or *mala masa,* i.e., the month which is deleted or dropped. In the year in which the *kshaya masa* is ordained, the actual number of months in a year is either 12 or 13, there being one or two intercalary months coupled with the *kshaya masa* or deleted month in the same year. Since the opinions of the various authorities as to intercalation differed in different parts of the country, Dassera and Divali were celebrated at two different periods of time in the different parts of the country.

Such intercalation is also resorted to in the solar cycle of the Gregorian calendar which subdivides a year into months, which are of unequal length, 28, 29, 30 or 31 days, and gives a total of 365 days in a year, short of the actual time taken in its journey by the earth round the sun by 5 hours, 48 minutes and 46 seconds. Since these extra hours could not be included in the calendar for a year, the device of intercalation was adopted and the system of adding one day every four years to the month of February came into vogue.

(vii) *Days.* Months are divided into *pakshas* or fortnights, weeks and days. The two *pakshas* or fortnights are *shukla* the bright half and *krishna* the dark half, each approximately of 14 or 15 days, seven days making one week.

(a) *Lunar Day or Tithi.* Days are both lunar as well as solar, lunar day being called *tithi* or *vasara* and solar one *divasa*. The path of the moon round the sun extends to 360 degrees, which it covers in one lunation of 29 days, 12 hours and 44 minutes, giving 12 degrees to a *tithi*. But the time taken to cover it varies owing to the eliptical form of the orbit of the moon. The duration of *tithi* or a lunar day, therefore, varies and is a trifle shorter than the *divasa* or solar day covering day and night from one sunrise to another, the average duration of a *tithi* being 23 hours 37 mintues i.e., 23 minutes less than a day.

(b) *Solar Day or Divasa.* The solar day is the period from one sunrise to another, each named after its ruling planet. Seven days make one week, commencing from Sunday and ending with Saturday. They are:

Var/Vasara	*Day*	*Planet*
Ravivar or Adityavasara	Sunday	Sun
Somvar or Chandravasara	Monday	Moon
Mangalvar or Bhomvasara	Tuesday	Mars
Budhvar or Saumyavasara	Wednesday	Mercuy
Guruvar or Brihaspativasara	Thursday	Jupiter
Shukravar or Bhriguvasara	Friday	Venus
Shanivar or Mandvasara	Saturday	Saturn

(c) *The Civil Day.* The civil days begin at sunrise. They follow the Christian almanac and begin from one and run into a series of consecutive numbers upto 28, 29, 30 or 31 according to the number of days assigned to each of the 12 months of the year, both of which are solar. The days are further subdivided into hours, minutes and seconds, by which all clocks are adjusted and civil activities regulated.

Unlike hours and minutes a *tithi* is subdivided into *ghatika, pala* and *vipala* related to the Christian calendar in the following manner:

One day and night=1 *divas* a or 24 hours=60 *ghatikas*; one *ghatika* is equal to 60 *palas*, i.e., 24 minutes; and one *pala*=60 *vipalas*=24 secodns. Two *ghatikas* make one *muhurta* or 48 minutes. Thus 2.5 *muhurtas* are equal to 2 hours. 2.5 *ghatikas* are equal to one hour, 2.5 *palas* are equal to 1 minute and 2.5 *vipalas* are equal to one second.

The term *ghatika* became current from the practice of measuring time by means of an earthen bowl or *ghatika* with a hole pierced in it and kept floating on water, till it gradually sank to the bottom. The time taken during this process was called *ghatika*. These and other terms are used in the Hindu *panchanga* which is adopted for fixing auspicious and inauspicious times for the performance of religious ceremonies and social and domestic events like casting of horoscope at birth, marriage, sacred thread ceremony, commencement of business, travel, residence in a new house, bride's departure for her husband's house, etc. But for civil purposes the western method of calculating hours and minutes is universally adopted in India. Every *panchanga* or calendar, which is being issued either according to Vikram era or Shalivahan era, therefore, makes it a point to mention along with *ghatika*, *pala*, etc. corresponding hours and minutes of the day according to the Christian era with which the people are so well familiar.

(d) *Intercalary or Delated Tithi.* All Civil days according to the solar system commence from sunrise. But since the time of sunrise varies according to season, the practice of referring to sunrise in terms of hours and minutes has come into vogue. Also since a solar day is longer than the lunar day, the lunar day or the *tithi* may either commence before or after sunrise. When a *tithi* begins immediately before one sunrise and ends after the following sunrise, the former runs into two *divasas* and is, therefore, called *vridhi* or intercalary *tithi*. But when a *tithi* begins after sunrise on one morning and ends before sunrise on the following morning, it cannot be coupled with any *divasa* and is, therefore, deleted as *kshaya tithi*.

VARIOUS ERAS

(a) *Vikram and Shalivahan Eras.* Among the numerous eras prevalent in India, the two most important are Vikram and Shalivahan eras, noticed before. The Vikram era started 56 years before the Christian era, is in force almost in the whole of northern India except Bengal. The Shalivahan era commenced from the 78th year of the Christian era, and is generally current in southern India except Malabar and Tineveli district. At present the Vikram era is ascribed to king Vikramaditya and the Shaka era is assigned to king Shalivahan. In the present state of Indian chronology, it is difficult to identify king Vikramaditya, who is dated in the first century B.C. According to the Jain tradition he may be identified with king Vikramaditya of Ujjain, who expelled the Shakas from there. The representation of Vikramaditya as Shakari corroborates this identification. Many scholars, however, contend that the Vikram era was originally instituted by the Malava Ganarajya and hence known as the Malava Gana era, and that it was named after Chandragupta Vikramaditya when he conquered Malwa, in about 400 A.D. Similarly the Shalivahan era was originally initiated by the Shakas and was known as the Shaka era, but in later times it got arbitrarily ascribed to king Shalivahan when the era was commonly used in south India. In course of time, the term Shaka came to denote any epoch in general and to be used for any outstanding event or epoch in the life of the people. For civil purposes, the solar years according to the Christian era are for the most part followed in India, not only for official purposes but also for all the day-to-day transactions and activities. Whereas for the performance of religious rites and ceremonies, observance of fasts, holding of festivals, and fixing the various details of private affairs and domestic life where auspicious timings have to be determined with meticulous care, it is the lunar year which is universally followed all over the country.

Various other eras in vogue in this country are Hijri, Bengali, Amli, Nawroz, Fasli, Shur or Shahur, Magi, Kollam or Parashurama, Raj, Christian, etc. All these eras commenced at different periods and came into existence to mark certain epoch- making events in the life and history of the people who adopted them.

(b) *Hijri or Hejira Era.* This era is Arabic in origin. Before its commencement, the era which was in vogue was termed Amulfil, changed to Hijri or Hejira after the death of Mohammed Paigambar to commemorate this *hijrat*, from Mecca to Madina, which took place in the 42nd year of his life, on 15th July, 622 A.D. It was from this day that the Hijri era came into being. A year, according to this era, is divided into 12 lunar months, giving 354, to 355 days to a year, the day commencing from sunset. This era was adopted in India during the reigns of the Muslim rulers. The 12 months of the Hijri era are:

(1) Muharram	(7) Rajab
(2) Safar	(8) Shaaban
(3) Rabi-ul-Awwal	(9) Ramzan
(4) Rabi-us-Sani	(10) Shawwal
(5) Jamadi-ul-Awwal	(11) Zilqaad
(6) Jamadi-us-Sani	(12) Zilhijja

1. Muharram: the pious month, during which any business or travel is prohibited
2. Safar: meant for travel, business, fighting, etc.
3. Rabi-ul-Awwal: commencement of the spring
4. Rabi-us-Sani or Rabi-ul-Akhar: end of the spring
5. Jamadi-ul-Awwal: commencement of the cold season
6. Jamadi-us-Sani or Jamadi-ul-Akhar: conclusion of the cold season
7. Rajab: month for making preparation for fencing the fields, etc.
8. Shaaban: harvesting
9. Ramzan: pious month of excessive heat
10. Shawwal : month for going out for hunting
11. Zilqaad : month to get the camels ready for travel
12. Zilhijja: month of pilgrimage

The months which mark the commencement and end of various seasons, such as spring, winter and summer, and also indicate the period of economic activities, such as hunting, agriculture, business, and travel and religious observances such as fasting or pilgrimage, were introduced during the time of Paigambar Ibrahim. They were formerly connected with the change in seasons. But later on, they came to be determined according to the first appearance of the moon or crescent on the second day of the bright half and thus became purely lunar months. In course of time, the months occurred in such a sequence that there was no relation whatsoever either to the cycle of seasons or the solar year, as the difference between the lunar and the solar years was not adjusted in the Hijri calendar.

Since this era does not make use of intercalation as is done by others, it falls short of one year every 30 years, as the year being lunar consists of 354 or 355 days. The result is that there is lack of coordination between the various seasons and the months of the Hijri era.

(c) *Bengali Era.* The Bengali era came into vogue in Bengal. It commences when the sun enters Mesha *sankranti* in the month of Chaitra-Vaishakh. This era started 693 years after the Christian era.

(d) *Nawroz.* Nawroz is the era in vogue in Kashmir, and commences about the same time as Chaitra (March).

(e) *Vilayati or Amli Era.* Commences from the birthday of king Indradyumna of Orissa, when the sun enters Kanya *rashi* in the month of Bhadrapad. It started 592 years after the Christian era.

(f) *Fasli.* This era was introduced by Akbar and is related to *fasal* or harvesting season. It commences from the first day of the dark half of the month of Ashvin and started 592 to 593 years after the Christian era.

(g) *Shur or Shahur Era.* This era commences when the sun enters the constellation of Mriga. The year is a solar year and the months are lunar months, such as Muharram, etc. This calendar was much in vogue during the regime of Marathas.

(h) *Magi.* This calendar, which is current in Chittagong area of Bangladesh, very much resembles the Bengali calendar, of which it is ahead by 45 years. It is still in vogue in Kerala and Malabar.

(i) *Kollam or Parashurama.* This era is current in areas from Mangalore to Kanyakumari in Tirunelveli district. The months are named after the *rashis*, such as Mesha, Vrishabha, etc. and the year commences from the day when the sun enters Kanya *rashi* in the month of Bhadrapad.

(j) *Raj Shak.* Shivaji started the era called Raj or Anand, in Shaka 1593, on Jyeshtha Sud 13. It was luni-solar but is not in vogue now.

(k) *Christian Era.* This calendar is associated with the birthday of the founder of Christianity, Jesus Christ. It is a solar year commencing from the first day of January, a week after his birth and consists of 365 days, as against 365 days, 5 hours, 48 minutes and 46 seconds of the solar year. This year is adjusted to the movement of the sun by adding one day to the month of February every four years, which is a leap-year. All European countries have adopted the Roman calendar for civil purposes, though the one adopted for ecclesiastical purposes is luni-solar, the difference between the two being adjusted from time to time by intercalation and in March 1582, by the suppression of ten days in the calendar. As the Gregorian calendar evolved by the Christian era is followed in India for all civil purposes, the dates and months according to the Gregorian calendar are also shown along with the months and days of the Hindu calendar.

Since calendars regulate twofold human activities, (i) civil and administrative on the one hand, and (ii) social and religious on the other, two different types of calendars are in use in India—the Gregorian calendar for civil purposes and the Hindu, Buddhist, Jain and Islamic calendars for religious purposes of fixing up dates and moments for the celebration of festivals. There is no correspondence between the two, as the calendars followed for religious purposes are luni-solar or lunar, and that used for civil and administrative is solar.

All these various eras were started by some monarchs or by some prophets or founders of religion to commemorate certain epoch-making events. The Vikram era was started by King Vikramaditya; the Shaka era by King Kanishka, Fasli by Akbar, Amali by King Indradyumna of Orissa and Raj or Anand by Shivaji. Eras associated with the names of incarnations of God are Rama and Krishna eras. The eras associated with prophets and religious preceptors are Buddha, Mahavir, Jesus Christ and Mohammed. The Buddha (Nirvan) Samvatsara and Vir (Nirvan) Samvatsara commence from the day when Gautam Buddha and Mahavir attained *nirvan*. The Christian era is associated with the birth of Christ and the Hijri era with the *hijrat* of prophet Mohammed to Madina from Mecca. While Rama Samvat started 12,569,064 years ago, Krishan Samvat dates back to 5,189 years. Yudhishthir Samvat started 5,064 years ago, Buddha Samvat 2,538 years ago, Vir Samvat 2,488 years ago, Shankaracharya Samvat 2,343 years ago, Vikram Samvat 2,021 years ago, Shalivahan Samvat 1,886 years ago and Chaitanya Samvat 557 years ago.

The Vikram New Year starts on three different dates, viz., (i) from Kartik Sud 1 (November) immediately after Divali, celebrated as Festival of Lights all over India, (ii) from Gudi Padva in the month of Chaitra (March), and (iii) from Ashadh Sud 1 (July). Vaishakhi, however, is important for the Sikhs and also marks the beginning of the Tamil New Year. The Halari Samvat followed in Kutch marks the commencement of the agricultural season and commences from Ashadh or July. The Zoroastrian era is believed to commence from 632 A.D. The Parsis have two New Years, viz., (i) Jamshedi Navroz, corresponding with the equinox on March 21, and (ii) the Kadmi New Year or the Pateti, which falls on August 31. These are not the only new years current in this country. A host of others are also coming into existence, each starting from a date either commemorating some event or denoting a particular purpose in view.

References

1. *The Random House Dictionary of the English Language.* (Bombay, Allieds Publisher 1972) p. 488.

2. *Hornby A.S. and others. The Advanced Learner's*

dictionary of Current English, (London, Oxford University Press 1977*)* p. 366.

3. *Encyclopaedia of the Social Sciences,* Vol. VI, 1959 pp. 199-201.

4. *Ibid,* p. 199.

5. *The Encyclopaedia Americana,* Vol. XI, 1961 p. 153.

6. *Encyclopaedia of the Social Sciences,* Vol. VI, 1959, p. 58.

7. For more detail *See* The *Indian Astrnomical Ephemeris.* (Delhi Indian Meterological Department, 2003). pp.476-57

8. Underhill, M.M. *The Hindu Religious Years* (1992), pp. 17-18.

9. *Ibid.* p.16.

RELIGIOUS CALENDER AND THEIR CORRESPONDING ENGLISH MONTHS

Hindu Calender

	Name of the Hindu Month	Correponding English Months
1.	Chaitra	March - April
2.	Vaiakha	April - May
3.	Jyesth	May - June
4.	Ashadha	June - July
5.	Sravana	July - August
6.	Bharapada	August - September
7.	Asuina	September - October
8.	Kartika	October - November
9.	Margasirsha	November - December
10.	Pausha	December - January
11.	Magh	January - February
12.	Phalguna	February - March

Muslim Calender

	Name of the Muslim Month	Correponding English Months
1.	Muharram	February - March
2.	Safar	March - April
3.	Rabi-ul-Awwal	April - May
4.	Rabi-us-Sani	May - June
5.	Jamadi-ul-Awwal	June - July
6.	Jamadi-us-Sani	July - August
7.	Rajab	August - September
8.	Shaaban	September - October
9.	Ramzan	October - November
10.	Shawwal	November-December
11.	Zilqaad	December - January
12.	Zilhijja	January - February

Sindhi Calender

	Name of the Sindhi Month	Correponding English Months
1.	Chet	March - April
2.	Vaisakh	April - May
3.	Jeth	May - June
4.	Akhar	June - July
5.	Sawan	July - August
6.	Eado	August - September
7.	Assu	September - October
8.	Kati	October - November
9.	Nahri	November-December
10.	Poh	December-January
11.	Mangh	January - February
12.	Phagun	February - March

Jewish Calender

	Name of the Jewish Month	Correponding English Months
1.	Tishri	September - October
2.	Heshvan (Maroheshvan)	October - November
3.	Kislev	November-December
4.	Tebet (Teves)	December - January
5.	Shebat (Shevat)	January - February
6.	Adar or Adar I Ve-Adar or Adar II	February - March
7.	Nisan	March - April
8.	Iyar	April - May
9.	Sivan	May - June
10.	Temmuz	June - July
11.	Ab (Av)	July - August
12.	Elul	August - September

MAJOR FESTIVALS OF INDIA

HINDU FESTIVALS

Hinduism, the chief religion, has shown extreme resilience in braving the impact of potential swings of major change, retaining its identity.

Apart from the various Hindu sects there are many cults of the tribal India, Jainism, Buddhism, the Arya Samaj, and Sikhism, all of which began as movements of reform and grew to become separate faiths.

The influx of the Tibetan refugees has brought back Buddhism to the land of its birth, though in a modified form, adding to the number of followers of Tibetan Buddhism, or Lamaism, as it is also called.

As a festival comes round, the concerned communities of Delhi don their best clothes to throng the streets to join the fun, to watch the spectacular pageants go by, to become part of the ceremonial procession, if only to drive dull care away. The rituals, however, are confined to the devotees whose festival it is. Jainism, Buddhism, Sikhism, Christianity, Islam, and Zorastrianism are monotheistic faiths. As a result they have a fewer number of festivals, compared with the Hindu faith, with its innumerable gods and goddesses and its myriad festivals devoted to them.

As mentioned earlier, festivals generally celebrate the seasons, the exploits of legendary heroes, birth anniversaries of mythic or historical personages and other events close to the hearts of the devotees, or maybe for their own sake. All the same, all festivals include a factor regulating life-style, enjoining the devotee to do, or to refrain from doing certain acts for the sake of spiritual rewards. Rituals thus ensure performance of certain duties by raising them to the order of a sacrament.

Life is composed of joy and fear. Festivities take care of both, especially when the festival is ritualized. Ritual is believed to appease the powers that be, thereby, putting an end to fear, or is supposed to attract the attention of the benevolent forces being invoked so that they may suppress the evil that haunts the devout. Invocation seeks fulfilment of a cherished desire that the God can bestow, while the celebration of the affair itself results in joyous festivity.

Apart from festivals that are sheer fanfare, sport, fun and frolic, the great bulk of them are essentially based on seasonal and agricultural myths, though over these has grown a heavy mantle of religious myths and legends, shifting the focus on to themselves. A single festival may have numerous legends explaining it, some simple variations on the same theme, others that are entirely separate. It is these legends that lend a quaint charm to most of the festivals of this country. But at the root of a large number of festivals is the force of the seasons.

Take for instance *Diwali,* the most widely celebrated of Hindu festivals, Coming after the monsoons, it is essentially a post-monsoon home-cleaning ceremony. Homes made dirty by the monsoon, are white washed, cleaned and decorated. Diwali comes at a time when the farmer is free. Agricultural implements are repaired and cleaned. Seeds too are taken care of. The fungus and cobwebs that were unattended to through the long monsoon are now cleared away. A few winged insects still haunt the homes and need to be got rid of. The *deepak*, an open-flame oil lamp, is lighted all over the city. Another clay lamp inverted over the lighted one collects a deposit of soot which will line the eye of many a damsel for the year to come. People dress up in colourful clothes. There is fun and frolic, meeting, greeting and feasting some respite to the farmer who has the seasons for his taskmaster, now allowing him this short holiday so that he can enjoy himself. Slowly, it seems, legends grew around this seasonal festival, ritualizing it to no mean advantage. Diwali ensures that the farmer shall revamp his home, worship his gods and goddesses, and revel, for the legend of Laxmi (goddess of wealth) visiting only clean houses this night compels the devotee to discipline.

Holi, the festival of colour, is a spring festival celebrating the return of colour to the land. Flowers of *tesu* and *mahua* trees, abundant in this season, were traditionally picked and boiled to extract a dye. Cold water coloured with the dye was thrown on people to wake them to the fact that warmer days had come and winter was dead. In this case too, a number of legends have grown about Holi, as have certain conventions that ensure that the people will have this one day to patch up enmities and meet one another, socially irrespective of caste. Everyone is covered beyond recognition with colour with *gulal* (powder colour) wet colour (semi-permanent) and even silver paint and polish among the roudy youngesters. The legends have their own stories to tell, and add the element of worship to Holi.

Pongal, observed amongst the South Indian is directly a harvest festival (coming after the winter harvest) which combines thanksgiving to the God of the harvesting with a day of feasting, followed by a day allotted to cattle veneration. The festival is an expression of the joy of the farmer at his stock of some six months of foodgrain in his granary. In the rush of the ritual he is compelled to take care of his bulls (which might otherwise have overlooked), and he spends one day in sport with his best bull. Jallikattu, this sport of bulls, is a joyful manner of testing and sorting brave bulls from the weak. The strong ones become known to be so, for the villagers of many surrounding villages also come there with their bulls. Later through the year, in the rutting season, the farmers will take their cows to the best bull—an ancient way of selective breeding!

The harvest is celebrated with full vigour in the South with song and dance. Post-harvest the farmer has time off, and the harvest having been gathered gives him the inclination to express his joy, which he does with folk-songs and dances, the members of his family also joining in the frolic. The vigour of the dance might be directly proportional to the quantity of the grain winnowed.

Sweets and eats prepared on a certain festive occasion celebrate the maturing and consequent availability of the items that go into their making, usually got from the recent crop. At seasonal festivals such seasonal items go into the making of votive offerings, which are also distributed as *prasad*. Examples are *pongal* at Pongal, *gujjias* at Holi, *modaks* of it at Ganesh Chaturthi, *ghewar* at Teej, and milk products at Janamashtmi, to name a few.

Festival dates according to different calendars. India follows a large number of calendars, and there lies the rub ! The official calendar is Gregorian. Hindu festivals, however, fall according to the *Saka Samvat*, which is a lunar calendar? to bring it in line with the seasons. But excepting for two dates (*Makar Sankranti* always falling on the 14th of January, and *Baisakhi* falling on 13th April), they do not match. So Hindu festivals fall on different dates of the Gregorian calendar each year. The Jains follow their own calendar, the *Veer Samvat*, which is out of line with the two mentioned above. The festivals of the Muslims are held according to their lunar calendar, the month being corrected by the actual sighting of the new moon, not when it occurs mathematically, the case of Id being cited as an example. So their festivals, nay whole months keep shifting vis-a-vis the Gregorian months, and their festivals may occur in any month of the official calendar. The festivals of those who follow Tibetan Buddhism (Ladakhis and the Tibetan refugees, for example) follow the Tibetan lunar calendar, which in turn has been derived from the Chinese one. Then there is the *Vikrami* calendar, all with its own computation. Can one ever be sure which festival falls on what date. To add to the perplexity, the Hindus compute a day from dawn, and not from midnight. And *gharis* and *palas* (hours and months) have to be taken into account as per astrological and astronomical reckoning. A festival can fall on two days, beginning at a moment on one day and stretching into the following day. In such cases there is utter uncertainty leading to great confusion, with some devotees celebrating on one day, the remaining wanting to do so on the other day. Well, it is all part of the festive face of India ! The Hindu month, too, cuts across two months of the Gregorian calendar, and that too in a shifting fashion. Therefore, it is difficult to follow anyone calendar in organizing the festivals into a list.

Be that as it may, a Hindu festival has the magical touch of transforming the simple peasant, and his family and relations into a group of delightful beings, gaudily dressed, carousing, rejoicing, and feasting with great gusto, as they worship their favourite *devis* and *devtas*.

Some well-known Hindu festivals are given in the following pages.

Akshaya Tritiya

Akshaya Tritiya believed to be the first day of Satya Yuga, occurs at the end of spring and beginning of *grishma* or summer. It is one of the four most auspicious days in the year among Hindus, viz., Bhai Bij (Kartik Sud 2), Dhuleti (Phalgun Vad 1), Akhatrij (Vaishakh Sud 3) and Dhan Terash (Ashvin Vad 13), when any important work can be started without reference to astrology to determine an auspicious moment. Apart from prayers, *darshan*, etc., all types of important work are commenced on this day; marriages are celebrated; children are sent to school for the first time; new shops are opened; ploughing of fields is begun and the ceremony of laying the foundation stone of a new house is performed. Importance attaches to a bath in holy rivers, to sacrifice of barley grains in fire, to performance of *shraddha* for the peace of the souls of departed ancestors and to worship of Shiva and Vishnu. It is believed that by all such performances people gain religious merit which is *akshaya* or everlasting and hence this day is named Akshaya Tritiya.

Among Hindu it is a custom at some places to give to Brahmins or family priests and earthen pitcher, a bamboo fan, a fruit, a handful of wheat and a copper coin for the pacification of the souls of the dead of the family, so that they may not suffer from the scorching heat of the coming season. This custom is called *udakakumbh pradan*—gift of earthen pot full of water—or *tadhodiyan* gift by which ancestors are said to be pleased. In some communities such as Kayastha, it is a custom that a clay elephant with a driver on it is set on a low stool near another mud image of a man, before which is set a dish with mixture of wheat flour, *ghee* and jaggery called *kuler* and green vegetables. Kanbis consider Akhatrij as a lucky day for starting agricultural operations, e.g., manuring, ploughing, etc. They worship their bullocks, put cotton threads or flower garlands round their necks or horns which they rub with *ghee*, paint their horns, hoofs and brows with red colour and feed them on grains. For herdsmen, Akhatrij is their sheep-shearing day.

This day is important to farmers and traders, as a forecast about the coming year is made from the winds. It is called *gadli* of Akhatrij. Villagers collect near the village boundary and make five small heaps of grains of different varieties on open ground to which are offered a copper coin, a betel-nut, some *ghee*, *gur* and cotton. Thereafter they return home. Next day they visit the place again. If these articles remain intact, they believe that the coming year will be good. If something is found missing or eaten by ants, they believe that the articles missing will be scarce and their prices will rise. If the cotton has flown away, it is believed that there will be bumper crops in the direction in which it has flown.

In some parts of Gujarat this day is celebrated by swinging on swings hung from branches of trees. The family is served with *galmana*, a sweet soup prepared from wheat flour, *ghee* and *gur* boiled together, or *shev* prepared from wheat flour with other varieties. This day is celebrated as Dolotsav as on Dhuleti in the temples of Dwarka and Dakor in Gujarat.

It is said that the tide in the sea on this day is the highest in the year. As the seas are stormy from this day up to Naliyeri Purnima (Shravan Sud 15) voyages are not undertaken during this period, and merchants and sailors keep their ships anchored at a safe port.

Akhatrij has also another significance, being the brithday of Parashurama, the sixth incarnation of Lord Vishnu. He was the sixth and youngest son of *rishi* Jamadagni, the newphew (sister's son) of the great sage Vishwamitra, who had married Renuka. In his times, Kshatriyas had become proud and arrogant. Forgetting their duty of protecting the public, assigned to them since the time of Manu, they were harassing them in numerous ways. Kshatriya king Sahasrarjun Kartavirya of Mahishmati—present Omkareshwer on the bank of the river Narmada—was very powerful. He had the might of a thousand hands. He was, therefore, symbolically believed to possess a thousand hands and called Sahasrarjun. Once he visited the hermitage of *rishi* Jamadagni who cordially received him and his party and served them with rich and delicious dishes. The king was astonished as to how a poor Brahmin could have all these costly things. On enquirty, he came to know that the *rishi* had a *kamadhenu* or celestial cow fulfilling all desires. He asked the *rishi* to give that cow to him, but was refused. He became angry, destroyed the hermitage, killed the sage and took away the cow by force. Parashurama was out at that time. When he returned, he learnt the account and also knew that on the demise of his father his mother Renuka had struck her head on the ground twenty-one times. He took a vow to destroy the Kshatriy as from the surface of the earth, which he wanted to give to the Brahmins. He pursued Sahasrarjun, caught him on the way and slew him with his axe, rescured the cow and returned to hermitage. The battle-axe or *parashu* was his only weapon and he was, therefore, named Parashurama. He then started his mission to wipe off such arrogant terrorists who had swerved from the path of duty. He destroyed Kshatriyas twenty-one times, and gave their kingdom to Brahmins. He is believed to be one of the seven immortal beings in this world, the others being Hanuman, Ashwatthama, *rishi* Markand, sage Narad, King Bhartrihari and Gorakhnath, who are said to give *darshan* even now to a really deserving devotee.

Amavas

Amavas is the last day of the dark fortnight of a lunar month when the moon does not appear, and is considered to be a day auspicious for religious ceremonies for the upliftment of the souls of the departed ones. On every Amavas special prayers are said by the Hindus, baths are taken and alms given.

This is celebrated among the religious minded sections of the Hindus in Delhi. Though every Amavas is sacred, yet some have gained special importance, namely, Mahalaya Amavas, Somavati Amavas and Kartik Amavas.

Mahalaya Amavas is the chief day for the worship of the dead and it occurs on the first day of waning moon in the month of Asoj. The whole of the fortnight preceding Mahalaya is called the *Pitri Paksha*, or the fortnight sacred to the memory of the departed ancestors. During the fortnight *shraddh* of the departed ancestors is performed and Brahmins are fed.

Somavati Amavas means falling on Monday. A legend connected with this goes as follows:

Bhishma, the old grand-uncle of the Pandavas, was lying on his death-bed. Yudhishtira, the eldest of the Pandavas, bewailed as to what use his victory was when all his kith and kin had been killed. Even the foetus which the Princess Uttara bore, had been killed by the enchanted weapons of Ashvathama. Yudhishtira was greatly distressed at the prospect of the extinction of his dynasty and sought advice from Bhishma as to what should be done.

Bhishma then described to him the *vrata* (fast) which grants long-living progeny. He said that on the moonless night falling on a Monday, one should go to a *pipal* tree (*Ficus religiosa)*, and there worship Vishnu. One should make offerings of jewels, or coins, or fruits, and go round the tree 108 times. Bhishma further suggested that Uttara should do this *vrata* and her foetus would regain life and the child would grow into a man of fame and virtue.

Yudhishtira then wanted to know who had introduced the *vrata* first. Thereupon Bhishma told him the following story:

There once lived a Brahmin named Devaswami in the city of Kanti. He had a virtuous wife named Dhanavati. She gave birth to seven sons and one beautiful daughter, named Gunavati. The sons were married. The girl was waiting to be married. One day a Brahmin guest visited their house. All the seven daughters-in-law and the daughter bowed before him. He blessed the daughter-in-law with long married life, but the daughter he prophesied that she would become a widow while performing the *saptapadi* during the marriage ceremony. Dhanavati became alarmed and begged of the Brahmin to tell her how to forestall the impending calamity. The Brahmin told her that if she could induce Soma to come to her house, the calamity could be averted. Soma was a *dhobi* woman by caste, living in Lanka (Sri Lanka).

Saying so the Brahmin departed. To save

herself from the catastrophe of widowhood the girl and her brother undertook a voyage to Lanka. They crossed the sea and, on reaching Lanka, they went to Soma's house where they swept and mud-washed it every morning for full one year. Soma was pleased with their service and agreed to accompany them to Kanti. Before leaving, Soma asked her daughters-in-law to preserve the body of anyone who might die in the family during her absence.

On seeing her daughter and son returning home with Soma, Dhanavati was overwhelmed with joy. She worshipped Soma and then selected a match for her daughter. But, as predicted, the bridegroom fell dead as soon as he commenced the *saptapadi*. All those gathered began to bewail but not Soma. She stood erect and holding the sacrificial cup in her hand, bestowed on the girl her own credit for having observed the *vrata* of Somavati Amavas. At that the dead man came back to life.

Soma then returned home. On her way she learnt that the giving away of the merit of her observance of the *vrata* had resulted in the death of all her sons, her husband, and even her son-in-law. Fortunately for her it was a dark Monday. 'Somavati' on that day. Soma went to a *pipal (Ficus religiosa)* and worshipped the tree. As soon as she performed the 108 peregrinations her lost husband, sons, and son-in-law came to life again. On reaching home, she informed her daughters-in-law that *pipal* was the abode of Vishnu, the Protector, and that if he be worshipped on that day, there would be no widowhood.

Kartik Amavas occupies a unique place. It is the Diwali night, and is celebrated with unique pomp and gaiety. The orthodox Hindus of India fast on Amavas.

Bhadarvi Amavasya

The last day of each month is considered holy according to Shastras, but that of Shravan is the most important of all the *amavasyas* of the year as it ends the austerities conducted during the holy month of Shravan such as religious observances or *vratas*, fasting, meditation, chanting of *mantras*, worship of deities, etc. The whole month is dedicated to the worship of Lord Shiva.

This day is also known as Pithori Amas. Pithori means the goddess of a *pitha* or seat. There are sixty-four such *pithas* or seat of goddesses in India situated at different places. They are called sixty-four *yoginis* or *matrikas*.

There is a story in *Bhavishya Purna* how a Brahmin lady worshipped these *matrikas* to make her eight dead sons alive. A Brahmin named Shridhar had married Sumitra by whom he had eight sons. The eldest, named Shankar, had married Videha who also gave birth to eight sons but none lived. When she could not endure the ill-treament from her mother-in-law, she resolved to commit suicide. She went away to a forest where she met a lady at a *math*, who told her that it was the residence of Vaital and *yoginis* who would devour her and counselled her to go away. When Videha narrated her story, the lady took pity on her and advised her to hide on the nearby *bili* tree, so that when all the sixty-four *yoginis* came at night and enquired about a newcomer, she might approach them and pray to them for a boon of the life of her dead children. The plan worked and the yoginis granted life to her dead children. This happened on Shravan Vad *amavasya*. In pursuance of this story, women who have no issue or whose children do not live, perform Pithori Vrata. They observe fast for the day and establish the *mandal* of sixty-four *yoginis*. They place eight copper pots full of water on a square piece of red cloth called *sthapan*, i.e., place, naming each after one of the eight goddesses, viz., Brahmi, Kaumari, Vaishnavi, Chamunda, Maheshwari, Varahi, Indrani and Durga and place fifty-six betel-nuts in the name of the remaining goddesses. They then invoke and worship them with the help of a Brahmin priest. Next day after worshipping goddesses ten maidens are invited, worshipped and feasted with sweets. After that the fast is broken and the *mandal* is given away to the priest with *dakshina*.

Not only Brahmins and women but Kshatriyas and Vaishyas also observe this day as a festival. Farmers decorate their bullocks and take them in a procession in the villages and do not yoke them for the day. After worship they feed them with rich food. This festival is, therefore, also known as Vrishabhotsav. In Maharashtra it is known as Pola.

This day is also one of the tree dedicated to *pitris* or ancestors, known as *tripindi* which occasion occurs thrice a year, viz., Kartik Sud 13, 14, 15 Chaitra Sud 13, 14, 15 and Shravan Vad 13, 14, 15. These days are known as *aravara* and the *amavasya* is called Tripindi Amas.

The month of Shravan is sacred both to Lord Krishna whose birthday occurs on the 8th in the dark half as well as to Lord Shiva who is worshipped throughout the month. Special *puja* is performed at Mahadev temples, especially on all the Mondays and on the *amavasya* day, with offerings of *bili-patras* or *Aegle marmelos* leaves. The devout undertake a vow to offer 125,000 *bili* leaves to Lord Shiva during the month, and accordingly offer 4,500 leaves every day with the chanting of *mantras*. In some temples the whole quantity is offered on the *amavasya* day by a team of Brahmins offering the leaves simultaneously. Some Brahmins also undertake to worhip Chintamani at Mahadev temples during this holy month. This is done by preparing small *shivalingas* from clay freshly brought every day, arranging them in different designs in the *sabha-mandap* of the temple and worshipping them with prescribed rites and *mantras*. As 125,000 *shivalingas* are to be prepared and worshipped during the course of the month, 4,500 *shivalingas* are prepared and worshipped daily. The different shapes and designs in which the *shivalingas* are arranged during the week are as follows:

Sunday	*Surya*	Sun
Monday	*Nagpash*	Snake
Tuesday	*Trikon*	Triangle
Wednesday	*Kashyap*	Tortoise
Thursday	Chatushkon	Quadrangle
Friday	Panchkon	Pentagon
Saturday	Dhanush-ban	Bow and Arrow

Worship in this manner is believed to fulfil the wishes of the devotee and hence the name Chintamani. Since the *shivalingas* are prepared every day from clay, the deity is also called Parthiveshwer. This form of worship keeps the Brahmin busy from 5 a.m. to 10 p.m. throughout the month, bringing the clay in the morning, preparing *shivalingas*, invoking the deity, offering *puja* or worship, chanting *mantras* and finally performing *visarjan* at night. This type of worship is offered in many a Mahadev temple all over India.

People in large numbers visit Mahadev temples for *darshan* throughout the month of Shravan, when the *pujaris* decorate them in a variety of ways and scenes from Hindu mythology are displayed. They depict such events as Gangavataran or the coming down of the Ganges from the heaven to the earth, with Lord Shiva in readiness to receive her, mount Kailash, the abode of Lord Shiva with several deities like Shiva, Parvati, Ganapati, etc. with the help of paintings. Fairs are also held on this day at a number of pilgrim places Mahalaya, Pitra Amavasya.

Anant Chaudash

The fourteenth of bright half of lunar month Bhadra, known as 'Anant Chaudash', falls in the month of Bhadra or Asvina (September) every year. In India this festival is celebrated only by those castes who are entitled to wear yagyopawit—sacred thread—except Arya Samajists. Brahmins, Kshatriyas and Vaishyas fall in this category. Anant is a sacred triple cord insignia of Lord Vishnu. It is tied on the right arm by men and on left arm by women. Some of the well-to-do persons encase it in silver or gold armlet.

Those wearing this sacred thread observe fast on this day and worship it in the afternoon. If it is put on in the form of thread it is replaced with new one and in the case of encasement the same is put on again after worship. The worship is done in Sanatanic way. Food is taken in the evening.

Some persons perform *udyapan* of this fast but it is done once in life. Sanatanists believe that virtues of observing fast are not acquired unless *udyapan* is performed. During this ceremony fourteen Brahmins are fed after worship and each of them is given betel nut, cloth, coins, dhoti, metal pot and *yagyopavit* as *dakshina.*

Baisakhi

Baisakhi, the 1st day of Baisakh, invariably falls on the 13th of April. On this day, the sun reaches the highest point of its orbit, called *ucca,* in the Hindu system, and *aux* in the medieval European system of astronomy. Delhi joins in the festivities of this festival.

In Punjab Baisakhi marks the ripening of the *rabi* harvest, the happy time for the peasant to gather the fruits of his labour, and in some parts of the State it is considered a good omen to apply sickle to the crop for the first time on this day. The virile peasant then comes out, attired in his best clothes, to express his joy by performing *bhangra,* the typical Punjabi group dance. The dancers and the drummer challenge each other to continue the dance, and the scenes of sowing, harvesting, winnowing and gathering of crop, are expressed by zestful movements of the body, and to the accompaniment of ballads.

Persons of all denominations in Delhi may participate in the Baisakhi celebrations. To the Sikhs, the day has also a religious significance.

It was on the Baisakhi day in 1699 A.D. that the tenth Sikh Guru, Guru Gobind Singh founded the Order of the Khalsa. The Sikhs were converted into a martial community by instituting the custom of *Pahul* (baptism), celebrating with Hola Mohalla at Anandpur Sahib.

Earlier, it was on the Baisakhi day that some two thousand years ago Lord Buddha received Enlightenment and heralded the dawn of a new society.

Arya Samajis observe Baisakhi day with *eclat* because it was on this day in 1875 that Swami Daya Nand set-up the first Arya Samaj in Mumbai.

On this day it is regarded auspicious to hear of the new *Bikrami Samvat* which, in fact, commences from the first of Chaitra. Chaitra is considered as *Kala Mahina* (black month), the most plausible reason being that the granaries are empty and there are lurking risks about the safe maturing of the standing crops. Be that as it may, the celebrations of the New Year of the Bikrami era are postponed to Baisakhi. On this day, after taking bath in a river, canal or tank, the Hindus and the Sikhs visit temples or gurdwaras to pay their obeisance and hear the new *samvat* from the priest. Fairs are organized at various places, especially in the western and central Punjab.

Basant

'Basant' is the Sanskrit name of spring season. Basanta Panchami falls on the fifth day of the bright half of Magh, occurring in the latter half of January and marks the commencement of the spring season. The arrival of the spring season, heralded by the melodious notes of the cuckoo and fragrance of mango blooms, has been a constant theme of delight to Indian poets: they have elevated Basanta Panchami to the dignity of a festival, for there appears to be nothing particularly religious about the day, and in many parts of India, it is observed as a mere secular holiday, with no celebrations connected with it.

According to the Hindu scriptures Basanta Panchami is sacred to Saraswati, the goddess of learning and fine arts. Saraswati combines in herself the functions of all the nine Muses of the Greek mythology, presiding over the whole domain of letters, arts, and sciences. She is represented as a maiden of snow-white complexion, arrayed in spotless white clothes and sitting on a white full-blown lotus floating on an expanse of crystal-clear water. Her *vahan* (conveyance) is the swan. In one hand she holds a book, in the other a *vina* (a fretted instrument of the guitar kind), for she is also the goddess of music. Offerings made to Saraswati are unripe ears of barley and grains of gram, sprays of mango bloom, sweets prepared from white sesame, and other edibles. Saraswati puja is also the day on which Hindu boys begin to learn their alphabet and quite a little ceremony is made of the matter.

Basanta Panchami is also associated with the worship of Vishnu, god of preservations.

By and far, Basanta Panchami is a seasonal festival and is the harbinger of spring, when weather begins to warm up and nature starts pulsating with new life. Plants begin to sprout and blossom. The birds chirp and dance about leaving the stress of winter behind. *Sarson* fields with yellow flowers dozing in the warmth of sun invite man to come out to partake of their joy. To match the yellow *sarson* flowers, men, women and children don *basanti* (yellow) clothes. Women turn out in *basanti* suits or saris. At the least they will have *basanti* scarfs. Men put on *basanti* turbans and caps; if nothing else, they will have *basanti* handkerchiefs. The children are also dressed in similar clothes. The day begins with a taste of *basanti palao* or *halwa.* In certain parts of Delhi as elsewhere, fairs are held and kite-flying is done. Transparent blue sky is filled with multi-coloured kites and the air rings with the shouts of *voh kata.*

In Punjab the festival is associated with the martyrdom of Hakikat Rai who on this day laid down his life, for not accepting the Muslim faith under coersion.

Bawan Dwadashi

Bawan Dwadashi (12th day of the bright half in the month of Bhadon) is observed in the memory of Vaman who according to the Hindu mythology was the fifth incarnation of Vishnu.

It is believed that Lord Vishnu had to appear in mortal frame to protect the denizens of heaven from the *daitya* (demon) king Bali, who through devotion and penance became a favourite of Lord Vishnu and started terrorizing the godlings.

According to the legend Vaman was born a dwarf to Kashyap Rishi (sage) and his virtuous wife Aditi. He appeared before king Bali in the garb of a Brahmin mendicant and begged for a piece of land measuring his three steps, which he needed to conduct studies of the holy Vedas. King Bali readily agreed to this request. His pontiff Sukracharya, however, smacked some foul play and warned the king that his guest was none else but Vishnu himself who had come to destroy his kingdom and reduce him to a position of subjugation to the gods. But Bali, unmindful of the impending catastrophe, stuck to his promise.

The legend goes on to say that when the king asked Vaman to demarcate the plot which he wanted to have, the latter then assumed a gigantic form and compassed the whole earth with one step and in the next compassed the heavenly regions. He then asked Bali where he could put the third step. Bali offered his head to receive the third step. Thereupon Vaman hurled Bali with the weight of his foot into the lower regions. At the same time, pleased with this exemplary magnanimity of Bali, he promised to guard him against all adversities.

In the Hindu scriptures this day has been described as of great significance, and those who observe fast on this day after bath at the confluence of rivers and give charities to Brahmins ensure a seat in heaven. On the Dwadashi day every confluence of rivers is supposed to be as sacred as the Ganges. Before breaking the fast on the 13th, the devotees again bathe at the confluence and worship the image of Vaman, which is wrapped in a cloth. A new earthen pot is placed on the spot selected for the worship, and it is bedecked with yellow silken cloths. After the prayers all these articles are donated to Brahmins. Donations sometimes also include cows, umbrellas, shoes, gold, clothes and bulls.

Bawan Dwadashi is celebrated with special fervour and enthusiasm in northern India. Some Hindus, especially ladies, observe fast. At night tableaux depicting various scenes from *Ramayana* and *Mahabharata* may be taken through the bazars, in a procession, generally headed by a band and *gatka* and singing parties. During the daytime a fair is held in which there are all kinds of stalls. Earthen idols of Lord Vishnu are purchased by most of the visitors.

Buddh Purnima

Buddh Purnima, the full moon day of *Baisakh* (April/May) of the year 563 B.C. is considered most auspicious by Buddhist tradition. It is a gazetted holiday and is celebrated in Delhi keeping the Buddhist tradition alive. Buddha, his wife Yashodhara, his disciple Ananda, his charioteer Channa, and his horse Kantaka are believed to have all been born on the same day, and at the same hour. The *Bodhi* tree at Gaya, under which he became the Buddha (the Enlightened One), too, sprouted at the same moment. *Buddha Purnima* was again the occasion of his enlightenment, and later, of his *nirvana* (death, and deliverance from rebirth).

The day gains manifold importance owing to these factors, and is a day for pious homage to Lord Buddha. Buddhism flourished in India under the royal patronage of Ashoka. With the passage of time the number of adherents has dwindled. The once massive public celebrations of Buddha Purnima have now become a calm, indoor affair.

However, pilgrims visit Lumbini (Nepal), the birthplace of Buddha, and Bodhgaya (Bihar) on this occasion.

Historically, the birth of Siddhartha, Gautam Buddha, the founder of Buddhism, his mother, Mahamaya, had a strange dream that a white elephant, a lotus flower held aloft in its majestic trunk, entered her womb! The dream was ably interpreted as a prophecy. The child she carried would become the ruler of the world, if his leanings were temporal; or a great sage, should he be of a spiritual bent of mind!

As he grew up, he was groomed to be fit to succeed the old king, his father. Material bondage followed in the shape of a beautiful wife, and later, in the gift of a son. Hopes were pinned on his becoming a great emperor, in the light of the prophecy.

But Siddhartha came face to face with the pain, misery, and harsh realities of life in the form of a frail old man, a corpse being taken through the thoroughfare, and finally a recluse in a pathless world.

Turning his back on his realm and family, he exchanged his princely robes for those of a mendicant beggar. The rest is history.

Devshayani Ekadashi

The Devshayani Ekadashi is observed in Ashadh Sud (June-July). In the month of Ashadh the sun enters the orbit of Karka and begins to move in the southern region. The night of gods begins from Ashadh Sud 11 and Lord Vishnu goes to sleep on this day, known as Devpodhi or Devshayani Ekadashi when the night of Gods commences. The period from Devshayani Ekadashi, i.e. Ashadh Sud 11 to Kartik Sud 11 is called *chaturmas* (i.e., four months) and prescribed for penance, austerities, religious observances, recital of *mantras,* bathing in holy rivers, performance of sacrifices, worship and charity. As this is the monsoon season, such austerities as fasting, etc., also help in maintaining health. Hindu ascetics and *sanyasis* otherwise enjoined to avoid a long stay anywhere halt for these four months at a selected place, generally giving religious discourses to the public.

On Ashadh Sud 11, the idol of Vishnu with Lakshmiji is worshipped. Devotees resolve to observe some vow, giving up some item of their fond diet, during *chaturmas.*They observe fast on this day and awake for the whole night in prayers. Observance of fast at lest on *ekadashi* during all the four months is most common.

Newly married women observe Akhand Agiarash, on all the *ekadashis* of *chaturmas* by fasting on *falahar*. They keep awake throughout the night, keeping a *ghee* lamp burning all the time and singing devotional songs. Next day they breakfast after offering worship to Lord Vishnu.

Diwali—the Festival of Lights

Diwali is both the climax and commencement of the yearly cycle of festivals. It marks the close of the old year and ushers in the new. It provokes thought and wisdom and generates hope and aspirations. As the past blends into the future, Diwali fills every moment with *joie de vivre,* with zest for life. It is a universal festival which even the lowliest of the low celebrates with the ostentation he can afford. There is, geniality and happiness everywhere, joy on earth and goodwill towards all mankind.

It is impossible to confine the enthusiasm of people for this festival all over to a mere day or two. It is, therefore, celebrated for five consecutive days from *Dhan Terash* to *Bhai Bij,* each day a happy holiday in itself. Diwali is thus a cluster of holidays, each of them being considered a part of Diwali itself. In western part of India, therefore, Diwali, the name given to Ashvin *amavasya,* also signifies all these holidays collectively, while in other parts of India Diwali is celebrated as an individual holiday. Though all the five days are known and celebrated as Diwali, each is known by a separate name and dedicated to a separate deity. The festivals of *Vagh Barash* and *Labh Pancham* precede and follow it closely. Though the festival is thus celebrated for about a week, the preparations start right from *Navratri* and *Dussehra,* with an aftermath or a glow of festivity lasting right up to Dev Diwali. Holi excepted, this period of a month and a half is the gayest and happiest in the year.

Nature itself facilitates the celebration of this festival of festivals. In a predominantly agricultural society the successful completion of agricultural operations is of the utmost importance. By the end of Ashvin, the harvests are ready, and the hearts contented. The farmer has a well-earned respite from the rigours of hard work during monsoon, and can look forward to a year of prosperity and comfort ahead. The unhygienic season gives way to a healthy one. The monsoon is over, and the dampness, mud, filth and insects are all gone. After the oppressive heat of September and October the refreshing cold of the following months is particularly welcome. After a disease-ridden monsoon, the season transforms itself into a healthy and energizing winter. Rivers, ponds and lakes are not only full, but also clear, and the sky which has cast off its prolonged gloom is bright and cheerful again.

Though entirely social in its outlook and mode of celebrations, like all Hindu festivals, Diwali is not without its religious significance. Stories related in the Shastras and Puranas about the various festive days associated with Diwali are many. A collection of all of them would itself be a Diwali Purana! People wake up early, complete their morning duties and go out for *darshan* at temples. It is believed that goddess Lakshmi descends from the heaven to the earth during these days to stay at neat and clean, snug and tidy houses. Hence, to receive her at their own dwellings, people decorate their houses with ornamental festoons of *asopalav* leaves and small earthen lamps *(kodiyan)*. Indeed, all the three principal goddesses have special days earmarked for their worship during Diwali festival. Lakshmi, the Goddess of Wealth, is worshipped on Dhan Terash, Kalika, the destroyer of evil on Kali Chaudash and Saraswati, the Goddess of Learning on the day of Diwali. They correspond to the trinity of the main Hindu gods whose *shaktis* they are—Lakshmi of Vishnu, Kalika of Shiva and Saraswati of Brahma. However, the religious aspect remains in the background of the universal jubilations during these days.

Preparations to welcome Diwali are marked by intense activity in every household. Even in the smallest village in the remotest corner of the country, floors and walls are freshly plastered with mud and cow-dung. Houses are white-washed, painted by some. All the brass and copper vessels in the house are washed and scrubbed bright. The streets are cleaned. Sweets and other delicacies are prepared in every house. New articles of household use are purchased if one can afford them. New garments are made, and new ornaments acquired. Every member of the family has some purchases made for him. Merchants close their yearly accounts and clear out their old stocks even by concessions sales to make way for fresh ones. These are busy days for the traders, especially those dealing in cloth, jewellery, metalware, footwear, cutlery, toiletry and sweetmeats. They display their wares artistically to promote a thriving business by catching the public eye. This festival is truly earmarked for the Vaishyas or traders and farmers, as Balev is for Brahmins, Dussehra for Kshatriyas and Holi for Shudras. Diwali is given to wealth and prosperity as Balev is to religious rites, Dussehra to war and weapons, and Holi to unbridled revelry. In its social and economic aspect, Diwali is an important post-monsoon harvest festival, occupying a significant position in an economy which is mostly agricultural. There can be no fitter occasion for such spontaneous celebrations and merriment on such a mass scale than the close of an active cultivating season marked by fulfilment of one's labour.

Diwali is, literally and correctly, the festival of lights. Myriads of lights glow everywhere, on the main doors, on balconies, and on *dip-malas* in temples. Earthen lamps are most popular, while the more fashionable people nowadays decorate their house-fronts with electric lights. These lights turn the dark night into one brighter than the moonlit. Symbolically also Diwali is the festival of all that light stands for—brightness, knowledge and happiness, disappearance of darkness, evil and misery.

Rangoli is another decoration of the house during the Diwali festival. The foreground of every house is levelled and mud-plastered and attractive designs are drawn with coloured powders with the help of symmetrical dots which are joined up in the required designs. A new design is drawn everyday. The more skilful women draw such beautiful designs as give an appearance of rich carpets spread out for welcoming visitors. Those who do not indulge in such elaborate designs put at least the *swastika* in vermilion at the door front which symbolizes all that is good and auspicious.

Domestic Aspect:—Diwali is also a children's festival. Even the grown-ups can forget the worries and cares of their humdrum life and be children again, to enjoy the festival with gay abandon. Children like fire crackers more than anything else and all round the day, and far into the night, the air resounds with the boom of crackers. Special bazaars of crackers and fireworks are put up in towns and cities.

Diwali is equally a family festival. Every member who is out wishes to return home and spend Diwali with his family. Indeed Diwali "is more than ever symbolic of all that is gracious and good in life, all the light and felicity so urgently needed in a tired and nuclear world".

Vagh Barash:—This is a minor festival, not actually a part of Diwali. But, as it immediately proceeds Diwali, festivities begin from this day.

This day is also known as Govatsa Dwadashi. According to Shastras, a cow with a calf, preferably of matching colour, is to be worshipped in the evening on its return from grazing with libations of water at its feet and flower garlands, and fed with a preparation of *adad.*

Cow milk and milk preparations like curd, whey, *ghee,* etc., are forbidden on this day. Shastras enjoin taking of an *adad* preparation at dinner. Cow-worship symbolizes the importance attached to cattle in an economy in which animal power is most extensively used in agricultural operations, and livestock is a useful subsidiary occupation with agriculture.

Dhan Terash:—This day is dedicated to the worship of goddess Lakshmi in the form of *dhan* or wealth. People worship coins, ornaments and other belongings as symbols of wealth. The day is, therefore, named Dhan Terash. In ancient times in an economy which was primarily agricultural, the cow was considered to be the real wealth of the people and was worshipped as a symbol of Lakshmi, on its return home in the evening from grazing. A herd of cows is called *dhan* from which also the day is called Dhan Terash. People adorn cows, paint their horns and hoofs and decorate their necks with strings of bronze bells. Shepherds paint the horns of their cattle, viz., buffaloes, goats and sheep. Even potters paint their donkeys as they are of great help in their business. In the evening, young boys make cows run by the buzzing sound of *bambuda* (a country-made instrument made from bamboo with cotton string tied at one end). This custom has long been followed for good omen.

It is said that Yama, the God of Death, promised that people who illumine their houses by lamps for five days from Dhan Terash onwards would be saved from accidental death and pains of hell. People, therefore, illuminate their houses and shops which become an attraction for the public who move out in large numbers to see the illuminations. The whole day is passed in pleasure and merriment. Even the cinema houses and theatres are found overcrowded. Members of family are served with sweets and children given articles of their choice, especially crackers. Buying of utensils is common with the city and its markets filled with people buying utensils.

Dhan Terash is also the birthday of Dhanvantari, the physician of gods. When the gods and demons churned the ocean, he rose from it with a pot of nectar on his shoulder. His birthday is celebrated by Ayurvedic physicians on Dhan Terash day.

Kali Chaudash:—Kali Chaudash is also called Kalaratri and Narak Chaturdashi. According to *Devi Purana* the last three days of Ashvin, viz., Dhan Terash, Kali Chaudash and Diwali are specially assigned to each of the three main goddesses Mahalakshmi, Mahakali and Mahasaraswati respectively. People worship goddess Lakshmi on Dhan Terash, Kali on Kali Chaudash and Saraswati on Diwali. Since this day is reserved for the worship of Kali, it is named Kali Chaudash.

Associated with the name Narak Chaturdashi, by which Kali Chaudash is also known, there is an anecdote in *Shrimad Bhagavat* about the demon king Narakasur of Pragjyotishpur, the capital of the region of that name, situated in the south of Bhutan, near Assam. He was a mighty king and also very wicked. He had conquered Indra, the king of gods, and snatched away his royal insignia and the *kundals* or earrings of his mother Aditi, and captured the place known as Maniparva (present Manipur) on mountain Amara. He had built fortresses on the mountain around his capital. He had conquered 16,100 kingdom and imprisoned the princesses of these kingdoms in his castle. They secretly sent a message to Shri Krishna for help. He invaded Pragjyotishpur with his wife Satyabhama and a mighty Yadava force. A battle ensured, and Satyabhama, with the backing of Shri Krishna killed the demon. They entered the city where they were cordially received by the public who too were tired of the demon's atrocities. Lord Krishna released all the 16,100 princesses from the prison and returned the insignia of Indra and *kundals* of Aditi to them. The princesses decided to marry Krishna, their saviour and benefactor. This event happened on the dark fourteenth of Ashvin and since then it is known as *Narak* Chaturdashi. *Narak* also means hell, and the slaying of Narakasur, a representative of hell, symbolizes the disappearance of evil from the earth.

Another story concerning the three days starting with Kali Chaudash relates to Bali, the powerful king of demons, who had conquered the *devas* led by their king Indra, captured his capital, Amaravati and began to rule the three worlds: heaven, earth and the nether region. Indra and other gods, advised by their preceptor Brihaspati fled to *Brahmalok*—the residence of Brahma and with him approached Vishnu and prayed for his protection. In order to acquire sufficient merit to conquer even *Brahmalok*, Bali started performing one hundred Ashwamedh sacrifices on the bank of the Narmada at Bhrigutirth with the help of Bhargava Brahmins, as advised by his preceptor Shukracharya. On the completion of the last sacrifice Bali was to become powerful enough to conquer any place he wished. To save the *devas,* Vishnu took birth by Aditi, the wife of sage Kashyap, as Vaman, his fifth incarnation on the earth. Vaman approached Bali who had made a vow to give anything asked for by Brahmins in alms. Vaman asked for only a portion of land measuring three steps of his. Bali agreed, and Vaman with his one step took up the heaven, with his second step took up the earth and with the third step on Bali's head sent him down to *patal,* the nether region, and advised him to rule there. Without the least hesitation he consented only on condition that he be allowed to rule the earth for three days in a year. Bali's rule was benevolent and his kingdom was free from vices like drunkenness, theft, cheating, and killing of animals. His subjects were virtuous, pious and contented. The last three days of the year are, therefore, reserved for his rule, as requested by him, and are celebrated as a festival by people in his honour.

Vam margis, tantriks and *shaktas* believe the night of Kali Chaudash to be particularly propitious for invoking spirits and call it Maharatri. At midnight of Kali Chaudash, *yakshas, gandharvas, kinnars, bhutas* and *pishachas,* etc., can be invoked at the burning *ghat* or cemetery. Hence the *bhiuas, jatis* and such others go to such places and propitiate them to obtain control over them and thereby acquire certain supernatural powers.

This day is also important for the worship of Bhairav and Hanuman. On this day Hanuman killed the demons Ahi Ravan and Mahi Ravan, the two warriors of Ravan, who had taken away Rama and Lakshman to *patal* to sacrifice them to their goddess. On their release, Rama and Lakshman offered him oil and red lead. Since then Hanuman is worshipped on this day with oil and red lead as this is believed to free people from terrors of diseases and evil spirits.

Great importance attaches to *abhyanga-snan,* bath after rubbing the body with oil, on this day. It is essential to take bath in *brahma, mahurat,* i.e., before sunrise, with earth dug up by a plough and *agheda* or *Achyranthus aspara* leaves. Lord Shiva, Yama and Aryama, the god of *pitris* or ancestors are then to be worshipped. It is said in *Brahma Purana* that it is essential to move in streets with lighted earthen torches called *merayas* on these days which are believed to show the path of heaven to ancestors. This is called *ulka darshan,* the sight of *ulka* or burning lights in heaven and on earth. New flags are hoisted on the top of temples on this day. People apply *kajal* (lamp soot) in the eyes to increase their light and lustre. It is customary to take *vadan (bhajis)* or pounded pulses, especially *adad,* at dinner with sweets. The dishes prepared on this day generally consist of *dudhpak-puri* and *bhajis* of *galka* or *Luffa aegyptica,* while in Saurashtra, sweetballs of *churma* (preparation of wheat flour, *ghee* and *gur*) and *vadan* are taken after offering the same to Hanuman, Mamalia and other local deities, and after putting two or three *vadan* in an open chowk and pouring the water around them. This custom of putting the *vadan* at the crossing of four roads is believed to drive away evil spirits.

The use of *adad* or *Phaseolus mungo* on this and other occasions has a special significance. It is believed to possess strength-giving properties. It is, therefore, prescribed especially for *naivedya* offered to those deities and even spirits who are credited with supernatural power and strength. Preparations of *adad* are necessarily included in the offerings to Mataji, the Mother Goddess, who is the embodiment of Shakti, the Supreme Power. Similarly, the use of *adad* is prescribed in the worship of Hanuman and Bhairav who are propitiated for power. *Tantriks* who aim at commanding influence over evil spirits and powers attach great importance to *adad* and invariably use it in many ways like sitting in a circle drawn with *adad,* offering *adad baklas,* etc., while performing their rites.

Diwali—Ashvin Vad 15 (Amavas):—The last day of the Hindu year of Vikram era commencing from the first day of Kartik is Diwali or Dipotsavi, the Festival of Lights. Lord Vishnu had rescued on this day goddess Lakshmi from the hold of King Bali. She moves on the earth during the Diwali days when the rule of Bali is restored; she resides in happy homes where there is no quarrel but only peace and harmony. According to another Pauranic story, Lakshmi was born on Ashvin Vad *amavasya* when she sprang from the ocean churned by gods and demons and married Vishnu. People celebrate her birthday by cleaning and decorating their homes. It was on this day that Rama returned to Ayodhya after his conquest over Ravan and the return of their beloved Ramachandra was celebrated by the people of Ayodhya by illuminating their houses.

Diwali was celebrated all over India even before the Vikram era. Cow-worship during Diwali days is considered important as cows were deemed to be the wealth of the people in olden days. At present also *gokrida* is arranged before the idol of Krishna in the open *chowks* of temples of Vaishnavite sect and *dip-malas* are lighted in the evening. *Dip pujan,* worship of light is performed in the evening. *Sathia* or *swastik* design is made near the household deity or some other convenient place in the house, and earthen lamps are placed on it and worshipped. The significance of this worship is to leave behind all misery, indigence and unpleasantness and welcome peace, prosperity and happiness expected in the coming year.

Diwali is very important to merchants. They close their yearly accounts on this day. In several parts of India, even though the new year begins in Chaitra, merchants observe Diwali as the last day of the commercial year for closing their accounts. *Diwali-baki* or loans outstanding on Diwali are not liked by merchants who try their best to repay their loans and recover their bills in the days preceding Diwali. They open new account-books with a ceremonial worship of Lakshmi and Sharada Pujan at their shops which are cleaned, decorated and illuminated for the festival. As the new account-books are worshipped during this ceremony, it is also known as *chopda* or *vahi pujan.* Relatives and friends are invited to attend the ceremony which is conducted by the family priest. All the three main goddesses are worshipped on the occasion, the ink-stand being considered a symbol of Kali, a silver coin that of Lakshmi and the account-book that of Saraswati. On the first page of the new ledgers the auspicious *swastika* is drawn and characters like *Om Shri* 1¼ are written with vermilion. Similar figures and characters and words like *Shubh* (auspicious) and *Labh* (gain), etc., are also painted with red ochre or vermilion on or near the door-frames of shops and houses. Dry fruits, sweets, coins, etc., are offered to the goddess Lakshmi. By these acts, the goddess is propitiated to get her blessing for good business during the ensuing year. Gifts in cash, sweets, etc., are given to relatives, servants, dependants and Brahmins. Sweets, toys and crackers are distributed among children. Greetings are exchanged. Merchants transact business of new varieties of goods and give some cash to one another to enter the account of sale and purchase in the new books as a token of goodwill. They also send some items of their merchandise to their permanent customers as *boni* or the auspicious first deal and enter their names in the new books.

On the day of Diwali the ceremony of *meraya sinchava* is performed at some places. If a couple has been married during the year, the bride and bridegroom have to stand on wooden stools facing each other with *meraya* or torches of sugarcane with dry coconut kernel bowls fixed at the top, filled with cotton seeds and a cotton wick in the centre. They pour *ghee* in each other's *meraya* while the family priest recites *mantras* of benediction. Thereafter relatives pour *ghee* in the *meraya* held by each and give some gifts to the couple. In the evening children move in the streets from house to house with earthen *merayas* filled with cotton seeds and cotton wicks lighted in the centre, wherein every housewife pours some *ghee* or oil. The mother of a new-born child also visits the houses of her relatives with her child in new clothes and ornaments and a *meraya* held in her hand. Women pour *ghee* in her *meraya* and give some present in cash or kind to the new-born child, and sweets to the mother.

Lamps are lighted at night, not only in every household but in every nook and corner of the house setting the dark night aglow—one which is brighter than any *purnima!* The whole atmosphere is filled with the booms of crackers and fireworks. Women keep working late into the night decorating their courtyards with *rangoli* designs. At midnight they go silently to dispose of the rubbish from the house at the crossing of roads and return without looking behind, uttering a verse meaning misfortune has gone and fortune arrived. Lights are kept burning the whole night.

Jains also regard Diwali as the *nirvan kalyanak* or the holy anniversary of the *nirvan* of Mahavir, the 24th *tirthankar.*

Dussehra

Dussehra or Vijay Dashmi is sometimes described as the Royal festival of the Hindus. It occurs on the 10th day of the bright half of the Bikrami month of Asoj (September-October). It is one of the greatest Hindu festivals and is celebrated with great zeal throughout Delhi, as elsewhere in the country.

According to one legend, the festival is in commemoration of Bhagiratha, an ancestor of Rama, successfully exhorting Ganga (the Ganges to flow on earth and give up her abode in heaven). Another legend narrates that on this day Goddess Durga beheaded Mahishasur, a buffalo-headed demon who terrorized the denizens of heaven, and the day is celebrated as *Durgotsava* (festival of Durga).

According to another story, which is commonly current in many parts of India, the festival is held in commemoration of the victory of Rama over Ravana, who precipitated a war by furtively kidnapping Rama's wife Sita under the masquerade of a Brahmin mendicant, when Rama was passing his days in exile along with her and Lakshmana in compliance with his father's behest. In order to recover Sita, Ram and Lakshmana invaded Lanka (Sri Lanka) with an army mainly comprising the Vanars (monkey race) and killed Ravana and his kith and kin. Symbolically it is the victory of truth and justice over evil.

The celebrations extend over a period of ten days during which the life story of Rama is enacted *(Ram Lila)*, as narrated in the Ramayana.

The tenth day, the Dussehra day, huge crowds assemble in parks and open spaces, where large effigies of the demon-king Ravana, Meghnada (his son) and Kumbhkarna (his brother), are put up. A battle is enacted the warring chiefs ending in the Ravana receiving a fatal arrow from Rama. The effigies are then put to fire to the accompaniment of fireworks.

People distribute sweetmeats to rejoice the victory of Rama. Children explode crackers. It is customary to suck the new-crop sugarcane on this day. Brahmin priests visit their patrons and offer them tender barley plants in return for monetary gifts.

Ganesh Chaturthi

Shastras and mythology say that in Kali Yuga, goddess Shakti and Vinayaka or Ganapati can not only be pleased easily, but also they are the only deities that quickly fulfil the desires of their devotees, and as such the worship of these two deities has its own importance. Ganapati or Ganesh is worshipped on his birthday on the bright fourth of Bhadrapad, which is observed as a public holiday.

There is a mythological story about the birth of Ganesh. Parvati, the consort of Lord Shiva, was once taking a bath. Alone at home, she created an image from the dirt removed from her body, gave it life and asked him to guard the entrance. In the meanwhile Lord Shiva arrived but the child did not allow him inside. Shiva became angry and threw the child into the waters of the Ganga where it became enlarged and assumed human body. Gods worshipped him and named him Gangaputra, the son of the Ganga, and married him to eight *siddhis* or attainments, viz., Anima, Mahima, Laghima, Garima, Ishatva, Vashitva, Prapti and Prakamya. Lord Shiva appointed him as the head of all his *ganas* and named him Ganesh or Ganapati. Pleased with the prayers of Brahma, Ganesh granted him a boon that he would assist Brahma in the creation of the universe. Then all the gods came to pay homage to Ganapati including Shanidev or Saturn who, while offering worship, looked down to the ground. Being asked the reason by Parvati, he said that he did not look up at Genesh as he had the curse of an evil eye, which would destroy any object on which it fell. Parvati laughed at this and asked him to have a sight of Ganesh. At his mere glance the head of Ganesh fell down from his body. Parvati lamented much for her rash action and requested Vishnu to fix a head on his trunk and make him alive. Thereupon Lord Shiva at once sent all his *ganas* to bring the head of any living being met first on the way. An elephant met the *ganas* who killed it and brought its head to Vishnu which was joined to the trunk of Ganesh. Vishnu revived him thus and blessed him with a boon that he would be worshipped first among all the gods including the supreme trio, viz., Brahma, Vishnu and Mahesh.

There is another and more popular legend as regards the birth of Ganesh in which it is stated that when Ganesh did not allow Shiva to enter the house he became angry and cut off the head with his trident. When Parvati came to know of this, she lamented and asked Shiva to make her child alive explaining to him how she had created him. Shiva, therefore, joined the head of an elephant brought by his *ganas* with the body and gav it life. Parvati was not satisfied with the ugly form of her son. But Shiva pleased her by appointing him as the lord of his *ganas,* with a boon that he would be worshipped first among all the gods.

The shrewdness of Ganapati is narrated in an interesting tale. When he and his elder brother Kartik Swami came of age, their parents Shiva and Parvati told them that he who went round the earth first would be married first. Kartik Swami set out on the journey on his swift carrier, the peacock. Ganapati, with his stout body and, tiny carrier, the mouse, had no prospects of winning the race. He, therefore, made three *pradakshinas* (rounds) of his parents, and, relying on the Shastras, pointed out that three *pradakshinas* of one's parents were equal in merit to a journey round the earth. Pleased at this, Ganapati was married to Siddhi and Riddhi.

Ganapati being the lord of knowledge and intellect, his assistance was invoked by Vyas Badarayana in writing his famous epic of *Mahabharata.* He agreed on condition that Vyas did not stop during dictation. Vyas agreed on the condition that Ganapati did not write any verse without understanding its meaning. Ganapati wrote so fast that he did not allow Vyas any time to think. Vyas thereupon made it a point to dictate a difficult verse whenever he wanted time to think so that Ganapati himself would pause to understand its meaning.

Once Ganapati was returning from *Brahmalok* to Kailash, his residence, when he had to pass through *Chandralok* or the residence of the moon on the way. Seeing the strange figure of Ganesh, the moon laughed jokingly. Angry at this, Ganesh cursed him that none would look at him. Chandra was ashamed and fell at his feet to be excused. By the advice of Brihaspati, the preceptor of gods, he performed religious observance on Ganesh Chaturthi, whereupon Ganesh granted him that people would not look at him only on Ganapati's birthday, i.e., bright fourth of Bhadrapad, for fear of suffering some calumny.

Ganapati is installed at the entrance of all Mahadev and Mataji temples and many Vaishnava temples including Swaminarayan. He has only one curved tooth and as such he is called Ekadanta or Vakradanta. He is also called Mahakaya owing to the vastness of his body. He has four hands and his complexion is red. He is pleased with red lead, red flowers, red clothes and *naivedya* of sweet balls. In spiritual sense the word Ganesh means Gunesha, the lord of three *gunas* or qualities, viz., *satva, rajas* and *tamas,* which are embodied in him. His curved tooth is believed to be the upper portion of *Pranava---'Om'.*

The vastness of Ganapati's belly teaches his devotees to be large-minded and tolerant. The devotee should hear all but speak little. The large head of an elephant is the symbol of prudence, knowledge and foresight. His carrier, the mouse, is the symbol of patience as also of *kala* or time. The mouse nibbles at everything day and night as *kala* destroys everything bit by bit. By making *kala*, his carrier, Ganesh has kept him in his control. Thus Ganapati, who is the Lord and leader of all *ganas,* i.e., sections, is the repository of all knowledge, prudence, patience, intellect and virtues. Being the husband of *ashta maha-siddhi,* eight major *siddhis* or attainments, he fulfils the desires of his sincere devotees. As he destroys all obstacles of his worshippers, he is known as Vighnesh, and worshipped before undertaking any work. Poets pray to him at the beginning of their poems, writers in their writings. All religious rites commence with the worship of Ganesh who guarantees the happy completion of all ceremonies and functions. In the invitation cards for auspicious functions such as marriage, sacred thread ceremony and others, the words Shri *Ganeshay Namah,* meaning obeissance to Shri Ganesh, are always inscribed at the top.

Generally the bright fourth of every month is observed as Ganesh Chaturthi known as Siddhi Vinayaki Choth, but that of Bhadrapad is Mahasiddhi Vinayaki Choth. A staunch devotee observes all the bright fourths. Ganesh Chaturthi of Bhadrapad is, however, particularly propitious for worshipping Ganesh for the attainment of bliss. It is said that the mind is in *turiya* condition and remains steady during worship on this day. A look at the moon is avoided on this day as it is the symbol of the mind which has a mercurial nature and a look at the moon may unsteady the mind.

Hindus in Delhi and all over India celebrate Ganesh Chaturthi. Shops selling clay idols of Ganesh in various shapes and forms are opened fairly in advance. Devotees purchase an idol of their choice, and bring it home in a procession in the morning of the bright fourth. They install it at home with proper rites and offer worship daily with red flowers, *durva* grass and red lead and *naivedya* of sweet balls. Social functions such as *bhajans*, lectures and religious discourses are arranged daily in the evenings. *Kumkum* powder and sweets are distributed as *prasad.* The image is worshipped for ten days. On the last day, i.e., bright fourteenth called Anant Chaturdashi, after the final worship in the evening, the idol is taken in a palanquin in a procession led by musical bands and *Bahaman mandlis* to the sea, river or pond and immersed in water. Those who cannot observe the *vrata* for ten days, worship the idol for one to five days, and at the end of that period conclude the worship in the same manner.

As at private houses of the devotees, Ganesh Chaturthi is also observed by various associations in public places. This joint celebration is an important social aspect of the festival, like that of Navratri. However, the religious rites of worship during Navratri are not generally performed in such public celebrations because they are to be performed strictly according to the prescribed procedure with meticulous care. On the other hand, Ganesh worship is comparatively simpler and, therefore, in public celebrations also a suitable large idol is installed and worshipped everyday.

There is a strange custom, not so much in vogue now, of throwing stones on the neighbours' houses at night. It is said to have originated from the curse of Ganapati to Chandra or the moon. People who have an accidental glimpse of the moon on this day, throw stones on the neighbouring houses at night to get abuses from neighbours, to avoid fear of more serious calumny. The day is, therefore, known popularly as as Dagada Choth, from *dagad,* meaning a stone in Marathi.

Jains also treat this day as a religious and festive occasion as it is the last day of their Paryushana, the days of religious austerities, known as Samvatsari.

Ganesha is known to be the remover of obstacles and hence called Vighneswara (Vighna meaning obstacle). Hence he is propitiated at the commencement of every rite. The worship of Ganesha represented by a conical mass of turmeric paste or cowdung, plastered into shape with the fingers, forms the first item of the ritual complex in every sacred occasion amongst the Brahmans and other higher castes in Peninsular India.

Ganga Dussehra

Ganga Dussehra is celebrated on the tenth day of Jyestha (May-June). River Ganga is worshipped as a mother as well as a goddess, particularly by people of Uttar Pradesh, Bihar and Bengal through which the river flows. On this day, if the devotee is unable to visit and bathe in the river Ganga, then Ganga jal (water) kept in most Hindu homes is used fo rpurification. A bath in the river is said to purify the bather of all sins. The Ganga is revered all over India even in places far from its course.

According to the *Agni Purana* and *Padma Purana*, the Ganga descended to the earth on Ganga Dussehra day and a bath in the holy river on this day is said to purify one of all sins. To die on the banks of the Ganga is considered most auspicious. If that is not possible, then the immersion of the ashes after cremation in the river Ganga is a must, as it then releases one from the cycles of birth and re-birth.

Initially, river Ganga flowed in the heavens. She was brought down to earth by the sever penances of sage Bhagiratha and that is why she is also called Bhagierathi. According to the story, of the descent of the Ganga, once a number of demons were harassing the hermits by disturing them in their ascetic duties. During the day, they would be chased into the ocean. But in the darkness of the night, they would emerge from the ocean and staret harassing the hermits again. In desperation the hermits appealed to Rishi Agastya. Agastya, known for his gastronomic powers, drank all the waters of the ocean. Though this was done in good faith, it resulted in depriving the world of the water needed for sustenance and the earth became parched and dry. Bhagiratha brought this drought to an end.

According to the legend, King Sagara of theIkshvaku dynasty ruling at Ayodhya in Uttar Pradesh had two queens, Keshani and Sumati, but neither had a child. Sagara performed severe austerities befor ehis wives could produce sons. But whereas Keshani gave birth to a son called Asmajas, Sumati bore 60,000 sons. Sagara performed the Ashwamedha sacrifice to declare his suzerainty over the neighbouring kingdoms. According to the prevalent custom, the sacrificial horse was let loose and allowed to wander into the neighbouring kingdoms. If the horse was caught, a battle ensued and the outcome edcided the winner. The 60,000 sons of Sagara were following the horse when they saw him enter a cavern where sasge Kapila was meditating. Not seeing the horse in the cavern, they presumed that Kapila ahd captured it. They did not kill Kapila as he was a sage but they started disturbing his meditations. Annoyed at being disturbed, Kapila with a curse burnt the 60,000 sons of Sagara. Time passed and later Bhagiratha, the great grandson of Sagara, chanced to come across the bones of his dead ancestors. He wanted to perform the shraddha of his ancestors but there was no water available for the ceremony. Agastya having drunk all the waters of the ocean, the country was passing through a severe drought. Bhagiratha prayed to Brahma, the Creator, to end the drought. Brahma asked him to pray to Vishnu, the Preserver, to allow the heavenly river Ganga, issuing from his big toe, to come down to the earth. Vishnu when prayed to by Bhagiratha agreed, but asked him to request Shiva, the third member of the Hindu trinity of gods, to allow the torrential river to fall on his head before it came to the earth as the river was very forceful and if she were allowed to come down unchecked, her fall would split the earth. Shiva agreed to take the gigantic weight of the cascading river Ganga on the matted hair piled high on his head. This ensnared and delayed the progress of the river which, in meandering through the labyrinth of his hair, lost its force and then gently descended to the Himalayas from whence it flowed to the plains bestowing its waters on the parched earth. And that is why the anthropomorphic image of Ganga is shown in the matted hair of Shiva who is also called Gangadhara. Being born in the Himalayas, Ganga is considered the elder sister of Parvati, who is also a daughter of the Himalayas.

The seven ways of worshipping the Ganga are : by calling out her name, 'Oh Ganga'; by having a darshan of her; by touching her waters; by worshipping and bathing; by standing in the waters of the rivers and by carrying clay dug out of the river. Ganga in her anthropomorphic form is shown as a beautiful young woman standing on a crocodile and holdin ga waterpot in her hands. Her image, with that of the goddess Yamuna, another sacred river deity, is often depicted on the doors of temples and palaces.

Govardhan Puja

The day after Diwali in the month of Kartik (October-November) Govardhan Puja is celebrated when Mount Govardhan, near Mathura, is worshipped. Pious people keep awake the whole night and cook fifty-six different types of food for the bhog to Krishna. This ceremony is called ankut which means a mountain of food. Various types of food—cereals, pulses, furit, vegetables, chutneys, pickles and salads—are offered to the deity and then distributed as *prasada* to devotees.

This festival is in commemoration of the lifting of Mount Govardhan by Krishna. According to a legend, before Krishna was born, Indra, the God of Rain, was the chief deity of Vraja. Then, Krishna instigated the people to stop worshipping Indra. Indra wanted to show his power over Krishan and brought about a cloud-burst which flooded the countryside for many days. People were afraid that the downpour was a result of their neglect of Indra. But Krishna assured them that no harm would befall them. He lifted Mount Govardhan with his little finger and sheltered men and beasts from the rain. This gave him the epither Govardhandhari. After this, Indra accepted the supremacy of Krishna.

Gugga Naumi

The cult of Gugga is classified under serpent worship for no better reason than that Gugga has a peculiar power of curing snake bite. As many as eleven legends have clustered round Gugga. He is also called Gugga Pir, Zahir Pir "the Saint Apparent". Some refer to him as *Bagarwala* "He of the Bagar" because of his grave near Dadrewa (Ganganagar District of Rajasthan) in the Bagar tract which he is said to have ruled over.

He flourished about the middle of the 12th century. He was a Hindu and his proper name is Gugga Bir (Gugga, the Hero). The Muslims also flock to his shrine and his name has been altered to Gugga Pir (Saint Gugga), while, in the opinion of many, he himself became a Muslim.

The legends connected with Gugga narrate the same events with minor variations. There is, however, a marked difference of opinion about the place of his birth and the name of his father. One of the legends names the place of his birth as Gard Darera, the second as Dadrera in Bikaner about 82.50 from Sirsa, the third as Daruhera in Hissar and the fourth as Garh Dandera near Bindraban. Similarly, the different legends give out different names of his father. He is named as Jewar, or Jhewar, or Jiwar, in some of the versions. Another version gives out the name as Vachha Chauhan, Raja of Jangal Desh which stretched from the Sutlej to Haryana. Still another version names his father as Devi Chand. Unlike the various names given about his father or place of birth, there is marked unanimity about the name of his mother. She is named as Bachhal. Bachhal's sister is named as Kachhal or Achhal. Achhal is said to be the wife of Jewar's brother, Newar. But in one of the versions she is said to be the second wife of Jewar.

The story goes that both Bachhal and Kachhal were without a son. Once Gorakh Nath came to Jewar's capital and camped in a garden which did not have a single blade of green grass due to continuous droughts. By a mireale it so happened that on the coming of Gorakh Nath the trees put forth green leaves and started blossoming. Impressed by this happening Bachhal went to Gorakh Nath and begged of him to vouchsafe her a son. Gorakh Nath asked her to come on an appointed day. Bachhal's sister, Kachhal, however, went to Gorakh Nath some time before the appointed hour disguised in her sister's clothes and received from the saint two barley corns. She ate them and in due course gave births to twins, who were named Arjan and Sarjan. Later, Bachhal went to Gorakh Nath at the proper time and Gorakh Nath having discovered the deceit played by Kachhal gave Bachhal a piece of *guggal* out of his wallet, saying she would attain her desire by eating it. Gugga, it is so said, derived his name from this *guggal*. However, according to one of the versions Gorakh Nath had given her ashes and not *guggal*. Still another version goes, that Gorakh Nath having known that Bachhal was destined not to bear a child took her to Bhagwan. The latter rubbed some dirt out of his head and gave it to Bachhal. Bachhal divided the *guggal* or dirt, as the case may be, into four equal parts and gave one to a Brahmani, another to a sweepress, the third to a grey mare, and kept the fourth for herself. According to one version Bachhal having been charged with infidelity was turned out of her husband's house and she set out for the house of her parents. On the road, the cart, in which Bachhal was riding, was halted for the midday rest, and the oxen taken out, whereupon a snake bit them and they died. Gugga now made himself, heard, and his power over snakes felt, though he was yet to be born. Bachhal weeping at the loss of the oxen fell asleep, and in dream Gugga directed her to cut a branch from a *nim* tree and call on Gorakh Nath to heal the oxen. Bachhal on awaking did so and the oxen came back to life. Thus Bachhal went to her parents safe, and there Gugga again spoke and protested that he would be for ever disgraced if he were born in his maternal grandfather's house. According to one version her husband realizing his mistake called her back. Anyway, in due course, Bachhal gave birth to Gugga, Brahmani to Nar Singh, the sweepress to Bhaju (Patiya Chamar) and the mare to a blue colt. When Gugga grew up, he was married to Sirial (or Siliar), daughter of Raja Sanjai of Dhup Nagar, or Surial, daughter of Sanjai of Bundi, or Surjila, daughter of Raja of Bangala, as has been given out in three different versions. His cousins Arjan and Sarjan demanded a moiety of the property but Gugga objected to any partition. However, according to one version Arjan and Sarjan were jealous of Gugga's marriage with Sirial. They wanted to get her by killing Gugga. They persuaded Gugga to go out for hunting with them and treacherously attacked him. Gugga slayed them both and returned home with their heads tied to the back of the horse. When Gugga appeared before his mother with the heads of his cousins she bade him not show his face to her any more. In his distress Gugga prayed to the earth to swallow him up but it refused to do so, as has been given in one of the versions, as he was a Hindu. Instantly the saints Khawaja Muhi-ud-din, Ratan Haji and Miran Sahib appeared and converted him to Islam. Gugga then recited the *kalma* and disappeared into earth. According to another version Gugga learned Yoga of Gorakh Nath, and the earth answered his prayer and engulfed him with his horse and arms.

In this context mention may also be made of the Jain version. It is said in the time of Nandi Braham who reigned some 2,500 years ago, Chand Kosia, a huge venomous snake lived in a forest near Kankhal. Whatsoever he looked at was burnt to ashes so that not even a straw was to be seen within 20 kms of his hole. When the twenty-fourth Avtar Mahabir Swami turned mendicant, he passed by Chand Kosia's hole, disregarding all warnings, and though the serpent bit his foot thrice he was not injured. Mahabir Swami asked him "What excuse will you give to

God for your ruthless deeds?" Chand Kosia on hearing this repented and drawing his head into his hole only exposed the rest of his body so that the way would be safe for travellers. Thenceforth he was regarded as snake god and wayfarers and milk-women passing that way sprinkled ghee, milk, oilseeds, rice and *lassi* on him. He now became known as Gugga.

Gugga finds a mention also in ancient Hindu scriptures. According to *Shrimad Bhagavat*, the Rishi Kapp had two wives: Kadro and Benta. Kadro gave birth to a snake and Benta to a Garur which is the conveyance of Bhagwan. The snake could transform it into a man at will and was called Gugga. The Hindus regard both the Garur and the snake as sacred.

Ninth of Bhadon was the date on which Gugga descended into earth. To commemorate this event, fairs are held at his shrine every year on this date. Those who do not attend the fair go out in search of holes that might contain some snake and pour on it diluted milk *(Kachi-lassi)*, and cooked vermicelli *(sewian)*.

Gurupurabs

Attempts to liberalize and reform Hinduism date back to Buddha and continued from time to time by many religious and social reformers. Jaidev (A.D. 1,100), composer of the *Gita Govind,* taught that Yoga was worthless in comparison with God's worship in thought, word and deed. Ramanand, at the close of the 14th century, freed his followers from caste restrictions. A little later Kabir (b.1,398) denounced idolatry and ritualism.

Nearly a century later in 1469, was born Nanak, the founder of Sikhism. His faith was sternly monotheistic. He preached the futility of religious vestments, of ostentatious prayer and penance, and pilgrimages. He declared that all men had a right to search for the knowledge of God, irrespective of caste. He led a married life and had two sons. Sri Chand and Lakhmi Das. But, as his spiritual successor, he designated his disciple Lehna who came to be known as Angad.

To Guru Angad is due the inception of the *Granth Sahib,* the holy book of the Sikhs, in which he embodied what he had learnt from Guru Nanak, and added devotional reflections of his own. To mark the sacred character of the work, he invented the Gurumukhi script, the "Guru tongue", by modifying the Sharada alphabet.

Angad in turn excluded his sons and designated Amar Das as his successor. The reforms made by his Guru were chiefly the separation of the Udasi order, founded by Nanak's son Sri Chand, from the laity; denunciation of Sati; and stressing Nanak's attitude to caste by making all his Sikhs (disciples) eat together. In 1574, Amar Das bestowed the guru-ship on his disciple and son-in-law Jetha, who came to be known as Ram Das.

To Guru Ram Das is due the foundation of The Golden Temple at Amritsar in 1579, on a site granted him by the Emperor Akbar, whose policy was to weld together all the creeds of India. Guru Ram Das taught no new doctrines but is still much revered.

So far the Gurus had aimed at continuing the guru-ship by designation, and not setting up a hereditary spiritual dynasty. But after Guru Ram Das the tendency to regard sainthood as vested in a saint's physical descendants asserted itself. Guru Ram Das selected his third son, Arjan Dev, to succeed him as Guru. Guru Arjan Dev enlarged the Granth Sahib, half of which is due to him. He was tortured to death by Jahangir in 1606.

Guru Arjan Dev's son Har Govind was constrained to maintain his throne by arms. The guruship was now launched on a new adventure—the foundation of a militant sacred dynasty. Guru Har Govind founded the first Sikh stronghold and was able to resist Shah Jahan and claimed three victories over the Imperial troops. He died in 1645.

Guru Har Govind's grandson, Har Rai, succeeded him and on the latter's death his younger son Har Kishan assumed the guruship. Guru Har Kishan's death in 1664 left the direct line extinct and the inheritance reverted to Teg Bahadur, Har Govind's second son, but he was executed by Aurangzeb in 1675 for having refused to accept Islam.

The tenth and the last Guru was Guru Teg Bahadur's son, Govind Rai, who took the affix

"Singh" (lion) in lieu of Rai, and remodelled the Sikh organization which he renamed Khalsa, "the Pure". He made the Sikh initiation *(pahul)* a rite of admittance into a militant order. Thenceforth a Sikh must wear the five *kakas,* the *kesh* (unshorn hair), the *kachha* (drawers reaching only to the knee), the *kara* (iron bangle), the *kirpan* (sword), and the *kangha* (half comb).

Guru Govind Singh waged an active defensive action against the Mughal power but his action were dispersed and his two sons put to death by the governor of Sirhind. Guru Govind Singh declared the line of Gurus as extinct and vested the guru-ship in the *Granth Sahib* as God's representative on earth. Sikhism was thenceforth to be a militant theocracy. After Guru Govind Singh, Banda formed an almost regular army, gained notable successes against the Mughals, sacked Sirhind and compelled the allegiance of the Hindu hill-Rajas. However, the Mughals finally succeeded in capturing him and he was executed in 1716.

To commemorate the Gurus, Gurupurabs (fairs in the memory of Gurus) are held in Famous among the Gurupurabs are those connected with the birthdays of Guru Nanak and Guru Govind Singh and martyrdom of Guru Arjan Dev and Guru Teg Bahadur. On these Gurupurabs, *Akhand Paths* (non-stop recital) of Granth Sahib, *Kirtan* and religious discourses are held in Gurduwaras and processions are taken out. Free meals *(langar)* are served and partaken of by all without any distinction of caste and status in life.

Hanuman Jayanti

Hanuman, was born on a Saturday in the month of Chairta (March). His birth anniversary is celebrated with visits to his temples and fasting. Hanuman is considered more a perfect devotee than a deity. He is famous for his learning, physical strength, celibacy, selflessness and devotion to Rama an incarnation of Vishnu, of the epic *Ramayana*. His physical strength is legendary. When he was born, he mistook the orb of the Sun for a fruit and leaped to catch it. The Sun took fright and hid itself, plunging the universe in darkness. Hanuman was about to swallow it but the gods intervened and saved the Sun and thereby the universe.

This yellow-bodied,red-faced deity, shown wearing a red loin-cloth and sometimes with a crown on his head, is usually worshipped with Rama and Sita, but is shown with them in a servile position. On his birth anniversary, the *Ramayana* and the *Hanuman Chalisa* are recited. For his unflinching devotion to Rama, he was given a boon by the latter that he would be remembered in the world, as long as the name 'Rama' remained on people's lips. His special days of worship are Tuesday and Saturdays when devotees throng to his temples shouting, 'Jai Bajrang Bali'.

Hanuman was born to Anjali, an apsara (celestial maiden) and Marut, God of Wind, which gave him the epither Maruti. Anjali by a curse had earlier been transformed into a monkey. Hanuman has an honoured place in the Hindu pantheon of gods, mainly becasue of his devotion to Rana and for locating Sita. who had been abducted by Ravana and taken to Lanka. Since Hanuman could not swim to reach Lanka, he leapt over the Palk Strait. Once in Lanka, he discovered Sita sitting in a grove of Asoka trees, Seeing Hanuman's monkey face, Sita mistook him for a demon who had been sent by Ravana to harass her. To allay her fears. Hanuman showed her Rama's signet ring that had been entrusted to him.

While leaving the grove, Hanuman was caught by the palace guards of Ravana and the latter ordered his tail to be set on fire. Hanuman reversed what was meant to be an ordeal and a punishment. With his tail on fire, he leapt from building to building and set the golden city of Lanka aflame.

He informed Rama of Sita's whereabouts and this led to a great battle. During the battle, Lakshmana,Rma's younger brother was seriously wounded and lay unconscious. To receive him, a special herb had to be obtained from the Himalayas and Hanuman, who could fly with the speed of the wind. offered to get it. But when he reached the mountains, there wre so many herbs that he could not find the right one. Time was running out and he pulled our a big chunk of the mountain and flew back to Lanka with it, in time to revive Lakshmana. In the end Rama kolled Ravana. The balltle was over and Sita was rescured.

Holi

Holi is the festival of romance and revelry gaily celebrated by Hindu communities all over India from Kashmir to Kanya Kumari and from Dwarka to Jagannathpuri, even by other communities such as Jains, and Sikhs who also participate in the celebration. The festival lasts for three days, namely, Gheraiya Chaudash or Phalgun Sud 14, followed by the *Purnima* or the day of Holi, and *Dhuleti* or Dolotsav on Vad 1. It is in essence a spring festival, a counterpart of the autumnal festival of Divali which also is celebrated for at least three days. This is a very ancient festival. Several stories of its religious significance are found in Hindu mythology.

According to *Bhavishya Purana,* King Yudhishthir once asked Shri Krishna why people celebrate the festival of Holi. Shri Krishna replied that a demoness named Dhundha or Hoda practised penance to please Lord Shiva, who gifted her with a boon that she would not be killed by gods, demons or human beings; by arms, weapons or charms; during day or night; in a forest or in a house; in the winter, summer or monsoon and by young or old; but that she would die at the hands of children at the conjunction of day and night (at twilight) and of two seasons. On hearing this she rejoiced, but began to kill all the children she came across. People, terrified by this outrage, approached King Raghu and requested him to rescue them from her terror. Raghu sought a remedy from his preceptor Vasishtha. He got dung-cakes and fuel collected and arranged in a heap. By the charm of the *rakshoghna mantra* she was attracted and induced to enter the heap. Raghu then asked the children to light the heap in the evening. Thus, she was burn and killed, and since that time the festival called Holi is celebrated.

Bhagavat Purana narrates another account about Holi. According to the divine prophecy Kansa was destined to be killed by his sister's eighth child who was Sri Krishna. Kansa, therefore, laid designs to kill Shri Krishna, as he was unable to lay his hands upon the child at birth even by imprisoning his sister and her husband. He sent the demons to look where Shri Krishna was reported to be living. The child, however, killed the demons, and the event is since then commemorated by celebrating Holi on Phalgun Sud 15.

Amongst the South Indians, it is observed as the day of *Kamadahan*—burning of Cupid, God of Love. When Lord Shiva was in penance, gods decided to get him married to Parvati, the daughter of Himalaya. Indra, the king of gods, asked Kamadev—Cupid—to approach Shiva and lure him away from his austerities. Cupid in the company of his friend Vasant (Spring), appeared before Shiva with a band of *apsaras* or celestial nymphs. The *apsaras* began to sing and dance and Cupid shot an arrow of flowers at the heart of Shiva, who awoke from meditation and saw Kama. He was angry and opened his third eye in the forehead, throwing flames of fire on Kama and burnt him. The *ganas*—followers of Shiva—dispersed his party abusing them in profane words. Since that time the festival of Holi is observed in memory of the event and people have an excuse once a year to indulge in vulgarity.

There is also a fourth Pauranic account widely current in Gujarat and Rajasthan. The demon king Hiranyakashyap had a son named Prahlad who was a devotee of Lord Vishnu, his deadly enemy. Prahlad continued to worship Vishnu in spite of his father's attempts to dissuade him. Hiranyakashyap resorted to several designs to kill him, but without success. His sister Holika, who had from Lord Shiva, a boon of immunity from injury by fire, came to his assistance. She took Prahlad on her lap sitting on a heap of wood and asked her brother to set it on fire. But, when the heap began to burn, Holika burnt and Prahlad remained alive by the grace of God. Holi is said to be lighted every year on Phalgun Sud 15 to commemorate that event.

Whatever may be the background of the celebration of Holi, the festival is in essence and spirit a spring festival. It is held at a time when the *rabi* crops like wheat, gram, *til,* etc., ripen and come to the market. Farmers are free from worries of looking after their fields and also have some cash in hand. Merchants, too have their stocks replenished with new crops and look forwared to the prospect of good business. The season is at its best with loveliness all-round. With the advent of spring, the cold of winter recedes. Forests, gardens, and orchards wear new garments of fresh leaves, flowers and fruits. Rivers, streams, ponds and lakes are full of clear and transparent water. It is in the fitness of things that Holi should be celebrated during this period as the festival of spring.

People in all walks of life, high and low, men and women, young and old alike—celebrate Holi. Even an ordinary man can spray red powder or sprinkle coloured water on those of higher status. In the countryside, women gather together and perform *ras*, *garba* and play at spraying of colours. Holi is thus a national festival just like Diwali. The celebration of Holi festival spreads over at least three days. The day preceding Holi, i.e., Phalgun Sud 14, is Gheraiya Chaudash, derived from *gheraiyas* or persons who indulge in spraying colours, performing folk dances in groups, and singing folk-song with flat drums called *daf*. At some places, a small heap of dung-cakes is lighted in the evening on Gheraiya Chaudash at the place where Holi is to be lighted on the next day. This is called Kamla Holi. The day of *Purnima* is celebrated as Holi, on which the Holi fire is lighted. The day after Holi is known as Dhuleti celebrated by spraying colours, throwing dirt, mud, etc., at one another.

Preparations start some days in advance. Some days before Holi, street urchins start spraying bathroom and colour on passers-by. At places youths start collecting funds and firewood. They may procure the latter even by pilfering stray wooden articles, unused doors, frames, beams, etc. Colour spraying is universal. On the Holi day a small pit is dug, over which a conical stack of dung-cakes and wood is built with a flag planted on the top. Bonfires are lit in the principal squares and localities of each town and village. At some places the fire is lit by an 'untouchable', a Vaghri or some other person according to local custom, and *puja* of Holi follows. People, especially women, go round *(pradakshinas)* the fire pouring water and offering flowers, mango blossoms, parched *jowar,* gram and coconut, etc., into the fire. It is considered an act of bravery to take out coconuts from the flames. Omens are seen about the coming monsoon from the direction in which the flag falls. A pot filled with water is placed in a pit under the Holi fire. Over it are placed four balls of clay covered by thread, representing the four monsoon months, viz., Ashadh, Shravan, Bhadrapad and Ashvin. It is believed that the extent to which the threads get wet indicates the extent of rain in the months represented by them. In the pit below the Holi, some people put in an earthen vessel grains of wheat, *jowar,* etc., soaked in water which are cooked by the fire overhead. This is called *ghughari* and is distributed as prasad the next day. Gheraiyas wake for the whole night to keep the Holi fire alight. In some places an effigy of Holi is prepared from rags and old clothes and burnt in Holi fire. While a total fast is generally not kept, many persons abstain from cooked food till Holi is lighted. During daytime the diet is restricted to the taking of parched *jowar*, gram and dates which are also distributed among relatives. Cooked food is taken only at night after having *darshan* of Holi and offering worship. In Pushtimargiya Vaishnava temples, Holi is lighted in the courtyard and idol of Lalji is placed near the Holi and worshipped.

In some communities is a custom to adorn the new-born baby with a white frock sprinkled with colour prepared by *boiling kesudan* or flowers of *khakhara* or *Butea frondosa* tree and adorn his ankles and waist with silver ornaments and take him to have sight of Holi. This is called *ghim* ceremony. Ornaments and frocks are generally given by the maternal side with dry fruits, parched *jowar* and gram and strings of sugar-candy. It is also customary to send *harda* to betrothed girls from the bridegroom's side. *Harda* consists of sweets, strings of sugar-candy, dry and fresh fruits available and a *sari*. A custom is prevalent in some communities to bring newly married couple for Holi worship. They sit side by side with corners of their clothes tied, worship Holi and then go seven times round the fire.

Jagannatha Yatra

Jagannatha yatra is best known in the world as the biggest festival of its kind. It is observed o the

Asadha Shukla Duritiya, i.e., on the second day of the bright fortnight of the month of Asadha (June-July). This annual festival at the first break of monsoon is the most ancient, most elaborite, biggest festival of Lord Jagannatha.

The Ratha Yatra (chariot procession) of Jagannatha stqarts from the Jagannatha temple of Puri in Orissa and goes to the countryside residence of the deities at Gundicha Bari, two miles away. Puri, on the eastern coast of india, is one of the four Dhamas or Mahakshetras (most important places of pilgrimage), the other three being Dwaraka in the west, Badrinath in the north and Rameshwaram in the south. Jagannatha temple is dedicated to Krishna, the eighth incarnation of Vishnu, as Lord of the universe. The presiding deity, Krishna, is worshipped with his elder brother, Balarama, also called Balabhadra,and sister Subhadra, also known as Ekanamsa.Subhadra is not even a minor deityand the presence ofher image with Krishna and Balarama is unusual and the only one to be found. It is believed that Arjuna, one of the Pandava brothers, and a friend and admirer of Krishna fell in love withSubhadra while he was visiting Krishna. Krishna encouraged Arjuna to elope with her. Even thogh Arjuna later married her, Balarama, Krishna's elder brother, was annoyed at this incident. His anger was directed against both Arjuna and Krishna.

The images of Krishna, Balarama and Subhadra are incomplete, as none of them have arms or legs. This is most unusual. Legend has it that once King Indradhumna saw a wonder box floatingdown the river. The box contained relics of Krishna. The king had a dream in which he was asked to have the images of the god carved out of the wood and to install Krishna's relics in them for worship. The king commissioned the divine architect, Vishwakarman, for the purpose. Vishwakarman agreed, but on condition that he would not be disturbed while he was carving the images. if he was, then he would stop working. The King agreed to the condition. Many years passed. Vishwakarman was locked in his workshop, carving the iages. King Indradhumna grew restless, and curious to see what progress had been made, walked into Vishwakarman was locked in his workshop, carving the imagers. King Indradhumna grew restless, and curious to see what progress had been made, walked into Vishwakarman's workshop. Vishwakarman was annoyed at the intrusion and refused to complete the job. The arms and the legs of the images had still to be carved. Indradhumna was very upset at having broken his own word. But Brahma came to his help and agreed to breathe life into the images.

The relics of Krishna are kept inside the images. Since the images are made of wood they have to be periodicallychanged. A special priest is deputed to transfer them from the old to thenew image, but he is blindfolded so that he does not see the relics. His hands are bandaged in layers of cloth so that the relics are not defiled by human touch. No one knows what the relics are, as the priest cannot feel them with his hands. The renewal of the images takes place only when certain astronomical conditions are present. The wood used for the images has to conform to certainspecifications. The occasion when the new images are installed is a day of festivity called Nav-kalebara.

On the anniversary of the full-moon day when Vishnuis supposed to have incarnated himself in the form of Jagannatha, the images ar brought to a platform and 108 pitchers of sacred water are poured over them. During the anointing ceremony Vedic mantras (hymns) are chanted, music is played and drums are beaten. After the ceremonial consecration of the images isover, they are painted with colour. This is done by the Daitas, who are the hereditary artisans for this job. Finally the deities are dressed in resplendent clothes. During this ritual of fifteen days, the devotees are allowed to have a darshan of the deities.

When the deities are ready for the ratha yatra,(chariot procession), they are placed in their respective chariots. Nandighosha, the yellow-coloured chariot of Jagannatha, is 14 metres high with 16 wheels, each 2 metres in diameter. Balarama's chariot in blue is also 14 metres high with fourteen wheels and is called Taladhvaja. Subhadra's chariot is the smallest, 13 metres high with twelve wheels and is called. Deviratha or Darpadalana. The chariots are drawn by devotees and there is such pandemonium that often some people get rampled under the colossal wheels.

According to another legend, Subhadra wanted to visit Dwaraka and her brothers, Krishna and Balarama, took her to Dwaraka on this day. The Ratha Yatra is in commemoration of that visit.A legend in the *Bhagavata Purana* says that Akrur was sent by Kansa, the King of Mathura, to Gokula to ask Krishna to visit Mathura. And on this day, Krishna and Balarama travelled in a decorated chariot to Mathura, followed on foot by the gopis and herdsmen. In olden times the normal mode of transport was by ratha and therefore on both occasions,i.e., Subhadra's visit to Dwaraka and Krishna and Balarama's visit to Mathura were by ratha.

Janmashtami

If there is any one person who has influenced the Hindu mind more than all the rest put together, it is Shri Krishna. It is, therefore, no wonder that his birthday on Shravan Vad 8 is celebrated as a festival not only in the whole of India but universally, and in some of the western countries too, where in recent times Krishna sects have establised their base.

In the Hindu chronology there are four ages or *yugas,* viz., Satya Yuga, Treta Yuga, Dwapar Yuga and Kali Yuga. In all these ages Lord Vishnu takes birth in one form or another, whenever the people are oppressed by the tyranny of ruling classes, for the protection of sages, saints, religious people and religion itself. Similarly, in the last days of Dwapar Yuga, the rulers of the times had become violent, arrogant and proud. Sages, saints and religious people were harassed and terrorized. Kshatriya kings like Jarasandh of Magadha, Kansa of Mathura, Bhishmak and his son Rukmi of Vidarbha, Shishupal, Dantavakra, Shalva and others had abandoned their duties and religion. They were oppressing the public by their might. Besides, demon kings like Trunavarta, Bakasur, Dhenukasure, Arishtanemi, Kalanemi and Narakasur had become terrors to the people. There was also constant fear of foreign invasions from the Yavan king like Kalayavan of Kandahar. The time was, therefore, ripe for the saviour to come to the rescue of religion. Helpless devotees prayed to Lord Vishnu for the protection of good and destruction of evil and for the re-establishment of religion in its real sense on the earth. Vishnu heard the prayers and took birth as the son of Devaki, the wife of Yadava Vasudev at midnight of Shravan Vad 8 as the eighth incarnation. Devaki was the sister of Kansa of Mathura, a tyrant, who had at the instigation of his father-in-law Jarasandh, the king of Magadha, dethroned and imprisoned his father Ugrasen. On being warned through an oracle, that the eighth son of Devaki, his sister, would be his destroyer, he put in jail his sister and her husband Vasudev.

He killed the first six infants of Devaki, and the seventh embryo was shifted to the womb of Rohini, the second wife of Vasudev, living at Gokul. Rohini gave birth to a son at Gokul named Balrama. He is also known as Sankarshana as the embryo was shifted. Kansa had asked the prison guards to be strictly vigilant and inform him immediately about the birth of a child at its first crying.

Before taking birth as their eighth child, Lord Vishnu gave *darshan* to Devaki and Vasudev and said, "I shall be born as your child as promised in your previous birth," and advised them to take the new-born child to Gokul and put it near Yashoda, the wife of Nand, and bring back the daughter born to her. After the birth of Shri Krishna at midnight, through a miracle all the guards fell asleep and the doors were unlocked. Vasudev took the child in a basket on his head and slipped out, and crossing the flooded Yamuna, reached the house of Nand in Gokul where also everybody was soundly asleep. He placed the child near Yashoda and brought back her daughter. When Kansa came to know of the new born baby, he instantly rushed to the jail, and took up the child from the hands of Devaki who prayed to Kansa to save her, as she, a girl, could do him no harm. But Kansa, heedless of her request, tried to dash the child on stone when she sprang from his hands into the sky warning him. "Fool ! your destructor has already been born elsewhere." Kansa in his anxiety ordered a thorough search for the child Krishna.

In Gokul, the birth of a boy to Yashoda was widely celebrated as a festival. As days passed,

Kansa tried in vain to kill the child through his demons whom the child Krishna killed without much ado. When he was twelve, Krishna was invited to Mathura by Kansa with the intention of getting him killed in a wrestling bout. Krishna and Balrama killed not only the wrestlers but also Kansa and released his parents and restored the throne of Mathura to Ugrasen. He then stayed at Mathura with his parents. Both the brothers were sent to the hermitage of Sage Sandipani at Ujjain for study. There they studied four Vedas, six Shastras and politics, and learnt sixty-four arts in sixty-four days. On completion of their studies they asked Guru Sandipani about *guru dakshina*, and, at his behest, brought back alive his only son drowned in a reservoir at Prabhas. Jarasandh, the father-in-law of Kansa, invaded Mathura seventeen times, but Krishna with his Yadava force defeated him every time. On his eighteenth invasion, Kalayavan also prepared to march on Mathura from another direction with a mighty force. Thereupon Shri Krishna left Mathura with all the Yadavas in order to save their energies being wasted in constant warfare. He settled on the west coast at Kushasthali, where he built a wonderful city in twelve square *yojan* area with the help of Vishwakarma, the gods' architect and named it 'Dwarikapuri'. Later on, he got Kalayavan and Jarasandh killed by trick.

Krishna killed Shishupal, Dantavakra and other evil rulers. He killed Narakasur,the demon king of Pragjyotishpur and released 16,100 maidens whom Narakasur had abducted and kept in custody. They all desired to marry Krishna their saviour. He married them and brought them to Dwaraka. On the expiry of the period of exile of his cousins, the Pandavas, Krishna went as an envoy to the court of Kauravas and asked them to give back the kingdom of Indraprastha to Pandavas, but as Duryodhan did not agree to part with any portion of his possessions, there remained no other alternative but a battle. Shri Krishna was related to both the parties and had to help them in battle. As the choice of Arjun, his ardent devotee and friend, he joined the Pandavas as Arjun's charioteer under a vow not to take up arms while his army of one *akshauhini* he sent to fight for the Kauravas.

In the beginning of the battle Arjun became nervous seeing in the battlefield his elders, brothers, cousins, relatives and dear ones, with whom he had to fight. He refused to fight even at the cost of his life. At that time Krishna advisde him and showed the path of duty. This advice in *Gita,* shows the way of self realization and self-development. It gives peace of mind and shows the path of action. It destroys ignorance and guides to salvation. For thousands of years *gita* has been the most sacred to every Hindu. It is the essence of Vedas. Hearing the advice of Krishna in the form of *Gita*, duty without attachment and without any concern for the result of his actions, the dejection of Arjun vanished. He realized his duty-the path action-and was ready to fight. In the great battle of Mahabharata that ensued, the Pandavas were victorious over the Kauravas.

After the holocaust of Mahabharata, Shri Krishna returned to Dwaraka. But his life mission was nearing its end. The Yadavas had become arrogant, lazy and drunkards. They fought with each other at Prabhas and died. Thus all the evil elements were wiped off from the surface of the earth. His mission fulfilled, Shri Krishna left this world, shot by a hunter at Prabhas Patan.

The significance of Shri Krishna's life and its indelible effects on the life of the people of India cannot be overemphasized. He was not only the greatest politician, diplomat and benefactor of mankind but also the greatest of *yogis,* ascetics, philosophers and saints. He lived his life for the destruction of evil and the promotion of good, for freeing *dharma* from the clutches of evil-doers and oppressors, for doing away with old and useless customs and establishing new and healthy ones. Through his many deeds from childhood to old age which are looked upon as miracles, he taught lessons of love, equality of all beings and sympathy for the lowest strata of society. If he had not done anything else but given the *Bhagavadgita* alone, he would even then have been worshipped as the best friend, philosopher and guide of the people. In *Gita,* he gives the message of *karmayoga*, i.e., doing one's duty without any attachment and concern for the results of one's actions and also promises that the person who unreservedly takes refuge in God is sure of his salvation and smallest of the good deeds does not remain unrewarded. *Gita* is thus a comprehensive philosophy of life and Shri Krishna, its author, has been worshipped not only as the perfect human being but also as a complete incarnation of God, or the *Purna Purushottama*. Throughout the ages great men have worshipped him in different ways and in different forms. Mira, Narsinh Mehta, Chaitanya Mahaprabhu, Tukaram, Tilak, Aurobindo Ghosh and Gandhiji were all great devotees of Shri Krishna and lovers of *Gita* which inspired them all. Numerous book have been written about Shri Krishan's life and mission. The chief of them are *Shrimad bhagavat, Mahabharata, Jaimini Ashvamedh, Vishnu Purana, Harivansh*, etc. Foreigners also have written on the life of Krishna and *Gita* which embodies his profound teachings in almost all the important languages of the world.

Owing to the predominance of Vaishnavism, which worship Lord Vishnu in one form or another, the worship of Shri Krishna is universally popular in India. The perfection of the Almighty reflected in the personality of Lord Krishna endears him to one and all. He is venerated by people of all sects and Janmashtami, his birthday, is celebrated alike in Vaishnava and Shiva temples, and observed austerely, in fasting and prayers. Early in the morning, people throng to the temples to offer worship. The most devout go to pilgrim places like Gokul-Vrindavan, Dwaraka, Dakor, Vadtal, Gadhada, etc., to celebrate the festival at his shrines. People observe fast for the whole day taking only *falahar* which consists of fruit and some non-cereal items once in the afternoon. The whole day is passed in reading religious books like the *Bhagavat Gita*, etc., and hearing religious discourses. In villages, the day is passed in singing *bhajan-kirtan*. Numerous fairs are also held on this day all over Gujarat. Gambling, common in the lower strata of society, was practised the whole night. Before merger of the former States, some small chieftains were holding fairs in their estates on this day arranging gambling for which contracts were given.

As Shri Krishna was born at midnight, his birth is celebrated in each and every Vaishnavite temple and in orthodox households with special *puja* offered at that time, though with the change of time the practice of household celebrations is gradually falling into disuse. The entire atmosphere is surcharged with intense religious fervour and enthusiasm. The whole day is marked by intense activity in preparation for the midnight celebrations. People keep themselves busy engaged in various religious pursuits till midnight. Temples and rooms set part for worship in private houses are decorated with festoons of *asopales* and flowers. *Bhajans* are sung. Holy books are read, and *Harikathas* are arranged. The principal shrines are visited at midnight to have the special *darshan* of the deity. Lord Krishna is worshipped in his *bal-swarup* of infant form. A small idol of infant Krishna, known as Lalji, is worshipped by *shodashopachar* or sixteen rites, anointed with sandal and saffron paste, dressed in costly garments and placed in a decorated cradle, sometimes made of gold and silver, swung by *pujaris, mukhiyajis* and devotees. After *arti, panchamrit* and *prasad* of *panjari* or *panchajiri,* a sweet-pungent powder of five constituents mixed together, viz. dry ginger, sugar, *dhana, kopra* and *khaskhas* are distributed to the devotees. The fast is broken the next day with a feast. Since the rituals emulate the festivities held at the house of Nandrai in Gokul when Lord Krishna was born, the *dhun* on everybody's lips is, "*Nand ghar anand bhayo, jai Kanaiyalal ki* "(There is rejoicing at the house of Nand; glory to the child Kanaiy). This day is, therefore, known as Gokulashtami or Janmashtami. The festival is celebrated at Mahadev temples with the *mahapuja* at midnight, but at Mataji temples with the cradle of Lalji lovingly and reverentially rocked by devotees. The celebrations of the birth of Krishna at the temples of other deities show the basic unity of religion in this country. God is considered the Universal Power or Eternal Truth Who manifests Himself in various forms, some calling Him God, some *Shakti*, some *Adi Purush*, etc. In Hinduism there is thus a happy synthesis of all forms of beliefs practised according to one's own stage of mental development.

It is worthy to note that Vallabhacharya, the founder of Pushtimargiya Vaishnavite sect, emphasized the worship of Krishna in his childhood, i.e., Krishna at Gokul. Importance is also given to the period passed at Golok or Gokul in play, games, grazing of cows and playing of *raslila* with *gopis*. In *havelis* and at the seats of Pushtimargiya sect Krishna is worshipped as Bal-Krishna. In Vaishnativite temples like Dwaraka, Dakor and Nathdwar, Krishan is worshipped in his youth as Dwarkadhish, Ranchhodji and Shri Nathji. At Jagannathpuri and other Jagdish temples he is worshipped in still another form. In Gujarat importance to Krishna *-puja* is given in the temples of Pushtimarg, Swaminarayan and Radha-Swami sects mostly in towns and cities. In Delhi crowds through temples whole day and keep fasts breaking them at 12 midnight. Spending the day having fruits and singing songs in praise of Lord Krishna.

Karwa-Chouth

The festival of Karwa-Chouth (or pitcher-fourth) falls on the 4th day of the month of *Kartik* (October-November), i.e., on the fourth day of the fortnight of waxing moon. Just 12 days after Karwa-Chouth falls the great festival of Diwali. The observance of the festival is restricted only to married women, the unmarried women and widows do not observe it. It is learnt that in Punjab even unmarried women and girls observe the festival — the difference being that whereas married women perform the worship only after the moon rises, those unmarried do so after the first star becomes visible in the evening sky.

Fast is observed for the whole day and it is broken only after due worship is offered to the moon or the first star, as the case may be. Small earthen pitchers with a tap-like projection on the upper half are painted by the women and in the tap-like projection are stuck the ears of *Kans* grass. In the Karwa (the pitchers with a tap-like opening) are put sweets and other delicacies but all items are 4 in number. One of the invariable articles kept in the Karwa are the balls prepared out of rice-flour and sugar. In the houses of the people of poor economic status, these may form the only sweets kept in the pitcher. These sweet balls of rice-flour are known here as *pinni*. The pitcher is covered with an earthen pan-like lid which is filled with rice and on the rice is kept earthen wick-lamp with 4 wicks. Two such pitchers are prepared.

As the night approaches, the central portion of the courtyard or some such place from where the moon would be visible as soon as it rises, is washed with cowdung solution and a design is made with rice or wheat flour. The two pitchers are kept there. Also kept there is the pot full of water (Kalash) on which is also burning a wick-lamp.

The night of Karwa-Chouth appears (how true is the Einsteinian principle of Relativity to the ladies to be the night when the moon rises very late. They arrange the worship paraphernalia as soon as it is dark and then go to this side of the house and that to look for the moon. The husbands usually keep a permanent watch on the moon looking at the impatience and keennees of their wives. Every woman desires to offer her worship to the moon as soon as it shows its face on the horizon. The sentiments are the offering worship to the young moon (*Bal-Chandrama*) would favour them with a youthful husband in the next life.

Out of the two figures, one is for the self and other is for the Goddess Gouri whose image is there on the worship place. As soon as the moon is visible, the pitcher is taken in both hands and the wick-lamp is waved and then water is poured at the tap-like projection of the pitchers. This simple worship being over, the contents of the pitcher are eaten by those keeping fast and other members of the household save widows and unmarried girls. Before breaking the fast are related the following stories:

I

Long long ago there was a king who had seven sons and one daughter, she being the youngest of them all. On coming of age she was married and on the first Karwa-Chouth festival, she was in her father's place. As every married woman, she was on fast for the whole day, her lovely young face a little pale with hunger and thirst. But the moon of the Karwa-Chouth was not showing its face in the sky.

Seeing the somewhat restless condition of their lovely sister, the seven brothers held a council and decided to prepare an artificial moon so that, duped by it, their sister may offer worship and break her fast. One of them climbed a distant tree, placed a lamp on one of its branches and put a round sieve before it. From a distance the improvisation gave the semblance of the young just-risen moon. Doing this, all the seven of them came shouting.

"Sister, O Sister the moon is risen. Offer soon your worship lest it may grow old".

And hearing them the princes came out and there in the distance was the moon amongst the trees. She offered her worship and partook of the meals. The real moon rose much later, but she did not know the truth.

Just as the moon rose, there came a messenger from her husband's kingdom with the urgent and unfortunate message—her husband was suddenly taken ill and was breathing his last. She was strucked with sorrow and her wailing could not be heard without the heart being broken. And then, as other women were offering their worship to the moon, it dawned on her that she had broken her fast long before the moon rose. How could that be for she had seen the moon there admist the trees.

Came forth the guilty brothers all in sorrow. It was their doing that caused the misfortune but there was nothing that could now be done to correct the wrong done.

The princess started immediately for the husband's place, the messenger going ahead with the instructions that the dead body should not be burnt before she reaches, for the princess will bring back her husband from the Lord of Death.

On reaching her husband's palace, she kept the corpse in oil to preserve it for one year. She had done a wrong and only the *Karwa- Chouth* can forgive her. The whole year, days in and days out, she prayed the *Karwa-Chouth*.

"O deity, I am faultless. I have done a wrong in all innocence, not knowing what I was doing. Forgive me for you are all merciful".

And the whole year she took great care of the body of her husband. So that it did not putrify and remained fresh. And thus passed one full year. She never considered herself as a widow—her husband was not dead for her. On the Karwa-Chouth day she kept fast and then as the moon rose in the sky offered her worship with all devotion praying to be forgiven. And when the worship was duly over, she went to the oil-bath where lay the body of her dear husband and there to the amazement of everybody was the prince—her husband—sitting saying that he was sorry he was sleeping all this long. He was feeling thirsty and requested for a glass of water. A wave of rejoicing ran through the whole kingdom. Karwa-Chouth had brought back her husband and given her a long long marital happiness. And Karwa-Chouth would go on giving long marital bliss to all who would worship and pray on this day.

II

Once upon a time, there lived seven brothers who had only one sister. This girl was pampered by the whole family — by the parents and the brothers alike. One day the girl, while fetching water from the well, heard an oracle, that there were four imminent dangers to her husband. She was married but the *dwiragman* ritual had not yet been done and as such she was living with her parents. According to the oracle, these dangers were:

(1) When he passes through the main door of the house, it would fall down killing him;

(2) If he is saved, then he would get drowned in the Ganges when he goes to bathe there;

(3) If he is saved from drowning then, he would swallow a babul thorn while eating his food, which would get entangled in his wind-pipe choking him to death;

(4) If he is saved from this also, he cannot escape the cobra that would bite him when he goes to sleep.

Hearing this oracle, the girl came home running and told her mother that she would immediately go to her husband's house. Everybody was dumbfounded because, the *gauna* or the *dwiragman* ceremony had not yet been performed and she could not be sent to her husband's house like this. Moreover, no message had been received from her husband's house. Sending her thus was a matter of disgrace. Everybody tried to convince her of this. But she would not listen and said that she would not even touch water here.

The parents and seven brothers then decided that after all she was so much loved and pampered and all her wishes had been fulfilled by that time. Even if it comes to disgrace, she should be sent to her in-law's house because the only sister that she was, she would not be allowed to suffer like that. The girl was married in the same town and there was not much of difficulty on that account; she could be taken there easily.

But when the brothers took her to her husband's house, everybody was astounded there also; how could a girl so come before *gouna* ritual? But the litter carrying her was already at the door and so the mother-in-law and other ladies went there to get her down and take her to the house. The girl however refused to get down. She said that the main gate of the house should be felled and a new one should be installed. Only then would she get down from the litter and enter the house. Everybody was annoyed. Firstly she comes here unsent for and now this demand.

The whole day passed and the girl kept sitting in the litter without food and water. The neighbours intervened, "After all" they said "you people have so much money and she is your only daughter-in-law. It will not matter much if you dismantle this old door and get a new one installed". The intervention of the neighbours had its results and the in-law's decided to dismantle the door but no sooner was the first blow struck, the whole frame fell. "What a good luck" they said, "this door was not going to remain here any more. It would have fallen any moment".

The daughter-in-law was taken inside. Going in the house she offered a worship to the door but she did not accept even water. In the meantime her husband prepared himself to go for bathing in the Ganges and seeing him, she immediately jumped up saying that she would accompany him. The mother-in-law was very angry already and said that such an act would be disgraceful for the women of the house and she could not thus accompany the husband. But the daughter-in-law was adamant. She would go and so unwillingly the consent was given.

The Ganges was in floods. As soon as the couple reached there, the girl worshipped the river and then only let her husband bathe in the river. After bathing he returned home with her. At the meal-time she insisted that she would eat with her husband. The mother-in-law had lost her patience by this time and said that she had nothing to do with her and she may do as she pleased. The girl unhesitatingly sat with her husband for food and immediately spotted the *babul* thorn in the vegetable. She picked it up unnoticed and tied it in the corner of her sari and got up. Everybody asked her to eat something but she only kept quiet.

At night she requested her mother-in-law to let her go with her husband to bed. This was the limit and the old woman was very much enraged. In her rage she gave her permission and the girl entered the bedroom with her husband. There she spotted the cobra in the corner and in a flash of moment covered it with a basket. Then she came out immediately and begged her mother-in-law's permission to go to her parent's house. The whole conduct was shrouded in mystery and the mother-in-law asked her why she had so come and why was she so going. She then said, "O revered mother, I had come to let your son live and let my husband survive. He had four dangers to his life as I heard in the oracle. She then told them why she got the door dismantled, why she accompanied him to the river, why she sat for eating with him and then she showed them the thorn. She told them the reason why she insisted to go to bed with him and told them to go and see the cobra in the bedroom. Everybody was amazed and the mother-in-law embraced her — "O my beloved daughter, you are Laxmi of this house. We could not recognise you". She then went back to her parent's house and returned in due time, after *gouna*, to live for many many years in happy wedlock".

Lohri

Lohri, like Basant and Baisakhi is a seasonal festival observed in Delhi as well as in Northen India . It falls on the last day of Poh (mid-January), when the sun touches the southern most point on the ecliptic and the duration of the night is the longest. Astronomically the winter is then at its peak. The word ' Lohri' seems to be the corruption of the words 'loh' and 'ari', literally meaning iron foe, or figuratively formidable or black foe, suggestive of the long, dreadfully cold night.

On the Lohri night bonfires are made private . It is a great fun, more so for the youngsters. Small quantities of peanuts, popcorn, parched rice, sesame seed, gur and sweets are thrown into the fire as offerings, and eaten by the persons who sit, sing and eaten by the persons who sit, sing and gossip around the fire. The superstitious people close their eyes and wish for their heart's desire as the Lohri fire burns.

Mahalaya—Pitra Amavasya

The new moon day at the end of the dark fortnight of Bhadra (Aswini in some areas) is called Mahalaya amavasya. The entire fortnight is called *pitru paksha* or Sola shraddha.

Ancestral worship forms the core of Hindu religious beliefs, Remembering the ancestor in a variety of ways, by propitiation and offerings, is an integral part of ritual complex of many Hindu religious rites. Every *grihastha* (householder) is enjoined by the scriptures to perform as one of his daily duties the five sacrifices, namely, to the *devas, pitrus* (ancestors), *bhutas, Brahma* and *manusya* (guests). Apart from this daily routine of sacrifices, certain special days have been stated to be particularly important for ancestral offerings. Every new moon day (amavasya) is one of them.

Ancestral worship on the new moon day of Bhadra is compulsory for all Hindus who are obliged to perform ancestral rites. The mantras (formulae) for the ritual are in Sanskrit and are followed by all Hindus mostly with the help of Brahman purohits. People from some families congregate at the nearest water source-a river or a tank and perform 'tarpana' rites in groups. Hindus of lower castes believe that a tarpana rite or shraddha on Mahalaya amavasya, will compensate the annual shraddha ceremony death anniversary which he might have neglected or forgotten.

An outstanding feature of the 'tarpana' rite is that it reaffirms the lineage ties by the performers mentioning the name of the original (mythical) lineage ancestor (gotra) and the names of the ancestors of three generations in the ascending order, i.e., father, father's father, father's, father's, father (i.e., ita, pitamaha, prapitamaha) respectively. The performer gives oblations of water with sesame seeds to each of the above individually. During the later part of his life, he may normally be expected to have one or more sons and son's sons. These latter will naturally become aware of the names of the members of the lineage of six generations in all from grandson upwards. According to the old adage a sonless person has no salvation, for he has failed to perpetuate the lineage with the result that the ancestors have been deprived of the offerings due to them and so every male member has a duty to perform towards the lineage "itself, past, present, and future".

Mahashivratri

This is a big festival of the Hindus in which Shiva is worshipped. There are three main deities in the Hindu Pantheon worshipped from time immemorial, viz., Brahma, Vishnu and Shiva. Since the creation of the universe this trio is said to have distributed the duties amongst themselves. Brahma is the creator of the world, Vishnu the preserver and Shiva the destroyer. Gradually Brahma ceased to be worshipped, while Vishnu and Shiva continued as deities popularly worshipped. Magh Vad 14 is the day of worship of Shiva at night and is known as Mahashivratri. The fourteenth day of the dark half of each month is called Shivratri, but that of Magh is Mahashivratri or the greatest of Shivratris, which is celebrated as a festival by Shaivites all over India.

It is said in the Puranas that on the night of Magh Vad 14, Lord Shiva had created his idol in the form of a *linga,* to show His might to Brahma and Vishnu who were fighting *inter se* for superiority. They both approached Shiva for a decision. Lord Shiva at once assumed the form of a *linga* and asked both of them to find out the upper and lower ends. The *linga* was spread over all the three worlds of *swarga, Prithvi* and *patal*-heaven, earth and nether region. Brahma and Vishnu failed and returned to Mahadev and praised him, and acknowledged his superiority among the trio. Since then, Shiva is worshipped in the form of a *linga* throughout India. Lord Shiva then created twelve such idols called *jyotirlingas,* in different part of India to worship as under :

1. Somnath at Prabhas Patan Saurashtra
2. Mallikarjun in Andhra Pradesh
3. Mahakaleshwar at Ujjain
4. Omkareshwar on the bank of Narmada
5. Vaijanath at Parli in Bihar
6. Bhimashankar in Dakini forest
7. Rameshwar in the South
8. Nagnath in Daruka forest
9. Vishvanath in Kashi (Varanasi)
10. Tryambakeshwar at Trimbak
11. Kedareshwar in the Himalayas
12. Ghusruneshwar or Ghushmeshwar Verul

These places are known as *Shivapuris*, and are the main pilgrim places for all Shaivites. Staunch devotees of Shiva wish to celebrate the festival of Mahashivratri at any of these places.

A Pauranic story of a Bhil hunter in *Linga Purana* describes the importance of Mahashivratri thus. In ancient times there was a Bhil, who was supporting his family by hunting. On a Mahashivratri day he went to a money-lender in his village to get some money. He waited at his house till evening without taking food, as all the members of the money-lender's family were occupied in the worship of God Shiva reciting the name of Shiva. He uttered the name unknowingly all the while. As the money-lender asked him to come on the next day, he returned home where all his family members were hungry. He went to the forest at night and spread his net and sat on a branch of a *bili* tree *(Aegle marmelos*) to look out for the prey. He began to pluck and throw leaves of the tree on the ground, where there was an unworshipped *linga* of Lord Shiva underneath. All the *bili* leaves thrown by the hunter fell on this Shivalinga. Fortunately some deer were caught in his net, but they requested him to allow them to go home for a final meeting with their families and promised him to return the next day. Due to fast on the previous day and unknowing worship of Shiva by *bili* leaves, his heart melted and he allowed them to go. He passed his night on the bili tree, dropping the leaves on the ground. Next day the deer returned and asked him to kill them and satisfy the hunger of his family. But the hunter was totally changed. He was full of mercy and set them free. Lord Shiva was very much pleased with him due to his observance of fast and worship of his *linga* at night by bili leaves, and sent a *viman*-aeroplane-to take him and the deer to heaven. The Lord placed them in the heaven as constellations and named them Mrigashirsha and Vyadha. These constellations can be seen by the naked eye at night in the sky from the month of Margashirsh to Jyeshtha, rising in the east. The month of Margashirsh is named from the constellation Mrigashirsa.

This day is observed as a public holiday, and the festival is celebrated in every Hindu home. There are three main features of the celebration, (i) observance of fast, (ii) worship of Lord Shiva and (iii) keeping awake the whole night. After a bath in the early morning the devout go to the temple and worship God Shiva with *bili* leaves and *dhatura* flowers, favourite of Lord Shiva. This worship may take place at home but preferably at some temple of Shiva, where worship is performed at midnight.

In Delhi Devotees observe fast and pass the time in worship reciting *panchakshara mantra* of Shiva—*Om namah Shivaya*, to lord wearing a rosary of rudraksha in the neck, and recital of either *Rudri* or *Mahimnastotra*. At midnight devotees gather at the temple of Shiva for *mahapuja* or ceremonial mass worship when the idol is bathed with *panchamrit*—a mixture of milk, *ghee,* curd, honey and sugar—and then again with the holy waters of the Ganga or some other river or sea and worshipped according to *shodashopachar* or sixteen rites with the chanting of mantras, etc. Temples are illuminated. Devotees pass the whole night at the temple. Mahashivratri is thus a night festival, as it is during the night that the most important *puja* takes place. The importance of the worship in the dead of the night is also emphasized in the story of the hunter narrated above. Next day after taking bath in the morning, people again have *darshan* and offer prayers. Brahmins are fed with sweets and given alms in cash. Thereafter they break the fast and return home after a community dinner.

The festival is not without significance to the agricultural economy. It is a post-harvast festival occurring at the conclusion of the *rabi* season, when there is no work in the field, and the farmer is free. People can, therefore, take time to relax. As a result, the festival is favourite both of the advanced as well as of the backward classes, who celebrate it with zeal irrespective of caste or sect.

The day is also important for the Arya Samajists, as Swami Dayanand, the founder of Arya Samaj, got divine inspiration to begin his search of truth on the night of Mahashivratri at his native place Tankara in Morvi taluka of Rajkot district. His farmer name was Mulshankar. He was by caste an Audichya Brahmin. His former members were devout followers of Shiva. They celebrated the festival of Mahashivratri observing fast the performing *puja* at night at a Mahadev temple. Mulshankar also used to attend the function. Once he saw the worshipping Brahmins dozing and a mouse running on *shivalinga* to eat grains placed on it. Mulshankar at once realized that there is no god in the idol otherwise he would not have allowed a mouse to run on his head. He lost faith in idol worship. He fled from home and went to the Himalayas in search of a preceptor . Everywhere he found *sadhus* and *sanyasis* taking undue advantage of the faith of devotees exploited in the name of idol worship. Therefore, he himself practised penance for years and,as a result of divine revelation, was inspired to fight idol worship root out evil and vicious practices prevailing at that time and propagate the true doctrines of Vedic religion. He started his mission from the Punjab where the Arya Samaj founded by him has a wide following.

Makara Sankranti

Makara Sankranti, traditionally believed to be the starting point of the sun's northward journey, is celebrated by Hindus according to the solar calendar on January 14. When the sun enters the orbit of a *rashi* from another it is called sankranti. The sun moves in the orbit of *rashi* for a month In it enters the orbit of Makara, and as such the day is celebrated as Makara Sankranti. The earth moves round the sun and takes one year to complete one round. The imaginary path of the movement of the sun is known as *krantivrat* in Indian astronomy. The path is divided into twelve parts. These twelve parts or *rashis* taken together are known as *rashi-chakra* or zodiac, each known by a special sign assigned to it. Accruing to the Hindu astronomy they are Mesha (Aries), Vrishabha (Taurus), Mithuna (Gemini), Karka (Cancer), Simha (Leo), Kanya (Virgo), Tula (Libra), Vrishchika (Scorpio), Dhanu (Sagittarius), Maker (Capricorn), Cumbria (Aquarius), and Mina (Pisces) respectively. The sun takes one month in its movement through one *rashi* while the moon takes two and a quarter days. Each planet also moves in the zodiac. The movement of the sun in the orbit of a *rashi* or sign of zodiac is called *sankramana*. When the sun enters the orbit of a particular *rashi* it is called the *sankranti* of that rashi. Thus the day on which the sun enters the orbit of Makara (Capricorn) is called Makara Sankranti. This path is also divided into two *ayanas*—zone—northern and southern. The northern zone begins when the sun enters the orbit of Makara. The sun seems to be making a northward journey and as such it is called *Uttarayana*, i.e., entrance into the northern zone. When the sun enters the orbit of Karka (Cancer) rashi in the month of Ashadh it is called *Dakshinayana*. In the *Uttarayana* the day becomes longer. Similarly in *Dakshinayana* nights become long and days short. Really speaking the sun enters the orbit of Makara on 23rd December and that of Karka on 23rd June every year. Formerly Makara Sankranti was observed on 23rd

December and not on 14th January as at present according to *sayana* principle. But our calendars are prepared according to lunar months under the *nirayana* system. which gives a difference of twenty three days between the two.

The day of gods begins with the winter solstice or the entry of the sun into the orbit of Makara, it has a special importance and is regarded as auspicious. It is also believed that the gods sleep from Ashadh for six months closing the doors of heaven, which open at the entrance of the sun in northern zone, i.e., in the orbit of Makara, when the gods awake from the long slumber. The month preceding Makara Sankranti, known as *dhanurmas* is considered inauspicious for beginning any new work. Religious minded people have an intense desire that their death may occur during the period of *Uttarayana*, during the day of gods. Bhishma, the great-grandfather of Pandavas and Kauravas, had passed a long period on the bed of arrows on the battlefield, and departed from this world only after the *Uttarayana* had set in, i.e., on the day of Makara Sankranti. As the Pandavas took a purifying bath in the holy waters of the Ganga on this day great importance is attached to a bath in the early morning in the holy rivers and the sea which have become centres of pilgrimage and occasions for people to assemble at fairs.

The use of *til* (sesame) is specially prescibed on this day and during winter. Importance is given to sesame seeds in Puranas also.

Religious people should clean their teeth with sesame oil, bathe after rubbing sesame oil on the body, sacrifice sesame seeds in fire, drink the water mixed with sesame seeds, take sesame preparations at dinner, and give *til* in alms. The use of sesame in these six ways destroys sins.

The season of *shishir* begins from this day. According to Ayurveda, people require to take oily diet in this season for body building and *til* seeds are considered best for the purpose. The use of *til* is, therefore, enjoined during the whole season for acquiring vitality. According to alopathy also, *til* contains vitamins A,B and C, and its use is beneficial.

Cows are worshipped in the morning and fed with boilded *bajri* or *jowar* known as *ghughri* and *tethawa.* Women give five earthen or metal vessels filled with wheat, fruit such as jamun and brries, sweetballs of *til* and gram, sugar-cane pieces, etc., to five married women, generally daughters and sisters to whom a new *sari* is also presented after feasting.

All these practices have a significant relationship to the agricultural economy of the state. By this time the *kharif* crops are ready and brought home. These are shared freely with the others as gift of grain earns great religious merit on this day. In an economy which is purely agricultural, domestic animals are not forgotten and grass is freely distributed to the village cattle. Makara Sankranti thus becomes a harvest festival in the true sense of the term.

In Vaishnaivite temples, deities are offered *khichadi* and *ghee* in the morning in dhanmas, i.e., month prior to Sankranti, and on the Makara Sankranti day *khichado*-a special sweet of wheat, *ghee* sugar and dry fruits. In former States, princes used to arrange *chorashi,* i.e., dinner of sweetballs to all the sub-castes of Brahmins in the morning. People give *guptadan* of cash, hiding coins in sweetballs.

Nag Panchami

Nag Panchami, the name of the festival implies that it is a day which is dedicated of the worship of snakes (Nag) and that the worship is to be on the fifth day (panchami) in the bright fortnight Sravana (July-August) Though the name denotes Cobra as the objects of worship, it embraces the entire species of venomous reptiles according to popular conception. It is known in some parts of the country as Vishari or Bishari puja—bisha meaning poison. Srinivas says, 'Cobras are revered throughout India and their worship takes different forms in different parts of the country.

Each household celebrating this festival gives a small present of flour and butter. The 'dough snake' is finally buried and women propitiate the spirit of the snake for nine days with offerings of curd. He explains that 'dough snake' is clearly a substitute for a real snake.

A number of legends have grown round *naga* worship and are currently narrated at the end of the performance of the rite emphasizing its importance for the preservation of human lives. This can be understood from the various objectives which the propitiants intend to attain by performing the rite. The apparent object of the worship is to obtain protection from serpents which are deadly dangerous to human lives. This is evident from the fact that the time of the festival (Sravana August-September) coincides with the advent of rains (Varsha Ritu) during which serpents come out of their holes to the surface of the earth and become a source of danger to human being, the danger being particularly great in marshy areas.

In some parts of the country, married women who are unlucky in the mattar of children, either being barren or whose children fail to survive after birth, take to cobra worship by installing stones carved with images of cobras at the foot of peepal trees after due ceremonies. It is also a very common custom among such women to pour milk over anthills at the root of a peepal tree in the belief that the milk will reach the serpents living beneath them. This aspect of cobra worship clearly leads to the inference that Nag Panchami celebrations may be regarded as a fertility rite. Vogel observes, "There exists a widespread belief that the same animal (cobra) has power to impart fecundity and remove barrenness".

The cobra is endowed with many uncommon attributes which arouse in the human mind an instinctive reverence not unmixed with fear, which has procured for it a place among powers greater than human. When man finds himself unequal to meet a danger from something which he regards as superhuman, he tries to appease it by propitiation. The deification of the cobra naturally follows from fear inspired by the animal as well as from its association with Vishnu, Shiva and Subramanya, gods of the Hindu Pantheon.

Navaratri, Durga Puja

Navaratri is observed twice in a year. It occurs during first nine days of *shukla paksha* in the months of Chaitra and Ashwin. While the former is called Vasantiya Navaratra and continues up to Ram Navami, the day when Lord Rama is said to have been born, the latter is Sharadiya Navaratri and precedes Vijayadashami.

Whether it is Ram Navami Navaratra of *vasant ritu* (spring season) or Devi Navaratra of *sharad ritu* (winter), both festivals are associated with Lord Rama: the first with his birth and the other with his triumph over Ravana.

Chaitra Navaratra usually falls in April. On Ram Navami, thousands of devotees bathe in the Sarayu river. A grand fair is held in Ayodhya and people throng temples. Devi Navaratra (in October) is also associated with the divine creation of goddess Durga through the powes of all the gods to annihilate the demon Mahishasura.

The worship of Durga, Kali, Laxmi and Saraswati is widely observed all over the country, especially in West Bengal. For nine days, people worship idols of these deities and finally immerse them in water. Young girls are also worshipped as symbols of pure female powers. It is celebrated at home and in temples of the Mother Goddess in her various forms, while the social and cultural aspect of the festival relates to its collective and public celebrations.

Mother Cult or Shakti Puja

The worship of Mother Goddess is indeed older than the dawn of history. Man, who started worshipping the elements of Nature, began to probe into them and came to believe that there is a power behind them. Nature, a manifestation of this power, is herself a loving mother who nurtures her children with affection and care. Mother Goddess thus represents the all-pervading power that destroys evil, punishes wrong-doers and protects her faithful children. She, therefore, came to be worshipped in her numerous forms.

The worship of Mother Goddess was prevalent not only in India but also in various other countries in ancient times. It is believed to have flourished hundreds of years before Christ in Pharas, Mesopotamia, Egypt, Syria, Asia Miror, etc., i.e., from the Mediterranean and Egypt to india. An inscription of Mesopotamia describes her as the remoer of the calamities of the people. The Shakta sect had spread from the region of the Nile to the Indus in ancient times.Stories in *Makandeva*, *Brahma-Vaivarta* and *Skanda Puranas* support this belief. Goddess Isis of Egypt, Ijani of Sumer, ishtar of Babylon, and

Hingula of Sind, etc. resembles Amba, Kali, Durga and other goddesses of India.

According to one opinion, goddess-worship was prevalent in India even before the advent of the Aryans who adopted it from the original inhabitants of the land, along with some other religious practices. References are found in the Vedas to goddesses like Gayatri, Ratri,Usha, Prithvi, Vagdevi, Aditi, Saraswati, etc. Some of the most beautiful poetic hymns of *Rig Veda* are dedicated to these goddesses. Some clay idols believed to be of Matri Devi have been found at Mohen-jo-Daro.The *Devi Sukta nor Rig Veda,* the *Shri Sukta* of *Sama Veda, Durga Sukta, Bhoo Sukta,* and *Nila Sukta* and Shakta Upanishads like *Sitopanishad, Devi Upanishad, Saubhagya Upanishad, Saraswati Upanishad, Bhavanopanishad, Bahvrichopanishad,* and Puranas such as *Makandeya Purana, Devi Purana, Devi Bhagavat,* etc. stress the motherly aspect of God. *Kenopaishad* also speaks of Uma Hemavati who imparted wisdom of the self to Indra and the gods. The five main deities of Hindu, religion called *panchayatan* are Shiva, Vishnu, Shakti, Ganapati and Surya. All these are the forms of *Parabrahma,* the Supreme Being or almighty. They are worshipped together or separately, by their respective devotees, as worship of this *panchayatan* on any of its individual deities earns salvation.

In course of time several forms were attributed to Shakti and she came to be worshipped in her numerous manifestations—some of them benign, as the dispenser of well-being, others ferocious, as the destroyer of evil. Some of her important forms are: Amb, Jagadamba, Uma, Gauri, Bhagavati,Bhavani, Lalita, Durga, Kali, Bahuchara, Kameshweri, Chandi, Chamunda, Tara, Tripurasundari,etc. Each one of these goddesses has her special form, emblems, weapons, and carriers, and generally represents one of the various aspects of Mother Goddess.

The importance attached to goddess-worship is seen from the fact that the tonsorial ceremony of Shri Krishna was performed at Ambaji. Nandraja with his relatives had gone there from Gokul and worshipped the Goddess. Adya Shankaracharya had composed prayers in her praise carried *Ananda Lahari* and *Saundarya Lahari.* King Vikram after whom the Hindu era prevalent is named, is also said to be a devotee of goddess Harsiddhi. All Kshatriya rulers are staunch devotees of Mother Goddess adopted under one name or another and regarded as their *kul-devi* or family goddess. For it is she who embodies all power and gives them the strength they need for the protection of their people. Shivaji was a devotee of Bhavani, who gave him a sword as a special favour. Ramakrishna Paramahansa, the great saint and reformer, worshipped the Mother Goddess and attained self-realisation. Followers of Shakti are called Shaktas.They believe her to be the supreme power on earth and identify her with Mother Nature herself. She is, therefore, called Jagat-janani or Jagadamba, the mother of the universe. Much religio-philosophical thought has been bestowed upon Shakti. She represents *prakriti*, the counterpart of *purusha*, jointly making possible the creation of the world. She maintains the sportive play or *lila* of the Lord. She is *ichchha shakti, kriya shakti nor jnan Shakti*, or the power of will, action and knowledge. She manifested herself to Shiva in *dash mahavidyas* or the ten forms, viz.,Kali, Bala, Chinmastha, Bhuwaneshwari, Matangi, Shodashi, Dhumavati,Tripurasundari, Tara and Bhairavi.

Just as a physicist visualises energy as a form of matter, the Shakta believes energy to be the ultimate form of all material objects. But even this is a limited manifestation of Shakti who is the Supremes Power or Maha Shakti. As the Shakti of the gods of the Hindu trinity, she is Brahma-Shakti or Saraswati, Vishnu-Shakti or Lakshmi and Shiva-Shakti or Parvati, Gauri or Kali. In conjunction with Shiva, however, she has a special significance. Shakti or power should always be with Shiva, godness or bliss.Shiva and Shakti are inseparable. Shakti has to be liked with goodness to be beneficial to mankind, and while Shiva, without Shakti, is witout action and, therefore, cannot achieve anything. Indeed, Shiva is also worshipped s Ardhanarishwer, half man, half woman. Shakti is the power or energy aspect of Ishwer, the Lord, or the cosmic energy. Shakti is inherent in God. Just as heat cannot be separated from fire, Shakti also cannot be separated from God—the Shakta or the possessor of Shakti. For, both are one and inseparable. Hence worship of Durga, Parvati or Kali is the worship of Lord Shiva.

Great is the glory of the goddess. The countless

universes are only the dust of the Divine Mother's holy feet. Her splendour is indescribable and Her greatness is un fathomable. The abode of Tripurasundari, the Divine Mother, is called Shri Nagara. This magnificent abode is surrounded by twenty-five ramparts which represent the twenty-five *tatvas*. The resplendent Chintamani palace is in the middle, the Divine Mother sits in the Bindu Pitha is Shri Chakra in that wonderful palace. There is a similar abode for her in the body of man also. The whole world is considered Her body. Mountains are her bones, rivers are her veins, the sun and the moon are her eyes, wind her breath and *agni* her mouth. Such a supreme goddess, the mother of all, should be worshipped with *divya bhava* or divine disposition, through *satsang* or company of good and saintly men, renunciation, *japa* or chanting and meditation, as a result of which a Shakta enjoys *bhukti* or worldly enjoyment and *mukti* or salvation. An advanced *sadhak* or worshipper feels himself one with the goddess, and chants, *'Saham',* 'I am She'. Every deity of worship has a special *mantra* or spell to be recited by devotees. That of Devi or Mother Goddess in Navarna *mantra* consisting of nine syllables, viz., "ऊँ ऐं ह्रीं क्लीं चामुंडाये विच्चे।" (*Om aim hrim klim Chamundayai vichche*) which contains the essence of the philosophy of Shaktism and means 'May I know and get the Shakti fulfilling desires and bestowing energy'. The goddess is propitiated by devotees at home or at temples by worship of *yantras* which are geometrical designs drawn to certain measure and form containing certain letters and numerical digits drawn on a metal plate. Thus Viso *yantra* is worshipped at Ambaji, Bala Tripura *yantra*at Bahucharaji and Kali *yantra* at Kalika Mata, Pavagadh.

Shaktism is not mere theory or philosophy. It prescribes systematic *sadhana* of *yoga*, regular discipline according to the temperament, capacity and degree of evolution of the *sadhak*. It helps the aspirant to arouse the Kundalini and unite her with Lord Shiva and to enjoy the supreme bliss of *nirvikalpa samadhi*. When Kundalini sleeps man is awake to the world. He has objective consciousness. When she awakes, he sleeps, i.e., falls in *samadhi* or trance and the body is maintained by the nectar which flows from the union of Shiva and Shakti. Shakti lies dormant in the Muladhara Chakra in the form of serpentine power or coiled up energy known as Kundalini Shakti. The real *sadhak* tries to wake up that Shakti by performing *nirvikalpa samadhi.* She is the primal force of life that underlies all existence. She vitalises the body through the Sushumna Nadi and nerves. She nourishes the body with chyle and blood. She vitalises the universe through her energy. She is energy in the sun, fragrance in flowers, beauty in nature, colour in rainbow, intelligence in the mind, potency in medicines, will and *vichar shakti* in sages, devotion in *bhaktas, samyama* and *sadhana* in *yogi* and Gayatri in Vedas.

A vast body of rituals grew up in Shakti-puja. Shakta Sampradaya adopted various forms of worship, some of which degenerated into undesirable practices. However, the noble idea underlying goddess-worship is also a practical manifestation of the gratitude of man for his mother. A person is more free with his mother than with any one else. He opens his heart more freely to his mother than father. न मातुः परदेवतम् । There is no one greater than the mother. It is the mother who protects, nourishes, consoles, cheers and nurse him. She is the first *guru* or preceptor. The first syllable which almost every human being utters is the beloved name of the mother—*Ma*. She sacrifice her all for the sake of her children. It behoves him, therefore, that the aspirant should approach the mother first, so that she may introduce her spiritual child to the father for his illumination and self-realisation.

Mythology

In *Saptashati*, the religious book of Shaktas, which is a part having seven hundred verses of the *Markandeya Purana*, there are three stories of the demons, Madhu-Kaitabh, Mahishasur and Shumbha and Nishumbha who represent evil elements. They had become powerful and had conquered the gods and made them slaves. Gods, symbolishing divine elements, were so much afraid of these demons that they forgot their own strength and power. Each time it was Shakti who saved them.

After the deluge of the universe, Lord Vishnu was resting in the ocean, reclining on the Shesh Nag. Brahma sprang from his navel thinking to create a new universe. At that time two demons Madhu and Kaitabh said to be born from the dirt of the ears of

Vishnu began to harass Brahma, who invoked the latent power of Vishnu by prayer.Thus invoked, Shakti inspired vishnu who fought with the demons and killed them. His latent power or Shakti was then worshipped as Mahakali, who is referred to as goddess Ratri in *Rig Veda*. The prayer offered by Brahma on that occasion is known as *Ratri Sukta* in *Saptashati* and is repeated daily by the ardent devotee of Shakti.

In the next *yuga* or age, the demon Mahishasur, having gained immunity from being killed by a mortal, conquered and enslaved gods who, led by Brahma, approached Vishnu and prayed to him for shelter from the terror of Mahishasur. Vishnu advised them to invoke their latent power. At that time a lustre sprang out from the body of Lord Shiva and all other gods, and the combined lustre took the form of a woman. All the gods gave her their clothes, ornaments and weapons and a lion as her carrier. Mahishasur and his demon warriors gave a fight to her. She slayed Mahishasur and his army after a nine-day long fight and is, therefore, called Mahishsaurmardini. Gods prayed to her to help them whenever required. Pleased at the prayers offered by gods, she granted them this boon. In this form, she represents Mahalakshmi, is worshipped as such and is Aditi of Vedas.

In the next millennium, two demon kings, Shumbha and Nishumbha gained supremacy over the gods who then assembled on a summit of the Himalayas near the Kailash, the residence of Lord Shvia, to find a way out of their misery. Remembering the praise of the goddess for assistance, they invoked her by prayer. In the mean while, goddess Parvati, the consort of Shiva who was passing by to take a bath in the river Ganga stopped and asked the reason of their gathering. Gods told her the reason.There-upon, the face of Parvati turned black and from her a goddess sprang out. Two demons Chand and Mund saw her and thought that she was fit to be a queen of one of their masters, Shumbha and Nishumbha. They immediately approached and told them about her. The kings sent a message with Dhumralochan asking her to choose one of them as her husband. She replied that she had a vow to marry her conqueror in battle. Shumbha and Nishumbha thereupon marched with a mighty force to fight with her. After a fierce battle the goddess killed them. She is worshipped as Mahasaraswati, who is Saraswati of the Vedas.

These are the main three goddesses worshipped as manifestations of Maha Shakti, viz., Mahakali, Mahalakshmi and Mahasaraswati. Afterwards, she came to be worshipped under various names. For example, she who killed the demon Durg is worshipped as Durga and the killer of the demons Chand and Mund is worshipped as Chamunda. As the daughter of the Himalayas and the consort of Lord Shiva she is worshipped as Parvati or Gauri.

As for the establishment of the various Shakti *pithas* it is said that when Uma or Sati, the consort of Lord Shiva, sacrificed herself in the sacrificial fire at the house of her father, Daksha Prajapati, because of the latter's insulting attitude towards, Lord Shiva was beside himself with grief, and started to roam all over the world, carrying the body of Sati. It was necessary to pacify him, otherwise his grief and anger would afflict the world. But he could no the calmed down unless the body was removed from him. Vishnu, therefore, threw his Sudarshan Chakra which cut the body into pieces, and at the fifty-two places where the pieces fell, Shakti *pithas* or seats of the deity were established. Shiva, gaining back his senses, repaired to the Himalayas to practise penance.

It is but interesting to note that some of the important temples of goddesses who protect their devotees are found at the top of mountains or on the border of the State.

Goddess-worship is prevalent in almost all parts of India since times immemorial.Indeed the Durga puja festival of Bengal, celebrated during the Navratri days is very famous. Similarly in the South, goddesses Kamakshi or Kamakhya and Minakshi are worshipped ceremoniously during these days. Goddess worship is also found in Nepal. Even in Sind in Pakistan there is a well-known temple of Hingalaj Mata having a large number of followers especially among the castes of Bhat and Bharvad, who used to frequent the temple on pilgrimage every year till the partition of the country.

Navratri is the most suitable occasion for doing intense *sadhana* as these nine nights are very sacred to Devi. During Navratri one should plunge in her worship, doing *anushthan* and praying her to establish righteousness or *dharma* in the world, to destroy all dark and hostile forces that disturb the peace of the world, to bring supreme peace and prosperity to all her children; to transmute the *asuras* or the demons or people with diabolical tendencies into *satvik* and to annihilate the *asuri* tendencies in human beings such as lust, anger, pride, hypocrisy, egoism, etc., which demons like Madhu, Kaitabh, Mahishasur, Shumba and Nishumbha represent.

Thus the nine nights, popularly called *nortan,* are specially dedicated to the worship of Shakti, or *prakriti.* Out of the four Navratris in a year, viz., in Magh, Chaitra, Ashadh and Ashvin, that of Ashvin called *sharadiya* Navratri is the most popular and universal in its celebration. For it it at this period of the year that *prakriti* or Mother Nature is at her best after the rains are over and crops are ready for harvesting. The *puja* then performed is called *mahapuja.* Each Navratri thus falls either in the beginning or the end of a season, when *prakriti* or nature blossoms in full bloom. Two Navratris fall in the beginning and end of spring and the other two in the beginning and end of the monsoon. The bounty of nature at these periods encourages people to worship the nature. Navratri is in essence a festival of seasons dedicated to Nature-worship

Gujrati's celebrates Navratri in three ways, viz., (1) at Mataji's temples, (2) in individual households, and (3) at public places in every street and locality by groups of people, men, women and children, through *garbas* and *ras* at night—a unique feature of celebration in the State. The ritualistic aspect predominates in the first two, while the social and cultural aspect in the last.

The rituals commence from the first or the second day, if it is in Ashvin, according to the custom in the family. The installation of the goddess takes place at a specially selected spot in the house which is cleaned and purified beforehand. A small platform, a couple of inches high, is prepared with earth brought from the fields and grains like wheat, barley, etc. are sown in it. They sprout up in a day or two and are known as *jawaras.* On the platform a *kumbh* or an earthen pot is placed, filled with pure water. A betel-nut and a silver coin are kept inside and a coconut on the top.The goddess is invoked in this *kumbh.* This is known as *sthapan*, generally performed with the help of a priest. *Akhand jyoti* or lamp is kept incessantly burning before the goddess. The pot where Mataji is installed is gaily decorated with silken curtains, flowers, *ashok* leaves, etc. Worship is daily offered and on the eighth, known as Havanashtami, a *havan* or *yajna* is performed in temples. On all these days *naivedya* is offered to the goddess as per local custom.

The same person has to perform worship on all the days. He has to observe restrictions regarding diet, etc., observing a complete fast on the eighth. On the ninth day, the final worship is performed and Brahmins are feasted after offering a full dish to Mataji. In the evenings *bhajans* and *garbas* are sung in the praise of the goddess beside a lamp placed in a perforated earthen pot, also called *garbo.* After the conclusion of the final worship on the last day, the *jawaras* are removed in the morning of the tenth day and immersed in a pond or well.

Besides these essential concomitants of Navratri *puja*, there are numerous other customs pertaining to them. These differ from place to place, temple to temple and family to family. The most common thing about them is the rigidity with which these customs and rituals are followed without the slightest change through generations. The ceremonies and practices, both religious and customary, are followed with meticulous care as it believed that the goddess would be displeased if the slightest neglect is shown in her worship.

The symbolism behind the ingredients of worship during Navratri is interesting. As the goddess is identified with Mother Nature herself, she is worshipped as the goddess of fertility and creation which is symbolised by *jawaras.* It is in essence the worship of Mother Earth for all the bounties she bestows on mankind. The *garbo* has been likened to the human body, the perforations representing the senses and the light within the soul which enlightens and enlivens the body. The *kumbh*, which is generally an earthen pot, symbolises both by its material and by its round shape, the universe. It also contains water which is essential for fertilising earth and raising crops for human sustenance. Light symbolises knowledge, victory of good over evil. It is by the *shakti* or energy of Mataji that light prevails over force of darkness all the world over. Importance is, therefore, attached to burning an incessant light before the goddes during Navratri.

Temple Celebrations

Of the four Navratris in a year, the one of Ashvin is considered the principle Navratri which the goddess herself is said to have favoured according to *Saptashati*. Therefore, by the term Navratri the people understand the Navratri of Ashvin unless specified otherwise. Ashvin Navratri is, therefore, celebrated at most of the temples. There are some temples, however, where the Chaitra Navratri is more important than others while a few celebrate all the four. The religious ceremonies performed are common to all. The *jawaras* are sown near the image of the goddess, *kumbh* established for daily worship, and an oil or *ghee* lamp kept incessantly burning before the goddess. *Saptashati* or *Chandipath* is also recited. At some places continuous chanting of the name or *mantra* of the goddess is arranged. The concluding ceremony of *havan* is generally a big affair, sometimes a *yajna* like Navchandi or Shatachandi, performed on the eighth or the ninth day with ceremonial rites. An altar is constructed in the centre of the open courtyard in front of the deity, and Brahmin priests, generally nine in number, conduct the ceremony. Reciting *Saptashati* they offer with each verse *ghee,* barley, sesamum and *khir,* a sweet preparation of rice and milk. The sacrificial wood comes from the following trees:

Kher, Acacia catechu

Palash, Butea frondosa

Pipal, Ficus religiosa

Vad, Ficus indica

Bili, Aegle marmelos

Umbaro, Ficus glomerata

Shami, prosopis spicigera

When the *havan* is over, a pumpkin is cut before the deity, at a stroke of the sword, symbolising a sacrifice in her honour, and a piece thereof is placed at a public square. It was formerly the practice to sacrifice animals on this day, which is said to have continued at some important Mataji temples till half a century ago. It came to be given up with the passage of time, and the practice of offeringa pumpkin instead as a symbol of animal sacrifice is now adopted. It is said that in some of the temples animal sacrifice is still in vogue during Navratri. The *havan* is concluded with the final offering of *ghee* and coconut with a loud recital of *Shakradaya Stuti,* the prayer sung by Indra and other gods after the goddess slew Mahishasur on the ninth day of Navratri. At this time the whole atmosphere is resonant with the rousing notes of the prayer describing the Mother's valour and benignity.

The temples of the goddess which are specially decorated and illuminated on the occasion are found heavily crowded with people longing for *darshan* of the deity bedecked in a new *sari,* ornaments, shining weapons, and flower garlands. Her carrier is daily changed such as bull, lion, eagle, chariot, etc. In some temples the deity is dressed to assume the forms of different goddesses daily, viz. Kali, Amba, Durga, Bala,Saraswati, Mahishasur-mardini, Indrani, Varahi, Narsinhi and others.Devotees who keep Navratri, arrange for a recital of *Saptashati* or *Chandipath* at home, while others engage Brahmins to recite it on their behalf at temples, pay them *dakshina* and feast them or give *sidhun* or uncooked food materials in lieu thereof. In the evening a *garbo*, a lamp or a *mandvi* is placed in the open square before the temple, and *garbas* and *garbis* are sung around it.

Household Celebrations

Devout worshippers of Mataji specially install the goddess at home and worship her for 7, 8 or 9 days according to the custom of the family. The ceremonies commence from 1st or 2nd of Ashvin, the first day being avoided by some as it is the day of *matamah* (maternal grandfather) *shraddha*, which can be performed only when the daughter, her husband and son are all alive at a time. The elaborate ceremonies of installation of *kumbh,* worship and *visarjan* are generally performed only among higher castes, especially the Brahmin castes, but there are some among the lower castes also who perform them. In most of the families, the celebration is compulsory according to family tradition handed down from generation to generation, while in others Navratri is celebrated in fulfilment of a vow or simply out of faith.

According to common practice, the place for worship is generally in an inner corner of the house, mostly near the family deity, where a part of the wall is white-washed, and trident, the weapon of the goddess, and Shri Chakra with the Navarna *mantra* therein is painted in vermilion as the symbol of the goddess. At some places a picture of the goddess is attached on the drawing on the wall,which looks like the *angi* of the goddess. In front of this symbol, the *kumbh* is installed in an auspicious *muhurt* on the first day. The family priest conducts the ceremony of invocation of the goddess. The head or any other member of the family who worships the goddess for all the nine days, is said to "keep Navratri". After worshipping Ganesh in the beginning, Varuna, the God of Waters, is invoked and worshipped putting some *panchamrit*, sandal paste, etc., in the *kumbh*. The surrounding ground is sanctified by sprinkling some holy water from the *kumbh*. The *kumbh* is then established on the platform of *jawaras*. The goddess is then invoked and propitiated with *shodashopachar puja* or sixteen rites such as bath with *panchamrit, abhishek* with chanting of *Shri Sukta*, and worshipped with sandal and saffron paste, *kumkum*, turmeric, red lead, *abil-gulal*, incense, flowers and garlands. *Naivedya, dakshina* and finally *niranjana* or *arti* are offered at the end. Near the *kumbh*, the lamp *nanda deep* burns unceasingly during Navratri. On the other side, a lamp is lighted in the *garbo*, in the morning and evening. the *kumbh* is worshipped daily by offering *kumkum*, flowers and *naiveya*. The services of the priest are also availed of for recital of *Saptashati* or *Chandipath* near the goddess, for the *havan* or sacrifice and for *utthapan* on the last day. The Navarna *mantra* is chanted a specific number of times before the goddess daily. The person who keeps Navratri observes fast during the festival. The severity with which the fasts are kept depends on family custom. Sometimes only *falahar* is allowed, or the worshipper is allowed to eat once a day. A total fast is generally observed on the first and eighth days, and on other days the worshipper takes what is offered to the goddess in *naivedya*. In the final worship on the ninth day *maha naivedya* is offered to the goddess. The items included in this *naivedya* also depend on family custom. For example, in some families they include all the nine varieties like *khir* or *dudhpak, puri, kansar, khichadi, talvat, galmana, pudla, vada* or *dalbhajis*, gram *bakla* and *divdanshivdan*. In others, any one or more of these nine items are offered according to the family tradition. Along with the *naivedya* pieces of pumpkin are kept as a symbol of animal sacrifice formerly in vogue. The *naivedya* is artistically arranged in the midst of lights in *divdan*. Dry and fresh fruits, sugar-cane, coconut, pan-supari and *dakshina* are also offered in *maha-naivedya*. After feeding a Brahmin, the worshipper breaks fast by taking *prasad* of the *naivedya*.

In some families ten *kumarikas* or unmarried girls of the ages 2 to 11 years, are worshipped along with the goddess as the symbol of *dash matrikas* or *dash mahavidyas*, called Kumari, Trimurti, Kalyani, Rohini, Kali, Chandika, Shambhavi, Durga, Bhadra and Lalita. At some places nine maidens representing the first nine goddesses who are called *nav durga* are also worshipped. These are the forms of the energy of gods who assisted the goddess in the battles with demons like Mahishasur, Shumbha and Nishumbha. They are enjoined to be worshipped with Vedic hymns and offered clothes, garlands, applying saffron and sandal paste and vermilion on their forehead. They are then feasted and given *dakshina* in cash or kind either collectively on the last day or individually on each of the ten days.

The ceremony of installing the *kumbh* or growing *jawaras* is not common to all households. It is observed in those families where it is enjoined by the family custom. For many others who keep Navratri, the most common practice is to have only a lamp incessantly burning for all the nine days, and to fast on the first and the last or all the days.

While the essentials of worship are the same everywhere, there are many variations in the practices associated with the Navratri celebrations. These are governed more by family traditions and customs rather than any regional pattern.

New Year's Day

The first day of the year is observed as New Year day. In various parts of India New Year is celebrated according to the beliefs of there communities. Accordingly, in West Bengal, however, the first month of the year is called Vaisakh, though the first day, i.e., the New Year's day coincides with the day of Chaitra, when the Sun enters the zodiacal sign of Aries (Mesha). It is called *Pahela Baisakh* (meaning the first day of Vaisakha), while in Madras State it is known as *Varusha* pirappu (Varusha-year, Pirappu-birth) or *Chithrai masa pirappu*. Whatever be the name by which the festival of New Year's day is known the theme characterizing it is uniform in that it is celebrated to welcome the year. From the data available, it may be said that the first day of the year is regarded as very auspicious and a day of rejoicing and merry-making. In Kerala State, the investigator has mentioned that ritual sowing for the year is initiated on the day of Meda Vishu, *i.e.*, when the Sun enters the sign of Aries (Mesha). In Coorg, ritual ploughing is initiated on this day.

The year for the Malayalam-speaking areas begins with Onam in the month of Sravana (August-September). The word Onam is a local variation of the Sanskrit term Sravana. The day on which the full moon and the constellation Sravana conjugate is held sacred for Vishnu. In Kerala, the day, as mentioned by the investigator, is in commemoration of the benevolent reign of the Asura king Bali. It is interesting to note that the day is observed as an occasion for strengthening social relations, such as cementing of feudal and family obligations. On this day, the serf brings gifts to his master and has the seeds of grain blessed by him: the head of the tarawad gives presents to its members. Hence the festival seems to have religious as well as social values.

Amongst Kashmiri Pandit community New Year is called Navroz and is celebrated on the first day of the Hindi Calendar Year Vikram Samvat around March/April. It is the first day of the Navratras. Andhra Pradesh and Mysore reckon their months according to Amanta system, *i.e.*, from new moon to new moon. The first day of the year is known as Yugadi, *i.e.*, beginning of Yuga, or Samvatsaradi—beginning of Samvatsara. It is also called *Chaitra Pratipada*. It is a day of festivity on which peace and plenty and a sense of leisure and relaxation prevail. It is an age-old custom that the members of the household should after the ritual bathing taste a solution of fresh tamarind pulp, new jaggery (molasses), fresh or tender leaves and flowers of neem with pieces of green mango added to it. In the rural areas of the two States, the solution is prepared in the form of a thin beverage called *bevu*,—bevu being the local name of the neem tree, and every householder offers it to his neighbours, relatives and friends as a gesture of good will. The ingredients of the beverage are the products of Spring, the season of Nature's visible rejuvenation and promise. They are also indigenous. The belief seems to be that tamarind, mango, and neem flowers which appear at the onset of Spring signify newness, of life and energy and that the ceremonial consumption of, the articles will revive and energise human beings also. Even in cities where the phenomena of the change of the season are not directly experienced, individual households have retained the custom of taking bevu. One of the items of the festival is the *Panchanga Sravana*, i.e., hearing of the year's events-the characteristics and outstanding peculiarities recited by the head of the family or the priest (Purohit).

In Gujarat, the New Year is celebrated in the month of Kartika on the day following Dipavali. The New Year day of the Vikram Era according to the system followed in Gujarat falls on Kartik Sud'. It is celebrated throughout the State by all sections of the public irrespective of caste or creed. Indeed, it is inseparable from and part of the Diwali celebrations which extend in the New Year. This day is also known as Bali Pratipada, and religious people worship the idols of Bali and his wife Vindyavati with that of Kuber, the God Wealth, and Lakshmi at their home. It is interesting to note that *Bestu Baras* in Gujaratin the month of Kartika and Onam in Kerala in Sravana are both associated with King Bali.

Nirjala Ekadashi

Nirjala Ekadashi is an important Hindu festival and is observed on the 11th day of the bright half in the month of Jeth. It is also called Bhimsaini

Ekadashi because of the following legend.

The legend goes that the Pandava brothers except Bhimsain observed the Ekadashi fast regularly. Fasting was, however distasteful to Bhimsain who was known for gluttony. But, then, life without fasts was 'life wasted' debarring entry to heaven. Caught in this dilemma he sought the advice of the sage Vyasa. The latter enlightened him on the comparative merit of all Ekadashis, holding Nirjala Ekadashi as propitious as all other Ekadashis put together, the sage advised him to observe fast at least on the Nirjala Ekadashi. Bhimsain followed the advice.

Krishan is said to have narrated the following story about the origin of Ekadashi to the Pandavas whom he had advised to keep Ekadashi fast in sin of killing their kith and kin during the battle of Mahabharata.

There once lived a mighty daitya (demon) named Mridumarrya. He was a staunch devotee of Shiva. His exemplary devotion secured for him the boon of immortality from Shiva. The boon turned the head of the demon and he became a terror both for gods and men. This upset Shiva and, fearing that the demon might vanquish even the Trinity of Brahma, Vishnu and Shiva himself, Shiva modified his boon saying that the demon would meet his doom at the hands of a female born without parents. This modification sent the *daitya* into a fit of rage and exasperation and he set out to take revenge on the gods. To begin with he challenged Indra who ran away for life and sought the protection of Brahma in his heaven, the Satya Loka. But soon the *daitya* reached there, and Brahma along with his wife Savitri took to heals and reached Vaikuntha, the abode of Vishnu. Before Vishnu could ascertain the facts, the *daitya* was already there. He challenged Vishnu to a combat. A desperate fight ensued between the two, and soon Vishnu found himself entrapped in the death-lock of Mridumanya. It was with great difficulty that Vishnu could free himself and he fled to the Kailash, the residence of Shiva, along with his wife, Lakshmi, and Brahma and Savitri. All the fleeing gods appraised Shiva of evil consequences of his boon and sought his protection. But Shiva too was helpless. The daitya reached there and asked the Trinity to surrender. The Trinity with their wives betook themselves to the summit of Trikut Mountain and took refuge in the hollow of a *dhatri* tree *(phyllanthus emblica)*.

It was then rainy season. The gods resolved to stay on in the hollow of the tree to save their lives and the lives of their wives. They got drenched and passed the day without food. They breathed a deep breath of relief when instantly a virgin appeared before them. With folded hands they implored her to save them from the *daitya*. The *daitya* was already standing at the mouth of the hollow of the tree and on being accosted the maiden, replied that she was his deliverer. Saying so, she pounced upon the *daitya* and with her sword cut off his head and went up to the firmament. Brahma, Vishnu and Shiva along with their wives paid obeisance to her. She said that her name was Ekadashi, that she had no father nor mother but was born out of their own breath, and exhorted them to observe the fast every fortnight, as they had incidentally done on that day.

The merits ascribed to the Ekadashi fast are of the highest order. It is held as tantamount to performing penance for 60,000 years; it is also equivalent to making a gift of a thousand kines to the Brahmins or feeding millions of starving beggars, and so on. It is also equal in efficacy to undertaking a number of holy pilgrimages, or wearing out the body by rigid austerities.

The month of Jeth is the hottest. One feels thirsty after every moment. To observe a fast without water is a real ordeal in those days and that is what a real fast on Nirjala Ekadashi entails. Hence the name Nirjala (without water).

Early in the morning the persons who undertake this fast take bath and visit the nearby temples for prayers. A large number of women sit there and listen to the story of the Ekadashi being retold. The devotees sing devotional songs and make offerings of hand-fans made of palm twigs, earthen pitchers and musk melons. The fast is broken at night when the moon appears, after saying prayers.

The fast is observed extensively both by men

and women, but the latter observe it in larger number and with more devotion. Chhabils are set-up in bazars and crossings where drink of sweetened water or sweetened *kachi lassi* (milk and water) is offered to the passers-by. In some commercial and business centres, commercial concerns remain closed and no business is transacted on this day.

Onam

Onam, this major four day festival is celebrated in full fenor by the Malayalies through out India.

The tradition of Kerala had handed down the sweet memories of a period of peace and plenty in the dim distant past when Mahabali, a celebrated emperor of the Asuras, was ruling over this land. His period is believed to have been the golden age in the history of this country. There is a popular folk-song which narrates the glories that were then Kerala.

Maveli natu vanitum kalam
Manusharellarumonnupolay
Aamodathoday vasikkum kalam
Aapathangarkumottilla thanum
Kallavumilla Chathivumilla
Ellolamilla Polivachanam
Kallapparayum Cherunazhiyum
Kallatharangal Mattonnumilla

When Maveli was ruling all men were equal. Then they were leading a life of happiness, nobody had any calamity. There was neither dishonesty nor deception, nor was there any instance of false utterance, counterfeit measures there were none, nor other kinds of dishonest practices. The ideals of Welfare State were then realised if we believe the folk-song. There was not a man, woman or child who suffered from want, fear or disease. Absolute economic welfare and social justice were ensured. No wonder, therefore, that the memories of such a period are enshrined in the folklore and tradition of this country.

But this golden age came to a tragic close, according to the legend, when Mahabali was expelled from his Kingdom by Vamana, the dwarf incarnation of Vishnu. The Devas, the eternal enemies of the Asuras, grew jealous of the prosperity of Mahabali's Kingdom, and they appealed to Vishnu to expel Mahabali. Vishnu acceded to their request and assumed incarnation as Vamana. He went to Mahabali in the guise of a Brahman *brahmachari* and begged of him for a small plot of land, not more than three feet, to put up a hermitage. The generous emperor, not knowing the design behind this, readily agreed to grant the request. Vamana, thereupon, assumed a most gigantic form and measured the whole earth with one foot. He covered the lower and the celestial regions with his first and second steps. To complete the three feet of promised ground, Mahabali had to place his head also underneath Vamana's foot. Vamana then pushed him down to *Patala*, the lower world. Thus by the designs of the gods, the glorious reign of the Asura emperor came to an end. But his grateful subects demanded with all popular might that their former ruler should be permitted to return to his country once a year. This request was granted. The time for his visit was fixed in the first Malayalam month *Sravana* (August-September), and this occasion became one of jubiliation throughout the length and breadth of the land, reminiscent of the prosperous times of Mahabali. This is an age-old tradition in Kerala known to every child, and is partly in consonance with the Puranic story relating to Vamana and Mahabali. According to the *Puranas,* Mahabali was expelled from his imperial position by Vamana as stated above, but they are silent as regards Mahabali's relations with Kerala and his annual visits to this country from *Patala.*

Whatever be the truth of this tradition, this keeps alive the memories of a period of peace and plenty in the history of this land conveying to the people an ideal of a Welfare State. There are also historians who feel that the *Onam* is a harvest festival (vide *History of Kerala* by K. P. P. Menon — Vol. IV — Page 287). This opinion derives support from the circumstance that the *Onam* is celebrated in *Chingom* (August-September), the harvesting season, when nature is particularly gay in Kerala. Although the relation of this festival with the harvest cannot be rejected as irrelevant, that cannot explain away the traditional genesis connecting this celebration with Mahabali.

Whatever be the origin of *Onam*, it has for the last several centuries become a grand national festival in which all sections of the people of Kerala participate with extreme jubilation. The most striking fact about this festival is that it is celebrated in commemoration of a glorious past when there prevailed an ideal state of prosperity and peace. This aspect has a special significance to the people of modern times when all our dreams are for the realisation of such a State.

The festival falls in *Chingom,* the Malayalam month corresponding to August-September. The festival is supposed to begin from the lunar asterism, *'Attham,* which falls ten days before the asterism *Tiruvonam*. The most important celebrations are on four days *Utthradam, Tiruvonam, Avittam* and *Chathavam.* But for the whole period of the *Onam* season there will be mirth and jollity among all people, especially among the younger folk. The preparation for the celebration usually begins from the *Attham* day. Houses are cleaned and food-stuffs for feasts are collected. The rich and poor alike make every preparation. There is a popular saying "*Kanam vittum Onam Unnanam*" i.e., conducting *Onam* feast one may sell away anything. It is an occasion for all people to show their mutual regard and liberality. In former times, under the feudalistic system, agricultural labourers of well-to-do families invariably used to offer presents to their landlords on the eve of the Onam day, and in return they received new cloths, paddy and vegetables for celebrating the *Onam*. Village artisans like blacksmiths, washermen and barbers also used to receive similar perquisites.

The Tiruvonam is the most important day. To quote Sri K.P. Padmanabha Menon "A quasi-religious portion of this ceremony is performed early in the morning that day." In the front yard of the house flower carpets are spread on every day from *Attham* and conical figures made of clay are put up. One of these is the idol of Thrikkakkara Appan, the deity of Thrikkakkara, where the festival is believed to have had its origin. In olden days, tradition says, that this festival was conducted in the Trikkakkara temple for 28 days when all the Kings of Kerala went there to participate in the celebrations. It is in commemoration of the journeys undertaken to Trikkakkara in olden times to participate in the *Onam* celebration, that *Atthachamayam* is performed by the Maharaja of Cochin and the Zamorin of Calicut even to this day.

On the Tiruvonam day early in the morning every one bathes and offers worship in the temples. Then the gayest apparel is put on. Presents are distributed to the younger members by the *Karanavan* or the senior member. Clothes of yellow colour are included among the presents as a characteristic feature. Then follows feasting at which a brass lamp is lighted and before that viands are served in a plantain leaf as an offering to Ganapati. Food is served on plantain leaves. Rice is the main item and along with it several sorts of curries or vegetable preparations are also served. *Upperies, pappadams,* pickles, *payasams* and *prathamans* (various kinds of puddings) are also invariably included in the menu. Meat preparations are however not served. Whereas in Delhi the celebration are carried out in a much lower profile than in the South. Therefore members of the family staying in other places generally go home to be present for the *Onam* celebrations. Details of the full festivities are listed below.

Sports and Amusements

After the feasting there will be sports and games, indoor and outdoor, in which every one participates according to his or her inclination. Among outdoor games *panthukali* (using a kind of football generally made of leather and stuffed with coconut fibre) is very common. *Thalapanthu* and *Kayyankali* (a kind of boxing) are also important games.

There is an old poetical work "Haryakshamasa Samaratsavam", asigned to the 16th century A. D., describing *onathallu* or mock fight, during *Onam* festivals. There is also reference to *anathallu* in an ancient Tamil work entitled "Maturai-Kanci," composed by Mankudi Marutanar, of second century A.D. (see *Kerala Sahitya Charitram* by Mahakavi Ullur. I. 35). Among other amusements *thumbi-thullal, karadikali, thiruvathirakkali* and *oonjal-attam* are very common. A description of the traditional items of entertainments associated with *Onam* is given below:—

Panthukali: This is known under several names like *thalapanthu, thalama,* etc. The ball used in this game is made of coir or rope or leather stuffed with coir of the leaves of Clerodendron. The players divide themselves into two parties, one party standing by the side of a stick perpendicularly planted on the ground which may be called the snake. In the first service the person who serves the ball turns his back and propels the ball in the hind direction holding his right hand above the head. The opposite party can either catch the ball in the air or if it falls down, drive it with foot which is then returned in the same manner by the serving party. This process continues either till the ball comes to a standstill at some point of shoots off the snake. In the former case the opposite party has a right to strike the stake with the ball. The server is out either when the ball shoots off the stake while driving with foot or strikes the stake when thrown. Each service is done three times. The second service is called *otta.* In this the server drives the ball with one hand standing in the front of the stake facing the opposite party. The third service is called *eratta* in which the server floats the ball in the air with his left hand and drives with his right hand. The next one is called *thodama* in which the server has to float the ball with his right hand, clap on his thigh with the same hand before the ball comes down and drives the ball with the same hand towards the opposite party. The fifth service called *kalamkeezhu* is much more complicated. In this the ball has to be thrown into the air from between his legs and driven as it comes down towards the opposite party. The last one is *odi.* This is most enjoyable to the server as he has only to drive the ball with his foot. The process of receiving the ball by the opposite party as described in the first service is repeated in all services. If all the services are successful the serving party wins the game. Similarly, if all the services are lost the party sustains a defeat. There are, indeed, local variations in the rules and terms set forth above. But the game is substantially the same in all parts of Kerala.

Vettukali: In this game two parties stand opposite to each other at a good distance. They choose as their playground usually an open field. A ball of the same material as mentioned in the previous case but of smaller size is propelled by hand by floating it with the left hand and during it with the right hand towards the opposite party. The ball is either hit back and driven again from the place where it falls or taken from the ground when it falls and driven in the opposite direction. The more a party succeeds in striking the ball with greater force which automatically means the driving of the opposite party more and more to the rear that party ultimately wins the game when the limit agreed upon between the parties is transgressed.

Karakali: This is nothing but native hockey, the ball being the root of a plant cut to shape and the sticks being cut out of the branches of *kara*, a thorny bush.

Kayyankali (Native boxing): The villagers interested in this game divide themselves into two parties, each one standing for a few combatants trained in *Kayyankali.* One party sends forth their first combatant who challenges anyone of the opposite party for a combat whereupon of the opposite party accepts the challenge. When they reach the centre of the ground they then begin the exchange blows in measured steps both with open and closed fists. While doing so each combatant tries to ward off the blow of his opponent and at the same time to deal his own blow on him. The process is repeated until one of them comes out victorious. The whole combat is subject to special rules. This game requires long training for the combatants. One of the manuscripts containing the secrets of success in this games "*Kayyankalichadangu*". There may be other manuscripts as well on the subject. Each party may have more than one combatant in which case after the victory or defeat of each set of combatants, a fresh set come forth and fight in the same manner. Each step of the combatants is attended by shouts of encouragement from the respective parties.

Attakalam: This has been described by Shri T. K. Gopala Panicker as follows:

"This is essentially a boyish pastime, though adults also at times take part in it. A large circle is drawn on the plain sand floor and people are selected for each of the two sections from amongst the assemblage. One section is then placed in a collective body inside the circle, while the other stands around the outside. The latter then try with, of course, as little personal injury to themselves as possible, to strike at, and bring outside, the former who are inside, each by each. In the interval between one outsider getting inside and touching the body of any one among the inside group, the latter are allowed to beat and worry the antagonist. But the moment he touches the person of the inside man, he obtains complete immunity from violence at the hands of the rest of the inside batch. But the person who is caught is at liberty to strike him and struggle to prevent his being driven out. If he gets turned out, then he is no more to remain inside; and when the whole of the inside section are thus driven out, the first batch has finished its turn and is then followed up by the other batch and if any body is left inside who cannot be driven out, his party is declared successful. Sometimes. persents are given to the winners as tokens of appreciation of their training and strength." A game more or less resembling this is found in Central Kerala called *thodum pidutham* meaning touching and holding. In this a party of youngsters stand inside a circle and the opposite party outside it. Those outside the circle try to touch the members inside the circle. On so touching, the person touched pursues the opponent and tries to catch hold of him and stop him. If he succeeds in this the opponent loses the game. Otherwise he sustains the defeat. Though no blows are exchanged in the struggle to stop the opponent the game is, nevertheless, risky as the struggle to escape the hold is often violent enough.

Villukottu: In this, a bow is made of strong and slightly elastic wood joined by a small cord made of bamboo material. It is played upon by means of a small stick when it produces a very delectable musical tune. Sometimes more than one bow are held by a number of persons who constitute a bow party. Generally, this is a game of children.

Thumbithullal: In this game, a girl sits in the centre of a circle closing her eyes with both the hands and a number of girls sit round the circle singing songs and clapping their hands to the rhythm of the song. After sometime when the song has reached its high pitch the girl in the centre begins to shiver and falls to the ground, often unconscious. Water is then sprinkled upon her, when she regains her normal condition.

Karadikali: In *Karadikali,* a person wears a mask resembling the face of a bear. His body is painted black and covered with dried plantain leaves, the idea being to get the appearance of a bear. He is accompanied by a small party of men who play drums or musical instruments. This party visits houses during *Onam* days on moonlit night and after dancing in a crude form for sometime, pass on to the next house receiving presents, if any, given by the households. This is a popular item in Central Travancore.

Thalipeelikali: This is current in North Kerala. Two sets of girls stand opposite to each other, one set holding a girl who is sought by the opposite party. The members of the opposite party in musical tunes enquire whether there is a girl with the other party and whether she would be parted within their favour, whereuopn the party holding the girl refuses to surrender her and sings to that effect. After a series of musical exchanges of demands and refusals, the opposite party looses patience and attempts to take the girl child by force which, indeed, is resisted by the party holding her.

Tiruvatirakali and Oonjalattam

A National Festival: From days of antiquity, *Onam* was regarded as a national festival in which not only all the sections of the people participated but which was also sponsored by the rulers of the land. The *Athachamayam* celebrations at Cochin and Kozhikode and the participation of the Rajas of Venad, Otanad. Matathinkizh and Desinganad, in the *Onathallu* described in the *Haryakshamasa Somarothsavam* point to the active association of the rulers of the land wih the celebrations. But, in course of time this participation of the State seems to have waned making it almost a people's concern. The festival however has never lost its importance or its grandeur so far as the celebrations are concerned. Recently, the awakening national consciousness has been responsible for resuscitating Onam and making it as much a national celebration as a people's festival.

Pongal Sankranti

In South India, Makara Sankranti is called Pongal Sankranti and is celebrated mainly in Tamil Nadu, Andhra Pradesh and Karnataka in the month of Magha (Jan-Feb), when the sun passes through the winter solstic, from the Tropic of cancere to the Tropic of Capricorn, Makara. This is a three-day harvest festival observed of the thirteenth, fourteenth and fifteenth of January. Bhogi Pongal, the first day, is a family festival meant for enjoyment. In vilages it is celebrated like the Lohri festival of the Punjab by lighting a bonfire, though this custom is not now often observed. It is called Bhogi Mantalu, when useless household articles are thrown into the fire made of logs of wood and cow-dung cakes. Girls dance round the bonfire, singing songs in praise of gods, the spring and the harvest. In Andhra Pradesh, In the morning, the girls burn their old clothes, and wear new ones after having taken an oil bath.

The second day of the festival is called Surya Pongal, and Surya the Sun is worshipped. Rie boiled with milk and jaggery is offered to Surya. People are greeted with : "Paal Pongitra" (Has the milk boiled over?)" and they reply: "Yes, it has." It is a day of great rejoicing. Old earthenware pots are broken and replaced by new pots. This function is called Pongal Panai when the pots are painted and decorated with *haldi* (turmeric), flowers and mango leaves. The festival is connected with the harvesting of the paddy crop and only the new paddy is used in the preparation of pongal. It is made with *til* (sesame seeds), *gur* (brown sugar), *channa* (chick peas), groundnuts and dry coconuts, and is distributed to friends and neighbours.

The third day is Muttu Pongal when people worship muttu (cattle. Cattle are given a ceremonial bath, their horns cleaned, polished, painted and decorated with flowers and they are given pongal to eat.Arati (worship) is performed before the cattle, so as to ward of the evil eye. There is a legend behind the worship of cattle. Shiva asked his bull, Basava, to tell the people to have an oil bath every day and to eat once a month. In advertently, Basava announced that everyone should eat daily and have an oil bath once a month. This mistake enraged Shiva who then pronounced the curse that Basava should go to earth and plough the fields from the month of Ashadha to Makara Sankranti and help people produce more food. In the bull-flights arranged as entertainment for the day, boys try to snatch the wads of currency notes that are tied to the horns of cattle.

Muttu Pongal, also called Kanu Pongal is celebrated by sisters for the welfare of their brothers. A large-sized plantain leaf is taken that is not broken or cut anywhere. It is washed and left on the ground in the backyard, near the basil plant (*Ocimum sanctum*) altar with a branch of the amla (*Embelica officinalis*). On this leaf are placed at four corners, the left overs of sweet pongal and the salty pongal called Vand Pongal, rice coloured red, yellow as well as white, with five betel leaves, two betel nuts, two pieces of sugarcane, turmeric leaves (*Curcuma longa*), and two or three ber (*Zizyphus mauritiana*). In Tamil Nadu women do this before bathing in the morning and light a lamp before it. In Karnataka and Andhra Pradesh, the festival starts after everyone has bathed. Arati is performed with *haldi* (turmeric), water, *chuna* (limestone) and rice and this water is sprinkled on the rangoli (floor decorations made with coloured rice powder) in front of the house. Before the arati is performed, all the young and old women of the house assemble and the oldest woman, who is not a widow, distributes a handful of the coloured rice to everyone and all of them sing an auspicious song. The rice is then put in the centre of the plantain leaf with the saying that "the house and family of the brother should grow from now onwards." Sisters apply a Tilak to the foreheads of the brothers, and give them fruit, sweets, *til* and *gur* (jaggery). The brothers thank their sisters for their good wishes and give them gifts.

Prabodhini Ekadashi

Prabodhini Ekadashi is observed on 11th day of Kartik Sud (October-November) every year. According to Puranic belief, Lord Vishnu awakes on Kartik Sud 11 from a long slumber of four months from Ashadh Sud 11. It is, therefore, popularly known as Dev-uthi Agiarash. The conclusions of the period of gods' night and their waking up from slumber is an occasion for celebration. It is also known as Tulsi Vivah, as the marriage ceremony of *tulsi, Ocimum sanctum,* or the holy basil plant is celebrated on this day in pursuance of the Puranic story of Sati Vrinda.

In Satya Yuga, there was a powerful demon king Jalandhar alias Shankhchud born in the ocean from the flame of the third eye of God Sadashiva which fell in the sea. As he was born in the ocean he was named Jalandhar. He had built his capital on an island in the sea called Jalandharnagar. It is believed to be the small ialand of Diu on the south of Saurashtra. Jalandhar subjugated all the three worlds by his strength. Gods could not resist his strength and fled to Brahma in the quest of a way to win Jalandhar in battle. Brahma, after deep meditation, declared that he would not be conquered by any power due to the chastity of his wife Vrinda, the daughter of the demon king Kalanemi. If her chastity be compromised by any means, then only would he die. Vrinda was a sati—a pious and chaste woman—and none dared to accost her through fear of her curse. At last the devas sought the refuge of Vishnu under the leadership of Brahma.

For the sake of gods, Vishnu sent replicas of parts of the body of Jalandhar with two monkeys. Virnda seeing what she thought to be the dead body of Jalandhar became ready to burn herself with her husband. In the meanwhile, Vishnu arrived there in the garb of a saint and the monkeys fled away. He joined the parts of the dead body and made it alive, by himself assuming the form of Jalandhar. Vrinda was thus taken in. She was very glad to see her husband alive and embraced him.The spell of her chastity was thus broken, and Jalandhar, engaged in battle with Mahadev at this time, was enfeebled and killed by the trident of Mahadev. His dead body was brought by his followers to Vrinda. She thus saw Vishnu in the form of Jalandhar and also the dead body of her husband, and was confused. But, as she was a sati, she at once came to divine the deceit of Vishnu, and cursed him that he would turn black and be separated from his wife, who would be taken away by a demon, and that he would have to seek assistance of monkeys to rescue her from the demon. But being a firm devotee of God, she also requested him to marry her in the next birth. Vishnu granted her wish and promised that he would marry her in the next birth when she would be *tulsi* and he would take the form of *shaligram*. Vrinda's curse came true in the incarnation of Vishnu as Rama in Treta Yuga, when he had to take the help of monkeys to recover his wife Sita from the demon king Ravan. Vrinda became *tulsi* in the next birth and Vishnu married her on Kartik Sud 11. Vaishnavas, while worshipping Vishnu, always place a *tulsi* leaf on his head as also on the *prasad* offered after worship.

People observe fast on this day and perform the marriage ceremony of *tulsi* with *shaligram*, a black stone image symbolising Lord Vishnu procured from the river Gandaki in Nepal. This ceremony is generally performed in temples also in the houses of profound devotees. The plant is also decorated with *sari*, *mindhol* and ivory bangles. A formal marriage ceremony is conducted by a priest. Devotees assembled at this function are given *prasad* consisting of sugar-cane pieces, coconut chips, fresh and dry fruits, sugar-candy, ground-nut seeds, etc.

In some places a regular marriage ceremony of *tulsi* and Vishnu is performed as that of human beings. Two different Ramji mandirs (temples of Rama) of different places take a joint decision to perform the marriage ceremony of *tulsi*. At one of these two places *tulsi* is planted on Ashadh Sud 11 and kept fresh by sprinkling water. On Labh Pancham (Kartik Sud 5), an invitation card is issued. In the morning of Kartik Sud 11, the *barat nor bridal* procession of Lalji—*a* small image of Lord Vishnu—proceed to the place where the *tulsi* plant is reared. The image of Lalji, well-decorated with silk clothes and ornaments, is placed in a palanquin borne on the shoulders of devotees. The procession, led by *bhajan mandlis* singing and dancing in front, rest at the outskirts of the village of *tulsi*, where they are cordially received by the devotees of the bride's side. The *barat* is then pompously taken through the streets in procession to the temple of *tulsi*. There Lalji is placed under the booth decorated with festoons of *asopalav* leaves and lights. The *tulsi* plant is brought under the booth and placed opposite Vishnu. The wedding ceremony is then performed by the religious priest. *Kanyadan* ceremony is performed from *tulsi's* side. Then the bride and bride-groom are taken to the *chori*, where they take four rounds of the sacred fire. After the marriage ceremony is over people's from both the sides stand opposite to each other with *merayas* in hands. A *meraya* is a torch prepared by fixing a dry *kopra* or coconut bowl on a stalk of sugar-cane. The bowl is filled with cotton seeds, with a lighted wick in the middle. The *mahant* of Vishnu's side then pours some *ghee* in the *meraya* of the *mahant* of *tulsi's* side, whereafter the devotees attending the ceremony pour *ghee* in both the *merayas* giving some gift in cash. This ceremony follows a similar practice in the Hindu marriage celebrated in Saurashtra. All attendants of both the sides observe a fast on this day. They are served with milk, tea, and *falahar* at the *mandir* of *tulsi's* side. Bhajans are sung in the *chowk* of the temple for the whole night. Next day the *barat* is served with sweet dishes as *parana* (breaking the fast), and then Lalji's party returns with the bride *tulsi* to their place.

The festival of Dev Divali or Divali of the gods is also celebrated on this day in the temples as also at home by some people by decorating the houses with *rangoli* designs in courtyards and illumination by earthen lamps, just as in Divali.

This is a post-monsoon festival. The crops have been harvested by this time and the season is, therefore, apt for festivities. Moreover, Hindus generally refrain from performance of marriages during the four preceding months of *chaturmas*, and it is only after Tulsi Vivah or the marriage of Lord Vishnu, that marriages are arranged.

Puranmashi

According to the calendar, a lunar month is the interval between two new moons, about 29/½ days. The word Purnamashi literally means 'end of month' and it stands for the full-moon night.

Ordinarily every Puranmashi is a day of fasting on which orthodox Hindu's take meals only once in the afternoon. The *katha* (legend) that is recited on this day says that once upon a time, Narada Muni, son of Brahma, came down from heaven to earth. He was much distressed to see the miseries of the world, particularly those resulting from the cycle of births and re-births. He approached Vishnu and implored him to show some way out of these miseries. Vishnu told him that in this *Kali Yuga* (Iron Age)there was rare *vrata* (fast) of Sat Narayana; it was simple and yet efficacious enough to ensure prosperity in this life and salvation thereafter. The *vrata* was to be performed on a Puranmashi. Vishnu then detailed to Narad as to how Sat Narayana was to be worshipped on that occasion.

Though every Puranmashi is important, yet some have acquired special importance and are considered of high spiritual merit; they are *Vyas Purnima, Shravan Purnima, Kartika Purnima*, and *Asoj* or *Sharat Purnima.*

Vyas Purnima falls on Asadh Puranmashi and it is a day dedicated to Guru Puja. On Shravan Purnima, the well-known *Raksha Bandhan* festival is held.

Kartik Purnima is also known as Tripuri Purnima, because the demon Tripur was done to death on this day. Asoj Purnima or Sharat Purnima is said to be connected with Krishna's Ras Lila, though some authorities hold that Ras Lila is associated with Kartik Puranmashi. Legends connected with both these Puranmashis are given below.

There was once a war between the gods and the demons. The latter being defeated appealed for help to Mai, a great magician. She gave them three impregnable towers of gold, silver, and iron. The demons concealed themselves within those towers and continued their relentless fight against the gods from there. In helplessness the gods approached Shiva and, with a devastating shower of his arrows, Shiva destroyed the strongholds of the demons and killed them all. But the cunning magician was yet to be defeated. She threw the dead bodies of the demons into the well of nectar and, lo! the demons came to life and resumed their fight against the gods. To outwit the magician, Vishnu assumed the form of cow, and drank the nectar from the well. Shiva then attacked the demons with formidable preparations and brought about the end of the 'Triple-towered demon' (Tripurasurea). This victory, according to traditional belief, was won by Shiva on the day of the fullmoon of Kartik.

Vaishnavas commemorate the Kartik Puranmashi as the day of Krishna's Ras Lila, a festival celebrating the mystical amorous 'dance' of Krishan in the company of the 'pastrol maids' of Brindaban.

The description of the *Ras Lila*, from the physical plane, has been well summarized by Coleman in his *Mythology of the Hindu* (pp. 42—43), from which the following is an extract:—

"On the night of Kartik Purnima, when the moon was shining in her meridian lustre, and a cool and sweet air breathed around, Krishna began to play ravishing note on his flute. On hearing it, the *Gopikas* immediately left their several occupations unfinished, and ran out to listen. Krishna asked them if all was well at home and then proceeded to give them some good advice upon their duties to the family. One of the *Gopikas* replied, 'When frenzy seizes the heart, all duties; all earthly motives are overturned and forgotten. If you order us to go back, we are lame; if you call us unto you, we fly.' Krishna finding that their passion for him was sincere, took each of them in his arms and treated them with equal tenderness, so that all the happiness and transport which are to be found in the world were collected in one place—in the hearts of the *Gopikas*. Wherever they turned, each found Krishna close to her, and the happiness of their love for Krishna was enhanced by the feeling that Krishan loved them equally in return. All of a sudden—just as their love was tinged with this touch of vanity—Krishna played them a trick: he vanished from their company, leaving them staring around in astonishment and despair, and interrogating every tree, flower, and blade of grass, to obtain information of their run-away swain. After a tiresome search, they found that another damsel, named Radha, was engaging his attentions, and they became frantic with grief till Krishna, taking pity upon them, again made his appearance, when they worshipped him with flowers, and expressed their love to him in different actions and attitudes. All this excessive joy terminated in a gay dance, in which Krishna multiplied his form in proportion to the number of the *Gopikas*, and giving each of them a hand, caused each to believe that he was close to her side. The exertion of the dance caused the moisture of perspiration to appear on the cheeks of the *Gopikas*, whose jet-black tresses trembled over their shoulders as their hair lay in dishevelled curls behind their head."

Krishna was a mere boy of 12 at the time of *Ras Lila*. So the spiritual significance of *Ras Lila* the burning passion of a devotee (*bhakta*) to meet his Master (*bhagwan*)—scan be grasped even from this summarized vision of *Ras Lila*.

In Punjab some Puranmashis are celebrated as birthdays of Gurus and Saints. Asoj Puranmashi is associated with the birthday of Rishi Valmiki Birthday of Guru Nanak falls on Kartik Puranmashi. On Magh Puranmashi falls the birthday of Guru Ravi Das. Birthday of Guru Nanak is celebrated by the Sikhs as also by a large number of Hindus; the highlights of the celebrations are processions, a holy dip in some tank or river or canal, recitations from Granth Sahib and free community kitchen (*langar*). Birthday of Guru Ravi Das and Rishi Valmiki are celebrated by the harijans; processions and *kirtan* form important part of the celebration.

Raksha Bandhan

Raksha Bandhan is an important Hindu festival and is observed on the full moon day of the month of Sravana (July-August). It is known by various names: Rakhi, Rakhari and Solono. The word Solono is corruption of the Persian term Sai-i-Nai, 'the new year' and it is a name given to the full moon of Sravana, because it marks the point of transition between the old and the new *fasli* or agriculture year. The classic name, Raksha Bandhan is derived from the principal ceremony of the day-the tying of an ornamental cord round the wrist.

The silk or cotton cord is called 'Raksha' because it is intended to serve as an amulet guarding the wearer from all kind of evil. These are usually dyed in yellow, the most auspicious colour among the Hindus; but very often they are blazoned with a variety of gaudy colours and ornamented with tassels, to suit individual tastes.

According to a popular notion, Raksha Bandhan is distinctively a Brahmin festival, the privilege of observing it being confined to Brahmins alone. This notion is based on an ancient saying which enumerates four chief denominational festival, corresponding to the four chief divisions of Hindus. Thus Raksha Bandhan is the festival for Brahmins, Dussehra for Kshatriyas, Diwali for Vaishyas and Holi for Shudras.

Brahmins of the priestly order and of the mendicant class wander about the town all day, carrying a bundle of Rakshas visiting the houses of the well-to-do, tying a Raksha round their wrist wherever they can and receive a cash present in return.

The legend connected with the origin of the festival is as follows:-

Once Yudhishtira inquired from Krishan as to how impending evils could be warded off throughout the year. Krishan advised him to observe Raksha Bandhan in consonance with the scriptures. He also narrated to him a story of a long-drawn series of battles between Indra and Daityaraj, the demon-king. The latter suceeded in annexing the kingdom of the former and drove him away. Indra felt very much frustrated. He waited upon god Brihaspati and sought his advice. The latter counselled Indra to wait for the most opportune time when alone he should make another bid to vanquish the demon-king.

On the full moon day of Sawan, Indrani and Brishaspati tied a Rakhi round the right hand wrist of Indra. It was a signal for Indra to wage war against Daityaraj. After a sangunary battle, Indra vanquished his adversary and re-established his superiority over Triloki, all the three world-Swargloka, Manushialoka and Narakloka.

At the time of tying a Rakhi the following couplet is uttered:

येन बद्धो बली राजा दानवेन्द्रो महाबलः।
तेन त्वां प्रतिबन्धामि रक्षमाचल माचलः।।

"Thus I tie the Raksha round your wrist—the same which was twined round the arms of the mighty Bali, King of the Danavas. May the protection afforded by it be eternal"

In Delhi, as in many other parts of the country, ceremony has assumed almost a different shape. Instead of the Brahmin, now the sister decorates the right wrist of her brother. After tying a Rakhi she applies a tilak and puts some piece of sweetmeat in his mouth. In return the brother gives her some gifts. This is symbol of the sister asking for her brother's protection and the latter promising it.

Where sisters can't go and tie rakhi personally, they send it by post. Brahmins too visit their patrons and present rakhis in return for a cash present. The festival is observed all over the State both by Hindus and Sikhs.

Ramnavami

This is the birthday of Shri Ramachandra, the seventh incarnation of Lord Vishnu, born as saviour of religion on earth in the Treta Yuga. Lord Rama has a special place in the heart of every Hindu and as such his birthday is celebrated as a festival all over India.

Before the birth of Rama, the social, religious and political condition of India was beset with evils. People had a constant fear of demons ruining their lives. It was essential for Vishnu to take birth on the earth, to wipe off the vicious circle of evils. He was, therefore, born as Rama at the house of Dasharath, the king of Ayodhya. King Dasharath had three queens, viz., Kaushalya, Sumitra and Kaikeyi, but no progeny. He, therefore, performed a Putreshti sacrifice as advised by his preceptor,

Rishi Vasishtha, and got four sons—Rama by Kaushalya, Lakshman and Shatrughana by Sumitra and Bharat by Kaikeyi.

Ramachandra showed nobility of character, magnanimity and valour from his very teens. *Rishi* Vishwamitra took him with Lakshman to his hermitage for the protection of his sacrifices from demons whom the brothers destroyed, freeing the *rishis* from their terrors. Vishwamitra took them to the court of King Janak of Mithila where the *swayamvar* of his daughter Sita was arranged. King Janak had a bow of Lord Shiva presented to him by Parashurama. He had decided to marry his daughter to a person who could wield the bow, to ensure the selection of a valiant and strong husband for Sita. All Kshatriya kings and even the demon King Ravan of Lanka attended the function to win the hand of Sita. But none could raise the bow even from the ground, Ravan actually tumbling down in the attempt. *Rishi* Vishwamitra then asked Rama to try. He took up the bow, and broke it into two pieces while trying to string it. All the assemblage praised the valour of Rama and Sita garlanded him. News was sent to King, Dasharath at Ayodhya. Rama married Sita and returned to Ayodhya.

King Dasharath then decided to retire and enthrone Rama. But Rama's step-mother Kaikeyi instigated by her wicked maid Manthara asked Dasharath to fulfil his two promises given to her in the past. Dasharath consented and Kaikeyi asked that Rama be banished to the forest for fourteen years and her son Bharat be given the throne. King Dasharath hesitated and entreated her to ask any other favours as he loved Rama very much. Moreover Rama being the eldest, it was proper that he should be enthroned. But she did not change her mind. Rama came to know of this and immediately-approached his father and requested him to keep his word and satisfy his mother because.

रघुकुलरीति सदा चलि आई।
प्राण जाई अरू बचन न जाई।।

"It has always been the custom in the family of Raghu that a promise must be kept even at the cost of life." King Dasharath at last consented and Rama with his wife Sita and brother Lakshaman went into exile and lived at Panchavati in Dandakaranya forest. Here, after luring Rama and Lakshaman away from their hermitage by an illusory golden deer, Ravan abducted Sita and took her to Lanka. Rama and Lakshman with the help of King Sugriva and his monkey chiefs like Hanuman, Angad and others pursued him, and attacked Lanka, fought with him, killed him and his brother Kumbhakarna and son Meghnad in the battle and gave the throne of Lanka to his brother Vibhishana, a righteous devotee of Rama, and returned with Sita to Ayodhya, where he was cordially received by the people and enthroned.

Rama was virtuous, pious and always sought the truth. He had vowed to have only one wife. He loved his subjects sincerely. He always gave due consideration to the opinions of even the lowest of them. He was thus an ideal man and an ideal ruler, worshipped as God even after thousands of years. Rashtrapita Mahatma Gandhi was staunch devotee of Rama, and his name was always at the tip of his tongue till his last breath. The rule of Rama was so perfect in every respect that *Ramarajya* is now synonymous with the ideal rule or state, and his birthday, called Ramnavmi after him, is celebrated as a principal festival of devotion to Rama all over the country.

On this day people get up early in the morning, take bath, proceed to the temple to offer worship to Lord Rama and read *Ramayana.* At noon the birth ceremony is celebrated in the temples and people have *darshan.* A small image of Rama is bathed with *panchamrit* and holy waters and placed in a decorated cradle. A fast is observed on this day which is passed in religious observances. In the evening devotees attend religious discourses arranged in temples, and most of them keep awake for the whole night singing songs relating to the career of Rama. They avoid all evil thought and action and give alms to Brahmins and the poor and feed cows with green grass and grains. Next day, after again worshipping and offering *prasad* to Rama at the temple, the fast is broken.

The whole story of Rama has been applied philosophically to the soul and the human body.

The soul is Rama, intellect is Sita, the ten organs represent the ten-headed Ravan; Lakshman and other brothers are virtues and the false conception of a golden deer symbolizes the worldly desires lurking in human minds.

Generally, two incarnations of Lord Vishnu are worshipped most in India, viz., Rama and Krishna. Rama is taken as *Maryada Purushottama* while Krishna as *Purna Purushottama.*

Ravi Das Jayanti

Ravi Das is the author of many hymns some of which have been inscribed in the Granth Sahib. He was a disciple of Ramanand and a contemporary of Kabir. His birth day is observed on Magh Sudi 15 (November/December).

When he reached his years of discretion he began to wait on saints. He presented them with everything he could lay his hands on at home. His father got annoyed at this and gave him a separate place to live in. His father's wealth and means were considerable, but he gave nothing to his son. The latter who by this time had been married, supported himself and his wife by making shoes, and lived very happily. Whenever he saw a holy man he supplied him gratuitously with covering for his feet. He built a hut, set- up in it an idol made from a hide, and applied himself to its worship. When he was reproached for making an idol out of hide he defended himself by descanting upon the various advantages of hides, e.g., drums used in worship were made from hides; the cow held sacred by Hindus has a hide; God is contained in animals which have hides, etc., etc.

Ravi Das was ever immersed in his devotions which ultimately led to the abandonment of his trade and the deterioration in his circumstances. He was reduced to extreme poverty. One day a wealthy visitor visited him. Ravi Das gave him bread to eat and lavished every attention on him. The visitor in return presented him with a philosopher's stone, explained its qualities and asked him to keep it carefully. Ravi Das replied that he did not require it, as his property and wealth consisted in the name of God. On the visitor's insistence Ravi Das asked him to deposit the precious stone in the thatch of his house which the visitor did. On this occasion Ravi Das composed a hymn of which English rendering is:

God's name is the great wealth of God's saints;

Day by day it increaseth and in no way decreaseth.

Nothing can steal it either by day or night;

Its possessor sleepeth secure in his home.

O God, what need of a stone hath he who possesseth this wealth?

After a lapse of thirteen months, the visitor again turned up and found Ravi Das as poor as before. He asked him what had become of the philosopher's stone. Ravi Das replied, "It must be where they did put it; I have been afraid to touch it". Upon this the visitor took it from the thatch and departed, fully satisfied that Ravi Das desired no earthly wealth.

One day the saint found five gold coins in a basket employed to hold accessories of worship. The result was that he began to fear even worship of God, lest it might bring him wealth and turn him away from God. Then God said to him in a vision, 'Although thou absolutely desireth nothing, yet accept the wealth I give thee now.' Ravi Das promised to do so. A pious admirer gave him money with which he built a *sarai* or rest-house, wherein he entertained holy men. He then built a temple and so decorated it with a canopy, fringes, cords of gold lace, wall lamps and chandeliers that visitors were attracted to it from far and near. After this Ravi Das also built a two-storeyed house for himself wherein he worshipped an image of God with devotion as before.

The Brahmins complained to the king of Banaras that there was no authority in the *Shastras* for a shoemaker to make an image of God, yet Ravi Das had without any fear or compunction set-up such an image and was worshipping it. This was a sacrilege and he should be punished for it, they prayed. The king summoned Ravi Das, but was so much impressed with the dignity and reasonableness of his defence that he declared him innocent of any offence against religion.

Jhali, the Queen of Chittaur, hearing of Ravi Das's fame, visited him and became his disciple. At this, her Brahmin attendants were greatly agitated and they complained of her to the Rana, her husband, who had accompanied her to Banaras. He sent for Ravi Das, and heard the charges of the assembled Brahmins against him. They represented the supreme importance of caste, and the impropriety of allowing a shoemaker to usurp a higher spiritual or social position than that in which he had been born. Ravi Das replied, 'What is dear to God is devotion; He payeth no heed to caste." Upon this the Brahmins proposed to refer the matter to the arbitrament of prayer. They read the Vedas for three full hours and repeated many spells, but did not succeed in inducing God to persuade the Rana of Ravi Das's guilt. When it came to Ravi Das's turn, he said 'O Great King, be true to thy name of Pardoner of sinners.' He then sang a couple of stanzas. The first line of the first stanza is :—

O come without delay or call me unto Thee.

The first lines of the second stanza are:—

O God of gods. I Thy protection crave:

Have mercy on me, knowing me Thy slave.

The Rana was convinced of Ravi Das's correctness of stand and innocence and expressed himself accordingly. Upon this, it is said, all present became believers in Ravi Das's, sanctity.

After this Queen Jhali left Banaras, and returned to her kingdom, where she decided on holding a thanksgiving festival. With great modesty and humility she invited Ravi Das to attend it. He accepted her invitation and went to Chittaur. His visit afforded her intense pleasure. She distributed a large sum of money in alms on the occasion, and invited the principal Brahmins of her state to meet the holy man. The Brahmins knew that the queen's *guru* had been a shoemaker; so they preferred to have their meals cooked themselves rather than to partake of food proffered by the queen. They accordingly had food cooked for themselves, but, when they sat down to eat it, it is said, they saw Ravi Das seated between every two of them. They then believed in his divine mission and fell at his feet. It is stated that many became his disciples there and then.

After the name of Guru Ravi Das, a sect named Ravidasi came into being. Its membership is limited to *Chamars.* Present in different parts of India. The common mode of observance of Ravidas Jayanti is: procession, *kirtan*, recitation from Granth Sahib.

Satyanarayan Puja

Satyanarayan Puja or Vrata is a purely domestic festival consisting of the worship of Satyanarayan or the Supreme God as an embodiment of Truth. Though a form of Vishnu, the deity is worshipped by all sections of Hindus, to whatever sect they may belong. The *puja* is performed according to prescribed rites, when relatives and friends are invariably invited which makes it a festive occasion. It can be performed on any day; no particular date is prescribed or prohibited; though the *Purnima* or bright fifteenth is considered propitious. It may be celebrated in fulfilment of a vow taken in respect of some wish or desire, or on acquiring some material benefit or the occurrence of some happy event. Many a time it is performed on the conclusion of some social event like marriage or sacred thread ceremony. Some persons take a vow to celebrate it on every *Purnima* day, while others perform it on any date convenient for the purpose.

Though temples dedicated to this form of Vishnu are relatively few in number, the worship of Satyanarayan has been popular since Pauranic times. *Skanda Purana* states that in Kali Yuga no other act is so meritorious as the worship of Satyanarayan for fulfilment of one's desires and for attaining of peace and happiness in this world and salvation hereafter. People have, therefore, much faith in Shri Satyanarayan. Some call him Kala, and some Satya Ishwer, while others call him Satyanarayan or Satyadev.

The ritual of the *puja* is neither lengthy nor cumbersome. No elaborate preparations are required to be made, and most important of all, the expense involved depends entirely on the capacity of the devotee. There is no strict obligation that a particular amount must be offered. All that is required is that it must be performed with full faith. The *vrata* is, therefore, not only easy and convenient to perform, but the devotee sees in it the fulfilment of the ideal that God is not pleased by rich offerings but by intense devotion and faith.

On the day fixed for the *puja,* the Brahmin priest conducts the ceremony. It is permissible for the householder to perform the *puja* by himself, but this is rarely done. From the morning the joy and enthusiasm in members of the family is quite apparent as they busy themselves with the preparations. Neighbours, relatives and friends are invited to attend the function. Plantain and *tulsi* leaves, flowers and garlands are brought. Doors of the house are decorated with festoons of *asopalav* or *Polyalthia longifolia* leaves. A wooden *bajath* or low stool is placed in the centre of the verandah or main room of the house after washing the place and plastering it with cow-dung. Some decorate the ground with *rangoli* designs. Four plantain leaves are tied to the four legs of the stool with their tops tied together to make a canopy, which is decorated with garlands, flowers, etc. A square piece of white cloth is spread on the stool and a design drawn on it with rice or wheat. A copper or silver pot covered by a copper or silver saucer full of rice is kept in the centre of the design. The materials of *puja* consist, among other things, of two more square pieces of white and red cloth known as *sthapan,* some rice and wheat, betel-nuts and leaves, flowers, garlands, waters of holy rivers, *panchamrit* or mixture of milk, *ghee,* curd, honey and sugar, sandal and saffron paste, an image of Satyanarayan generally embossed on a gold leaf, two coconuts and some cash in silver and copper coins. *Naivedya* or *prasad* to be offered consists of *shira* or *halwa,* a sweet preparation of wheat flour, *ghee,* and sugar, dry and fresh fruits, coconut chips, sugar, etc.

The head of the family and his wife who generally perform the *puja* together, observe fast on the day. They take a purifying bath and put on clean clothes, preferably silken. On a wooden *bajath* covered by red cloth, an image of Ganapati is placed on a design drawn with wheat. On another stool rice is spread on white cloth and nine betel-nuts are placed as the symbols of the nine planets, which are to be propitiated.

Before the *puja* starts, Lord Varuna or the God of Water is invoked in a water pot in which a silver coin and a betel-nut are placed. He is then worshipped with *panchamrit,* rice, flowers, etc. The articles to be used in the *puja* and the surrounding ground are then purified by sprinkling water from the pot over them.

Ganapati is worshipped first with *panchamrit,* red lead, *kumkum, durva* grass and red flowers and *naivedya* of *gur* and a betel-nut, betel-leaf and some cash are offered. The nine planets are then worshipped in the same manner. Then follows the *puja* of the golden image of Satyanarayan. Oblations of water with flowers are offered to him as *arghya.*The image is then bathed with *panchamrit,* and then with holy waters with chantings of Vedic *mantras. Abhishek* then takes place by pouring of water through a conch chanting *Purusha Sukta* of *Yajur Veda.* Thereafter the image is again bathed with pure water and placed in the saucer on the pot on the stool. Sandal and saffron paste is applied with *kumkum, abil* and *gulal* and flowers and flower garlands are placed on it with a leaf of *tulsi.* A sacred thread and *dhotar* are then placed around it, and one thousand *tulsi* leaves are placed on it reciting *Vishnu-sahasranama,* i.e., one thousand names of Vishnu. Incense sticks are burnt before the image and *ghee* lamps are lighted and kept burning till the completion of the *puja.* The deity is then offered betel-nut and some cash placed on a betel-leaf. Generally from a rupee and a quarter to five rupees and a quarter are offered. Then *naivedya* of fruits, etc., is offered with a coconut.

Hearing of the *katha* or discourses on Satyanarayan given in five chapters in *Reva Khand* of *Skanda Purana* is an essential concomitant of the *vrata.* Each chapter contains a story depicting the glory of God Who is truth incarnate, the merit attached to His worship and the importance of truth. It is incumbent not only on the persons performing the *puja,* but also on the invitees to listen to this *katha* from the mouth of the priest.

The first two chapters narrate the stories of an indigent Brahmin of Kashi and a poor woodcutter who performed the *vrata* with all their heart and were thereupon favoured by the God with happiness and prosperity. According to another story described in the next two chapters, a Bania merchant and his wife Lilavati took a vow to observe the *vrata* if blessed with a child. Lilavati thereafter gave birth to a daughter named Kalavati. However, the merchant went on postponing the Satyanarayan Vrata, and, completely forgetting about it after Kalavati's marriage, set out on a business voyage with his son-in-law to a distant place. By the wrath of Lord Satyanarayan, therefore, they were accused of a theft at the king's palace, and thrown in gaol. Meanwhile, calamity befell Lilavati and Kalavati at home, and they lost everything they had. Once Kalavati saw a Brahmin perform the worship of Satyanarayan, and faith kindled in her, she persuaded her mother to perform the *vrata.* Lord Satyanarayan, pleased with their worship, advised the king in a dream to free the innocent Banias and return their confiscated wealth. On release they loaded their ship with merchandise and set sail for their home. To test whether the merchant had reformed, God Satyanarayan approached him in the form of an ascetic and enquired what he carried in the vessel. The Bania told a lie that the ship contained only tree-leaves and creepers.God Satyanarayan, displeased with this falsehood, turned his merchandise into leaves and creepers. He repented much, and sought forgiveness of the ascetic who advised him never to tell a lie and to worship Satyanarayan. After he performed the *vrata,* the merchant found his wealth restored to him, with which he returned to his native place. When the news of their arrival reached home, Kalavati, who was performing the Satyanarayan Vrata, impatiently ran to the harbour to meet her husband without completing the *puja.* The ship thereupon vanished, and only after she returned home, and completed the *puja,* did she find her husband with the vessel on shore. The merchant thereafter became a firm devotee of Lord Satyanarayan and was rewarded with prosperity and happiness. The last and the fifth anecdote in the *katha* is about king Tungadhvaja who showed disrespect to Shri Satyanarayan, and consequently lost his hundred sons and his kingdom. When he atoned for it and performed the *vrata,* he regained his lost kingdom and sons, and became Swayambhu Manu in the next birth.

After the reading of these five chapters of the *katha, mahaprasad* or the most important final offering of *shira* and fruits is made. The *puja* culminates with *arti,* i.e., waving of light before the deity with the chanting of songs. The *arti* is then moved among the assemblage, when everybody puts some coins in the *arti* plate. *Prasad* is distributed among the participants and neighbours. It is essential to receive the *prasad* with reverence and eat it. The invitees and others are then served with tea or sweet milk before departure. At some places, *bhajan-kirtans* are also arranged after *puja* till late at night. The priest and relatives are served with a feast, but this is not compulsory. Over and above the *dakshina,* the cash and other articles offered to the god go to the priest. Satyanarayan Vrata may be performed individually or collectively.

While the anecdotes in the *katha* are meant to impress upon the popular mind the importance of Satyanarayan worship, the significance of adherence to truth is not difficult to comprehend. Hinduism has always stressed the supremacy of truth over falsehood. In *mantras* like: *Satyameva Jayate* (truth alone triumphs) and *Satyam Param Dhimahi* (we contemplate or seek the supreme truth), it has advocated the search after Truth as a road to salvation. The Satyanarayan Vrata, in its present form, gives popular expression to the passionate devotion of the Aryans to Eternal Truth and combines austerity with festivity.

Teej

Teej, Teejon or Haryali Teej is a seasonal festival of Punjab falling on Sawan Sudi 3 (beginning of August) and is celebrated with great spirit in Delhi as in other parts of India. Since the festival falls on a Teej (third of a lunar month), it has come to be known as such. The rainy season starts gathering momentum near about the said date and the trees withered away by the scorching spell of summer, put forth tender and green leaves. The entire face of the countryside is changed. The heat bestirs the people out of their houses to take shelter under trees or to take bath in the welcome showers of the rainy season.

In northern parts of India to celebrate this change in season, every young girl from the countryside eagerly waits for Teej. It is an occasion for the newly married girls to go back to their parents for celebrating the first Teej with their girl friends. The brother of the newly wed goes to take her back some days before Teej and someone from her in-laws follows her with gifts of ornaments, clothes and sweets. On Teej, bevies of young girls attired in the best of their clothes and wearing new multi-coloured glass bangles start pouring in, in some mango grove overlooking a river, stream, canal or pond, where stout swings are hung from the trees for the girls to swing. They swing with agility and sing songs of their love gone to war or to far off lands to make a fortune. They pour out their hearts in folklores and give vent to their pent-up feelings. It is a time for emery frolics and girls get a chance to have a dig at their exacting mothers-in-law, unmanageable fathers-in-law, inexperienced *dewar* (young brother of husband) or jealous *nanad* (sister of husband). Sometime they sing of the good old days of innocent childhood. The humour, pathos and passions contained in these songs are really touching.

Kheer and *Malpura* are the special dishes of the day. Married girls when going back to their in-laws are given gifts of clothes and sweets. Mehndi (henna) is applied on the palms of women to add to the festivity.

Valmiki Jayanti

As the history goes Valmiki was a Bhil, a race of mountaineers, who used to rob and kill travellers passing through the forest. One day, seven Rishis journeyed by and when Valmiki attacked them, they asked him why he did so, as they had nothing worth stealing. He replied that he had vowed to kill all whom he found in the forest. The Rishis then enquired if the relations for whom he had been committing all those hideous sins would help save him from going to hell. Whereupon he asked his parents and wife if they would help him in case of need, but they declared they would not. Valmiki then told the Rishis that he was friendless, and they urged him to give up his evil ways, and to repeat *'mara', 'mara'* continuously. But rapidly recited *'mara', 'mara'* sounds like 'Ram', 'Ram'. He thus repeated God's name, sitting at one place for twelve long years. His body covered with dust was converted into a *valmik* or ant-hill. On their return the Rishis found him in this posture and named him as Rishi Valmiki.

Rishi Valmiki once went into the forest in search of firewood and grass for his daily sacrificial ritual. He saw a happy pair of *Krauncha* birds matting on the branch of a tree. Suddenly, the male bird struck by a hunter's arrow fell to the ground and the female bird uttered a deep cry of anguish and terror. Moved by this tragic happening, a spontaneous utterance welled up from Valmiki's heart and emerged from his lips, condemning this terrible crime. Immediately after he spoke he noticed that the flow of spontaneous expression had a perfect rhythm and melody. His *shok* (grief) had taken the form of a new *shlok,* (verse/meter) unknown to Sanskrit literature. After having discovered the *shlok,* Valmiki set out in search of an appropriate subject for describing which he could make use of the meter. The story of Rama fired his imagination and he thus produced *Ramayana*. For having written the first epic Valmiki is known as *Adi Kavi* or First Poet.

Rishi Valmiki is said to be a contemporary of Rama and his hermitage was situated in the deep jungles. When Rama banished Sita, she took refuge in Valmiki's hermitage. There she delivered two sons who were named Lava and Kusha. Rishi Valmiki brought them up and made them adept in the use of bow and arrow. They became great warriors and tied the sacrificial horse of Rama's *Aswamedh Yajna.* They defeated Rama and his army.

The Churah caste trace their origin to Valmiki and regard him their patron saint.

It is said that Valmiki's hermitage was situated at a place 11.50 kms. away from the present Amritsar. The place is today known as Ram Tirath. There is a big tank situated at the site, and in addition there are several temples. A temple dedicated to Valmiki has been constructed only recently at the site where Valmiki is said to have written *Ramayana*. A big fair is held every year at

Ram Tirath on Kartik Puranmashi. In Delhi Recitation from Ramayana, *bhajans, kirtan* and religious discourses are. Rishi Valmiki's birthday falls on Asoj Puranmashi and is celebrated by Harijans by taking out processions and holding mass *kirtans*.

Vat-Savitri Purnima

Vat Savitri Purnima is observed on Jyeshtha Sud 15 (June) eyery year. The Festival takes its name after Vat-Savitri Vrata, the principal austerity prescribed for married women for marital bliss and long life of their husbands. The *vrata*, which consists mainly of worship of *vat* or banyan tree, was originally performed by Savitri, a famous *sati* of Hindu mythology who succeeded in retrieving the life of her husband even from Yama, the God of Death. It is, therefore, called Vat-Savitri Vrata. Savitri was the daughter of King Ashwapati of Satya Yuga. As she was born as a result of a blessing of Savita, the sun-god, she was named Savitri, which means the daughter of Savita.

She was not only beautiful and intelligent, but also profoundly religious. Acording to the system of choice marriage prevalent at the time, Savitri, when she came of age, was sent in company of old and wise ministers to select a life-partner.They visited a number of kingdoms, territories and hermitages of sages but could not find a proper match for Savitri. Finally, on their return journey they came to the *ashram* of Dyumatsen, the king of Shalva. Defeated and dethroned by his enemy, King Rukmi, he and his wife, overcome with age and blindness, lived in exile in the forest. Satyavan, their only son, was virtuous and devoted to them. Attracted by his good qualities, Savitri selected him as her husband. The party returned home and told her parents about Savitri's choice. Meanwhile,sage Narad arrived there and coming to know about the marriage, advised that though Satyavan was in every way a suitable husband for Savitri, it was not desirable to marry Savitri to him as he had a very short life, and was destined to die within a year. However, Savitri was not to be dissuaded from her choice. She was a *sati*, and would not think of any one else as her husband, once she had given her heart to Satyavan, be his life as short as it may. She was, therefore, married to Satyavan. Narad blessed them and advised Savitri to worship *vat*, the banyan tree, and observe the *vrata* for three days on Jyeshtha Sud 13, 14 and 15, as *vat-vriksha* is the residence of Lord Vishnu, and its worship is equivalent to the worship of Vishnu himself. Savitri then began living a simple and pious life in the forest, in the service of Satyavan and his old parents. Five days before the day on which Satyavan's death was forecast by Narad, she started auster penances and religious observances as advised by the sage. From Jyeshtha Sud 11, she began to observe strict fasts, and worshipped God Shiva with full faith. On Jyeshtha *purnim* a she worshipped the banyan tree as directed and resolved not to leave her husband even for a moment. She accompanied him to the forest for fetching flowers, fruits, sacrificial fire-wood etc. Suddenly Satyavan fell down on earth under a banyan tree. Savitri instantly took his head on her lap and began to pray to Lord Shiva to save his life. As she was a real *sati*, she could see Yama taking away the soul from the body of Satyavan. Without being nervous, she rose, put the head of Satyavan. on a heap of flowers, and followed Yama. He advised her to turn back, but she continued to move beside him, all the while praying to him. On the way she obtained three boons from Yama, viz., eyesight of her in-laws, the lost kingdom of her father-in-law and a hundred sons to her parents. At last when they came near the gate of *Yamalok* or the residence of Yama, she told Yama, "You are the son of Surya, and I am also the daughter of the same God. As we are brother and sister, you should treat me with indulgence." Yama was pleased with her and bade her ask a fourth and final boon and then return. She thereupon asked for a hundred sons by Satyavan. Yama, bound by his promise, had to grant this wish. Thus by performing the religious observance as advised by Narad, Savitri averted the death of her husband.

The festival is dedicated to the worship of the *vad* tree, the Indian fig or *Ficus indica*, which is considered to be an emblem of Shiva who wears matted hair, like the tangled roots of the tree. It is very sacred to Hindus, as it is believed that all the three gods of the Trinity, Brahma, Vishnu and Shiva, reside in this tree. Women worship it for marital bliss. Its wood is used in sacrificial fires. Its milky juice is believed to have medicinal and energy-giving properties. It is one of the principla shade-bearing trees, which gives welcome relief from the scorching heat of the sun. In gratefulness for the many benefits derived from them, man has worshipped trees from ancient times. *Vat* or *vad* is one of many such trees which also include *pipal, shami,* etc.

Three days are assigned to this *vrata* in the scriptures. Ladies observe fasts for the last three days of the bright half of Jyeshtha. After a cold bath at a river, lake or well, they water a banyan tree and worship it with rice, sandal paste and lamp and offer *naivedya.* Then they take one hundred and eight rounds of the tree, winding on it an unbroken cotton thread, with the prayer, "Oh *vat-vriksha*, Brahma, the creater, resides at your root, Vishnu, the protector, in your trunk and Rudra, the destroyer, at your top, and hence pour this holy water and wind this cotton thread, taking you as an emblem of the Holy Trio." They then return home, hear the story of Savitri from a Brahmin and keep awake the whole night. Next day the Brahmin is fed and given alms. If possible, sixteen couples are given new dressed and feasted by those who can afford. Then the fast is broken.

This observance is performed especially in Gujarat and Maharashtra, at least for five consecutive years after marriage.In the fifth year, after final worship of the tree, a new *dhoti* is wrapped on the trunk of the bunyan tree which is taken away by the Brahmin conducting the *puja*. In Bengal ladies worship their husbands after bathing them with scented water and garland them.

Jyeshtha Sud 15 is said to be the birthday of Lord Vishnu, and as such also it is celebrated as a festival since very olden times, generally in the Vaishnavite temples and Pushtimargiya *havelis*. The festival of *jaljatra* is observed mostly in Vaishnavite temples and in some Shaivite temples too. On the eve of *purnima*, pious Brahmins, after a purifying bath, take clean silver or brass pots to reservoirs without touching anybody on the way, chanting prayers to Vishnu. There they fill the pots after invoking Varuna, the God of Water. On return to the temple, the pots are placed on purified water stands decorated with flowers. The water of the pots is then scented with sandal and saffron paste and flowers. After midnight they begin to sprinkle the holy water on the deity chanting *Purusha Sukta* of *Yajur Veda*. They also sprinkle coconut water and *panchamrit* or the mixture of milk, *ghee,* curd, honey and sugar on the deity after *abhyanga snan* and again bathe the idol finally with pure water. The idol is then adorned with costly garments and ornaments. This ceremony lasts till morning. The ceremony is also performed in Shaivite temples but in a different form. After worshipping Lord Shiva with holy water, *panchamrit* and *abhishek* with chanting of *Namaste Sukta* of *Rudri* called *Rudrabishek*, the *shivalinga* is drowned in the water brought from reservoirs with the belief that there will be plenty of rain in the coming season of monsoon, if the Lord is immersed in water in this way.

SINDHI FESTIVALS

The partition of the Indian sub-continent into India and Pakistan resulted in a great exodus and mass migration of Hindus from the parts which are now known as Pakistan. The Hindus of the Sind province of Pakistan, better known as Sindhis, migrated to almost all parts of India and have rehabilitated themselves in the new-environments.

Sindhis celebrate almost the same festivals which other Hindus observe. However, there are a few festivals which are a speciality of Sindhis who have a calendar of 12 months as under :—

Serial No.	*Name of the month*		*Corresponding English months*
1.	Chet	.....	March-April
2.	Vaisakh	....	April-May
3.	Jeth	.....	May-June
4.	Akhar	.....	June-July
5.	Sawan	.....	July-August
6.	Eado	.....	August-September
7.	Assu	.....	September-October
8.	Kati	......	October-November
9.	Nahri	.....	November-December
10.	Poh	.....	December-January
11.	Mangh	.....	January-February
12.	Phagun	.....	February-March

It may be noted that the Sindhi month begins with the Shukla Paksha, (i.e., bright half) and not with the Krishna Paksha, (i.e., dark half). The following are some of the important festivals observed by the Sindhis in India.

Chaliho

This festival was celebrated in a grand manner in Sindh. Now it has lost its importance because of the changed circumstances. "The period of inundation is celebrated by observation of the Chaliho festival or the festival of the forty days of the flood. It commences on the full moon day of Akhar (June-July). The women mix rice and turmeric, dry them and then add cloves and cardamoms to it. They make grain oblations to the river deity from it, thrice a day during the inundation period, on the bank of a lake or canal and go through the usual form of worship. On every Friday, or the Birthday of river-god, victuals are offered to the waters and distributed among the people. The day of the full moon and the new moon and Fridays are sacred to the river-god; and when they fall during this period they are specially celebrated by taking five, or seven, one, or four corner lamps of wheat flour to the adjacent pool or canal where they worship the river deity and distribute the victuals after offering some to the waters.

The last day of the 'Chaliho' festival commences with the putting of forty kinds of eatables, specially fruits in an earthen vessel and mixing with wheat cakes one for each member of the family. The vessel is painted in red with five or seven *Swastika* designs and covered at the top with a coconut. Round about are tied the necklaces prepared of cloves, cardamoms and mango leaves then the vessel is carried by a woman on her head to the nearest tank or canal accompanied by another woman who carries five or seven four-cornered flour lamps burning with wicks of safflower colour. After taking bath she applies mark on the forehead and paints *Swastika* on her forehead with powder of red-oxide. The women thus gathered sing 'Panjra' songs in praise of the river-god, dive in the mid-stream with clothes on and sink the vessel under water. Grain oblations are made to the river deity and flour lamps are floated on water. Then they return and observe the birthday rite (Bij) of river-god and distribute victuals *(sesa)* after offering to water. This festival may be observed by some males also by sitting, on the bank of a canal or tank for forty days and keeping vessels full of water nearby. They make oblations to the river deity thrice a day and go through the usual form of river worship. The last day of 'Chaliho' celebration is the day of taking leave from water as the floods are now supposed to retreat[1].

Cheti Chand

This festival, which happens to be the New Year's Day, is observed on Bij Tithi of bright half of Chet, the first month of the year. The New Year's Day, it is believed, happens to coincide with the birth anniversary of the river-god. Ladies observe a fast on this day. (In fact all days that are sacred to the river-god are observed as fast days by ladies). The river occupies an important place in the life of the persons of Sindh since she is the source of all life. This day is observed as the birth anniversary of a great saint known as Uderolal (who is said to be an incarnation of god Varuna), around whom many tales are woven. In the beginning of the 11th century, Markh whose capital was at Thatta was the king of Sind. He was a fanatical Muslim and Hindus were persecuted by him as well as his followers. The king wanted that all Hindus should embrace Islam and passed an order to that effect. The Hindus were astonished at this strange proclamation and requested the king to grant them religious freedom. The request was turned down. However, the king gave them a period of three days for consideration. The Hindus gathered at the bank of the river and prayed for 3 days, at the end of which a voice was heard from the river saying "After eight days I shall be born at 'Nasarapur' and my name shall be Uderolal". As told, after eight days, the river-god, Uderolal, was born to Devki Mata, wife of Ratan Rai, Thakur of Arora Caste at Nasarapur in the evening of Friday, which happened to be the New Year's Day of 1007 of the Vikram era. The river-god is also known as Daryalal or Amarlal which is a much more popular name. The newly born child soon began to speak as a grown up man after a short time. When the King came to know about the birth of the child, the king and his Vazir named Ohio, wanted to capture the child who himself appeared suddenly before them from the river at Thatta. The king wanted to convert him to Islam but failed. The king could not catch him since he changed his form in quick succession. Ultimately Uderolal warned the king about the forcible conversion of Hindus to Islam which the latter ignored whereupon Amarlal ordered fire to destroy the town. This had its effect and the king repented and granted equal freedom of worship to all. The king was so much awed by the miracles of Uderolal that he revered him as a devotee of god and named him "Khwaja Khizir." The Sindhis, celebrate this day in gratitude of saving them from the tyranny of the Muslim ruler. On this day Sindhis take out a procession of the Sea God which ultimately ends at the river bank. They carry Bahranas (symbol of temple of river or sea god) by installing a picture of sea-god (Lal-Sai) with perpetual light in it. They also sing *panjra* (five line poems) in praise of the river-god to the accompaniment of music. Young men dance to the tune of wooden stick in their hands. This dance is called "Chej". On its way the people greet the procession. Sukho and Sesa (boiled Kabuli gram or boiled beans and sweet water) are distributed. Women offer flowers and coconuts to the "Bahrana" and while the procession moves forward they shout:

"Lal Ja Jati, Chou Jhoole-Lal" (Oh ! Ye traveller of the Sea ! May my God swing on water).

When the procession ends at the bank of the river, a *Puja* is performed and the "Bahrana" is assigned to water.

It is believed that Uderolal who practised the river cult gave seven things which occupy an important place in the celebration of the festival of Cheti Chand. They are:—

(i) Lamp, the symbol of Uderolal.

(ii) Priestly dress.

(iii) A big metal pot (deg.) in which rice is boiled for distribution.

(iv) A sword (for protection).

(v) A water pot.

(vi) A drum stick for performing "Chej" dance and

(vii) The "Darbha" grass.

Since the "Cheti Chand" happens to coincide with the "Gudhi Padwa" day (or New Year's Day) of Maharashtrians, the Sindhis of Maharashtra have started celebrating it in a great gusto and enthusiasm.

Guru Nanak's Birthday

One of the peculiarities of Sindhi culture is that they observe the main festivals of Sikh religion and amongst them the birth-day of Guru Nanak, the 1st of the ten gurus of Sikhism. is celebrated with much fervour and on a grand scale. This festival falls on Kati Sud 15, i.e., full moon day. The celebrations of this festival, which is called

"Gurupurabh" among Sikhs and Sindhis, commences 48 hours before the actual day when the recitation of *akhand path* of Granth Sahib begins at a convenient place. Four or five persons are posted to recite from the holy scripture, turn by turn, for about two hours, each. A person is appointed to coordinate the function and look after the comforts of the persons who recite from the Granth Sahib. *Dhupias* (incense burners) burn incense beside the "Swari of Maharaj" (the throne where the holy book is recited day and night till the *bhog* ceremony is over). "Jyoti" (flame) fed with pure ghee is kept burning during the period of *akhand path*. The entire recitation of the holy book takes 48 hours for completion. After 24 hours have elapsed the ceremony of *Madh Path* (the recitation of half the holy book) is performed with the blowing of conch shells, ringing of bells, etc.

After the completion of the recitation of the holy book (which is over on the day of the festival, i.e., Kati Sud 15) a *kirtan* is held at the same place followed by a *Katha*. The life story of Guru Nanak is told by prominent persons. A *Kavi Darbar* is also held. The *Karah Prasad* is then distributed among all those who are present. The end of the function is *guru ka langar* (i.e., free kitchen) which is open to all persons without any distinction of caste, creed or religion. All the persons sit in a *pangat* (row) and eat the same food which is all vegetarian. It consists of rice, curry, chapati, bhaji, chatani and sweet bundi.

The place where the function takes place is gaily decorated and in the mid-night a swing with the photograph of Guru Nanak is brought. Rose petals are showered on it.

Maha Laxmi

This is one of the festivals which is observed by Sindhis in honour of goddess Laxmi, the consort of Vishnu, or the goddess of wealth. This festival falls on Assu Vad 8. Sixteen days earlier, i.e., on Assu Sud 8 all the members of the family tie a thread around their wrist which is called "Sagro". It is made out of 16 yellow threads (of cotton) and has sixteen knots. In case of unmarried persons, two "Sagros" are tied. On the day of Maha Laxmi, people go to the house of a Brahmin priest and carry with them sweet cakes and lamps prepared out of flour. They untie the 'Sagro' and on reaching the Brahmin's place, they hear the story of Raja Mangli who had two queens. One of them (who was dear to the king) threw away the thread (Sagro) of Maha Laxmi in the horse stable which was picked up by the maidservant and handed over to other queen. She wore it round her wrist and since that day she was loved more by the King. On the other hand the other queen (who discarded the 'sagro') was deserted and driven out by the King. She had to suffer a great deal because wherever she went, she brought calamity. Ultimately a saint found out the reason. The queen had insulted the goddess by throwing away the thread (sagro). The thread of Maha Laxmi was tied to her wrist and she, thus, won back the King. After the conclusion of the story, the persons return home leaving the sweet cakes, etc., at the Brahmin's place. A part of the sweet cakes is taken back as a *prasad*.

Nowadays it is seen that the 'sagro' is not kept on the wrist for 16 days. They generally tie it on Assu Sud 8 and remove it either of the same day or the day following.

Thadari. This festival is observed on two different dates. The first one, which is called Nandhi Thadari (lesser Thadari) is observed on Sawan Sud 7. The other is celebrated on Sawan Vad 7. Both the festivals are celebrated in honour of the consort of Shiva or the female energy, the mother-goddess in the form of Sitala, the small-pox goddess. On the previous day the ladies prepare sweet cakes called "Bhajivans" and also a curd-preparation. On the festival day it is customary not to burn fire and the stale food (cooked on the previous day) is consumed *(thadho)*. The ladies sing songs and go to a temple and make offerings. The peculiarity of this festival is that generally women even gamble on this day. It is believed that goddess Laxmi (goddess of wealth) passes through the palm of one who gambles on this day. The children and grandchildren approach their parents and grandmother demanding money. Married daughters with their children, visit their parents place.

Tijri. Among Sindhis this festival which is observed mainly by married women and unmarried girls falls on Sawan Vad 3. A few days before the festival, women sow wheat or jowar seeds in earthen pots and allow them to sprout. On the day of the festival they decorate their palms with "mehndi". They observe a fast on the day and in the afternoon the earthen pots containing the sprouts of wheat or jowar grains (sown earlier) are kept in a swing. They rock the swings with pots on, singing songs and performing a dance called "Jhimir". They drink sweet water, i.e., *sharbat.* In the night, they worship the moon on its appearance by offering milk, flowers, rice, etc., and break the fast.

This festival is observed by married girls for the long life of their husbands while unmarried ones pray for a good husband.

Besides the above, the Sindhis also observe the following festivals :

Akhana Tij. This festival is observed on Vaisakh Sud 3. On this day, the Sindhis offer earthen pots to Brahmins. This festival is the same as that of Akshaya Tritiya of Maharashtrians.

Dusehra. This festival is observed for a period of 10 days beginning with Assu Sud 1 to Assu Sud 10. The first nine days are called Navratra and the last day is Vijaya Dashmi. On the last day people gather at a river bank and a Kandi-Puja is performed. The effigies of Ravana, Meghnad and Kumbhakarna are burnt.

Diwali. This festival is celebrated for 3 days. Assu Vad 30, Kati Sud 1 and Kati Sud 2. The merchant class celebrates it by opening new accounts and the worship of goddess Laxmi is held on Laxmi-pujan day, i.e., Assu Vad 30. Designs called *putra* (like geometrical drawings) are drawn on the wall of the room where usually food is cooked. The models of houses are also worshipped. A peculiar custom amongst Sindhis is that they put milk, gold or silver coins, ornaments in a vessel and dip a finger in it and they apply it to their fore-head and mouth. They usually say:

Diyari Jo Diyo Ditho Nandho
Vaddo Chibhand Mitho.

(After Diwali, the fruit of Chibhand becomes sweet.)

A burning torch light called *melahwana* is kept outside the house in the evening. The head of the family distributes sweets and some presents or cash (called *kharchi*) to the children of the house. The 3rd day is Bij and on this day sisters come to the house of brothers who offer them presents. It is called a sister's day.

Ganesh Choth

The fourth day of the dark half of the month of Bado is observed as Ganesh Choth. The females observe a fast on this day and break it after the moon-rise. A story goes that a merchant was returning home after spending many years abroad. On his way he saw a serpent in a fire. Though the merchant rescued the serpent yet the latter, true to its nature, decided to bite him. The merchant told the serpent that it may do so only after he had seen his wife and children. The merchant then returned home and told the thing to his wife. On that night when the merchant was fast asleep on a cot his wife kept the following 4 things at the four legs of the cot : milk, flowers, vermilion and a dagger. The serpent arrived and was pleased to see the milk, flowers, etc. It consumed the first three articles one after the other and was satisfied. When the merchant got up in the morning he found a necklace in place of the dagger. His wife told him that because of devotion of Ganesh his death was avoided.

Gop-Ashtami

This festival is observed on Kati Sud 8 when the cow is worshipped. A fast is observed and in the evening people feed cows with grass, etc.

Holi

This festival is celebrated on Phagun Sud 15. On the full moon day women prepare cakes or cutlets and tie them with a cotton string. The cakes or cutlets are then baked in such a way that the string remains intact. In this case the string is the symbol of Bhagta Prahlad and the cutlets or cakes represent Holika. Fire is lit in the evening.

The next day is called "Dhuryo" when coloured water is sprinkled over each other. The day is spent in merry-making.

Janmaashtami

The birth anniversary of Lord Krishna is celebrated on Sawan Vad 8.

Nag Panchami

Sawan Sud 5 is celebrated as Nag Panchami which is also called as "gogro" or "gogyo" the cobra (serpent king) is worshipped on this day by offering milk, etc.

Ramnaomi

This festival, which falls on Chet Sud 9, is celebrated as the birth anniversary of Lord Ram, the seventh incarnation of God Vishnu.

Tirmuri

This festival is observed on 13th January. On this day tiny *Til* balls, (i.e., *Bhorinda*) are sent to friends and relatives as a symbol of goodwill.

NAV-BUDDHISTS FESTIVALS

As per Buddhism, every full moon day of the month (Purnima) is an auspicious day and as such it is observed as a festival. Some specific events have happened on these days and in honour of those events the day is celebrated as a festival. As this religion has been revived in India in Maharashtra, since 1956 only all the full-moon days are not observed as festivals though most Buddhists observe a fast on every Purnima day. They worship the moon on its appearance and after worship they break the fast. Non-vegetarian food is strictly avoided on these days. In the same manner many Buddhists observe a fast on each Thursday and avoid non-vegetarian food. This day is observed in memory of the late Dr Ambedkar, their leader who breathed his last on a Thursday. On this day they worship the image of Dr Ambedkar and the fast is broken in the night.

The following are reported to be the most important festivals celebrated by the Nav Buddhists.

Ambedkar Jayanti

This festival is observed on 14th April every year to commemorate the memory of the late Dr B.R. Ambedkar (popularly known as "Babasaheb Ambedkar"). The day is celebrated as the birth anniversary of Dr Ambedkar who was born on this day in the year 1891. A great procession of photograph of Dr Ambedkar is taken out and a public meeting is usually held at prominent places where the teachings and life of Dr Ambedkar are explained. Many pay a visit to the statue of Dr. Ambedkar and pay their respects by offering prayers, flowers, etc, In every house of a Nav-Buddhist the photograph of Dr. Ambedkar is garlanded.

Vaishakh Purnima

The full moon day of the month of Vaishakha is an auspicious day for the Buddhists because many important events took place on this day. Lord Gautam-Buddha was born on this day at Lumbini. He also attained perfect knowledge or enlightenment at Uruvela near Buddha- Gaya in Uttar Pradesh on this day only. He also left this material world (*Nirvan*) on this day at Kushinagar. All these important events have enhanced the importance of Vaishakha Purnima.

The Nav-Buddhists celebrate this day by worshipping either the image or photograph of Lord Buddha at the Buddha temple or at a public place or at home. They also carry out a procession of the photograph of Lord Buddha and Dr Ambedkar, the great leader. A fast is observed on this day, and it is broken in the night by consuming vegetarian food. A public meeting is held where the teachings and life of Lord Buddha are narrated. Prayers and worships are offered on this day to the image of Lord Buddha.

JAIN FESTIVALS

Shwetambar and Digambar are two major divisions of the Jains. During the lifetime of Mahavir there were no sects among Jains. After his death, Jainism spread throughout the length and breadth of India. This made it difficult for the religious heads at different places to look after and organize their followers, who were distributed as they were in different parts of the country, developed variations in religious practices. Further, the religious doctrines and tenets was enunciated and taught by Mahavira were not codified but were memorized by his disciples and handed down from one generation to another. When they were reduced to writing, the text was not acceptable to some who maintained that it was not accurate. The interpretation of these canons also led to controversies. Towards the end of the first century, the ascetics and then the community were split into the two main sects, viz., Shwetambars meaning having white clothes and Digambars meaning with the directions as their clothes, i.e., no clothes at all. While there is little difference as regards the essentials of doctrines followed by these two sects, the major point of difference between them is whether the injunction to renounce all worldly possessions for achieving salvation should be carried to the extreme by dispensing even with clothes and practising nudity.

The following main beliefs to which the Shwetambars do not subscribe distinguish them from the Digambars :

(i) The monk who possesses any property whatsoever and develops an attachment for it cannot attain salvation. He should, therefore, forego even clothing.

(ii) Women are not entitled to *moksha* in this life.

(iii) Once a saint attained *Keval Jnan,* i.e., omniscience, he needed no food taken by morsels, but could sustain life without eating.

The Shwetambars have three subsects, viz., (i) idol worshippers called Deravasi or Murtipujak or Pujera; (ii) non-idolatrous Sthanakvasi, Dhundiya, Sadhumargi, or Bistola, and (iii) non-idolatrous Terapanthi.

The Sthanakvasi sect, formed in about 1476 A.D., arose from an earlier reformist sect called Lonka, founded by Lonkasha, a well-read merchant of Ahmedabad. They do not worship idols. The Sthanakvasi Terapanthi sect was founded in Vir Nirvan Samvat 1817 by Swami Bhikkhanaji Maharaj who had thirteen disciples and who laid stress on a like number of religious principles when he perceived some deviation in the religious practices of Sthanakvasi ascetices. It is believed that the impact of the Muslims was one of the factors which contributed to the formation of the non-idolatrous sects.

Among Digambars there are five subsects, which differ in the manner of worship. They are (i) Bisapanthi, (ii) Terapanthi, (iii) Taranpanthi, (iv) Gumanpanthi and (v) Totapanthi.

The principal places of pilgrimage for Jains are Parshanath hill in Bihar, Hastinapur in Uttar Pradesh. Sravana Velagola, wedged between two rocky hills. Indragiri and Chandragiri in Karnataka and in Gujarat Mount Shatrunjay in Bhavnagar district associated with the first *tirthankar* Rishabhdev and Mount Girnar in Junagadh district, where Neminath, the 22nd *tirthankar,* attained *nirvan*. These holy places are visited by Jains from all over India. Other well-known Jain shrines in Gujarat are at Talaja in Bhavnagar district, Bhadreshwar in Kutch, Bhiladiyaji and Kumbharia in Banaskantha, Taranga Hill, Pansar and Mahudi in Mehsana district, Bhoyani in Ahmedabad district and Jhagadia in Broach district.

Festivals among Jains are generally associated with austerities and fasting, and always with worship. Indeed, it is the successful completion of austerities in many cases that is a cause for jubilation, feasting and ostentation. The austerities are generally very severe. The devotee is required to avoid, in addition to roots which are prohibited on ordinary days, leafy vegetables, dry fruits, tasty food preparations, milk and curd and, in extreme cases, even water. Those who are incapable of such extreme penance try to observe it with whatever severity they can. The reason is the great emphasis placed on *tap* or penance as a means to earn religious merit. Thus the religious aspect is quite prominent in Jain festivals, though some of them have a social aspect also. Mention must also be made of the invaluable contribution Jainism has made not only to the philosophical thought and literature of the land, but also to the development of its art and architecture which have given many a beautiful specimen to the State and the country.

Ashtahnika

This is an austerity considered by followers of the Digambar sect as next in importance to Paryushana. It is observed three times in a year, during the week beginning from the bright eighth of Kartik, Phalgun and Ashadh. People fast with varying strictness of austerity during these days as in Paryushana.

Diwali

Diwali is another festival common to Jains as well as Hindus. Jains celebrate it as *nirvan-din* or the day of emancipation of Lord Mahavir, the 24th and the last *tirthankar*. His *nirvan* which took place at the age of about 72½ years in 527 B.C. marks the commencement of the Jain era, Vir Nirvan Samvat. When he died, after delivering a final sermon at Apapapuri which lasted continuously for sixteen *prahars*, the celestial beings, eighteen kings from Kashi, Koshal, etc., and others who were present, lighted lamps saying, "Since the light of intelligence is gone, let us make light with material objects." Light was also emitted from the *vimans* or aeroplanes and from precious jewels of the gods who came to participate in the ceremony.

Mahavir's *nirvan* took place in the night of Diwali. When Gautam Swami, a great saint, who was away at that time, came to know of it, he was overcome with grief and began to mourn, whereupon the Supreme Truth dawned on him and he attained *keval jnan*. Kartik Sud 1 is, therefore, the festival commemorating the *keval jnan* of Gautam. For the Jains, Diwali is also associated with this event, which is celebrated as the festival of light by illuminating their houses with numerous lamps. In villages children move from house to house with *merayas* or torches on which the householders pour oil.

After the time of Mahavir's birth at midnight, and in the very early hours of the next morning, people worship Lord Mahavir with sweetballs which are called *nirvan-ladu*, chanting mantras in honour of Mahavir and Gautam Swami. They then meet their relatives, friends and acquaintances and exchange New Year's greetings. People also prepare sweet dishes at home during Diwali and subsequent days to celebrate the attainment of salvation by Mahavir.

At some places, ceremonies like Lakshmi Pujan which have no place in the Jain faith are also performed. Karmik Sud 2 is also celebrated by Jains as Bhai Bij, as Sunanda, the sister of Mahavir, hosted her other brother Nandivardhan on that day to end the mourning and comfort him in his grief at the *nirvan* of the *tirthankar*.

Thus, Jains celebrate the festivals of Diwali, New Year and Bhai Bij in a manner similar to the Hindus, but against a somewhat different religious background.

Jnan Panchami

The fifth of every lunar fortnight is considered a *Jnan-tithi* by Jains, a day on which they are enjoined to endeavour to acquire more and more knowledge. Jnan Panchami, however, is the principal of all the *jnan-tithis*. Some call it Saubhagya Panchami also, because its celebration denotes *saubhagya*. or good fortune. No person can attain progress without acquiring knowledge. The festival underlines the importance of spiritual knowledge in uplifting the soul. The legend of Varadatta and Gunamanjari is narrated in this connection. Varadatta was a king's son who could not learn anything from his preceptor and who was afflicted with leucoderma. Gunamanjari was a wealthy merchant's daughter who was dumb and diseased from birth. When the parents of both Varadatta and Gunamanjari asked a learned Jain saint about their affliction, he said that Varadatta was a Jain sadhu in his former birth who had shown disrespect towards knowledge. Similarly, Gunamanjari was a merchant's wife who had neglected to send her children to school and insulted their preceptor. They were, therefore, destined to suffer in the present birth. As an atonement for their sins. He prescribed the austerities on the bright fifth for five years and five months by the chanting of a *Mantra* and observing a partial fast. Religious books are worshipped on this day. Insence is burnt before them, five *swastika* designs are drawn with rice. Five types of grains, flowers and sweet dishes are offered, and a lamp of five wicks lighted. By observing this austerity, both Varadatta and Gunamanjari were freed from their afflictions and became happy.

If every bright fifth cannot be celebrated like this, then the one of Kartik should be celebrated every year. On this day in the libraries of Jain institutions, all the books are taken out and dusted, and insects removed from them. In order that devotees can see such manuscripts, the most important of them are displayed and worshipped in a *mandap* specially erected for this purpose. This festival has been of immense use in maintaining these treasures, because on this day once every year every book is carefully cleaned. Every Jain is enjoined to offer special worship on this day, pay respects to *sadhus* or *sadhvis* and to make some endeavour to acquire more knowledge. Those who can afford, spend money for the cause of education and knowledge. Digambar Jains observe a similar festival on Jyeshtha Sud5, called Shruta Panchami. Their saints Pushpadanta and Bhutabali on this day completed the writing of the sacred book, *Shatakhandagama,* which was then worshipped by all Jains.

Kartik Purnima

This day marks the close of the austerities of *chaturmas* or the four monsoon months starting from Ashadh Sud 15. It is particularly important for the holy Mount Shatrunjaya in Bhavnagar district, where in ancient times Dravid and Varikhilya, the grandsons of Rishabhdev, the first *tirthankar*, attained *siddhipad* on Kartik Sud 15 along with numerous other *munis*. After they had shared their father's kingdom, Dravid became jealous of the prosperity of his younger brother Varikhilya, who was the more intelligent of the two, and enmity ensued between them. At last they realised their mistake and penitently renounced the world, accepted *diksha* (initiated to holy order) and ultimately became *siddhas.*

Devout Jains, who have undertaken the austerities of *chaturmas* from Ashadh Sud 14, end them on this day. During these austerities many articles like leafy vegetables, dry fruits, etc., are prohibited in food. These can be eaten from Kartik Sud 15 after the observance of *chomasi* or quarterly *pratikraman* or expiation of sins on the previous day, i.e., Sud 14.

To observe *pratikraman,* people undertake *chhath* or two days fast on Kartik Sud 14 and 15. The devout perform *paushadh* or living the life of a *sadhu* in an *upashraya* for a whole day or 24 hours. The day is important also for *sadhus* who are under the restriction of halting at one place during *chaturmas* but otherwise enjoined to be continuously on the move. On Kartik Purnima they again start on their *vihar* or journey to some other Jain tirtha. For the rest, for whom even this is not possible, a function is organized.

Mount Shatrunjayone (the holiest of the Jain places of pilgrimage), also opens on this day after remaining closed for the four monsoon months. 15,000 to 20,000 pilgrims, therefore, undertake the pilgrimage to that 'City of Temples'. Those who cannot undertake this journey visit some other Jain *tirtha.* For the rest, for whom even this is not possible, a function is held on the outskirts of the town. Paintings of Shatrunjay on cloth called *pat* are exhibited in an open space. Sometimes the *pat* has pictures of other *tirthas* also. Devotees flock to have *darshan* of the *pat* and earn religious merit. To remind them of the free distribution of refreshments to all pilgrims to Shatrunjay at the foot of the hill, similar refreshments or a sweet drink is sometimes distributed in these places also to the devotees coming to see the *pat.*

Kartik Purnima has a special significance for Gujarat as the birthday of Hemchandracharya, the well-known Jain *muni,* who lived some 800 years ago. He was born at Dhandhuka in Ahmedabad district on Kartik Sud 15, V.S. 1145, as the only child to his wealthy parents and was named Chang. *Muni* Devchandrasuri who realized the potential greatness of the child when he was only five years of age, begged Chang from his mother Pahinidevi and made him his disciple, changing his name to Somachandra. For the next sixteen years, he remained engrossed in studies and austerities. At the age of twenty-one he was made an *acharya.* A great Jain saint, he came to be equally well-known as a profound scholar with a catholic outlook and tolerance towards other beliefs. His *Siddha-Haima Vyakarana*, a Sanskrit grammar; was so greatly appreciated by Siddharaj Jaysinh of Patan that he ordered the book to be placed on an elephant and taken in a procession through his capital. Notable among his other standard works is the *Dvyashraya Kavya,* a poetic work with double purpose, namely to illustrate the principales of his grammar and to narrate the general history of Gujarat during the Solanki period up to Kumarpal. Siddharaj is known to have been considerably influenced by him. His successor Kumarpal accepted Hemchandra as his preceptor. The Acharya's influence on the political and cultural life of the people of Gujarat at that time was very great. He was a great religious leader, an erudite philosopher, a statesman and an adviser to kings. He is known as Kalikala-Sarvajna (the omniscient in Kali Yuga). After leading an illustrious life of 84 years, he died at Patan in V.S. 1229.

Mahavir Jayanti

Chaitra Sud 13 marks the birth anniversary of Mahavir Swami, the 24th and the last Jain *tirthankar.* The five main events in the life of every *tirthankar*, viz., conception, birth, *diksha*, *jnan* and *nirvan* are called *kalyanaks* which are festivel days for the devout. Chaitra Sud 13, the janma-kalyanak of Mahavir is celebrated by Jains of all sects throughout India with pomp and ceremony. Lord Mahavira was born as Vardhaman is 599 B.C. in Videh (present Bihar). His father Siddharth was a Kshatriya king. Both he and his wife Trishala were devout followers of Lord. He had fourteen significant dreams which indicated his future greatness. After his birth the family gained in wealth, fame and merit. He was, therefore named Vardhaman. He rejoined in making sacrifice for others and displayed exceptional abilities in studies. Though apathetic to marriage, he respected the wishes of his parents and. according to Shwetambars, married Yashoda at the age of thirteen, and a daughter Priyadarshani was born to them. Though married, he wished to renounce the world in search of the path of salvation. His parents died when he was twenty eight years old. After two years he succeeded in obtaining the permission of his elder brother and others to take *diksha* and adopt the ascetic way of life, which he did at the age of thirty years of Kartik Vad 10. His next twelve years were spent in severe penance and deep meditation. He bore hardships, restrained the impulses for the purification of the soul and remained unperturbed even in the most provocative circumstances. Thus proceeding on the way to deliverance he understood the eternal truth, earned omniscience and attained the highest knowledge and intuition called Keval Jnan on Vaishakh Sud 10 under a *sal* or *Shorea robusta* tree near the village Jrumbhikagrama on the bank of river Rujupali. Thus at the age of forty-two he became a *jina* and *Arhat*—a *kevalin*, omniscient, all seeing and all-knowing. He then started his career as a teacher explaining to the people the way of salvation as he knew it. During the next thirty years he visited Vaishali, Vanjigram, Rajgriha, Nalanda, Mithila and various other places, finally attaining *nirvan* on Ashen Ad *amavasya* in 527 B.C. at Pavapuri.

Lord Mahavira, is believed to be a contemporary of Buddha, and one of the greatest teachers of mankind. He preached the five great vows by adding *brahmacharya* (chastity) to the fourfold self-restraint already prescribed by Lord *Parshvanatha*, viz., (1) *ahimsa* (non-violence,(2) *satya* (truth), (3) *asteya* (abstinence from stealing), and (4) *aparigraha* (non-attachment to worldly things). It is believed by some that the fifth vow of *brahmacharya* was included in the fourth, viz., *aparigraha.* Mahavira further preached that beatitude cannote be attained through mundane happiness but through mortification of flesh. He exhorted his disciples to develop their power of reasoning and argument. He keenly watched the conduct and progress of his disciples to ensure exemplary behaviour on their part. He vouchsafed the gift of supernatural vision even to the householder without any distinction of caste, creed or sex and opposed hereditary priesthood and restricted the practice of religious penance of fasting unto death to those of his disciples who scrupulously followed his personal example. At the time of his death thousands of ascetics, male and female, and lakhs of householders were among his followers, chief of whom were eleven *ganadhars* guiding and instructing recluses under their charge.

The ceremonies to celebrate the *jayanti* are explained in *Panchashaka* of Haribhadra. In Delhi people gather for *darshan* at the temple of Mahavira or, in absence of it, any Jain temple in the town. Besides religious ceremonies at shrines, processions and *prabhat feris* (morning processions) are taken out through important streets, at times with the idol of Mahavira seated in chariot, of whom people have *darshan* on the way. Meetings are organized wherein discourses about Mahavira's life and teachings are given, and other religious and cultural programs are also held. A public holiday is declared in the State on this day.

Digambar Jain also celebrates Virashasana Jayanti on Shravan Vad 1, the day on which Lord Mahavira, after achieving omniscience, gave his first religious sermon on mount Vipulachala near Rajgriha in Magadha.

Maun Ekadashi

Margashirsh Sud 11 is a day of silence for the Jains. According to Jainism, *maun,* i.e., observing silence, is a means of self-purification which also gives mental peace to the individual who observes it. Lord Mahavir is said to have practised it much during his penace. 150 *kalyanaks* (i.e., holy days marking the anniversaries of birth, *nirvan,* etc., of *tirthankars*) fall on this day and hence it is considered to be very sacred. It happens to be the *kalyanak* or anniversary of the birth, *diksha,* and *keval jnan* of Mallinath, the 19th *tirthankar.*

Once upon a time when Neminath, the 22nd *tirthankar,* went to Dwarka, Shri Krishna requested him to name a day on which he could undertake austerities and attain religious merit. Indicating Margashirsh Sud 11 as a very auspicious day for this purpose, as a fast undertaken on this day earns merit equal to 150 fasts, and earns even greater merit if observed with silence. Neminath narrated the example of Suvrat Sheth who attained much wealth and glory by performing this *vrata.*

A wealthy Jain merchant named Sur, acting on his preceptor's advice, performed *paushadh* (living like a *shraman*) for a day on Margashirsh Sud 11 observing complete silence, repeating this for 11 months for 11 years, after which the austerity was terminated with celebrations. He therefore, attained godliness after death and lived in *devlok* or heaven for a prolonged period. Thereafter, he was born as a son of Sheth Samruddhadatta, a very wealthy merchant, and named Suvrat. He married eleven good wives who gave him eleven sons, and earned eleven crore *sonaiyas* (gold coins). Impressed by his truthfulness and benevolence, the king gave him the position of the *nagarsheth.* On hearing the importance of Maun Ekadashi from a *sadhu,* he was reminded of his previous birth and started observing this *ekadashi.* He was so strict in the observance that even when he saw thieves taking away his property on one such day, he did not utter a single word. He was rewarded for his penance as the thieves were miraculously caught the next day. They were released at his special request and reformed themselves. Once when he and his family were in *paushadh*, fire broke out in the city. It was fast approaching the *upashraya*, but he did not give up the religious performance though advised to leave the place and save his life. Miraculously, the fire did no harm to him. Finally, by performing the austerities of Maun Ekadashi, Suvrat Sheth attained *keval jnan* and *moksha.* On Neminath's advice, Shri Krishna is said to have also observed this *vrata* in which the people followed him. The lives of Neminath and Shri Krishna are therefore, narrated on this day.

Oli

The two Olis observed by Shwetambar Jains are called *shashvati parvas* as they are believed to have been observed eternally in the same form during the times of all *tirthankars*. Shwetambars consider it next in importance only to Paryushana and celebrate it. The rich and poor alike celebrate for nine days from Sud 7 to *Purnima* twice a year in Chaitra and Ashvin. During these days, worship of *navapadas* is performed with the austerity of Ayambil. The *navapadas* are: (1) Arihant, (2) Siddha, (3) Acharya, (4) Upadhyay, (5) Sadhu, (6) Darshan, (7) Jnan, (8) Charitra, and (9) Tap. The first five are known as *Panch Paraneshthins,* while the remaining four are the steps to attain these accomplishments. All these are represented on the Siddhachakra or saint-wheel, a circular figure embossed or engraved on a silver or copper plate worshipped in every Shwetambar temple. At the centre is the figure of Arihant and surrounding it are the remaining eight *padas*, of which the *paraneshthins* are represented by figures and the rest by words. As it embodies all the nine *padas* in it, Siddhachakra is taken to contain the quintessence of Jainism. the Worship of Siddhachakra, which is sometimes painted with different colours, is performed during Oli. When it is painted, specific colours are earmarked for each of the nine *padas* as follows :

1. Arihant White
2. Siddha Red
3. Acharya Yellow
4. Upadhyay Green
5. Sadhu Black
6. Darshan White
7. Jnan White
8. Charitra White
9. Tap White

The austerities of Oli are observed for nine days in Delhi each of which is assigned to one of the nine *padas* in the Siddhachakra, which is worshipped on that day by special *mantras, stavan*, etc. The devotee observes partial fast on these nine days during which he eats only once a day, avoiding articles like sugar, gur, oil, milk, curd and things which taste pungent and sour as these are believed to disturb the impulses. Some persons go even further and restrict their diet to some article which has the same colour as is assigned to the particular *pada* of Siddhachakra to which the day is dedicated. Thus, only rice may be taken on the first day dedicated to Arihant having the white colour assigned to it, and so on.

On the last day of this festival, the Siddhachakra is worshipped at the *upashraya* in a special manner. A devotee may arrange for it to be drawn on the floor with different kinds of grains, selected according to the colours assigned to the nine *padas*, like rice, *urad, moong*, etc. This is called *mandal*. The expenditure depends upon the capacity of the man, as sometimes six to seven Bengali *maunds* (200-250 kgs.) of grains are used and even silver and gold leaves are applied on the top. Dry coconut kernel bowls are placed on the nine *padas*. The room of the *upashraya* where this *mandal* is drawn is decorated with flags and pictures. People come for *darshan* and worship of this *mandal*. The articles used in it are given away to the *pujari* of the temple on the next day. Once during the nine days of Oli, Siddhachakra is taken outside the town in a procession and bathed in water. This ceremony is known as *jalayatra*.

In ancient times, King Haripal and his wife Maynasundari performed this Vrata whereby he was cured of leucoderma. In commemoration of that event, the *ras* of Shripal Raja, which describes the importance of Siddhachakra is read on this day. Some persons perform these austerities continuously for nine times covering a period of four and a half years. They sometimes begin these austerities in Ashvin as Shripal Raja also undertook it first in Ashvin.

The Ayambil can be observed anytime in the year but it is specially prescribed during Oli. Of late, the custom of observing it collective has come into vogue. For this purpose special *Ayambil-shalas* are established where special kitchens are run and the prescribed food served to the persons undertaking the austerities. Munificent donations are made by the rich for opening such *Ayambil-shalas*. This sort of convenience is a great facility to the devotees and promotes a sense of brotherhood in the community.

Paryushana or Pajusan

Paryushana or Pajusan, the most sacred of all the festival of Jains, is the occasion for continuous religious activities. Even those who do not or cannot normally perform religious acts on other days, do so at least during Paryushana. It is celebrated with strict austerities by all, but on different dates by the two Jain sects of Shwetambar and Digambar.

Shwetambars observe this *parva* from Shravan Vad 12 to Bhadrapad Sud 4, especially for the atonement of their sins during the previous year. People go to *upashrayas* as often as possible during these days to listen to the scriptures being read out to them, while some spend their whole day in *upashraya*. *Paushadh*, or living like an ascetic in an *upashraya* for twenty-four hours, earns special religious merit. For the first two or three days the *sadhus* explain to the devotees the significance of this *parva* and exhort them to perform religious acts. Thereafter, discourses are given on *Kalpasutra*, an important Jain scripture written in Prakrit. Since *Kalpasutra* contains 1,200 verses, this is known as *Barsa-vanchan*. The lives of the first and the last *tirthankars*, and of the *ganadhars* or principal disciples and ancient saints, and the preaching of *tirthankars* are narrated in *Kalpasutra*, numerous manuscript copies of which, many of them beautifully illustrated, are preserved in Jain *jnan-bhandars* or repositories of rare manuscripts. At several places *Kalpasutra* is also taken out in a procession on third day of Paryushana.

Five religious acts are specially enjoined during Paryushana, the first of which is the proclamation of *amari* or *ahimsa* (non-violence). People are enjoined by a proclamation not to harm or kill any living being. In ancient times, Samprati Raja had proclaimed *ahimsa* in his kingdom. Kumarpal, the king of Gujarat in twelfth century, also propagated non-violence in his domains. Emperor Akbar was also much impressed by the ideal of *ahimsa*, which was explained to him by Hirvijay Suri, a Jain ascetic whom he had specially summoned from Gujarat in V.S.1639, on hearing of his great qualities. Pleased with him, he issued an injunction against animal slaughter during Paryushana. He also released all prisoners and freed all the birds caught by or presented to him. Later on, he extended the injunction against *himsa* or violence to some other holy occasions also. In order to ensure that no animal life is taken during Paryushana days, the leaders of the Jain Community ensure with the help of the local authorities, prevention of slaughter of animals during Paryushana by persuasion, and even by payment of some compensation, if necessary.

The next direction relates to love and welfare of the co-religionists, for whose benefit money is recommended to be spent. Strict fasts are enjoined to be undertaken during Paryushana. Those who cannot fast on all the days should keep six fasts at least on the first, third, fourth, sixth, seventh and eighth days. Everybody fasts on the last day popularly called Samvatsari, considered to be the most sacred of all. Some devotees observe partial fasting as in Ayambil austerities undertaken during Oil.

Samvatsari denotes the Samvatsari or annual *pratikraman* or expiation of sins, directed to be performed during Paryushana. It is the last of the five periodical *pratikramans* enjoined, viz.

1. Devasi every evening, for the atonement of the day's sins;
2. Rai every morning, for the atonement of the night's sins;
3. Pakkhi fortnightly, on the 14th of every lunar fortnight;
4. Chomasi four monthly, on the bright 14th of Kartik, Phalgun and Ashadh; and
5. Samvatsari yearly, on the bright 4th or 5th of Bhadrapad.

Observance of *pratikraman* includes fasting and *paushadh*. On the Samvatsari day, as an atonement for his sins, every person must ask forgiveness of his elders, relatives, friends and acquaintances for any offences. This is called *khamavavun* or pardon. It is an important concomitant of the festival, performed on its conclusion. For this purpose people visit their relatives or write greeting cards to them with the words *michchha mi dukkadam*, or i.e., "all my sinful acts be pardoned".

In the fifth place comes *chaityaparipati*, which means visiting all the Jain temples every day, covering all of them in the Paryushana days. Over and above these, various other ceremonies like collective ceremonial worship, night-vigil, etc., are also prescribed, and are performed by the more religious of the community.

The fifth day of this *parva* is conventionally celebrated as Lord Mahavir's birthday, though it really falls on Chaitra Sud 13. On this day a *rath-yatra* or chariot procession is taken out after worshipping in the temple at noon the silver plated pictures depicting the fourteen dreams seen by the mother of Mahavir before his birth. A metal idol of the *tirthankar* is placed in a silver dish in the chariot specially decorated for the occasion. Before the procession starts, devotees make bids for having priority in leading the procession. This is known as *uchhamni*, a common practice among Jains followed on many religious occasions, the amounts realized being used for religious purposes like *puja*, repairs to temples, etc. The highest bidder is allowed to lead the procession, sitting by the idol in the chariot. All the Jains join the procession, with men at the head, followed by the chariot, behind which women walk singing songs in praise of Lord Mahavir. Conches are sounded in the procession as a mark of joy. The procession goes through the main streets of the town, ending at the residence of the highest bidder where the idol is kept for a day and then returned to the temple.

Among Digambars, Pajusan is observed form the fifth to the fourteenth of the bright half of Bhadrapad every year. In the morning of each of these days after the eightfold worship is over people who assemble in the temple are explained one out of the ten *dharmas* laid down in *Tatvarth Sutra*, one of the holy scriptures of the Jains. Attention of the people is thus focussed on the ten *dharmas* or reflections. Paryushana is, therefore, known also as Dasalakshana Parva. A complete fast is observed by many on all these days while some observe a partial fast by taking food once a day. Anant Chaturdashi, the last day of this *parva,* is considered particularly sacred and people attend the temple for the whole and perform special ceremonies prescribed. A fast is generally observed by all on this day.

Paryushana, being the most important festival of the Jains, is observed by all, high and low in Delhi. The rich, besides observing the austerities, also make donations for charitable causes.

Rakshabandhan

This festival is celebrated especially by Digambars in common with Hindus, but for different reasons in Delhi. It was on this day that great sage named Vishnukumar by his spiritual power saved the lives of seven hundred *sadhus* whom King Bali of Hastinapur was about to offer in a human sacrifice. Vishnukumar is, therefore, worshipped on this day along with these seven hundred monks. The festival is celebrated to foster affection towards religion and induce the people to follow the example of Vishnukumar and be ever prepared to protect their temples, institutions, *sadhus* and co-religionists.

Other Minor Festival

There are numerous other minor festivals observed by Jains. The full-moon days of the Kartik, Phalgun, Chaitra and Ashadh are observed by Shwetambars as special fasts when they worship at the temples, lighting lamps. Out of these the first and third are more important as these days are considered auspicious for a pilgrimage especially to Shatrunjay hill, the former on the opening of the pilgrimage, and the latter on its closing on account of *chaturmas.* From Phalgun Sud 14, leafy vegetables, dry fruits, etc., are to be avoided for eight months till Kartik Sud 15. From the next day of Holi (Phalgun Sud 15) special discourses are arranged in the *upashraya* and devotees in a group visit the main Jain temple in the town.

Akshaya Tritiya

Akshaya Tritiya is celebrated both by Hindus and Jains, but on different grounds. For the latter, who consider it one of the most auspicious and sacred days. It is the day on which Rishabhdev, the first of the 24 Jain *tirthankars* accepted sugar cane juice for the first time after continuous fasts for six months, from King Shreyana of Hastinapur. According to another version, Rishabhdev in his former birth saw a farmer beating an ox which was eating corn from the threshing floor. He advised him not to beat the animal but tie a bag on its mouth. It sighed more than 360 times, and in the next birth Rishabhdev had to fast for a whole year as he could not get suitable food in *bhiksha*, after which he received sugar-cane juice from Shreyans. In memory of this event, the idol of Rishabhdev is bathed in sugar cane juice and worshipped.

The devotees who perform the *Varsi Tap* or the austerities lasting a year terminate it on this day. The *vrata* is begun on Phalgun Vad 8 and completed on Vaishakh Sud 3 of the following year. It begins with fast for two days on Phalgun Vad 8and 9 called *chhath*, after which the devotee fasts on alternate days. On all non-fasting days he is allowed food only twice a day. He was to keep fast on the 8th and 14th of each lunar fortnight even through these may be non-fasting days according to their turn. The yearlong austerities are ended on Akshaya Tritiya by drinking sugar-cane juice from a small silver pot at the hands of friends and relatives. Formerly devotees used to go to Hastinapur for this purpose as Rishabhdev had concluded his penance there. But now they go to Siddhakshetra or Mount Shatrunjay (Bhavanagar district) along with their relatives friends, etc., for this purpose. About twenty thousand persons congregate at Shatrunjay on this day. Money is spent lavishly in these ceremonies in distribution of gifts, coconuts, etc. The person who successfully completes the austerities is also felicitated and honoured.

The festivel serves to remind people that Shreyans obtained *akshaya punya* or indestructible merit by offering only sugar cane juice to Rishabhdev, and to inspire them to offer gifts, of whatever value according to their capacity, to the deserving persons and obtain everlasting merit in the same way.

Dwadesh-Parvi

The eighth, fourteenth and fifteenth of every lunar fortnight are called *charitra-tithis* when special efforts are to be made to improve *charitra* or character; and every second, fifth and eleventh are *jnan-tithis* specially indicated for acquisition of knowledge. These twelve days in month are called *dwadash-parvi* or the twelve festivals. Jains believe that the fate for the next birth is determined on an auspicious day on the completion of two-thirds of the remaining one-third are over, and so on. Every third day is, therefore, included in the *dwadash-parvi.**

Kalyanaks

Also considered sacred are the Kalyanaks days when the five most important occasions in the life of every one of the 24 *tirthankars* fall, viz., conception, birth, *diksha, jnan* and *nirvan*.

Meru Terash

Paush Vad 13 is celebrated as Meru Terash. It is the *janma-kalyanak* of Rishabhdev, the first *tirthankar*. Special worship is offered at temples where seven silver pots are placed one above another in the form of a conical pile which is called Meru, and decorated with flags on all sides. This is done following the belief that after his birth, a *tirthankar* is taken to the mound Meru and bathed there by the gods.

Paush Dashmi

Margashirsh Vad 10, called Paush Dashmi (following the *purnimanta* months followed in Marwad), is the *janma-kalyanak* or the birth anniversary of Parshvanath, when devotees chant his *mantras*, and observe *ekasanu* or partial fast, eating only once a day. This *vrata* is performed continuously for ten years after which it is celebrated on a lavish scale.

MUSLIM FESTIVALS

The Sunni and the Shiah are two leading sects of the Muslim faith. Both of them are found in India and in large numbers in Delhi. The Sunnis are those who follow the Sunna or customs set-up by Prophet Mohammed by means of prescriptions, prohibitions and examples, including the recognized pre-Islamic usages, handed down to them by reliable oral transmission. The Shiahs (meaning separatists) separated from the Sunnis and, after the death of Ali, the son-in-low of the Prophet and fourth caliph of Islam, repudiated the first three caliphs-Abu Baqr, Omar and Usman as usurpers. This denunciation of the first three caliphs is the chief difference between Shiahs and Sunnis. Subsequently the Shiahs attributed to the head of their community the knowledge of interpreting the Koran occultly, and held that the occult interpretation of the Koran was known exclusively to the Imams (heads of the community) who had powers to alter the spiritual and temporal law. The Sunnis object to this and hold that the power to make any such change ended with their Imams—Shafai, Abu Hanifa, Malik and Hambal after whom there are four schools of Sunni Muslims called Shafai, Hanafi, Maliki and Hambali, most of the Sunnis in Gujarat being Hanafis. Later, the Shiah Imams acquired a superhuman character as the Shiahs held them to possess divine light. Some Shiahs went so far as to regard Ali and the Imams after him as incarnations of the God head itself. The majority of the Shiahs of this Imam sect who are in Persia, with a following in India, Iraq and Syria, recognize twelve Imams the last of whom Mohammed-al-Muntazar disappeared in 873 A.D. His return is still awaited.

One of the important groups of the Shiahs is that of the Ismailis who broke away over the succession to the sixth Imam, Jafar Sadiq. Most of the Shiahs chose Musi Qazim who was the second son of the deceased Jafar Sadiq as their Imam, while the Ismailis adopted Ismail, the son of his eldest predeceased son as their Imam. The Ismailis remained as one group till 1094 A.D. when, on the death of Al Mustansirbillah they were divided into two parties: those who chose Nazar, the elder son of Al Mutansirbillah as their Imam acquired the name of Nazarians and those who took Al Mustaali, the younger son of the deceased, as their Imam are known as Mustaalians. The Nazarians are represented in India by the Khojas and Mustaalians by the Daudi Vohras. The cause of Nazar, the elder son, was promoted very enthusiastically by one Hasan Sabha, who styled himself as Shaikh-ul-Jabal, Lord or Old Man of the Mountain. Among his successors there was Hasan (1163 A.D., 559, forth in the line, who promulgated his own doctrines and assumed the Imamate himself. His Highness Aga Khan, the Imam of Ismaili Khojas, traces his descent from Ali, through this Hasan.

Khojas are an enterprising business community, whose affairs, religious and social, are managed by regional councils functioning under the supreme council, the word of the Imam being final in all cases. Daudi Vohras also are a shrewd business community. Their leader, both in religious and social matters, is the Head Mulla of Surat. Short of worship, he is treated with the greatest respect and his authority in religious and civil matters is final.

The Shiahs exclude certain passages from the Koran, which they say were written by Usman, the third caliph, and add a chapter in praise of Ali which they contend was excluded by Usman. Their interpretation of the Koran differs from that of the Sunnis. They do not believe in saints. The Shiahs count the month from the last day of the dark lunar fortnight, while the Sunnis count it from the shining of the crescent. The Shiahs pray three instead of five times a day and, in praying, hold their hands open by their sides instead of folding them below the breast as the Sunnis do. To the simple Sunni *kalemah* (profession of the faith) which reads, "There is no God but Allah and Mohammed is His Prophet", the Shiah adds "and Ali the companion of Mohammed is the Vicar of God". The Shah goes on pilgrimage to Shah Najaf, the supposed place of Ali's martyrdom, 198 kms. south-west of Baghdad, and to Karbala to bow the forehead on the mounds of clay there and to drink the holy clay dissolved in water-practices which the Sunnis consider forbidden.

Before the time Pir Dadu (about 1550 A.D.), the form of worship prescribed to the Khojas was daily attendance at the *jamatkhana* or community prayer house and the repetition of utterance of the name Pir-Shah or Shah Pir on a rosary of 99 or 101 beads. Pir Dadu ordered his followers to pray three times a day like the Shiahs and repeat the said name in the prayer. The Khojas pray sitting mentally addressing their prayers to the existing Imam and make prostrations at specified intervals.

Thus, the Sunnis, the Khojas and the other Shiahs, though believers in Islam, differ from one another to some considerable extent in their profession and belief. On account of these differences, some of the festival described below are exclusive features of particular sect. Even so, major festivals like Muharram, Id-ul-Fitr and Id-ul-Zuha are observed by all.

Gyarwin

Gyarwin or the eleventh day of Rabi-us-Sani is celebrated by Sunni Muslims as the birthday of Gawsul Azam Saiyad Abdul Kadar Jilani, a Sufi saint popularly known as Piran Pir (saint of saints) born at Jilan (also called Gilan) in 470 A.H. His father was Abu Saleh Musa Jangidost, a very pious and God-fearing saint, and a direct descendant of Imam Hasan, the grandson of Prophet Mohammed; and his mother Ummul Khair Fatima, the daughter of Abdulla Asoomai, a very devout saint, was descended from Imam Husain, the younger brother of Imam Hasan. In his childhood he lost his father and began to stay with his mother's father who too expired soon afterwards so that his mother took care of him. Up to the age of 11 he continued to acquire religious and worldly education in his native place Jilan. By this time he had developed the habit of telling only the truth and also bearing all troubles with a peaceful mind. Thereafter, as he set out for Baghdad for acquiring higher education, his mother gave him 40 dinars (gold coins) which she sewed to his underwear. He joined a caravan going to Baghdad. On the way, 60 well-armed dacoits looted the caravan. One of the dacoits asked him whether he had anything with him. He said that 40 dinars lay sewn under his armpit. The dacoit thought that the boy was merely joking. Another dacoit asked him the same question some time later and received the same reply. When the leader of the dacoits came to know of this, he sent for the boy and got his garments searched. On finding the dinars, he was astonished and asked the boy why he disclosed about the money when he had hidden it very carefully. Abdul Kadar said that his mother had instructed him never to tell a lie and that he could not disobey his mother under any circumstances. The straightforward and truthful boy deeply impressed the head dacoit who repented his misdeeds, and following their leader, all the dacoits resolved to give up plundering, returned the booty to the caravan and became disciples of Abdul Kadar Jilani. When he reached Baghdad, a heavenly voice forbade him from entering the city, and permitted his entry after seven years. This interval of seven years he passed in the jungles along the Euphrates in meditation, often maintaining himself on leaves or going without any food. This strengthened his patience, fortitude and reliance on God. When he was 18 years old, he entered Baghdad and remained with saint Hammad bin Muslim and acquired from him and from some others very deep knowledge of religious and spiritual secrets.

He was now very devout and passed his time in austerities and worship of God. A true mystic with his heart replete with the love of God, he had no interest in worldly matters. For forty years from the age of 51, (i.e., from 521 to 561 A.H.), he delivered discourses in Baghdad to numerous persons including very learned men who profited much from his contact. He laid stress on the fact that a real Sufi (a mystic) must of necessity be pure of heart, true to God, courteous to the people and obedient to God's commandments meant for the people at large. He preached good behavior and gentility towards men and animals, refraining from every act likely to hurt the feelings of any individual, participating in another's joy without communicating one's sorrow to others, shunning jealously and regulating one's life in accordance with the tenets of religion. He explained that so long as he does not abandon the love of worldly things, a seeker of God is cut off from Him by a curtain. He had attained such spiritual heights and yet was so careful in carrying out all orders of God that all the saints of his time are said to have accepted him as higher than they. This is why he is known as Piran Pir (saint of saints).

He performed many miracles. During a time of scarcity, he once gave about 9 kgs. of wheat to one Abul Abbas Ahmed, with instructions to keep the foodgrains in a closed vessel, keeping only a small gap from which to take out the quantity needed. Abul Abbas Ahmed and members of his family continued to use the wheat for as long as five years. Once when the wife of Abul Abbas opened the vessel to see how much wheat remained, she found the same quantity as was originally placed in it. Thereafter, the balance lasted the family for only a week. When the story was narrated by Abul Abbas to Piran Pir, the latter said that the wheat would have lasted forever, had the vessel not been opened.

Again when there was a heavy flood in the river Euphrates and the waters were rising higher and higher, the people of Baghdad approached Abdul Kadar Jilani and requested him to save them. He went to the bank of the river and pointing his staff towards it asked it not to rise beyond its limits. The waters immediately receded to their ordinary level. Some of his other miracles illustrate his power over natural elements like rain, faculty of memory, spirits like genii and even the power of bringing a dead fowl to life.

He is the founder of the mystic (Sufi) order called Qadariya which is known for its philanthrophy, piety and humility. He had 27 sons of whom eleven carried on his work and with other disciples, spread his teachings in other parts of western Asia and Egypt. The head of the order and the keeper of his tomb at Baghdad is a direct descendant of his. He died at the age of 91 years in 561 A.H. and his tomb at Baghdad is visited by numerous pilgrims every year. There are his *chhillas* or shrines at several places in Gujarat.

On the 11th of Rabi-us-Sani, meetings are held in mosques and elsewhere, in which his preachings are recalled and his merits recounted. In Delhi the Sunni Muslims light even or twenty-two lamps in their houses. Some rich persons hang frames resembling leafless trees, with eleven lamps therein, called *mehdi* and cover them with presents of fruits and sweets for children. *Malids* (a sweet preparation of wheat flour) is taken on the occasion of this feast.

Id-E-Milad and Bara Wafat

Id-e-Milad is the day of the birth anniversary and Bara Wafat is the day of the death anniversary of Prophet Mohammed. Both these events occurred on Monday, the 12th of Rabi-ul-Awwal, the third month of the Hijri year previously known as the year of Amulfil. Prophet Mohammed was born as a posthumous child at daybreak on 22nd April 571 A.D. in Mecca. The name of his father was Abdulla and that of his mother Amina. According to a legend, when he was born, his head was bowed in veneration to God and when he lifted the head he uttered *'La ilaha illallaho wa inni rasulullah'* (There is no God but Allah and I am His prophet or messenger). At the age of six he was taken by his mother to Madina (then called Yasrab) but on her way back to Mecca she died when he was seven years old. Thus, left an orphan at a very early age, he was looked after by his grandfather Abdul Muttalib who too died two years later, leaving him to the care of his uncle Abu Talib alias Abde Manaf (the father of Ali, known as *Shere Khuda* or the Lion of God).

When he was still a boy of about ten years, Mohammed used to remain in contemplation of God and, when called upon by other boys to go to play, he used to say that man was created not to play but to do good deeds. When he grew up, he had a very sweet and attractive tongue, and in his dealings with people he showed absolute honesty so that he began to be known as *'al-amin'*, i.e., the honest. At the age of 25, he married a 40 year-old widow named Khadija. The only child of his that survived was Fatima who, at the age of 15 years, was married to Ali, the son of Abu Talib. At this time, the practice of slavery was deep-rooted in Mecca. He struggled hard to abolish this evil and released a slave named Zaid, the son of Haris, who was a slave to his wife's cousin, without taking any ransom and married him to a suitable girl. Other evils like fighting to death over trivial matters, excessive drinking and gambling with even women and children at stake, plundering, etc, were rampant and women were looked upon with contempt and had no right or voice in any matter. The ignorant Arabs buried new-born girls alive, drove away widows into jungles, ate carrion and there was no law or order of any kind. Mohammed spent 15 years in serving people and in praying. At the age of 38 he began to hear voices from the invisible and to have dreams that came true. He frequented the cave of mount Hira where he spent several days together in meditation and supplication to God.

From the age of 40 onwards, the Prophet began to receive *vahi* or God's commandments sent to him through angel Jibraeel (Gabriel), which he received at intervals over a period of 23 years. The orders received from God from time to time have all been incorporated in the Koran and details of certain matters not to be found in it are available in Hadis (traditions), which together form the full code of conduct for a Muslim. Some members of his family were the first believers in Prophet Mohammed's teachings and gradually others were also enlisted in the Islamic faith. In the beginning, however, the Meccans, who could not understand the message, oppressed those few who had embraced Islam and planned to murder Mohammed. In the meanwhile, the Prophet who was advised by God to leave Mecca managed to reach Madina and this event is known as *hijrat*, which marked the commencement of the Hijri era. Many persons in Madina joined the Prophet who carried on his mission of preaching the principles and requirements of Islam undauntedly and tirelessly. In his dealings with people he showed much humanity and nobility. Though he became famous and powerful, his successes did not change his noble qualities. He was very kind to his servants as if they were his children. He gave food and clothing to whomsoever came to his house and sat on the bench placed near it. Children were very dear to him; he played with them. The most important of his injunctions were:

(i) Believe in the Almighty as the only God and in Mohammed as a Prophet of God.

(ii) Pray to God five times a day.

(iii) Be kind to the poor and give them alms.

(iv) Keep fasts during the month of Ramzan.

(v) Finances permitting, make yearly pilgrimage to the holy city of Mecca.

Numerous miracles are recorded as having been performed by the Prophet. Once an army of 1,400 persons was in great hardship for want of water. As soon as the Prophet placed the end of his forefinger on the grounds a stream of water sprang forth and there was enough water for all. Again 1,000 persons were once fed by the Prophet to their satisfaction out of only four seers of barley bread and yet the stock of bread did not diminish. Joseph Gaer says, "After the death of all the great leaders of the past, their followers related wondrous miracles about them. There are the *Jatakas*, the birth legends, of the Buddha. There are the tales of miracles about the birth, life and death of Moses, Zoroaster and Jesus. But about none of the religious leaders of the past are there so many legends of miraculous happenings as about Mohammed. In Arabia, in Persia, in China and in every land where Mohammed's teachings have followers there are books of legends about the Founder of Islam".

The Prophet died on Monday the 12th of Rabi-ul-Awwal at the age of 63 years. Islam, having been placed on a firm footing, spread far and wide over the globe in subsequent years.

In Delhi the Muslims celebrate the birth of Prophet Mohammed on the 12th of Rabi-ul-Awwal every year. Alms are distributed to the poor, *qasidas* (verses in praise of the Prophet) are recited and meetings of Muslims and non-Muslims are organized, where lectures recounting the Prophet's virtues and preachings are delivered. Holy relics such as hair of the Prophet's beard or his foot-prints (where they have been preserved) are exposed to public gaze with great veneration. It is in carrying out the instructions given by the Prophet through the Koran and the traditions established by him that the real celebration of the occasion lies. As the day of Id-e-Milad is also that of the death of Prophet Mohammed, Muslims recite *fatiha* (the opening chapter of the Koran) and pray for the peace of his soul giving some food, particularly rice cooked in milk, to the poor.

Id-ul-Fitr or Ramzan Id

Id-ul-Fitr popularly called Ramzan Id is a festival celebrated on the first day of Shawwal, the tenth month of the Hijri year since the time of Prophet Mohammed. *Fitr* means breaking the fast or refraining from fasting, while *Id* means happiness. The festival thus marks the end of the fasts kept during the preceding month of Ramzan. Muslims regard this month as one of great bounty from God. The texts of previous scriptures were revealed by God to various prophets who preceded Prophet Mohammed, viz., Ibrahim (Abraham), Moosa (Moses), Dawood (David) and Isa (Jesus) in Ramzan. The Koran revealed by God to Prophet Mohammed also began to be revealed in the month of Ramzan and the whole of it was fully revealed by stages in twenty-three years. Muslims practice self-denial throughout this month by abstaining from eating, drinking, smoking, chewing, snuffing or smelling anything whatsoever throughout the day, i.e., from before dawn till sunset. In addition to the usual prayers offered five times a day, i.e., in the morning before sunrise, soon after the noon, in the afternoon, just after sunset and at night (about 2 hours after sunset), special additional prayers are recited by them every night in Ramzan. Mosques are illuminated with intense devotion to Allah, the Almighty God, during the entire month. It is believed that there is one night hidden among the Ramzan nights, which is known as a night of power, Shab-e-Qadr or Laylat-ul-Qadr when prayers and devotion to God earn religious merit equal to one thousand times that of during any other night. God showers His mercy and blessings on all who pray to Him during that night. No one knows for certain which particular night in Ramzan is Shab-e-Qadr but the general belief is that the 27th night following the 26th fast in Ramzan is the night of power and is spent in prayers, devout supplication to God and meritorious and charitable deeds calculated to earn the pleasure of God. The Daudi Vohras observe the night of power on 23rd Ramzan, keeping awake, offering prayers and giving charity.

As soon as the month of Ramzan is over and the crescent on the western horizon heralds the advent of the day of Id-ul-Fitr, the Muslims celebrate it (the first day of Shawwal) as a day of thanksgiving to God for having enabled them to successfully perform the austerities. They clothe themselves in new and costly garments, eat sweet dishes, greet one another and rejoice in a mood of relaxation after the self-denial practiced in Ramzan. As a token of thanksgiving to God, each Muslim gives to the poor 3 kgs of wheat or 6 kgs of barley or its value in cash or any other kind of foodgrains of that value. This charity is prescribed for every Muslim and also for all the members of his family. It is called *sadaqah* which is usually given before going to the special prayer of Id. Some sweet thing, usually sweet milk with dry-dates and *shev* cooked in it, is taken before going for the Id prayers. The special additional prayer is offered some time after the usual morning prayer and takes place in *idgah* (the place built for offering prayers of Id-ul-Fitr and Id-uz-Zuha) which is an open air mosque outside the town, having a stone of cement pavement higher than the adjoining ground by about four feet, and a wall with a small turret at each end on the western side. In the *idgah* there is a pulpit with three to five steps rising from the pavement near the wall for preaching sermons immediately after the prayers. Those who do not go to the *idgah* offer the Id prayers in the Jama Masjid or any other mosque in the town. After the Id prayers and sermons are over, those present shake hands, and some of them, particularly the elders, embrace one another. As they do so they congratulate one another on the occurrence of Id. Some money is given by all to the poor who wait outside the *idgah* or other place of worship for alms. After returning home from the prayers every Muslim gives some money to the children in his house who are dressed in new and colourful clothes. At a convenient time during the Id day, one goes to the residence of elders, relatives, friends and well-wishers for congratulating them on the day of Id. The visitor is treated to some sweets and children accompanying him are given some money to be spent as they think best. Those who are not able to visit their relatives, friends and others on account of long distance, send decorative greeting cards containing Id felicitations, good wishes and prayers.

Besides putting on good clothes, many use scents and perfumes on the Id day; dainty and delicious dishes are prepared and children are taken to the market for the purchase of toys and other articles of their choice. The day is spent in feasting, praying and receiving wishes and making presents. All look and feel gay and happy. Id is such an occasion for merriment that a fast on that day is strictly forbidden. All the Muslims, whether Sunni or Shiah, celebrates this festival with much gaiety and fervour, the only difference between the Sunnis and the Shiahs being that the latter celebrate it a day earlier and do not go to the *Idgah*.

Id-uz-Zuha or Bakri Id

Id-uz-Zuha or Id-ud-Duha popularly called Bakri Id or Id-e-Baqr is a day of thanksgiving to God by means of sacrificing to Him some animal like a goat, sheep, camel or bull on the 10th of the month of Zilhijja, the twelfth month of the year which is considered propitious for pilgrimage to Mecca. The practice of sacrificing an animal to God dates back to the time of Prophet Ibrahim (Abraham) who lived long before Prophet Mohammed. Ibrahim who had no son prayed to God for a son when he had attained a very old age. God was pleased to accept his prayer and a son was born to his wife who was also old. As he was begotten in the old age of his parents, as a result of special prayer, the son who was named Ismail was very dear to his father Ibrahim. When Ismail was a boy, his father had a dream for three consecutive nights to the effect that it was God's desire that the boy should be sacrificed to God. Both Ibrahim and Ismail were devout worshippers who would never go against God's wishes. When, therefore, the father told the son about the commandment of God, the latter advised his father to carry it out, adding that he would find him patiently resigned to God's wish at the time he was sacrificed to Him. Both of them went out to a jungle and as Ibrahim was running a knife across the throat of Ismail, with closed eyes, uttering *Bismillah, Allaho Akbar!* "In the name of Allah, God is Great!," a heavenly voice congratulated him for carrying out God's mandate though it was really difficult and asked him to open his eyes and see what was before him. Ibrahim found his son Ismail alive and quite uninjured and in his place, he saw a sheep lying sacrificed. Ibrahim felt very grateful to God. This occasion is commemorated by all the Muslims as Bakri Id. Whether they are in Mecca for pilgrimage or anywhere else in the world, the Muslims sacrifice a goat, sheep or any other animal to God on this day. At Mecca the sacrifice is offered in the valley of Mina near Mecca as it was in Mina that Ibrahim had offered his son in sacrifice. Others do so at their own places.

Before offering the sacrifice, all Muslims go to the *idgah* or any big mosque for the *namaz* (prayer) of Id, after the close of which, two sermons are read from the pulpit to all the worshippers, as is done after the prayers of Ramzan Id. The Id prayers are offered sometime after the usual morning prayers. The contents of the sermon on each of the two Ids are appropriate to the particular Id. A partial fast is observed on that day from early morning till the Id prayers are offered and worshippers return home and sacrifice the animal earmarked for the purpose, which has been well fed and taken care of during the preceding period. From the 10th to 12th of Zilhijja all animals may be sacrificed on any day (but not night) though it is preferable to do so on the 10th. The animal offered as sacrifice must be free from all bodily defects and, in the case of a small animal like a goat or a sheep, must not be less than one year or more than five years of age. Two or more persons cannot sacrifice one and the same goat or sheep but the cost of a big animal like a bull or a camel can be shared by seven persons, i.e., they can jointly sacrifice one big animal on behalf of all of them. At the time of sacrificing the animal an Arabic verse in the Koran is recited which means, "Verily, I turn my face to that Being Who has created the heavens and the earth and I am His obedient follower and not one of the ungrateful. Verily my prayers, my sacrifice, my life and my death belong to God, the Lord of both the worlds, Who has no partner. This is what I have been bidden and I am the first of those who have resigned themselves to God" and it is added "Oh, God! everything is from and for You". The meat or flesh of the animal sacrificed is distributed among friends, relatives, and the poor, a small portion being retained by the person sacrificing it for use by himself and his family members. According to the Koran, neither the flesh nor the blood of an animal sacrificed to Him reaches Him but the piety and the virtue (underlying the notion of carrying out His commands) alone reaches him.[1]

The sacrifice of Ismail offered by Ibrahim at the command of God teaches all to place the love of God above everything else, to which sentiment this festival of prayer and sacrifice is dedicated.

Muharram

The first month of the year according to the Hijri calendar is Muharram in which, according to the saying of Prophet Mohammed, unbounded righteousness and reward are secured by offering prayers to God. The Prophet said that it was on *ashura*, the tenth day of this month, that God created the heavens, the oceans and the mountains and also the first man and prophet called Adam and the subsequent prophets Ibrahim or Abraham, and Isa or Jesus. Although the exact year in which resurrection or *qayamat* will take place has not been revealed by God to anyone, the Prophet has said that it would occur on a Friday falling on the tenth of Muharram.

The significance, however, attached to this festival is in memory of the martyrdom of Husain, the second son of the Prophet's daughter Fatima, to serve the cause of truth and justice. Husain was born in the year 4 A.H. and was killed at Karbala in the year 61 A.H. He passed the first seven years of his life with his grandfather, Prophet Mohammed, the next thirty years with his father Ali, the subsequent ten years with his elder brother Hasan and during the last ten years of his life he was the head of the house of Bani Hashim to which the descendants of Ali belonged. The story leading to his martyrdom is given below.

Historical Background: Hasan, the elder grandson of the Prophet, was lawfully entitled to become the *Khalifa* or the governor and protector of the Islamic domain after Ali. In order to avert internacine strife, he entered into an agreement with Amir Muaviyah to the effect that the latter should be the *khalifa* during his lifetime. Amir Muaviyah agreed that, after his death, his heirs would have nothing to do with the *khilafat* or the rights and duties connected with it and that the office would vest in whomsoever was elected by the Muslims for the purpose. Amir Muaviyah did not abide by the agreement and during his life time and after the demise of Imam Hasan, he decided after, his death, his son Yazid would be the *khalifa*. When Muaviyah died, Yazid usurped the *khilafat* and called upon all Muslims to swear allegiance to him. Imam Husain, the younger brother of the deceased Imam Hasan, declined to do so, to protect the rights of the Muslims to elect a *khalifa* and to prevent the *khilafat* from passing to despotism and dictatorship as Yazid was a despotic king of the house of Bani Umaiyah of Syria and did not belong to the house entitled to the *khilafat*. In addition to this fundamental objection to the acceptance of Yazid as a *khalifa*, there was another reason why he could not be so accepted. He was quite unfit to hold the responsibilities of *khilafat* as he had succumbed to such grave vices as drinking and gambling. When the people in Kufa, an important centre of Islam having many followers of Ali, came to know that Imam Husain had protested against the usurpation of the *khilafat* by Yazid, they requested him to come to Kufa from Madina where he lived, and assume their leadership. Imam Husain deputed a relative named Muslim, son of Akil, to Kufa where the people promised him that they would remain faithful to Imam Husain if he came to Kufa. On receiving word to this effect, Imam Husain started for Kufa with all of his members of his family and relatives. Yazid came to know of this and appointed his cousin Ubaidullah as the Governor of Kufa. Ubaidullah got Muslims murdered and indulged in many tyrannical actions against the fickle people of Kufa who could not withstand the oppression of Ubaidullah and joined him against Imam Husain who had to encounter the forces of Ubaidullah in the vicinity of Kufa. Ubaidullah stationed men along river Euphrates flowing at some distance so that Imam Husain and his companions might not get any water to drink. In the meanwhile, Ubaidullah was pressing Imam Husain to declare allegiance to Yazid. Imam Husain and his followers went through all the ordeals firmly and patiently but categorically refused to accept Yazid as the *khalifa.* The tortures to which Imam Husain and members of his family were subjected by Yazid before he was killed by Shimr are heart-rending. Even the young baby of Imam Husain, known as Ali Asgar, was slain. "The children and women of the noblest house on earth deceived, deserted and tortured with thirst; the child's arms; streched forth for the blessing of the Imam lopped at the wrist; the babe shot in its father's arms; the noblest and bravest leader of Islam trusting to no weapon but to the justness of his cause, betrayed and surrounded; his choice of death to dishonour; his lonely last onset; his wounds, his death, his mutilation, all these miseries caused not by an ememy of the Faith but by a kinsman, a former friend and fellow champion. Oh the pity of it ! The pity of it !"[1] This martyrdom has immense significance for Islam. If Imam Husain and his small band of 72 persons had surrendered to Yazid instead of sacrificing their lives for the cause of truth, Yazid would have extirpated Islam from the face of the earth and its followers would have been stamped with the seal of wickedness and meanness.

Mourning: These tragic horrors of the plain of Karbala are commemorated by the Muslims the world over during the month of Muharram in which they occurred. Of the two principal sections of the Muslims, viz., the Sunnis and the Shiahs, the Sunnis believe that after the death of Prophet Mohammed the three *khalifas*, Abubakr, Umar, and Usman were lawful successors of the Prophet before Ali, the fourth *khalifa,* came to the *khilafat.* The Shiahs, however, contend that the three *khalifas* before Ali were usurpers defrauding Ali of his right to the *khilafat*. As Imam Husain was the son of Ali whom both the Sunnis and the Shiahs regard as a lawful *khalifa,* the month of Muharram particularly the first ten days are observed by Muslims of both these sects, as a period of mourning. Unlike the Sunnis, the Shiahs (who include Daudi Vohras) extend the period to forty days of which the first ten are a time of special mourning and on the tenth of the succeeding month of Rajab they repeat dirges and offer prayers for the souls of Hasan and Husain. The Shiahs feel the keenest grief and practise self-denial, observe Muharram as a period of mourning during which they sing elegies, keep fasts, offer prayers and recite *fatiha* and other portions of the Koran for the peace of the souls of Imam Hasan and Husain and consider Karbala as a place of pilgrimage. Mournful elegies and dirges known as *marsias* describing in appealing verses the tyranny perpetrated by Yazid against Husain and his family members before putting them to death and the unflinching patience, perseverance and fortitude shown by Husain and others who died in Karbala rather than surrender to untruth and the greedy usurpation of *khilafat* by Yazid are sung also by the Sunnis some of whom observe fast in Muharram and go through other forms of prayers for the peace of the souls of the martyrs of Karbala.

Tazias: In most of the big cities, towns and villages inhabited by Muslims in India there is the annual practice of taking out a procession of *tazias* through the principal streets to a river or, where there is no river, to a lake or a tank in which the *tazias* are immersed. The making of *tazias* dates back to the time of Amir Timur who invaded India in 1398 A.D. After returning to Samarkand from a pilgrimage to Karbala, he built in 1400 A.D. a miniature model (called *tazia*) of the tomb of Husain. He did this with the intention of accentuating the mourning during the first ten days of Muharram. *Tazia* is a Persian word meaning weeping, beating the breast and expressing grief. It was usual to weep and grieve from olden times but the system of taking out *tazias* originated in Timur's time. On account of the Mogul influence, some Hindus also began to participate in this, to prepare *tazias*, themselves and to have faith in them. *Tazias*, also called *tabuts* (coffins), are made of bamboo and tinsel and represent the shrine of Husain at Karbala. Rising above a projecting base, there are two or more storeys in a *tazia* which is crowned with a dome, the whole structure standing on four short legs. The work of tinsel around the wooden framework contains exquisite designs and gives it an appearance of a beautiful piece of architecture. It takes about a month to complete the structure of a *tazia*.

Individuals prepare *tazias* at their own cost if they have taken certain vows but generally the cost of *tazia* is met by contributions made by the people of one word or community. Thus, in a single town or city, there are many *tazias* scattered over different localities. The *tazias* are kept in the houses of the owners and, in some cases, in mosques for several days and, on the night of the 9th of Muharram, they are taken round the principal streets. Some persons who take vows send avowed offerings to the place where the *tazia* is made when the person making the *tazia* recites *fatiha* (first chapter of the Koran), breaks a coconut and distributes the juice with *sherbat* or milk in small cups to those present. If a vow has been taken to perform some act of penance or self-torture, the person who has taken the vow watches the *tazia* sanding for a night or more in a corner keeping vigil for the whole night, goes wherever the *tazia* is taken stopping where it stops. Such vigil is performed generally on the night of *shahadat* (martyrdom), i.e., 9th of Muharram, popularly known as *katal-ki raat*. On the 10th day, people who have kept vows come to the resting palace of *tazias*, offer coconuts, *agarbattis*, etc., and some money to the owner who rolls on the ground before his *tazia*. At the appointed time each of the *tazias* is taken out on its way to a river or tank (popularly called *karbala*). Each is accompanied by a band sounding plaintive tunes and gigantic drums producing grave sounds. At a certain place all the *tazias* join together, one after another, forming a continuous procession accompanied by numerous devotees. There are trucks carrying gymnasts and acrobats who display their feats to the people who gather in large numbers to see the procession passing, waiting for hours in the balconies or verandahs of houses, or on the pavements on both the sides of the roads or lining either side of its route. The processions in big cities like Delhi are accompanied by decorated vehicles (trucks) containing large vessels of *sherbat* or cold water for the thirsty. At various places in cities, towns and villages, arrangements for supplying *sherbat* or cold water are made. Water is sprinkled on the roadways along which the *tazias* are to be taken to *karbala* or the place of immersion. This is done in memory of the hardship experienced by Husain and his companions who suffered the pangs of thirst continuously for three days before death. High poles having swords at their tops are also carried with the procession. The swords are known as *zulfiqars*, after the name of the sword of Ali, who was known for his bravery, and has been called *Shere Khuda* or the Lion of God. Ali's son Husain also showed commendable bravery in fighting the foe at Karbala and the *Zulfiqars* carried with the procession are emblematic of his courage. With the procession taken out on the 10th and even during the preceding nine days, some persons play tigers, after painting their bodies with stripes, etc., like those of a tiger and putting on a mask of tiger's face, nails and even a tail.

Burrak: Burrak, each having the body of a horse but the face of fairy and two wings, are also prepared of wood and tinsel and moved about by persons who put on the structures round their own bodies by placing themselves the hollow in the middle of each *burrak*. Being the celestial creature which carried Prophet Mohammed to the seat of God on Shab-e-Meraj or the Night of Ascension, the *burrak* is taken by some to be symbolic of the ascension to God of Imam Husain who died a martyer while in prayer.

Passing through many principal streets, the procession at last arrives at *karbala*, i.e., river or tank where the *tazias* are immersed in the water of the river or the tank and the devotees disperse. Only very small *tazias* costing about two rupees each, purchased ready-made by persons in fulfilment of their vows, are made to drift away with the current of water. These are sometimes buried in the bed of the river or tank. Big and costly *tazias* are brought back to their places after water is sprinkled on them so that the wooden structure is utilized in subsequent years by decorating it with fresh tinsel every year. The silver *tazias* are kept in safe custody and used every Muharram.

Dulas: During the first ten days of the month of Muharram, some persons who have taken a vow to do so, play the role of *dula* or bridegroom. This practice is connected with the belief that when the martyrs of Karbala were besieged and hemmed in within their camp, a marriage between Kasim, the youthful nephew of Husain, and Sakina, the daughter of Husain, was prevented by the slaughter of the bridegroom. Some Muslims in the Deccan are said to have come into possession of the cast shoe of the bridegroom's horse, which was brought to India as a relic from Karbala and is supposed to have something of the bridegroom's sprit and is known as Nal Saheb or Lord Horseshoe. The holder of Lord Horseshoe is believed to receive the spirit (called *hal*) of the bridegroom into himself. In Gujarat, a fire is kindled in a pit which is dug to a depth and width of a foot. The person who has taken a vow to become a *dula* (bridegroom) goes round the fire seven or eleven times. a silver or iron rod two to three feet long ending in a massive crescent or horseshoe and covered on all sides with peacock feathers is placed before burning incense. If the man moving round the fire or any of his friends notices the bridegroom-spirit moving the devotee, the rod is waved with the feathers fanning him gently by moving it up and down near his face. The people standing round the *dula* keep up a chorus of "*dula, dula, dula*...." to the measure of which the devotee sways in increasingly violent oscillations. When he is filled with the full power of the spirit his eyeballs turn up and get fixed in a stony stare and his body becomes cold. He is then made to keep his face buried among the peacock feathers. The spirit seizes him after some time and he rushes out heedless of water or fire. As he starts rushing, one of his friends holds him from behind, supporting and steadying him, and guiding his aimless impulse to the *akhadas* or places of other *dulas* and *tazias*, where fresh incense is burnt before his face. On his way from place to place, women pray for the blessing of children or the casting out of an evil spirit. The *dula* directs that a flower may be picked from the jasmine garlands that deck his shoe-rod and this secures a son to the woman praying for one. The *dula* falls to the ground senseless when he returns to his own place or *akhada* and regains consciousness after an hour or two. Only those who have vowed to be *dulas* can become possessed.

Fire-Walking: At some places, Khojas, who are Shiahs, prepare *khandaks* (trenches), each about 10 to 12 feet long 2 to 3 feet deep and fill them with fire which is kept burning for the whole day from morning to night feeding it constantly with logs of wood. This ceremony is performed on the 7th, 8th and 10th of Muharram in memory of the fire trenches dug round their camps in Karbala to protect the families of Husain and his companions from sudden onslaught by the enemy, believing that only the pious persons remain unhurt by fire. About 10 o'clock at night the leading mourners take bath at the mosque and start for the place where *khandak* is burning, carrying *panjas* or replicas of human hands. They cross the trenches full of burning charcoal bare-footed, reciting dirges bemoaning the sad death of Husain but remain unhurt by fire. In this ceremony they are followed by others present who participate in this ceremony irrespective of age. After the ceremony, a procession is taken out between 11 p.m. and 3 a.m. headed by standard-bearers carrying the *alams* (standards or poles) mounted with the *panjas* or replicas of the human hand, made of gold, silver or copper. They remind the devout of the cruelty perpetrated by Husain's enemies who mercilessly cut off the hands of Abbas when he was returning with water from the river Euphrates, for the thirsty children of Husain and his companions. Such processions are taken out again on the 20th of the next month Safar, i.e., 40 days after 10th of Muharram.

These practices are outward expressions of the profound grief felt by the Muslims during Muharram, at the tragic martyrdom of Husain which stands alone in its unparalleled pathos. It is said that prior to the advent of Islam, when Iranians were the followers of Prophet Zoroaster, they used to mourn over the innocent and tragic death of Prince Siavakhsh, the son of King Kai Kaus, and when they embraced Islam they accidentally found another hero, greater in their esteem and affection, in the respected and beloved grandson of their prophet. The death of Imam Husain at Karbala is one of the most tragic events in the history of Islam about which Gibbon says, "In a distant age and climate the tragic scene of the death of Hussain will awaken the sympathy of the coldest reader".

Indeed, Hussain appeals to humanity at large irrespective of caste, creed and colour. The immortal voice of truth that went forth from Karbala has reached distant corners of the world and will continue ringing through ages.

Shab-E-Barat

Shab-e-Barat, which means the night of assignment, is the fifteenth night of Shaaban, the 8th month of the Hijri year. It is believed that on Shab-e-Barat the share and fortune of every individual including every unborn soul are fixed and registered in heaven. It is also a belief that on that night the tree called *sidratul-muntaha,* each leaf of which contains the name of one person, is shaken and persons whose names are registered on the leaves that fall down meet their death in the following year. This festival is also connected with the memory of the dead relatives whose souls are believed to visit their surviving relatives on this particular night.

On the occasion of Shab-e-Barat, special prayers are offered after the sunset prayer, praying for longevity, good health and freedom from indebtedness. The Almighty is moved with reference to the verse in the Koran in which He says that He annihilates whatever He wills and sustains whatever He wills, and He is beseeched to avert all calamities like earthquakes and wars whether known or unknown to the devotee, and to grant him good luck and maintenance. The whole night is spent in prayers as it is believed that God through His angels continuously invites His creations, the human beings, to bring to Him their difficulties by the following questions from sunset to daybreak:

(i) Is there anyone asking for my pardon so that I may pardon him?

(ii) Is there anyone asking for maintenance so that I may grant him maintenance?

(iii) Is there anyone asking for health so that I may grant him health?

(iv) Is there anyone asking Me to remove his difficulties so that I may remove them?[1]

It is the practice to visit graveyards on this night and there to recite some portions from the Koran and pray for the peace of the departed souls.

Delicious food like *halwa,* a sweet preparation, is prepared and distributed to the poor and the friends. Some let off fire-works on this night. Fasts are also observed by some both on the 14th and the 15th of Shaaban.

As Fatima, the daughter of Prophet Mohammed, was married to his cousin Ali on the 15th of Shaaban, the Daudi Vohras celebrate it as a day of rejoicing with sweets and by letting off fire-works. Special prayers are also offered at mosques on this day.

Shab-E-Meraj

The 27th of Rajab, the seventh month, is celebrated by the Muslims as the Night of Ascension on which Prophet Mohammed was seated on a heavenly creature called *burrak* and taken to all the seven heavens by the angel Jibraeel (Gabriel). The angel could not accompany the Prophet beyond the heavenly tree called *sidratul-muntaha* so that the Prophet went alone on a throne of light to the seat of God, called *arsh.* Here numerous heavenly secrets were revealed by God to the Prophet who, on return to the *sidratulmuntaha,* came back to Mecca in company with the angel. During his journey, the Prophet met many departed prophets and saw a large number of heavenly places and objects which ordinary mortals cannot see. In Delhi Pious Muslims keep an all-night vigil on 27th Rajab, passing it in prayers, devotion and reading and meditating on the Koran and on the next day observe a fast.

OTHER MINOR FESTIVALS

Sunnis

In addition to the common festivals mentioned above, the Sunnis celebrate the 13th of Safar, the second month, in commemoration of the recovery of Prophet Mohammed from a severe sickness on that day. This day is popularly called Tera Tezi or Talan Tezi on which day parched gram and molasses are eaten. The last Wednesday of the month of Safar, called Akhari Char Shamba, is also observed by some Sunnis who prepare sweetmeats and enjoy a feast in the fields and gardens outside the town in memory of the Prophet's recovery from a dangerous disease.

Shiahs

Besides keeping major festivals like Muharram, Id-ul-Fitr and Id-uz-Zuha in common with the Sunnis, the Shiahs also observe the following additional festivals.

The 27th Muharram is sacred to the Daudi Vohras as the famous saint Fakhruddin, a descendant of Raja Tarmal, became a martyr on that day near Galiakot in Rajasthan at the hands of certain barbarians. The saint's tomb in Galiakot is visited by many in fulfilment of vows taken.

The 20th of Safar is observed by the Daudi Vohras as the Chehlam (40th day after death) of Imam Husain who was buried at Karbala on that day. They keep mourning in remembrance of the martyr and feed the poor.

The Daudi Vohras celebrate the 4th of Rabi-us-Sani as the birthday of Imam Maulana Taiyab, the 26th Imam among the descendants of Prophet Mohammed. Dressed in new clothes, they arrange large gatherings and community dinners. The 20th of Rabi-us-Sani is also celebrated by the Daudi Vohras as the birthday of Mazun Saheb, Saiyadi Mohammedbhai, the heir apparent to Vada Mullaji, the Head of the Vohra community, by holding meetings and community dinners.

On the 10th of Jamadi-ul-Awwal, the death anniversary of Fatima, the daughter of Prophet Mohammed and mother of Imam Husain,they recall the good deeds done by her and feed the poor.

The 27th of Jamadi-us-Sani is the death anniversary of Sayyedna Kutbuddin, entombed at Ahmedabad, who was arrested and put to torture resulting in his death in the time of Emperor Aurangzeb. Many Vohras from long distances visit the tomb of martyr on this day when food is served to the visitors and the poor are fed in large numbers.

13th, 14th and 15th of Rajab are called Ayyamul Biz when the Daudi Vohras observe fasts. On the last of the three days, they meet at noon in the mosque to offer prayers to God.

Ali, the fourth Caliph, was wounded on the 19th of Ramzan (9th month) and died on the 21st of that month These two days are kept as holy days by the Shahs who give food to the beggars and pray for Ali's soul on both the days.

Among the Daudi Vohras, the 27th of Zilqaad is a day of rejoicing as it is the birthday of their Vad Mullaji or religious Head, Dr. Sayyedna Taher Saifuddin. All the members of the community, attired in good clothes, assemble to felicitate him. Functions like community dinners are also held and sweets are distributed to children.

18th of Zilhijja, the 12th month, is an important Shah holiday called Id-e-*Ghadir*, the lake holiday. On this day, the Prophet who was sitting near a lake announced that Ali was his own flesh and body. The Shiahs interpret the Prophet's announcement as meaning that he desired Ali to be appointed as his secular and spiritual successor.

The Shiahs also observe the 28th of Zilhijja as a sacred day and rejoice for three days as the *khalifa* (caliph) Umar was murdered on that day by Baba Shujauddin Abu Lulu, a fireworshipper converted to Islam. For as stated above, the Shiahs consider that Umar (the second *khalifa)* was one of the three usurpers who defrauded Ali of his right to succeed the Prophet as the first *khalifa.*

Ismaili Khojas

While the Ismaili Khojas, who are Shiahs, observe the common Muslim festivals, their main festivals are the 11th March, the Imamat Day or the day of Takht Nashini (Accession to the throne or gadi of the holy *imamat*) of His Royal Highness Prince Karim Aga Khan, the 49th Imam of the Ismailis, and 13th December which is his birthday.

These festivals are celebrated with religious devotion, rejoicing and thanksgiving. His Royal Highness the Aga Khan is competent to change the date of celebration of accession to the throne of *imamat*.*

Christian Festivals

In modern times the Christian religion has three main sects, viz., Roman Catholic, Protestant and Eastern Orthodox. The Eastern Orthodox section includes the Syrian (Jacobite and Mar Thoma) churches, which are very strong in Kerala. Among Protestants, there are at least seven different churches, which, though different from each other, work in cooperation on friendly terms, and indeed several of them are taking part in the present negotiations for merging numbers of Protestant churches into one single "Church of North India." They all differ widely in their practices from the Roman Catholic church, but differ less widely from one another.

One of the most striking differences between Roman Catholics and Protestants is in the matter of worship. The ceremony most frequently observed by Roman Catholics is the Sacrifice of 'Mass', which is conducted in Latin. The Protestant churches do not celebrate Mass at all, but celebrate instead the Sacrament of 'the Lord's Supper' (also known as 'Holy Communion'), which is conducted in the language actually spoken by the worshippers. The Protestant churches celebrate the Lord's Supper only at intervals of a month, or sometimes several months; while the Roman Catholic Church celebrates Mass on every Sunday and every festival, and the Roman Catholic priests actually celebrate it everyday. Therefore, on a festival, when members of both the sects gather for worship in their own church buildings, whereas the Roman Catholic celebration will almost always take the form of Mass, the Protestants will not necessarily have the corresponding observance of the Lord's Supper. Very often the Protestants will hold an ordinary service instead of the Lord's Supper. The word 'service' in this sense means a meeting, at which a minister of the church presides and hymns are sung, prayers are offered to God, passages from the Bible are read, a sermon is preached by the minister, and the members who are present give offerings of money to support the work of the church. So, among Protestants, the normal way to celebrate a festival is to have a service of worship; and on certain special occasions (for example, at Easter) the Sacrament of the Lord's Supper is also observed during the service. The service, whether with or without the Lord's Supper, is always conducted in the Language actually spoken by the people.

In the matter of celebrating Christian festivals there is not much difference between the various Protestant churches, and there are only minor variations among them. But there is one Protestant church (namely, the Church of India, Pakistan, Burma and Ceylon, also known as the Anglican Church because it took its origin from the Church of England) which observes a larger number of festivals than the other Protestant churches. The reason for this is that this church is accustomed to using a printed Prayer Book in which directions are given for observing a large number of festivals by worship-services with special prayers and readings. The other Protestant churches, however, do not use that Prayer Book. The Anglican Church normally observes, for example, the period of Advent leading up to Christmas, the period of Lent leading up to Easter, and such days as Trinity Sunday (commemorating that God is Father, Son and Holy Spirit, the Trinity 'Three in One') and the memorial days of various saints; whereas these are not very widely observed by the other Protestant churches.

The festivals observed by Protestant in India are the same as those observed by all Christians (i.e., Roman Catholic churches, Protestant churches, and Eastern churches) throughout the world. Similarly, most of the religious festivals observed by the Roman Catholics in India are the same as those celebrated by Catholics all over the world, and have scarcely any variation as regards the manner of their celebration.

Christian festivals are nearly all related to the life of Jesus Christ, and commemorate its outstanding events like his birth, death, resurrection and ascension into heaven.

Ascension

Christ continued to show himself in visible form to his disciples for a period of forty days after his resurrection. But after forty days, when he had promised that he would send his Holy Spirit to them, he ascended upto heaven, and a cloud hid him from their sight. In Delhi this event is remembered by Christians on the festival of the Ascension, which falls always on a Thursday, exactly forty days after Easter. It is the last Christian festival recalling the events of Christ's life on earth. This festival is celebrated by only a few Protestant congregations. That day at Mass in Roman Catholic churches, the Paschal Candle, which is kept burning throughout Eastertide, is extinguished after the reading of the Gospel, to express that Christ's physical presence on earth was discontinued.

Christ King

The festival that closes the year for Roman Catholics and which is celebrated with more exterior solemnity by them in India is the Kingship of Christ on the last Sunday of October. That day every Catholic community in India organizes a solemn procession carrying the Blessed Sacrament through the streets in the resplendent monstrance, amidst lighted candles and the singing of hymns. In many places the route is strewn with flowers or little children shower petals on the Blessed Sacrament.

Christmas

The first festival season, therefore, is the Christmas season, also called Natal, which is concerned with the birth or Nativity of Christ. In Delhi this extends through the month of December, especially the latter part of the month, the two chief days being Christmas Eve (24th December) and Christmas Day (25th December) which is celebrated as the actual birthday of Christ, and which is observed as a public holiday. Boxing day, the 26th of December, is a sectional holiday. The period preceding Christmas, i.e., from the beginning of the month till 25th December is called Advent. Among the Protestants, Advent is celebrated by the Anglican Church, in accordance with its Prayer Book, but is much less observed by the other churches.

Apart from the markets being decorated for the festive season, The religious observances of this season include the customary decoration of the inside of church buildings with gaily coloured flags, lanterns and lights. A popular form of decorations, both in church buildings and in private homes, is a bright star, which commemorates the unusual star which appeared in the sky at the time of the birth of Christ, and which was seen by the 'wise men' from the Eastern countries who went to Bethlehem to give precious gifts to the child Jesus soon after his birth. Some Christians also like to keep in their homes a little model of the stable in Bethlehem where Jesus was born, showing the child lying in the straw in the manger, with the figures of animals standing nearby, and also Mary, the mother of Jesus, with Joseph her husband. A special feature of the Christmas season is the singing of Christmas carols (songs about the birth of Christ), and it is customary for parties of Christians to go out at nights and visit one another's homes to sing such carols, especially on Christmas Eve. Roman Catholics and Protestants alike share in the common tradition of singing Christmas carols, i.e., special songs celebrating the coming of the Saviour to the world in the form of a child. This tradition has come from Europe; and these carols are sung Western tunes. Then on the morning of Christmas Day special services of worship are held in all churches. In these services the hymns, prayers, Bible-readings and sermons are naturally all centered on the story of Christ's birth. In some churches it is the custom, during the Christmas morning service, for members to bring forward 'white gifts' (that is, for example, money in a white envelope, or any gift wrapped in white) and hands them to the minister for the support of the church's work . In some churches, also, it is the custom to bring little children to be baptized during the Christmas service. Since at Christmas, Christ came to earth as a little child, Christmas has come to be specially the 'children's festival'; and it is, therefore, appropriate that children should be baptized on that day, thus being made members of the Christian Church.

As regards the special observances, it is traditionally a time of great rejoicing for all Christian people. People get new clothes, put up decorations in their homes, and prepare special sweets and other delicious food. Absent members of Christian families make special efforts to come home for Christmas; and all Christians like to have a holiday from their work, from Christmas Eve right through the following week until New Year's Day. Feasts are held on Christmas Day usually in the home of each family, but in certain villages the congregation has the custom of holding a common feast on that day for all the members. Another notable feature of the season is the exchanging of greetings and good wishes. This is done by word of mouth, when friends meet one another on Christmas Day; but it is also done very extensively by sending Christmas cards by post, especially to relatives and friends who may be far away. Christmas cards flood the mails those days, and there is no lack of Christmas cards, tastefully designed with Indian motifs by Indian artists, many of whom are Christians themselves. In fact, Indian Christmas cards are greatly appreciated abroad. Moreover, it is a widespread custom that Christians show their love for one another by giving gifts at Christmas. One of the aspects of the festival which is specially enjoyed by children is the receiving of gifts from their parents and friends. The popular legend of Father Christmas (an old man with a white beard, dressed in a red cloak and hat, who is supposed to go round the world at Christmas time, bringing gifts for children) has been introduced to India from Europe and America. This legend actually originated from St. Nicholas, the Russian saint who lived in the fourth century and who used to give gifts to poor children at Christmas time. The name Santa Claus, by which Father Christmas is often known, is a corrupted form of the name Saint Nicholas. In accordance with this tradition Christians often try to help the poor at Christmas time by giving them food, clothing or money. We may also mention another tradition which has been brought in from Europe, namely, Christmas trees, which Christian families set-up in their homes, hanging on them coloured lights, and candles, and parcels of gifts which are to be given on Christmas Day. Another type of observance in which children sometimes take part, at the Christmas season, is the performance of little 'Nativity plays', that is, short dramas, enacting the story about the birth of Jesus Christ which are found in the Bible.

For the Catholics, Advent is the period of preparation for the celebration of the birth of Christ and is solemnly observed. The Church vestments used in this season are purple, a colour suggesting penance, and the feeling that dominates the prayers is one of expectation and hope: hope that the Saviour announced by the Prophets will come to the world to redeem man from his sins.

At the end of this season of Advent, there comes the celebration of Christmas. On that day, since the birth of Christ is believed to have occurred at midnight, the daily Sacrifice of the Mass is not offered in the morning as usual, but at midnight between 24th and 25th December. The midnight Mass is often celebrated in the open air for the benefit of the hundreds of villagers who come for the occasion from all the villages around. The church compound is gaily decorated with lights, green leaves and flowers. Before the midnight Mass, the crowd enjoys a religious drama, staged each year in turn by the people of one of the village. Carols are sung throughout the Christmas season (25th December to 6th January) both in church and at home at Christmas parties.

Every Catholic home also puts up a crib inside the house and an illuminated star in a prominent place outside. The crib is a representation of the sense of the Nativity or the birth of Christ: the Child Jesus lying in a manger, between his mother Mary and Joseph; and an angel from heaven appearing to the shepherds, and hosts of angels singing the Christmas message to the world— "Glory to God in the highest and on earth peace to men of good will".

Various presents are placed on a richly decorated tree (usually the branch of a fire tree or an imitation) and distributed in a party among those attending it. Such parties may be organized for family and friends or may be part of a 'Social'—a Christmas party. There will always be one specially organized for children and also for the poor, that they too may share the joys of Christmas.

Easter Sunday

The dates of many Christian festivals have to be calculated by counting backwards or counting forwards from the date of Easter, which is the principal festival. Easter itself is always the first Sunday after the full-moon which happens upon, or next after, the twenty-first day of March; and if the full-moon happens upon Sunday, Easter Day is the Sunday after. This day normally falls somewhere in the first three weeks of April, but it can sometimes fall as late as April 25th, and can sometimes fall as early as March 22nd.

Early in the morning on the first Easter Day, Christ rose from the dead and showed himself to several of his disciples; and during a period of forty days after that, he repeatedly met his followers at various times and places. Easter, being the day of his resurrection, is an occasion of great joy for all Christians. In Delhi as in India it is the custom to put up gay decorations in all church buildings. Some congregations hold a Sunrise Service, because it was in the early morning that Christ's resurrection took place, and in some congregations this service is held outside in the open air, where the members can actually watch the sun rising. Then, in all churches, the chief service of the day, at which there is a very large attendance, is held at about 8 or 9 a.m. In a number of churches it is customary to observe the Sacrament of the Lord's Supper during this service. In some churches Easter is a day when Christian parents bring their children to be baptized by the pastor. Also, in those churches where meetings are held every night during the Holy Week, a final special meeting will be held on the evening of Easter Day. At all these services there is an atmosphere of great joy and thanksgiving, and the resurrection of Jesus Christ is the principal subject of the hymns, prayers, Bible-readings and sermon.

The social customs connected with Easter are not as many as those connected with Christmas. It is, however, an occasion of general rejoicing for Christians and the following day, Easter Monday, is often also celebrated as a holiday. Many people send Easter cards to their relatives and friends.

Among Roman Catholics, the celebration of Easter Sunday starts with the Easter Vigil the night before. In memory of the resurrection of Christ, who is the 'light of men', there is first the festival of lights. This consists in the blessing of the new fire and the blessing and lighting of the 'Paschal Candle', from which each one lights his. The Paschal Candle represents Christ, and the candles that the people hold in their hands represent the light they have received from him. The festival of lights is followed by the festival of water, i.e., of Baptism, by which the Christian is made to share spiritually in the new life brought by Christ's resurrection. Finally, at midnight, the sacrifice of the night is offered amidst the joyous pealing of bells and the singing of the 'Alleluia'.

In some parts of India, the three Catholic church services corresponding to the three days of Maundy Thursday, Good Friday and Easter Sunday are also held in the open air, due to the great crowds that attend them. People wish each other a 'Happy Easter'.

Good Friday

The Friday in Holy Week, being the actual day of Christ's death, is known as Good Friday, and for Christians it is the most solemn day of the whole year. It is a public holiday. Most Christian churches hold a special service in the morning. Many churches also hold another service lasting from 12 noon till 3 p.m.—those being the three hours during which there was darkness while Christ was hanging on the cross until he died. At this three-hour service it is a common custom for the people to think specially about the 'Seven Words', that is, the seven sayings which Jesus Christ uttered at various times after he had been nailed to the cross. As Good Friday is such a solemn day, some Christians in Gujarat fast for the whole day. In Roman Catholic churches, the death of Christ on the cross is commemorated by the singing of 'Passion' (the story of the crucification and death of Christ) and by the unveiling and veneration of the cross.

In addition to the above-mentioned observances on the Sunday, Thursday and Friday of Holy Week, the custom has been established in many parts of India that Christians gather together for special meetings in the evenings on everyday during Holy Week. Special sermons are delivered at these meetings, and many congregations invite a preacher from some other place to come and give a series of sermons, night after night.

Holy Week

This is the last week Lent, immediately preceding Easter. It is the time when Christians specially remember the events which took place during the last week of Jesus Christ's earthly life, and in particular his sufferings (which are referred to as his 'Passion') and his death.

Lent

'Lent' is the name given to the period of 40 days leading up to Easter observed as a commemoration of the 40 days which Jesus Christ spent in the wilderness, fasting and meditating and encountering temptation by Satan, in which Jesus was victorious over Satan. The tradition is that during this period Christians ought to practice special self-discipline, for example, by fasting, and by penitence for their sins, and by seeking to take their own share in Christ's suffering. But as a matter of fact, in Gujarat, the church of India, Pakistan, Burma and Ceylon is the only Protestant church which normally observes the period of Lent. The prayer Book, which is used by that church, includes directions for services to be held on the first day of Lent (known as "Ash Wednesday", because of the ancient custom when people sprinkled ashes on their heads on this day as a sign of penitence) and on each of the Sundays which occur during Lent.

For the Roman Catholics, Easter, though not as popular and colourful as Christmas, is the most important festival, as it celebrates important events in the life of Jesus Christ directly connected with the redemption of man, viz., his death and resurrection. Indeed, it is the biggest feast of the liturgical year, as it commemorates the resurrection of Jesus from the dead, which has been called "the central fact of history." The resurrection of Christ as promised by him restored the faith, courage and morale of his followers who were disheartened by his crucifixion. They then carried the message of Christianity to all parts of the world, on which mission, St. Thomas, one of the twelve apostles of Christ, came to India. Resurrection is not merely a historic fact, but, understood spiritually, it represents the victory of truth over falsehood, and light over darkness. It shows that even death was not the final word in the struggle of Christ, but, as the Eastern hymn puts it, "Death and Life were locked together in a fearful struggle; the Lord of life who was dead now reigns alive". The resurrection of Christ, therefore, "gives new hope to man, it is a pledge of our own over all that brings death". Even in the darkest hour of despair, it enables the true believer to look forward to a triumph over suffering. Christ showed by the resurrection that "suffering could be transcended", for Good Friday on which he was crucified, was not the end, but was followed by Easter Sunday when he rose again. The event emphasized that "in suffering is concealed with tremendous intensity, the world's power of ascension", and "upon it rests the whole body of Christian morality and sociology".[1]

Preceding as it does the anniversary of this most significant event of Christ's life, Lent is a period of prayer and penance. The most popular practice of this period is the Way of the Cross, a devotion which consists in recalling fourteen different 'stations' or happenings in the Passion of Christ

Maundy Thursday

Accounts can be found in the Bible of what Jesus did on each of the days of the Holy Week, but apart from Palm Sunday, the two most important days are Thursday and Friday. On Thursday evening Jesus and his twelve disciples met together for a meal the Last Supper. He washed the feet of each of the disciples, thus setting them an example in humility and service, saying to them, "If I have washed your feet, I who am the Master and the Lord, you in your turn ought to wash each other's feet." He also gave them bread to eat and wine to drink, saying, "Do this in remembrance of me" thus instituting the Sacrament of the Lord's Supper, which Christians still observe by taking bread and wine after offering special prayers. Later on Thursday night Jesus was arrested by the Jewish authorities. During the night he was tried and condemned to death. Early on Friday morning the Jewish chief priests got the permission of the Roman Governor to have Jesus executed, and on the same day he was crucified, and died in the afternoon, after which his body was buried.

On the Thursday of the Holy Week-that being the day when Christ instituted the Lord's Supper—some Christian churches observe the Lord's Supper.

In Roman Catholic churches, the highlight of the day is the celebration of the Mass, which is itself a memorial of that event. The typical feature of the Mass is that, in the course of the ceremony, the priest washes the feet of twelve persons, usually children.

New Year

The beginning of the calendar year on 1st January has no connection with any special event in the life of Christ, and thus cannot be called a Christian festival in the same sense as Christmas or Easter. In India people like to celebrate this festival in gay spirits and come out in large numbers to markets and eating joints to revel in the festivities. It is widely celebrated by Christians in many lands, and the fact the New Year's Day comes only one week after Christmas has caused it to be taken as part of the same general holiday season. In some parts of India it is a sectional holiday. The end of the old year and the beginning of the new one is naturally a time when people look both backwards and forwards. They look back to the past with thanksgiving to God for the joy and successes they have experienced and with penitence for the sins they have committed. And they look forward to the future, asking for God's help and protection, and resolving to live a better life than they have lived hitherto.

Many Protestant congregations hold what is called a 'Watch Night Service' on New Year's Eve (31st December), beginning at about 11 or 11.30 p.m. The service includes special prayers in which, as explained above, the worshippers look back to the past year and forward to the year that is about to begin. The central point of the service comes at midnight, when the New Year actually starts. The service ends with a rededication of the people's lives to the service of God in the future.

Then, at about 8 or 9 a.m. on New Year's Day, another big service of worship is held in the church building. Here again there are special prayers, hymns, etc., and the minister gives a special sermon appropriate to the occasion. The people also make a point of greeting all their friends and relatives, to wish them a happy and prosperous New Year. There is a growing custom of sending New Year cards in the same way as Christmas cards are sent. Many Christians like to make some 'good resolutions' at New Year time, making up their minds that with God's help they will carry out certain things which they believe life wants them to do. On New Year's day there is an opportunity for Christians to visit one another and put an end to any misunderstandings or quarrels that may unfortunately have arisen between them during the previous year.

The New Year seasons, like that of Christians, is a time of general feasting and rejoicing.

Palm Sunday

The first day of Holy Week is Palm Sunday, so called because on that day Jesus Christ made his triumphal entry into the city of Jerusalem, riding on a donkey. While his disciples walked with him, the common people welcomed him by cutting branches from Palm trees and waving them in the air or spreading them on the ground before him, shouting for joy. A number of children came into Jerusalem with Jesus on that day, and went with him to the temple, where they shouted and sang. Therefore, it is now a custom in some places for Christian children to go in a procession to the church building on Palm Sunday, carrying palm branches and singing hymns of praise. And in many places even if no such procession is held, it is the custom to use palm branches to decorate the church building; and at the worship service held on that day, the hymns, prayers, Bible-readings and sermons are on the subject of the events of the first Palm Sunday.

The Roman Catholics also re-enact the event in a ceremonial procession, carrying palm branches and acclaiming the Messiah: "Blessed be he who comes in the name of the Lord".

Pentecost

The word 'Pentecost' is derived from the Greek word which means 'Fiftieth'. This festival falls on the fiftieth day after Easter (the tenth day after Ascension Day), that is, on the Sunday seven weeks after Easter. It was on this day that the Holy Spirit came upon Christ's followers in Jerusalem, in accordance with Christ's own promise. From that time onwards the Holy Spirit has been given to all those who believe in Jesus Christ; and He (the Holy Spirit) dwells in their souls, to inspire and guide and strengthen them. Therefore, at the services held in Christian churches on the day of Pentecost each year, Christians give thanks for the coming of the Holy Spirit; and the hymns, prayers, Bible-readings and sermon are concerned with Him (the Holy Spirit).

Weekly Sunday

It is appropriate to mention here that the reason why the early Christian believers chose Sunday as the weekly day for Christian worship was that Christ rose from the dead on that day. Therefore, in fact Christians celebrate Christ's resurrection not only once a year on Easter Day but every week on Sunday, which is the 'Weekly Easter'. The Sunday was instituted very early in the Christian era to keep alive the hope of his 'return in glory to judge the living and the dead'. Every congregation of each church holds a worship-service on Sunday morning, and some congregations hold a second service in the evening too. In addition to the services, each congregation holds a Sunday School at some convenient time on Sunday. This is arranged so that children can be taught about the Bible and the Christian religion; and in some places adults as well as children attend and receive instruction. The teachers of classes in the Sunday Schools are volunteers, both men and women. Sunday is the weekly feast day for all Roman Catholics, which they observe by participating in the sacrifice of the Mass and abstaining from work.

Other Minor Festivals

In addition to the various festivals described above, various special Sundays are celebrated at different dates by different congregations of the Protestant churches in India. These special days are not connected with any particular event in the life of Christ, and they are not necessarily observed on any fixed date or by all congregations.

Bible Sunday

The people's thoughts at the services on this day are specially centred on the Bible, which of course has a very important place in the Christian religion. Prayers are said on behalf of the Bible. Society which produces and sells copies of the Bible, and offerings of money are given to support its work.

Children's Sunday

At the services on this day children from the Sunday School perform songs, dances, Bible-readings, recitations and religious dramas; and the sermon is specially addressed to children.

Harvest Festival Sunday

This is observed specially in village congregations in South Gujarat. After the harvest has been safely reaped, the Christian farmers gather together in the church building to give thanks to God for His blessing on their work, and they bring with them gifts of grain, vegetables, fruits, etc., which are afterwards sold, and the proceeds used for the work of the church.

Hospital Sunday

At the services on this day, there is special thought about the healing of the sick and the work of hospitals. Prayers are offered for God's blessing on this work, and the offerings of money which are given at the service are sent for the support of such work. In places where there area Christian hospitals, Hospital Sunday is a very important day in the church, and people often bring gifts of equipment which can be used in the hospital, and doctors and nurses take part in the conducting of the service.

Youth Sunday

Young men (and women) read passages from the Bible at the services on this day, and lead the congregation in offering prayers and singing hymns, and the sermon is specially addressed to young people.

Week of Witness

This is a special week (usually in February) which is observed by most of the Protestant churches, in obedience to the command which Christ gave to his disciples after his resurrection from the dead: 'Go forth to every part of the world, and proclaim the Good News to the whole creation'. Everyday, during this Week of Witness, Christian men, women and children go out in groups into cities and villages. By singing Christian hymns, by preaching, and by selling copies of portions of the Bible, they endeavour to make known to their fellowmen the Good News of Christ's life, teachings, death and resurrection.

The following Saints Days are particularly remembered in the Church's calendar. They are:

St. Andrew	November 30
St. Thomas	December 21
St. Stephen	December 26
St. John the Divine	December 27
Holy Innocents	December 28
St. Paul	January 25
St. Matthias	February 24
St. Mark	April 25
St. Philip and St. James	May 1
St. Barnabas	June 11
St. John the Baptist	June 24
St. Mary Magdalene	July 22
St. James the Great	July 25
St. Bartholomew	August 24
St. Matthew	September 21
St. Michael and All Angels	September 29
St. Luke	October 18
St. Simon and St. Jude	October 28
All Saints	November 1

For all the Festivals and special days mentioned above, proper forms of service are appointed for Churches.

PARSI (ZOROASTRIAN) FESTIVALS

The Parsis are a unique ethnic and religious group of the people , particularly of the western part of India. They are descendants of a band of Zoroastrians who first sought refuge in India after they had to leave Persia in consequence of the defeat of the Sassanian King Yazdezard by the Arabs in the battle of Nehawand in 641 A.D., when some Iranians who wanted to save their faith set sail towards India. They came to Sanjan, 120 kms. south of Surat. According to one opinion it was at Diu in the Saurashtra peninsula that they first anchored and after passing nineteen years there proceeded to Sanjan. The traditional date for the landing of Parsis at Sanjan is Shravan Sud 9, V.S. 772, i.e., 716 A.D. According to another opinion the year was V.S. 992 (936 A.D.). When they sought permission of Jadirana, the local Yadava ruler, to settle there, the latter laid down the following five conditions:

(i) He would ascertain that their religious practices were not objectionable.

(ii) They should adopt the local language, Gujarati, as their mother-tongue

(iii) Their women should adopt the costume the Hindu women of the region.

(iv) They should not bare arms, and

(v) They should hold marriages in the evening.

On their agreeing to these conditions, their request for asylum was granted. A pillar called Kirti Stambh set-up at Sanjan in 1920 commemorates this event. Six hundred years after the Parsis settled at Sanjan, they were driven away from that place by a general of Alauddin Khilji (1295-1315 A.D.). At that time, they took their sacred fire *Atash Behram* with them to the hills about 13 kms. east of Sanjan. After remaining in hiding for twelve years, they settled in Bands with the sacred fire which they carried with them wherever they went. Subsequently, a magnificent fire temple was built by them in Navsari in which they kept the sacred fire for about 250 years. Then there was a dispute leading to a quarrel between the priests of Navsari and those who had come there from Sanjan. In 1733 A.D. the Sanjan priests, taking their fire with them, went to Surat but returned to Navsari three years later. In 1741 A.D. they went to Bulsar for a year and on 28-10-1742 moved to Udwada where the original Sanjan fire has since been enshrined. Udwada has since then been the place of pilgrimage for all the Parsis who, from all over the country, visit it for worship at this most important firetemple. Situated on the Mumbai-Baroda main broad gauge line of the Western Railway, it is 183 kms. north of Mumbai and 87.5 kms. south of Surat. It is on the seashore and has a salubrious climate. There are some excellent modern hotels for the pilgrims.

On the decline of Surat as a port and the rise of Mumbai, many Parsis from Surat district migrated to Mumbai and settled there. Parsis are a fair-skinned, enterprising, good-humoured and strictly endogamous race. Most the Parsis in the India live in south Gujarat, though they are to be found in other districts of Gujarat also particularly in urban areas. Besides their main occupation of business and service, they pursue agriculture and are found scattered in villages of Surat district. Some are excellent garden cultivators reputed for raising beautiful roses, particularly in the northern proximity of Mumbai.

Parsis are called fire-worshippers by some, but in fact they are God-worshippers and follow the Zoroastrian faith which lays great stress on righteousness in thought, word, and action. Their scriptures are known as the *Zend Avesta*, or the translation of the *Avesta* or sacred texts. Their ancient Iranian culture resembled in several respects that of the Aryans of yore. Of the two sects., viz., Shahenshahi and Kadmi, the former predominates in India. The difference between the two sects is that the calendar of the Kadmis is one month ahead of the Shahenshahis as the latter abandoned the practice of adding an intercalary month after the completion of 120 years.

Gahambars

These are seasonal festivals celebrated six times a year and held in high esteem by the Parsis. 'Gahambar' means 'proper season time'. Animate objects have to depend upon the timely onset of the seasons for their prosperity and well-being. Seasons were originally marked by the Gahambars. Each Gahambar is celebrated for five days, when the Parsis meet as a fraternity, offer to God prayers and thanks for His six principal creations as also for the six seasons, and join in a common feast.

The first Gahambar, called Mediozarem or mid-spring, takes place from the 11th to the 15th of Ardibehesht, the second month, when heaven is believed to have been created. The second Gahambar called Medioshem or mid-summer lasts from the 11th to the 15th of Tir, the fourth month, when water is traditionally believed to have been created. According to tradition the earth was created from the 26th to the 30th of Sharivar, the sixth month, which are the days of the third Gahambar named Peteshem or the in-gathering. The fourth Gahambar is Yathrem or summer's farewell, lasting from the 26th to the 30th of Meher the seventh month, when according to tradition the trees were created. Mediarem or mid-winter is the fifth Gahambar lasting from the 16th to the 20th of Deh, the tenth month, when animals were created. The sixth Gahambar is known as Hamaspethmedem or winter's farewell and is celebrated to commemorate the creation of man, during the last five days of the year, which are in addition to the twelve months each having thirty days, so as to complete a year of 365 days.

In Delhi as in other parts of India a single individual or a group of Parsis can celebrate a Gahambar. They may offer food, money, wine or anything in kind or cash. They give alms and food to the needy to show their gratitude to God for His bounteous gifts of nature.

Gathas

In the Parsi calendar, the year has 12 months of thirty days each, making 360 days in all. Five extra days are, therefore, added at the end of the twelfth month Aspandad so as to make up a total of 365 days to correspond with the time of the earth's revolution round the sun. These five days are named after the five holy *Gathas* which are hymns composed by Prophet Zoroaster himself. The names of these Gathas are Ahunvad, Ushtavad, Spentomad, Vohukhshathra and Vahistoyast, respectively. Unlike other days, these five days have no names either after the Holy Amshaspands (immortal furtherers) or the Yazads (the Worshipfuls). As they are named after the holy hymns of the prophet, they are also held sacred. These five days together with the last five days of Aspandad, the last or twelfth month, in all ten days, are held sacred for the *muktad* (*muktatma* or released soul) and indicated for the ceremony in honour of the dead. In Gujarat, the *muktad* days are generally seventeen, as the first seven days of the first month of the new year are also added to the ten days.

A brick platform or an iron or brass stand is raised in a neat and clean place in the house. Many brass or silver or glass vessels filled with water are arranged on this stand. Fruits are placed near them and flowers are laid on and near them. A lamp burns continuously day and night near the platform and at night many lamps are lighted. Sandalwood and incense are burnt in an urn; rich food is placed near the platform; and ceremonies are performed in honour of ancestors and dead relatives whose souls are believed to visit the homes of their family during these days. The last of the five hymn days was formerly called Pateti or Day of Penitence but the New Year's Day is subsequently treated also as such. The seventh day Amardad of the first month Farvardin is the last of the seventeen days of *muktad,* when the souls of the dead which come to this world on the first *muktad* day return to the other world. On this day, known as Amardad Sal, Parsis formerly used to go to gardens and celebrate a feast for thanking God on the completion of the *muktad* days.

Jamshedi Navroz

Jamshedi Navroz is celebrated on the twenty-first of March, the day of vernal equinox, when the sun enters Aries. This Navroz is distinct from the Navroz of Farvardin which marks the beginning of the year according to the Parsi calendar. While Jamshedi Navroz is always determined according to the Gregorian calendar, the New Year's Day is fixed according to the Parsi calendar. According to a legend it was Jamshed, the third king of the Peshdadian dynasty of Iran, who fixed this day as the New Year's Day, and celebrated it by performing a *jashan* as a token of offering thanks to Ahuramazd (Almighty God) for His mercy in giving bountiful crops and for welcoming the advent of sunny spring after the chilly winter. The Kadmi Parsis known as Iranis celebrate Jamshedi Navroz more enthusiastically than the Shahenshahi Parsis. The calender of the Kadmis runs one month ahead of that of the Shahenshahis and their festivals (other than Jamshedi Navroz), therefore, occur a month earlier on account of the Shahenshahi Parsis having abandoned the practice of adding an intercalary month to the Parsi year after the completion of 120 years. Both the Kadmi and the Shahenshahi Parsis observe the Jamshedi Navroz on 21st March according to the Gregorian calendar as it is related to a solar phenomenon.

That this Navroz (New Year's Day) was founded by King Jamshed is believed to be merely a popular myth by some as it does not find any mention in the *Avesta* and Pehlavi scriptures of the Zoroastrians. It is said that on the recommendation of Omar Khayyam, King Jalaluddin of Iran introduced Navroz popularly known as Navroz-i-Jalali, as it was convenient to do so for the purpose of collecting revenues. Navroz, therefore, commences a fiscal year and not a religious year. *Ain-e-Akbari* records that Akbar the Great had adopted this festival of Navroz or the New Year of the ancient Persians, and that is was "celebrated with feasting for nineteen successive days, during which time immense sums of money and valuable articles" were distributed.

In any case, the Parsis of India celebrate it as a day of great significance by going to the fire-temple and offering prayers to Almighty Ahuramazd, and visiting friends and relatives to exchange greetings.

Jashans

A *jashan* is a festival of Parsis fixed for celebrating an important event by offering prayers to God the Almighty, when four priests knowing the major portion of the Zoroastrian scriptures by heart recite it orally without committing a single mistake. The event may be joyful or melancholy. A *jashan* performed on the death anniversary of a person is called the *jashan* in his honour, a *jashan* performed to celebrate the Independence Day would be called the *jashan* of Independence Day, and so on. Among the Delhi Paris it may be performed not only at a fire-temple, but also in any place like a room in the house, which is clean and pure. Fruit, flowers, milk and *sherbat* are the articles used at a *jashan,* fruit and flowers symbolizing the vegetable kingdom, and milk, the animal kingdom, while *sherbat* is a source of exhilaration and joyful attitude of mind. All these articles are offered to God and distributed among relatives and friends after the ceremony conducted by the priests is over. On rare occasions, community dinners are arranged by collecting contributions from the participants.

A specific day in each month is indicated for celebrating *jashan*. Seven of the thirty days of a month in the Parsi calendar are named after Ahuramazd and six Amshaspands, the Holy Immortals; twenty days are named after the first twenty of the twenty-three Yazads, the Worshipfuls; and the remaining three days (viz., the eighth, fifteenth and twenty-third days) have names derived from those of the ninth, sixteenth and twenty-fourth days. Seven of the twelve months of the year also named after Ahuramazd and the six Holy Immortals and the remaining five have names of Yazads, the Worshipfuls. The day of the month having the same name as the month is treated as a holy day when the high priest, the other priests and the leading Parsis congregate in the hall of the fire-temple carrying trays of fruit and flowers before them. One of the priests feeds the fire-urn with sandal and frankincense. All recite hymns of praise and thanksgiving in honour of the guardian angel of the month. On the completion of prayers, the fruit are handed round enabling all present to taste them. This ceremony is called a *jashan* or a feast. Seven of the days having names of months are observed as *jashan* days. The first of these is called All Souls' Day or

Farvardin Jashan falling on Farvardin, the 19th of day Farvardin which is the first month of the Parsi year celebrated in honour of all the *Frohars* or *Fravashis,* believed by some to be the souls of the dead. Others believe them to be guardian spirits each of whom is in charge of a human soul, alive or yet to be born. On this day Parsis go to the Tower of Silence, offer prayers for dead relatives and friends and hold *jashans* in the yard around the Tower of Silence.

In Delhi as in other parts of India A ceremony of this kind with the same object and called by the same name (i.e., All Souls' Day or Farvardin Jashan) is also performed on Farvardin the 19th day of Adar, the ninth month.

The sun feast called the Meher or Meherangan Jashan falls on Meher, the 16th day of Meher, the 7th month. This *jashan* is very popular in Iran where the sun or sun-angel was held in high esteem at one time. The victory of Faredun over Zohak and some others of the most memorable events in ancient Persian history are believed to have taken place on the day of this *jashan*. Worship of light and observance of truth and brotherhood are associated with this *jashan.*

Avan, the 10th day of Avan, the 8th month, is a sacred day when the Avan Arduisur Jashan is performed in honour of the Water Spirit or the angel presiding over water. On this day, Parsis go to the sea-shore, a river-bank or a lake and pray to the water-angel. Coconuts, sugar and flowers are offered to the sea, river or lake. Those who have vowed to do so if they gain prosperity, make *poli* (sweet cake) and send some of it to friends.

The fire feast or Adar Jashan falls on Adar, the 9th day of Adar, the 9th month, when the Parsis go to the fire-temple with offerings of sandalwood and pray before the fire. Adar is the angel presiding over fire and is likened to the son of God. Fire is pure, removes filth and sustains life in cold regions. It is, therefore, honoured as the son of God, as if it were His representative and is believed to be the source of all happiness, strength and protection. Besides praying in the local fire-temples, many Parsis go in the month of Adar to the fire-temple at Udwada which is their only place of pilgrimage and to which many Parsi devotees from all over the country repair with faith and devotion. On the Adar Jashan, well-to-do Parsis distribute money in charity to the poor Parsis and priests.

The Bahman Jashan falling on the 2nd day of Bahman, the 11th month, is performed in honour of the animal guardian. Special kindness is shown to animals who are served with fodder, milk, etc., throughout this month. Dogs are also fed well. Devout Parsis shun meat, beaf or other flesh throughout the Bahman month or at least on 2nd, 12th, 14th and 21st days of it as they are sacred to Bahman, the animal guardian.

The Aspandad Jashan falling on the 5th day of Aspandad, the 12th month, is the earth *jashan*. A *jashan* is performed on this day to remind one of the protection afforded by the earth which sustains houses, fields, etc, and which grows foodgrains, fruits, etc., and for thanking God for the gift of the bounties of the earth to mankind. It is also known as the *jashan* of agriculturists. On this *jashan* every Parsi family brings from its priest some dry sand, purified by him by reciting certain prayers over it and a piece of paper with the following text in Pehlavi written on it in red: "By the name of the Creator Ahuramazd, on the day Aspandad of the month Aspandad, I close the mouths of all hurtful animals, evil spirits *devs,* perverting spirits, *darujs,* sorcerers, elves, oppressors, the wilfully blind, the wilfully deaf, evil-doers and robbers. I do this in the name of Ahuramazd, of the valiant Faredun, of the Testar Star, of the Sataves Star, of the Vanant Star and of the Haptairing Star". The sand is sprinkled in the house and the paper is fixed on the main door as it is the belief that by doing so reptiles and other harmful insects would remain away from the house. According to the book of customs called the *Rivayats,* storax, horn of cattle, frankincense, wild rue and cotton seeds were formerly fumigated in the house so as to ward off biting reptiles and obnoxious creatures. In addition to these, the horns of cattle and the beaks of cocks and other birds were painted with scarlet colour, signifying thereby the birthday of animals and birds.

Five other *jashans* are performed on the following days in Delhi.

(i) Ardibehestt Jashan is performed in honour of Ardibehesht Amshaspand who presides over fire, on the third day of Ardibehestt, the second month, by offering prayers in the fire-temple.

(ii) Khordad Jashan is performed in honour of Khordad Amshaspand who presides over water, on the sixth day of Khordad, the third month.

(iii) Amardad Jashan is in honour of Amardad Amshaspand who presides over vegetation and is performed on the seventh day of Amardad, the fifth month.

(iv) Sharivar Jashan falls on the fourth day of Sharivar, the sixth month, and is performed in honour of Sharivar Amshaspand who presides over metals and is the lord of wealth.

(v) Deh Jashan is performed in honour of Ahuramazd, the Creator, on the 1st, 8th, 15th and 23rd days of the tenth month named Dae or Deh.

Khordad Sal

Khordad Sal is celebrated on the 6th day named Khordad of the first month Farvardin of the Zoroastrian calendar, the birth anniversary of the prophet Zoroaster. His parents lived in the town Azerbaijan, west of the Caspian Sea. The name of his father was Porushasp of the Spitama clan and that of his mother Dughdova. The year of his birth is not known definitely and placed by various opinions in 660 B.C., 1000 B.C. or even 6000 B.C. by some Greek historians. It is said that when he was born, Durasan, the chief magician of Iran, began to tremble in great fear and, with the assistance of three other magicians, caught hold of the child and placed it on a great fire but the child played happily in the midst of the flames as if in sprays of water from a fountain. When babe Zoroaster was unhurt by the flames of fire, Durasan and his assistant magicians placed him in the middle of a highway where a large herd of cattle was to pass. The cow heading the herd, however, stood over him till the herd had passed away and thus saved him. The magicians, thus frustrated in their evil plans, placed the child in a den of wolves but they got fixed to the ground and could not move. Angels in the form of two goats are said to have fed the child in the den.

When Zoroaster was seven years old he was sent away to study under Burzin-Kurus known for his wisdom throughout Persia (Iran), with whom he studied religion, farming, cattle breeding and healing for eight years. For the next five years, he healed the wounded during the invasion of Iran by the Turanians and helped the sick and the poor during the famine following the war. He then married a girl named Havovee and for ten years more he went on serving the people. Subsequently he went to Mount Sabalan for meditation and after passing a long time there he came to the conclusion that there is only one omnipotent God Ahuramazd, "the creator of the universe, the giver of good, the hearer and answerer of prayer", Who created two forces, one Good and the other Evil, which rule this world. He returned from the mount ready to teach his religion to the people of Iran. At that time impiety, cruelty and black magic were rampant in Iran. He preached that good thoughts, good words and good deeds lead to God Ahuramazd. He stressed that purity of thought, charity and help to the needy, good deeds like cultivating the land, growing trees, breeding cattle, doing other useful and gainful work or labour, being kind to all useful animals and, above all, devotion to truth are necessary for man to reach God. He advised his followers that to be good, a man need not renounce the world· but must shun all evil in thought, word and deed. Man should be kind to others including animals but not to evil doers as this increases evil. He was against asceticism, or renunciation of the world and self-mofication, as such, ascetics and the like are a burden to the society. No one should practice fasting or celibacy but at the same time he stressed the need of control over the mind. According to him the value of life should not be diminished by saying that life is unreal as this results in stagnation. His philosophy was constructive in every field and he desired that man should exert himself so as to be a superman. Inertia is a great evil and a true devotee of God is always ready to do all the good work he can in this world.

It is said that Zoroaster smiled when he was born and wanted all to be smiling by doing work useful to the people and community, shunning cruelty, wickedness and viciousness which are a negation of all happiness. Though against renunciation of the world, celibacy and fasting, Zoroaster was a sound advocate of spirituality and purity of mind which can be attained through control and sublimation of human emotions. Pure thought is the basis of good speech and good conduct and it is impossible to attain spiritual perfection without purifying the mind and sublimation of emotions. He added that worship of the Almighty softens the heart and, therefore, everyone should worship Him whenever possible, particularly in the morning and at night.

Zoroaster's teachings have been collected in the scripture called the *Avesta* which became known all over Iran and subsequently in Turan, Greece and India. When Zoroaster was kneeling before the sacred fire in the temple of Balkh, a Turanian soldier rushed into the temple and stabbed the old prophet who succumbed to death.

According to a verse in one of the *Gathas* (hymns) written by Zoroaster, only he is happy who can make others happy. The Parsis who follow Zoroaster are well-known for their charity and assistance to others. Of them Mahatma Gandhiji once said, "I am proud of my country, India, for having produced the splendid Zoroastrian stock, in number beneath contempt but in charity and philanthropy perhaps unequalled, certainly unsurpassed". Zoroaster explained that no reward should be expected for the good done to fellowmen, that dissatisfaction should be banished as it creates imperfection, that service to His creatures is the true service to God and that God can be approached only by doing good deeds. Zoroastrian scriptures specifically lay down that one can save oneself by one's own good actions and that neither the prophet nor any other heavenly being can save the wicked.

The Prophet's birthday is celebrated with much love and reverence for him as he pointed out the path of *ashoi* or righteousness. It is celebrated with as much pomp and rejoicing as the New Year's Day. The Parsis go to the fire-temple and garland the portrait of Zoroaster. If it has not been possible to wish *sal mubarak* to anyone on the New Year's Day or any of the four days following it, it is wished on the Khordad Sal which is the sixth day of the new year.

Besides being the birthday of the Prophet, many significant events are said to have occurred on this day in the history of Iran from where the Parsis originally hailed.

The ceremonies for the *muktad* (the released souls—the departed souls) which are carried on by the Parsis for seventeen days end on the Khordad Sal day, when they pray to God to give them strength to perform the ceremonies for the departed members of their family in the next year also and to confer on them illustrious children who would add to the glory of the family and the country. On this day, the last of the *muktad* days or All Souls' Day, the souls of the departed descend on this mortal world. Ceremonies are performed at home or at the fire-temple. A ceremony called *stum* is performed in the evening and meat, boiled eggs, vegetables and sweets are offered to the visiting souls. Food to be offered in the ceremonies is prepared with well water fetched by a Zoroastrian and never from tap water, because well water is considered pure whereas tap water which is usually stored in some reservoir is considered stagnant and impure.

Pateti and Navroz, The New Year's Day

The first day Hormazd of the first month Farvardin, commonly known as Pateti, is the New Year's Day of the Parsis. Previously, the last of the five Gathas or hymn days which is the 365th day of the Parsi or Zoroastrian calendar was called Pateti (derived from *patet kartan* meaning to repent) or the day of penitence for the sins committed during the closing year. The first day of the New Year was known as Navroz or New Year's Day; but subsequently the latter is treated both as New Year's Day and Pateti. On this day, Parsi men and women in Delhi as in other parts of India, rise early, take a bath and clothe themselves in their best. Women and children put on ornaments. They decorate their houses with festoons of leaves. The day starts with prayers of repentence at home whereafter they go to the fire-temple with offerings of sandalwood. Here they read or recite texts from their scriptures in front of the fire-alter and offer sandalwood to the holy fire which is considered a symbol of pristine purity. They kneel before the holy fire which is the symbol of God and apply ashes to their foreheads as mark of humility before the almighty. They pray and thank Ahuramazd (the Almightly) for bestowing on them His choicest blessings for the year. The atmosphere at the fire-temple is absolutely calm and serene as if the devotees are in tune with the Infinite. The weak, decrepit and those otherwise unable to visit the fire-temple pray at home. While going to the fire-temple the laymen as well as the priests dress themselves in spotless white which is the colour considered by the Zoroastrians to be a symbol of physical and spiritual purity. In the street and at the fire-temple they give alms to the poor.

After prayers in the fire-temple they visit friends and relatives who treat them with fruits, sweets, etc. When two Parsis meet, they greet one another by uttering *sal mubarak* (i.e., may the new year be bountiful to you) and as their hands are interlocked while performing the *hamajor* by joining hands, they bless one another saying, "Let us give our strength to purity. May God guard you. May you live long and happily". After the visits are over they spend the rest of the day in feasting and merriment and attending garden parties with their families. The theatres are packed with Parsis and gaily attired Parsis fill the best of the restaurants. Friends and relatives exchange greeting cards, reciprocating New Year's greeting and good wishes.

Zarthost-no-Diso

Zarthost-no-Diso is the death anniversary of the Prophet Zoroaster or Zarthost falling on Khurshed, the eleventh day of Deh or Dae (Ahuramazd), the tenth month. While the Prophet was praying in the fire-temple, he was assassinated by an enemy named Turbaratur. At this time, the pious Prophet threw his rosary on the murderer who was burnt to death. The Prophet was 77 years and 40 days old when he died. The Parsis pray for the peace of the prophet's soul and observe the day solemnly. Lectures are arranged by scholars and priests who recount the teachings and the ways of the life of the Prophet with a view to inspire the audience to take a sip from the fountain of pure goodness and righteousness and mould their lives accordingly.

JEWISH FESTIVALS

Except for a very small number of Jews of Iraqi or European origin in Greater Mumbai, the bulk of the Jewish population of India belongs to a single homogeneous section which is known in Western Maharashtra as Bene Israel. This section has for centuries past adopted Marathi as its mother-tongue and has lived in close and intimate cultural contact with the Hindu and Muslim people of the Konkan, while strictly adhering to the tenets of Judaism. It is, therefore, felt appropriate, in describing Jewish festivals as observed in India to do so with relation to the customs of the Bene Israel. So far as religious ritual goes, there is little variation from the observances of Jews in other parts of the world; but the discerning reader will not fail to notice certain distinctive Indian features, so far as social usages are concerned. In particular, the Bene Israel had adopted their own Marathi names for their festivals and these names are still in frequent use, particularly in the Konkan Districts, though the Hebrew or English equivalents tend progressively to replace them. These are celebrated all over India.

The Jewish calendar as it now exists is based on astronomical principles and is luni-solar in character. The length of each month, which commences as near as may be to the new Moon, is based on the time taken by the moon to go round the earth, viz., 29 ½ days. As each month must have an integral number of days, some Jewish months have 29 days and some 30. Ordinarily twelve months make a year, which has 353, 354 or 355 days, according as it has 5, 6 or 7 months of 30 days each. As the number of days in an ordinary year falls short by 10 to 12 days of the 365¼ days needed by the earth to go round the sun, harmonisation of the lunar years with the solar years is effected over a cycle of 19 years by inserting a thirteenth month of 30 days between the fifth and sixth months in the 3rd, 6th, 8th, 11th, 14th, 17th and 19th years of each cycle. This particular place of insertion was chosen as it was at one time the end of the ecclesiastical year. As it is, it now makes an interruption. The month affected is that of Adar, which becomes, in a year of thirteen months, Adar II or Ve-Adar, though it retains the festivals due to be observed in the month. By this very ingenious contrivance, it is ensured that the observance of the festivals, several of which are linked with the seasons of the year, do not fall seriously out of alignment.

The names of the twelve months of the Jewish calendar and their corresponding English months are given below:—

Name of the Jewish Month	*Name of Corresponding* English Months
1. Tishri	September-October
2. Heshvan (Maroheshvan)	October-November
3. Kislev	November-December
4. Tebet (Teves)	December-January
5. Shebat (Shevat)	January-February
6. Adar or Adar I Ve-Adar or Adar II	February-March
7. Nisan	March-April
8. Iyar	April-May
9. Sivan	May-June
10. Tammuz	June-July
11. Ab (Av)	July-August
12. Elul	August-September

Note :—In a year with 13 months and in the year following, some Jewish months may commence or end in periods later than those shown above against their names.

As the Jewish Day commences and ends at sunset, each festival commences at sunset of the preceding day according to the common computation and ends at sunset. Thus, the Sabbath, which is observed on Saturday each week, actually commences at sunset on Friday of our ordinary calendar and ends at sunset on Saturday.

The Jews, Bene-Israel as they are called in India, observe the following important festivals and fasts during a year:—

Fast of Ab

This is an important fast among the Jews. This fast which falls on the 9th of the month, Ab, is also one of the four fasts of National mourning. According to Biblical mode of expression, it is called the "Fast of the Fifth Month". It is also called "Birdiacha San" by the Bene-Israel. It is so named because this fast is broken on the evening of the 9th of Ab by consuming rice with curry of Birdi (Wal), a kind of pulse. "Wals" are kept in water day and night, till they sprout. The outer covering is removed and then they are cooked with spices, etc. A legend is told about this festival. The forefathers of Bene-Israel of India were the survivors of a ship wreck when only 7 couples could reach safely to the shore. They landed at Navgaon village in Kolaba district. Since they were hungry they ate 'Wal' (in raw state). The day on which they landed at Navgaon was 15th of Ab and hence on this day, Bene-Israel even now, consume "Wal". This version, however, is not accepted by some Jews who think that the consumption of "Wal" in raw state is done to commemorate the memory of their forefathers who were compelled to eat anything that was available during their hardships.

The food, which is consumed on 8th of Ab is served on plantain leaves to symbolize the fact that Israelies had no household utensils from which to partake of food at the time of the loss of their dominion and power. During the preceding eight days, the Jews abstain from consuming meat, wearing new clothes, celebrating marriages, etc.

This fast has historical importance. It is a major fast day in Jewish tradition. Known in Hebrew as *Tisha b'av,* it commemorates the destruction of the first and the second temples, the two events, though almost 500 years apart, took place on the same day, i.e., 9th of Ab. This is an occasion of immense pain and sorrow. Jews squat on the floor without any footwear and offer prayers bewailing the destruction of the temple.

In the month of Elul, i.e., the last month of the year, many devout Bene-Israel observe fasts for 40 days beginning with the 2nd of Elul to the 10th of Tishri on which day the fast of Yom Kippur is observed. The fasts are observed on all days except Sabbath (i.e., Saturday) and the two days of Rosh Hashanah,i.e., New Year's day.

The month of Elul precedes the month of Tishri and because many festivals and fasts are observed in the month of Tishri, the month of Elul gets a special significance. In the past the Shofar (a ram's horn) used to be sounded at morning religious services from 1st of Elul to prepare the people for the month of Tishri.

Those who are unable to observe the fast for 40 days are said to observe them at least on Mondays and Thursdays.

While fasting they take their meals only once a day after sunset.

Fast of Gedaliah

This fast, which is observed on the 3rd of Tishri, is one the four fasts of National Mourning. It is observed in memory of the murder of Gedaliah, the governor of the Jews. He was appointed by Nebuchadnezzar. His assassination brought great hardships to the Jewish people. In Delhi the Fast of Gedaliah is broken by consuming "Khir" (a sort of pudding made out of rice, coconut milk, sugar, etc.,) and because of this custom it appears that the day is known as (Khiricha San). A dish full of "Khir" with a few branches of "Sabja" (Basil) is kept on the table. A censer with frankincense is also kept burning. A prayer is offered for the relief of the souls of dead relatives.

Fast of Esther and Feast of Purim

These two festivals are observed on 13th and 14th day of Adar, respectively. (Adar II or Ve-Adar in a year with an additional month). A fast is observed on the 13th and a feast on the 14th. It coincides generally with the Hindu Festival of Holi.

Historically this festival goes back to the ancient days following the dispersion of 586 B.C.E. when a large Jewish community developed in the Persian Empire, Esther, whose other name was Hadassah, was the Queen of Persia. She was a Jew. At that time Haman was the King's Prime Minister who was all powerful. Esther's cousin, Mordecai, was somehow not in the good books of Haman, the Prime Minister. He, therefore, decided to kill Mordecai. This, however, was not sufficient. Haman, wanted to exterminate all Jews. He at last obtained an order from the King to destroy all Jews and 13th of Adar was selected for the massacre. This news, however, reached Mordecai and through him Esther, whose timely intervention saved the lives of the Jews. Haman was exposed and was ultimately hanged.

This fast commemorates the day that Haman had selected to kill the Jews. It also recalls the fast that Esther had ordained upon the Jews an appeal to God to help her save them.

The feast of "Purim" is also known as the "feast of lots". Haman wanted to make his plot of annihilation of Jews successful and accordingly he had cast lots to decide the best day on which Jews could be killed. In Persian "lots" are called "purim". This gives the explanation for the feast being called "Feast of Purim".

On the 14th of Adar, i.e., on the feast of "Purim", presents of sweetmeats prepared at home are sent by one family to another.

Feast of Hannuccah

This is called the "festival of lights" and resembles to some extent the Diwali festival of the Hindus. It is observed for 8 days from the 25th of Kislev to the 2nd or 3rd of Tebet as Kislev has 30 or 29 days. It is celebrated with much zeal and fervour and dedicated to the idealism and heroism of the Jewish people as exemplified by the struggle and suffering of the Maccabeus. When King Alexander of Macedonia conquered Syria and Palestine he treated them with kindness. After his death his conquests were divided and Palestine, where many of the Jews lived, came under rulers who attempted to hellenise them and force them to forsake their religion. Early in the Second Century B.C., during the reign of Antiochus Ephiphanes, the suffering of the Jews became unbearable. Antiochus compelled them to do many things which were forbidden by their religion, e.g., eating is forbidden of flesh of swine, not respecting Sabbath, etc. All his efforts, however, proved fruitless because the Jews were faithful to their religion and hence he sent his army into Jerusalem (168 B.C.E.) and killed thousands of Jews. The army also desecrated the temple. However, a few Jews gathered around Mattathias, a respected elder belonging to a priestly family, and defied the King's orders. Judas Maccabeus, one of Mattathias' brave sons, led a small group of Jews and conducted a heroic struggle against the Syrian army. Finally at Emmaus Judas completely defeated the Syrian army in the year 165 B.C.E. and recaptured Jerusalem.

When Jerusalem was recaptured by Judas Maccabeus, they went to the temple. The priests started preparation for the ceremonies of rededication, but could not find oil for the temple menoram (lamps). They found only one small cruse of oil which was sufficient for burning the light for one day. But a miracle took place and the oil burned for 8 days.

Among the Jews of Delhi as in other parts of India, these 8 days are days of rejoicing and praise and on every night of these 8 days lights are lit near the door of the houses in order to display and reveal the miracle that was performed for Israel in olden days. It is customary to light Hannuccah lights on this festival. Hannuccah is a stand made of metal or wood where eight small tiny glasses are either kept on or fixed to the stand to enable them to hold the candles or oil in them. There is an additional small tiny lamp/glass known as " Sammesh" lamp. The time of lighting them is immediately at the appearance of the stars. The order of lighting the lights is as follows:—

On the first night, i.e., the night of the 24th of Kislev, a light shall be lit towards the right and on the second night one light added at its left and lit first and then the former. On the 3rd day i.e., 26th of Kislev, one more light shall be added at the left and this one shall be lighted first and then the lights at its right, one after another . This process will be continued for the remaining five days , adding one light on each day. Thus we get:—

24th of Kislev	..	One light
25th of Kislev	..	Two lights
26th of Kislev	..	Three lights
27th of Kislev	..	Four lights

28th of Kislev	..	Five lights
29th of Kislev	..	Six lights
30th of Kislev or 1st Tebet	..	Seven lights
1st or 2nd of tebet of Kislev	..	Eight lights

The lights are lit at a height of about 5 feet from the ground in a frame specially provided for the purpose against the interior wall to the right as we get out by the front door. These lights are required to be stationed in such a way that their light should fall on the Mezuza at the front door.

The festival is spent in merry making and in most joyous way. Nowadays there are public functions for 8 days when various items of entertainment are staged, e.g., Fancy dress competition, *Bhavageet* competition, Debate, etc. Sweets and presents are distributed to the children.

Fast of Tebet

This fast, which is observed on the 10th day of Tebet is one of the four fasts of National Mourning and is known in Biblical phraseelogy as the "Fast of Tenth Month." India this fast was not observed by the BeneIsrael of Maharashtra in olden days but was introduced among them by David Rahabi. This fast might have been instituted to commemorate the first seige of Jerusalem by Nebuchadnezzar, king of Babylon, in the sixth centurey, B.C.E.

Feast of Passover

This festival is also known as "Pesach". In Delhi as in other parts of India the Jews abstain from using sour liquid, as well as any leaven, during the preiod of the feast. This festival commences on the 15th of Nisan and lasts for 8 days. The festival of Passover has many beautiful symbols and observances, and most significant of all is the seder service held at the home for the first two evenings of the holiday. It is in the nature of historical drama enacted at the festal table around which are gathered the members of the family. The head of the family leads in the narration of the story of the Exodus from Egypt and the family, particularly the little children, take an active part. This holiday is celebrated in memory of the deliverance of the ancestors of the Jews from Egyptian bondage . For 8 days, from 15th Nisan to 22nd Nisan, the Bene-Israel eat unleavened bread.

This feast is one of the three Pilgrim Feasts, the other two being that of Sukkoth and Shahbuoth. These 3 Pilgrim feasts have agricultural as well as historical background. The Passover Festival marks the beginning of liberty of Israel and the end of Egyptian bondage.

A great marvel is connected with this festival. When the Egyptian King was persecuting the Jews prior to their liberation, he was told not to harass them. However, the pleadings had no effect.

The task of liberating a host of men in bondage was assigned to Moses, the towering figure of the Old Testament. When Moses saw an Egyptian beat a Hebrew, he killed the former and had to flee to Midian, where God gave Moses his divine mission to "bring forth my children, the sons of Israel, out of Egypt". Moses approached Pharaoh and asked him to liberate Hebrews, but Pharaoh refused and God struck Egypt with 9 plagues such as infestations of frogs, flies, insects, sky-darkening, sand storms, etc. Still there was no change in Pharaoh's heart but the 10th plague, the destruction of the first born children of Egypt had the desired effect and Pharaoh at last allowed the Jews to go.

In order to distinguish a Jewish house from an Egyptian, one God asked the Jews to mark their houses in a particular manner so that he would "pass-over" their houses when the 10th plague took its effect. The "pass-over" festival is, therefore, called so.

The Feast of Pentecost or Shabuoth

This festival, which falls on the 6th of Sivan and lasts for 2 days, was not originally observed by the Bene-Israel in India.

It has a historical importance for the Jews. It commemorates the giving of the Torah, (i.e., the Mosaic law), by the Almighty from Mount Sinai. It thus, marks the spiritual birth of Israel. By virtue of Torah, Israel has been a spiritualised force in the world and bears a profound message for our times.

This festival has no local name.

It is also called as the "Feast of Weeks". This festival has an agricultural, religious and national significance in Jewish history. In Biblical times this festival was mainly an agricultural feast. It is known in the Bible as "the feast of the Harvest" and also as "the day of the First Fruits".

The Feast of Tabernacles

The festival of Sukkoth of Tabernacles is celebrated for 8 days, from the 15th of Tishri to the 23rd of Tishri. This festival, which is known by different names, has historical and agricultural background. The feast of Tabernacles reminds the Jews of ancient times when their ancestors were wandering from place to place to escape the wrath of the Egyptians. During their journey they stayed in tents of booths and the protection offered by the tents or booths would have been insufficient but for the God's help. The Bible says "The fifteenth day of this seventh month shall be the Feast of Tabernacles for seven days unto the Lord." "Ye shall dwell in booths for seven days; that your generations may know that I made the children of Israel to dwell in booths, when I brought them out of the Land of Egypt."

In former days a Succa or booth used to be built with the help of leaves of the trees near the house. However due to changed times a booth is constructed nowadays near the synagogue where the local Jews congregate to offer prayers. Some also pass the night in the Succa.

The other name given to the festival of Sukkoth is "The Feast of Ingathering". In the land of the ancestors of the Jews the month of Tishri is the harvest period of crops. The agricultural aspect of this festival is given an expression in a custom followed by the Jews. When they go to the synagogue to offer prayers on this festival they carry invariably 4 different things wrapped together. These four thing are :—

(i) Citron,

(ii) Branch of Palm tree,

(iii) Myrtle branch,

(iv) Willow of the brook.

These four items represent the different kinds of Jews in this world. Citron has good taste and sweet smell. So there are Jews in this world who are learned and good. The Palm tree has taste but no smell and hence represents Jews who are learned but not good. The Myrtle, which has a smell but no taste, reminds us of Jews who are good but are not learned. The last, i.e., willow of the brook has neither smell nor taste. There are Jews who are neither good nor learned. Thus, we must live with all kinds of people.

This festival is also known simply as "Feast".

The last two days of the festival are known as Shemini Azeret (22nd of Tishri) and Simath Torah (23rd of Tishri). Simath Torah marks the end of this festival when a great feast is held known as the "Feast of Rejoicing of the Torah".

Simath Torah marks the completion of the cycle of reading from the Torah or the Laws as recorded in the Bible at the synagogue services and the commencement of a new cycle. Amid great rejoicing Scrolls of Law are taken out of the Ark in the Synagogue and carried in procession round the central reading platform. Keen bidding takes place for the right to carry the Scrolls, and considerable sums of money thus accrue to synagogue funds. It can never fall on a Saturday.

Fast of Tammuz

This fast which falls on the 17th of the 10th month Tammuz is one of the four fasts of National Mourning, the other three being, the Fast of Tebet, the Fast of Ab and the Fast of Tishri. In Biblical phrase the fast is called the fast of the "Fourth Month".

It has historical importance. In the days of the First Temple, the Babylonian army besieging Jerusalem breached the walls on the ninth of Tammuz. Almost five centuries later, the Romans breached the walls on the seventeenth of Tammuz. Since the second destruction of the temple was of more lasting effect, the fast was decreed for the seventeenth of Tammuz.

Among the Delhi Jews. The fast is observed in a most solemn manner.

The period between 17th of Tammuz and 15th

of Ab is given a special treatment in sense that all auspicious functions like marriage, etc., or purchase of clothes are not undertaken. They are, so to say, inauspicious days.

New Year's Day of the Trees

On the 15th of Shebat, the Bene-Israel of Maharashtra celeberate a festival which called by them "Eliyahu Hannabichaoorus", but, in fact, is observed as the Rosh Hashana Leilanoth, i.e., New Year's Day of the trees. It is also called as It is said that Elijah the prophet appeared to some Bene-Israel at a village, Khandala, of Alibag Taluka, Kolaba district, and then ascended to heaven. On this day, the Bene-Israel purchase various kinds of fruits and place them in a plate along with "*Malida*", i.e., a composition made of bread of rice flour besmeared with sweets. New fruits are purchased by Jews since it is a season of harvest of fruits in the land of their fore-fathers. The plate is placed on a white clean sheet. A twig of *sabja* and a censor with frankincense burning are also kept. They invoke Elijah the prophet and say "Veitoenlekha", i.e., the verses of blessing Prayers in gratitude are offered to the Almighty who has given so graciously everything for men's use and benefit. After the prayers the contents of the plate are distributed among the members of the family.

Among the Delhi Jews by observing this festival the debt which mankind owes to the trees and forests is remembered. Trees give us not only shade and fruits but are useful in many other ways.

Rosh Hashanah

The 1st of Tishri or New Year's Day. Jewish New Year's Day used to be called "Navyacha San" in the past. According to Jewish tradition the first of Tishri ushers in the Days of Awe, known in Hebrew as the "Yommim Noroim". It is an occasion on which every Jew must strive to reconcile himself with the Almighty and with his fellowmen. In Delhi Prayers are offered at the synagogue, the Jewish place of worship. On return from the synagogue, on the New Year's Eve, a service is held in the evening when the following seven things are kept on a table:—

(i) Sweetened apple (i.e., apple and honey),
(ii) Green garlic (with roots and leaves),
(iii) Beet root,
(iv) Dates,
(v) White pumpkin,
(v) Fish,
(vi) Head of lamb (or goat).

After prayers the articles are shared by all those who are present. The meals are taken after this function.

The Rose Hashanah is marked by much joy amongst the Bene-Israel. A feast is held where mutton or sweet, in two or more varieties, are highlights of the dinner. Family reunions are a special feature, son, daughters, and sons-in-law coming in from far and near. New clothes and ornaments are worn. Fruits and home-made delicacies are sent after the mid-day meal to relatives and friends. Presents are given, specially of jewellery, to married daughters and sons-in-law in the first year of their marriage.

This festival is also known by three different names and each name has a special meaning attached to it. It is known as the Day of Judgment when God—the King of Kings—judges the actions and deeds of the people done during the last year. It is also called the Day of Remembrance i.e., it has a reference to the days when Abraham prepared to sacrifice his son at God's command. The other name given to the New Year's Day is the day of Blowing the Shofar. The blowing of a Shofar is an important feature of the day's celebrations. The Shofar is a musical instrument made out of a ram's horn by flattening it by heat. In the olden days, the blowing of the Shofar served many purposes, viz., heralding the new year, the crowning of the King, etc. When the Shofar is blown on the New Year's Day, it means that a day of peace, prosperity and happiness will be ushered in.

This festival helps the solidarity of home life and contributes to the well-being of the family and the community.

The 1st of Tishri always falls on a Monday, or Saturday.

Yom Kippur

A fast is observed on this festival which occurs on the 10th day of Tishri. Since the Jewish day lasts from sun-set,the fast of Yom Kippur starts from the sunset of the 9th of Tishri and ends at the sun-set, of the 10th day of Tishri. As the Jewish calendar is arranged, the fast can commence only on a Tuesday, Friday or Sunday at sunset. This festival is also known as the Day of Atonement and the 9th of Tishri is called The Eve of Atonement. It is the great day of reconciliation between man and man and man and God. As a fast day it is spent in a solemn manner. The Jews offer prayers for the forgiveness of sins which they might have committed and they solemnly resolve to abide by the law of god.

On the 9th of Tishri (which is also called "Malma" by Bene-israel) the Jews take a bath, first in hot water and then in cold, the procedure being called "Tebila, or "Cleansing". During local inquiry at Panvel, district Kolaba, it was observed that the local Jews there take only cold water bath, on this occasion, preferably in a river, tank or the sea. After the bath, they go to the synagogue and offer prayers with the congregation. While going to the synagogue they wear white clothes. They take their meals in the morning and again at about 5 p.m. of the 9th of Tishri and fast till the evening of the next day, i.e., the 10th of Tishri. The fast actually lasts for more than 24 hours since the meals are taken after sun-set of the 10th of Tishri. In the past, when there was no synagogue and Hebrew prayers were not known to Bene-Israel, they generally kept themselves behind closed doors throughout the day and it is perhaps because of this practice that the festival was known in the past as "Darfalnicha San". After the meals were taken (i.e., before sunset, on the 9th Tishri) everything in the house used to be shipshape and the doors shut and all the members of the house used to gather in the centre room or hall and make devotions according to traditions. They used to wear white dress and neither did they touch people of other religions nor did they exchange words with them. They used to keep indoors on this day lest they should come in contact with impure persons, or lest some foul words should pass through their mouths on this day. A strict fast was observed by all adult men and women, and children abstained from food until well past noon when they were given "Puris" (i.e., a sweetmeat made from rolled kneaded wheat flour stuffed with a mixture of *soojee,* sugar, etc.).

However, the custom of closing the doors, keeping aloof from others, etc., is not followed so strictly now. Nowadays, they go to the synagogue and offer prayers and observe a fast for a period of 24 hours.

The fast is broken after the customary prayer is said, by consuming *sharbat* made of black grapes, puris, etc. They greet each other by joining of the palms. A light supper is cooked after sunset. It consists of rice cooked in coconut milk (obtained by mixing the shreaded kernel in water and squeezing out the juice) and a curry of mutton, fowl or fish.

The next day, i.e., the 11th of Tishri, called as "Shila san" or Simbat Cohen is wholly spent in merriment and entertaining relatives and friends in each other's homes. A special dinner is cooked and served. All wear their best clothes. Alms are given to the poor as well as old clothes like saris, etc.

NATIONAL FESTIVALS

Bal—Divas or Children's Day

One of the numerous facets of the late Prime Minister Pandit Jawaharlal Nehru's personality was his profound love for children. He was a child among children, who never missed an opportunity to be one with them. They in turn affectionately called him Chacha or Uncle Nehru. According to him the nation must look after the welfare of its children who are the future citizens of the country. The country can ill afford to neglect them.

Instances of immense fondness and regard for children are numerous. Nothing would come in the way of his meeting has young friends and warmly reciprocating their love and affection for him. In the middle of a procession he would stop suddenly to receive a flower bouquet or garland from a child or hug him. Only a few days before his demise, he allowed a young boy to meet him on the rostrum in the midst of the A.I.C.C. meeting at in May 1964. A large number of children wrote to him to convey their greetings, and always drew a warm response. It was, therefore, in the fitness of things, that his birthday on 14th November should be celebrated as Bal-Din dedicated to the welfare of children. Mass rallies of children are arranged at many places on this day, and sweets are distributed amongst them. Children's entertainment programmes like fancy-dress competitions, children's dramas, etc., are organized. Organizations of children or institutions dedicated to child welfare like Bal Bhawan, Bal Vikas Samiti, etc., hold various functions on this occasion. Special children's programmes are broadcast over the radio. During the past ten or twelve years, special efforts are made by the various agencies of community development to promote child welfare.

This day is special for children and schools distributes sweets and show them some cartoon or movie or hold some competition. The children's drawing and painting competitions organized by the well-known Shankar's Weekly have evoked keen response not only from the country, but also from all the world over. The birthday of Nehru Chacha is thus celebrated with great enthusiasm by children everywhere and marked by activities aiming at the welfare of this young section of society so close to his heart.

Gandhiji's Birthday: Mahatma Gandhiji was born on the dark twelfth of Bhadrapad in V.S. 1925, i.e., on the 2nd October, 1869 A.D. After his rise on the political scene of India, Gandhiji came to be more and more respected both for his saintly qualities and his able leadership in the national struggle for freedom. His birthday, therefore, became a national festival long ago in the early twenties of the present century. Some of his followers had originally named it Mohan Dwadashi after him. Gandhiji did not approve of it as he did not wish that a *jayanti* should be celebrated to honour an individual like him.

The festival assumed great popularity during pre-independence days and many activities relating to the social and economic welfare of the people were undertaken in connection with the celebrations on this day. They included continuous spinning 24 hours. The spinning wheel was looked upon by Gandhiji as the symbol of the country's independence. It signified self-purification, self-help and self-reliance. It also was an expression of one's desire to help the poor, *Daridranarayan,* through revival of cottage industries. All staunch followers of Gandhiji therefore, took a vow to spin *antis* or skeins of yarn equal in number to the years since Gandhiji's birth and donate it to some Gandhian institution. The programme of cleaning the public streets, tanks, Harijan *vas* (localities) and other places was undertaken for the triple purpose of inculcating among the people an awareness about cleanliness, dignity of labour and removal of untouchability, a very important phase of social uplift for which Gandhiji worked throughout his life. Various activities aiming at the welfare of the Harijans and bringing them and the *savarnas* of caste Hindus nearer to each other were undertaken on this day. Social workers visited the Harijan *vas* in groups and undertook *safai* or sweeping and cleaning in the locality. Dinners were arranged where Harijans were invited to participate along with caste Hindus without any distinction. The more enlightened workers invited individual Harijans to their place for dinner and for spending some time with them. Temples to which entry to Harijans was barred were thrown open to them by the efforts of workers who led them in a procession for effecting the entry. Of late, such programmes are arranged during the Harijan Week celebrated by the Government generally towdards the end of January. Various other constructive programmes were also initiated or executed on this day as advised by Gandhiji as a part of the national movement. The celebrations on this day which roused the masses in pre-Independence days now attract a comparatively smaller number.

The festival stands for national unity and integration, self-dedication and complete negation of ill-will. It is a festival for introspection and sublimation of the soul, cultivating respect for all religions and pursuit of the various ideals Gandhiji laid down for the nation.

Gandhiji's birthday according to the Gregorian calendar, which falls on the 2nd October, is also celebrated as a national festival. It is a public hoiliday, popularly known as Gandhi Jayanti. The days intervening between Bhadrapad Vad 12 and 2nd October, though varying in number from year to year, are celebrated as Gandhi Saptah or week. At institutions established by Mahatma Gandhiji or associated with the nationalist movement, the whole week is celebrated with constructive programmes like spinning, *safai*, popularization of *khadi*, debates, discourses and meetings, etc. The inmates and constructive workers of such institutions and *ashrams* give themselves up to these activities for the whole week. Typical examples of the celebrations are those held at Rashtriya Shala at Rajkot, where Mahatma Gandhiji undertook a historical fast in 1939 for the cause of a responsible Government in the former Rajkot State, and which was then the centre of all political movement in that region. Generally an eminent leader of all-India status is invited to Rashtriya Shala to mark the conclusion of the celebrations, which include prayer meeting, mass spinning and public meeting. In the Sabarmati Ashram at Ahmedabad also various programmes are arranged on this occasion. The period from 11th September, the birthday of Vinobha Bhave, to Gandhi Jayanti, 2nd October, is celebrated as Sarvoday *parva*. Various programmes like *prabhat feri* or morning procession, *bhajans*, continuous spinning, exhibition, cultural programmes and discourses by prominent Gandhian workers are arranged. The Harijan Ashram has special significance on this occasion as it is the palace where Gandhiji established his headquarters on return from South Africa in 1915. The Ashram which was then known as Sabarmati Ashram has within its precincts his humble residence known as Hriday Kunj from where he directed various national movements till he undertook the famous Dandi March for the Salt Satyagraha in 1930. The Ashram now called Harijan Ashram forms the pivot of various Gandhian activities, particularly in the field of Harijan uplift and social welfare. In Delhi, a visit to the Raj Ghat, the final resting place of the Mahatma by leaders from various political parties as well as the PM and President is followed by various celebrations.

Independence Day

The 15th of August has been named the Independence Day since the country achieved Independence on that date in 1947. It was on the midnight of 14th August 1947 that the transfer of power to popular ministries at the Centre and in the States took place, elevating India to Dominion Status, with a Constituent Assembly of its own which would frame its future Constitution. The event resulted in the partition of the country into two, viz., India and Pakistan, both of which were granted Independence. The spontaneous and overwhelming jubilations on the night and the day following were truly memorable. Torchlight processions were taken out after Union Jack was replaced by the National Flag. It was an occasion of unbounded joy and elation for a people who had come into their own after centuries of foreign domination. The entire country rose as a man to celebrate this most outstanding event in the history of Indian people. The whole of the next day, 15th August, was spent in merriment and cultural and entertainment programmes arranged in every locality, the celebrations being rounded off by fireworks at night.

In Delhi, the Prime Minister gives a speech to the country from the historic Red-Fort. Since then the day is celebrated as the Independence Day which is observed as a public holiday. The celebration begins with the official function of flag-hoisting at the State, district and taluka headquarters. The national flag is flown on top of buildings public and private, and cultural programmes are arranged.

Martyr's Day

This day commemorates the death of Mahatma Gandhiji, the Father of the Nation, who fell to an assasin's bullets while on his way to a prayer meeting on the evening of Friday, the 30th January, 1948, at Birla House New Delhi.

Though the struggle for freedom was successful, and Independence achieved, he was not pleased with the course of events as it was not the Independence he strived for. He, therefore, devoted himself to fighting communal frenzy that was let loose in the subcontinent in the wake of partition and worked incessantly to promote communal harmony, removing bitterness and discord between the two major sections of the Indian people till the day of his martyrdom.

On this day, all the known and unknown soldiers in the fight for freedom who laid down their lives for their country's Independence are paid homage by observing complete silence for two minutes at 11 a.m. For this purpose there is a complete stoppage of work in offices and establishments, and the traffic also comes to a standstill. Prayer meetings are also held.

The Republic Day

The Republic Day falling on the 26th January is the most important national festival. It was on this day in 1950 that the Constitution of Independent India was adopted amidst universal jubilation by the Constituent Assembly, formed on the advent of Independence in August 1947. The Constitution embodies the aspirations of the Indian people, long subjected to the humiliation of foreign dominance, not only to guard its haard-won freedom, but also to guarantee the fundamental rights to every citizen and to achieve all-round progress according to the directive principles laid down therein. It was on this day that this country became a soverign democratic republic called India or Bharat. This event is commemorated by the celebration of the Republic Day every year on January 26.

The day was not without significance even before 1950. In December 1929 at the Lahore session of the Indian National Congress, presided over by the late Pandit Jawaharlal Nehru, a resolution was passed unequivocally declaring complete Independence as its goal. In order to implement the policy behind the resolution, it was decided to observe 26th January 1930 throughout the country as the Purna Swarajya Day. On this day a declaration in terms of the resolution was read out in public meetings all over the land as a pledge to work ceaselessly for Purna Swarajya or complete Independence. These solemn declarations "revealed what a five of pent-up feeling, enthusiasm and readiness to sacrifice there lay beneath the seeming torpor and despair of the people. The fires of patriotism and sacrifice were covered by the embers of loyalty or submissin to Law and Order. All that had to be done was to blow off the ashes covering the red-hot cinders of emotion and fervour".[1] The day was since then known as the Independence Day, celebrated by the people as such even before the advent of freedom. The celebrations generally started with *prabhat feris* or morning processions in the early hours of dawn followed by flag salutations. Programmes of mass spinning and special sales of *khadi* were arranged, and meetings were held in which national affairs were discussed, people were explained the basic principles of the freedom movement and the pledge to achieve complete Independence renewed.

The festival acquired added significance as the Republic Day of free India, which is declared a public holiday. A lead is given in the celebrations by the Government through various official functions. In the morning at the capitals of States and every district and taluka headquarters, national flag—hoisting ceremonies are performed followed by a parade of the armed forces and the police. This is witnessed by huge congregations and followed by mammoth processions in which the public participate with great enthusiasm. Floats are also taken out which represent various themes of national importance, related to planning and development. Flag salutations are also held all over the country and sweets are distributed to children. In the evening an official reception takes place, in which the invitees participate. The national flag is flown on public and private buildings. Apart from these official functions, various cultural and other programmes are arranged by organizations and associations. These include public meetings, entertainment programmes, folk-dances, etc. At night there are illuminations, and in large towns competitions for the best illuminations and decorations are organized.

Each State is also represented on this occasion at the Republic Day parade in New Delhi by the inclusion of a float and by special troupes participating in cultural programmes. National award in recognition of services rendered in several walks of public life are also declared by the President of the Indian Republic.

The festival thus affords an opportunity to the people to rededicate their lives for the welfare of country and give vent to their feelings of patriotism.

ALPHABETICAL INDEX
OF
FAIRS AND FESTIVALS
VOLS. 1 TO 5

A

Aali Masjid, **Vol. 4**, 271
Aattu, **Vol. 3**, 249
Abbi Matha Fair, **Vol. 2**, 213
Abdapir Fair, **Vol. 5**, 389
Abhaya Puja Festival, **Vol. 6**, 170
Abhimwara Mahadev Fair, **Vol. 4**, 452
Abhujmarias Festivals of, **Vol. 5**, 441
Adavirayangudi Jatra, **Vol. 2**, 217
Adavisiddeshwara Matha Jatra, **Vol. 2**, 218
Adhikari Babu's Utsav, **Vol. 6**, 170
Adi Pooram Festival, **Vol. 3**, 273, 290
Adi Shaktyattmaka Sri Annapurneshvari, **Vol. 2**, 214
Adi Subrahmanyeshwara Jatra, **Vol. 2**, 214
Adi Tapas, **Vol. 3**, 299
Adi-Gaddige Shri Guru Dattatreya Phalahara Matha Festival, **Vol. 2**, 213
Adikesava Perumal Temple Festival, **Vol. 3**, 291
Adi-Puram Festival, **Vol. 3**, 273, 290
Adrishyananda Math Jatra, **Vol. 2**, 218
Afzal Shah Biyabani Urs, **Vol. 2**, 6
Agastheswaraswamy Festival, **Vol. 2**, 6
Agasteswaraswamy Kalyanam, **Vol. 2**, 9
Aghoareshwara Jatra, **Vol. 2**, 214
Agnihotra, **Vol. 3**, 300
Agrahanya Purnima Fair, **Vol. 6**, 40
Agtarang Fair, **Vol. 4**, 141
Ahilya Utsav, **Vol. 5**, 390
Ahmad Shah Urs, **Vol. 2**, 215
Ahmad Shah Wali Bahamani Urs, **Vol. 2**, 216
Ahmad-Bava Fakki Urs, **Vol. 2**, 215
Aindra Fair, **Vol. 5**, 85
Aishan Saheb, **Vol. 4**, 270
Akadi Festival, **Vol. 2**, 9
Akal Takht, **Vol. 4**, 318
Akepur Jatra, **Vol. 5**, 390
Akhan Jatra, **Vol. 6**, 74
Akhana Tij, **Vol. 2**, 102, **Vol. 4**, 62
Akhatrij, **Vol. 5**, 85-86
Akhin Pardhi Festival, **Vol. 6**, 77
Akshaya Tritiya, **Vol. 1**, 41-43, 114-115, **Vol. 4**, 16, 68, **Vol. 5**, 85-86, 231
Akshaya Trutiya, **Vol. 6**, 77
Akshya Thrithiyai, **Vol. 3**, 301
Alakakhu Festival, **Vol. 6**, 419
Alivelu Akkamma Jatra, **Vol. 2**, 10
Allar Fair, **Vol. 4**, 141
Aluvamanal Puram, **Vol. 3**, 24
Alwar Festival, **Vol. 3**, 301
Amali Agiarash Festival, **Vol. 5**, 87
Amareshwara Jatra, **Vol. 2**, 218
Amareswara Temple, **Vol. 2**, 102
Amarnath Yatra, **Vol. 4**, 270
Amavas Fair, **Vol. 4**, 321
Amavas, **Vol. 1**, 42-43, **Vol. 4**, 16 *See also* Bhadarvi Amavasya, Somavati Amavas
Amba Devi Fair, **Vol. 5**, 231-32
Amba Devi Temple Fair, **Vol. 2**, 219
Ambaji Fair, **Vol. 5**, 87-97
Ambareshwar Fair, **Vol. 5**, 233
Ambedkar Jayanti, **Vol. 1**, 105, **Vol. 4**, 63
Ambu Festival, **Vol. 3**, 273, 276
Ambuvan Fair, **Vol. 6**, 292-95
Ammadevaru Car Festival, **Vol. 2**, 219
Ammadevaru Temple Fair, **Vol. 2**, 219
Ammankoda Festival, **Vol. 3**, 27
Amongmong Festival, **Vol. 6**, 419
Amriteshvara Temple Jatra, **Vol. 2**, 219

Amriti Fair, **Vol. 6**, 170
Amruthkunda Jatra, **Vol. 2**, 219
Anandanarayanapuram Thirumala Devaswom Utsavam, **Vol. 3**, 79
Anandpur Sahib, **Vol. 4**, 346-48
Anant Chaudash, **Vol. 2**, 44, **Vol. 4**, 18
Anant Chaudash Fair, **Vol. 4**, 331, 452
Ananta Vrat, **Vol. 2**, 220
Ananta Vrata, **Vol. 6**, 77
Ananta Vratha Festival, **Vol. 3**, 291
Anantapadmanabha Temple Fair/Festival, **Vol. 2**, 220
Andhra Vishnu Kalyanothsavam, **Vol. 2**, 11
Andhra Vishnu Temple, **Vol. 2**, 13
Ani Thirumanjanam, **Vol. 3**, 273
Anjaneya Jatra, **Vol. 2**, 220
Anjaneyaswami Car Festival/Jatra, **Vol. 2**, 220, 221
Ankamali Church Feast, **Vol. 3**, 80
Ankamma Tirnuala, **Vol. 2**, 10
Ankos Shah Vali Urs, **Vol. 2**, 13
Annakuta Festival, **Vol. 6**, 170
Anniversary of Sheikh Zain-ud-Din, **Vol. 4**, 270
Antarghattamma Jatra, **Vol. 2**, 221
Antige-Pantige Festival, **Vol. 2**, 221
Antri Mata Fair, **Vol. 5**, 390
Aoling Monya, **Vol. 6**, 419
Aparadh Bhanjan Fair, **Vol. 6**, 171
Appar Jayanthi, **Vol. 3**, 303
Appaya Dikshitar Jayanthi, **Vol. 3**, 304
Arakkal Temple Utsavam, **Vol. 3**, 81
Arangan Mahadeva Temple Utsavam, **Vol. 3**, 81
Aranya Siddheshwara Jatra, **Vol. 2**, 222
Ardhodhaya Mahodhaya Period, **Vol. 3**, 294
Arif-ul-Hassa Syed Sikander Ali Shah Urs, **Vol. 2**, 222
Ariyotlu Bhadrakali Temple Pattu, **Vol. 3**, 27
Arudhra Darsanam, **Vol. 3**, 273
Arudra Festival, **Vol. 3**, 294
Arwa Festival, **Vol. 6**, 40
Ascension, **Vol. 1**, 131-132, **Vol. 4**, 91
Ashadhi Fair, **Vol. 5**, 323
Ashadhi New Year Festival and Rath Yatra, **Vol. 5**, 97
Ashadi and Kartiki Ekadashis, **Vol. 5**, 234
Ashokastami, **Vol. 6**, 77, 78
Ashoora, **Vol. 4**, 270
Asht Bhuja Devi Fair, **Vol. 4**, 452
Ashtahnika, **Vol. 1**, 108, **Vol. 4**, 65
Ashivin Purnima Fair, **Vol. 6**, 5, 40
Ashwathanarayana Car Festival, **Vol. 2**, 223
Asoka and Bodh Gaya, **Vol. 6**, 24
Asrar-I-Sharif's Urs, **Vol. 4**, 271
Assissi Church Feast, **Vol. 3**, 82
At-Challa Temple Fair, **Vol. 6**, 171
Athachamayam, **Vol. 3**, 28-34
Athakhoda, **Vol. 4**, 141
Atmaram Baba Fair, **Vol. 5**, 389
Atmaram Fair, **Vol. 5**, 391
Attukal Bhagavathy Temple Ponkala, **Vol. 3**, 83
Avani Avittam Festival, **Vol. 3**, 299
Avani Moolam, **Vol. 3**, 273
Avani Mulam Festival, **Vol. 3**, 297
Avu Devatha Festival, **Vol. 2**, 14
Ayyapan Temple Utsavam, **Vol. 3**, 167
Ayyappa Fair, **Vol. 2**, 223

B

Baba Atal, **Vol. 4**, 319
Baba Attar Singh Fair, **Vol. 4**, 322
Baba Balraj Fair, **Vol. 4**, 322
Baba Brahmdas Fair, **Vol. 4**, 322
Baba Buddha Fair
– Bir Sahib, **Vol. 4**, 322
– Ramdas, **Vol. 4**, 322
Baba Buddhan Ali Shah Urs, **Vol. 4**, 271
Baba Chand ki Roshni, **Vol. 4**, 452
Baba Diwan Saheb Urs, **Vol. 5**, 235
Baba Fakiruddin Saheb Urs, **Vol. 2**, 14
Baba Farid Shaherjang's Urs, **Vol. 5**, 391
Baba Ganesh Dass Fair, **Vol. 4**, 115
Baba Garib Das Fair, **Vol. 4**, 453
Baba Handal Fair, **Vol. 4**, 323
Baba Hardi Rishi Fair, **Vol. 4**, 273
Baba Ishaq Ali Shah alias Bal Jati Shah Urs, **Vol. 5**, 394
Baba Jagdhar Fair, **Vol. 4**, 453
Baba Jiwan Shah's Urs, **Vol. 4**, 273
Baba Jwala Singh Fair, **Vol. 5**, 324
Baba Mast Nath Fair, **Vol. 4**, 115
Baba Nara Singh Dass Fair, **Vol. 4**, 115
Baba Prabhu Jatra, **Vol. 2**, 223
Baba Prayag Das Temple Fair, **Vol. 4**, 453
Baba Rah's Urs, **Vol. 4**, 276
Baba Rameshwar Dass Temple Jatra, **Vol. 4**, 115
Baba Sagan Fair, **Vol. 4**, 453
Baba Sahaj Ram Fair, **Vol. 4**, 454
Baba Saheb Fairs, **Vol. 5**, 395

Baba Shahabuddin Saheb Oulia Urs Fair, **Vol. 5**, 395
Bab Shakarbaras Fair, **Vol. 4**, 454
Baba Shami Dayal Fair, **Vol. 4**, 116
Baba Sodal Fair, **Vol. 4**, 328
Baba Sri Chand Fair, **Vol. 4**, 324
Baba Sukha Nand Fair, **Vol. 4**, 324
Baba Tajuddin Urs, **Vol. 2**, 15
Baba Tragianwala Smadhi Fair, **Vol. 4**, 325
Baba Vir Singh Fair, **Vol. 4**, 325
Baba-ka-Mandir Fair, **Vol. 4**, 454
Bachhretu Naun Fair, **Vol. 4**, 141
Bada Osha, **Vol. 6**, 78
Bada Osha Festival, **Vol. 6**, 81
Bada Osha Jatra (Mancheswar), **Vol. 6**, 81
Badi Asthami Fair, **Vol. 4**, 454
Badrinath, **Vol. 4**, 537
Bageshwari Devi Fair, **Vol. 5**, 396
Bahiram Fair (Karanja), **Vol. 5**, 237
Bahreshwar Mahadev Fair, **Vol. 5**, 105
Bahu Fort Fair, **Vol. 4**, 278
Bahula Chauth, **Vol. 4**, 142
Bahura-Chouth Festival, **Vol. 5**, 397-99
Baijnath Mahadeo Fair, **Vol. 5**, 399
Baikunth Chaturdashi Fair, **Vol. 4**, 532
Baira Jatar, **Vol. 4**, 142
Baisakhi, **Vol. 1**, 44-45, **Vol. 4**, 18, 143, 279
Baisakhi Fair, **Vol. 4**, 130, 142, 325
Baitarani Jatra, **Vol. 6**, 81
Bakreshwar Nath Fair, **Vol. 6**, 172
Bakri Id, **Vol. 1**, 122-123, **Vol. 4**, 182
Bal Divas, **Vol. 1**, 155, **Vol. 4**, 109
Balaji Fair, **Vol. 5**, 238-40
Balak Rupi Fair, **Vol. 4**, 143
Balamuri Fair, **Vol. 2**, 223
Balandar Fair, **Vol. 4**, 143
Balanghi Mutairenal Festival, **Vol. 6**, 454
Balayogi Teertham, **Vol. 2**, 15
Baldeoji Fair, **Vol. 4**, 454-55
Baldev Chhat Fair, **Vol. 4**, 116
Bale Miyan Fair, **Vol. 4**, 455
Bale Miyans Urs, **Vol. 4**, 455
Balev Festival, **Vol. 5**, 98
Bali Jatra, **Vol. 6**, 75, 78, 80, 82
Baloba Fair, **Vol. 2**, 224
Balsundri Devi Fair, **Vol. 4**, 532
Balunkeswar Shiva Temple Jatra, **Vol. 6**, 82
Bam Fair, **Vol. 4**, 143
Banabihar Fair, **Vol. 6**, 455
Banashankaramma Jatra, **Vol. 2**, 224
Bandar-Chooka Fairs, **Vol. 5**, 399
Bandevi Fair, **Vol. 4**, 455
Bandi Habba Festival, **Vol. 2**, 225
Baneshwara Fair, **Vol. 4**, 381-84
Bang Kayang, **Vol. 4**, 144
Banganga Fair, **Vol. 4**, 384
Bangara-Tirupati Jatra, **Vol. 2**, 226
Banlagi Fair, **Vol. 4**, 144
Bannumma Fair, **Vol. 5**, 240
Bansi Fair, **Vol. 4**, 456
Bapum Reshi, **Vol. 4**, 279
Bara Miyan Fair, **Vol. 4**, 456
Bara Rauza Fair, **Vol. 4**, 327
Bara Wafat, **Vol. 1**, 119-122, **Vol. 4**, 77
Barabar Hills Jatra, **Vol. 6**, 5
Baradol Festival, **Vol. 6**, 172
Barara Fair, **Vol. 4**, 144
Barari Devi's Fair, **Vol. 4**, 144
Baretha Fair, **Vol. 5**, 400
Barey Pir's Urs, **Vol. 4**, 456
Bari Fair, **Vol. 4**, 144
Barman Fair, **Vol. 5**, 391
Barnapur Fair, **Vol. 4**, 457
Barnot Fair, **Vol. 4**, 145
Baruni Fair, **Vol. 6**, 83, 173
Baruni Jatra, **Vol. 6**, 83
Baruni Festival, **Vol. 6**, 337
Baruni Snana, **Vol. 6**, 83
Barunishan Festival, **Vol. 6**, 174
Bas Puja / Madan Kam Puja, **Vol. 6**, 295
Basant Panchami / Fair, **Vol. 1**, 45-46, **Vol. 4**, 18, 145, 329, **Vol. 6**. 9, 125 *see also* Sripanchami
Basava Teertha Jatra, **Vol. 2**, 229
Basava-Jayanti Fair, **Vol. 2**, 227
Basavangudi Temple Festival, **Vol. 2**, 229
Basavanna Devara Jatra, **Vol. 2**, 231
Basavanna Jatra, **Vol. 2**, 231
Basavanna Temple Jatra
– Korva, **Vol. 2**, 231
– Nandi Kurli, **Vol. 2**, 232
– Nidtha, **Vol. 2**, 232
– Sultanpur, **Vol. 2**, 232
– Turamari, **Vol. 2**, 233
Basaveshvara Jatra, **Vol. 2**, 233
Baseli Puja (Chaiti Ghoda), **Vol. 6**, 78-80

Basi Charak Festival, **Vol. 6**, 174-76
Basilica Church Feast, **Vol. 3**, 304
Basora Festival, **Vol. 4**, 116
Bata Osha, **Vol. 6**, 83
Batamaloo Saheb, **Vol. 4**, 279
Bat-Tala / Paush Sankrantir Fair, **Vol. 6**, 456
Bawan Dwadashi, **Vol. 1**, 46, **Vol. 4**, 19, 116
Bawan Dwadashi Fair: Nahan, **Vol. 4**, 145
Bawangaja Jatra, **Vol. 5**, 392
Beebrian Fair, **Vol. 4**, 327
Beeralingeshvara Jatra, **Vol. 2**, 233
Beeredeva Jatra, **Vol. 2**, 234
Beeredevaru Jatra, **Vol. 2**, 235
Beh-Dieng-Khlam Festival, **Vol. 6**, 383
Belhi Devi Fair, **Vol. 4**, 457
Belli Basavanna Jatra, **Vol. 2**, 235
Belur Math Fair, **Vol. 6**, 176
Bendoji Baba Fair, **Vol. 5**, 241-43
Beri Baba Buddha, **Vol. 4**, 318
Berinag Fair, **Vol. 4**, 533
Betegara Muttappa Jatra, **Vol. 2**, 235
Bhadarvi Amas, **Vol. 1**, 43-44, **Vol. 5**, 99
Bhadra Amavasya, **Vol. 4**, 146
Bhadra Kali Fair, **Vol. 4**, 146, 327, 457, **Vol. 5**, 400
Bhadrakali Sarannavaratrothsavam, **Vol. 2**, 16
Bhadrakaliamman Festival, **Vol. 3**, 261
Bhadwa Mata Fair, **Vol. 5**, 392
Bhagabat Fair, **Vol. 6**, 84
Bhagandeshwara Temple Fair, **Vol. 2**, 236
Bhagat Singh Fair, **Vol. 4**, 327
Bhagavathi Fair, **Vol. 2**, 238
Bhagavathy Kavu Padayani, **Vol. 3**, 84
Bhagavathy Temple Pooram, **Vol. 3**, 85
Bhagavathy Temple Utsavam, **Vol. 3**, 86, 88
Bhagavati Temple Festival, **Vol. 5**, 54
Bhagabati Fair, **Vol. 6**, 41, 176
Bhagoria-hat Festival, **Vol. 5**, 400
Bhagwati Bala Sundri Fair, **Vol. 4**, 117
Bhagwati Devi Temple Fair, **Vol. 5**, 14
Bhai Behlo Fair, **Vol. 4**, 328
Bhai Duj, **Vol. 5**, 103
Bhai Gurdas Fair, **Vol. 4**, 328
Bhai Mani Singh Fair, **Vol. 4**, 328
Bhairaveshwara Jatra, **Vol. 2**, 239
Bhairavnath Fair, **Vol. 5**, 243
Bhairo Nath Temple Fair, **Vol. 4**, 9
Bhairoba Jatra, **Vol. 2**, 238
Bhakta Jalaram Fair, **Vol. 5**, 104-05
Bhalkeshwara Jatra, **Vol. 2**, 239
Bhandari Community, **Vol. 5**, 35
Bhandi Habba Jatra, **Vol. 2**, 240
Bhangui Community, **Vol. 5**, 57
Bhaona, **Vol. 6**, 296-99
Bharani Deepam, **Vol. 3**, 307
Bharani Festival, **Vol. 3**, 34
Bhareshwar Mahadev Fair, **Vol. 5**, 105
Bhari Devi Fair, **Vol. 4**, 147 *See also* Baravi Devi Fair
Bharwad, **Vol. 5**, 22
Bhatheli Festival, **Vol. 6**, 299
Bhatru Dwitiya, **Vol. 6**, 84
Bhattarika Temple Festival Sasinga, **Vol. 6**, 84
Bhavani Shankara Jatra, **Vol. 2**, 240
Bhaya Sokhar Devi Fair, **Vol. 5**, 40
Bheemana Festival, **Vol. 2**, 17
Bheemeshwara Jatra, **Vol. 2**, 239
Bhel Fair, **Vol. 4**, 147
Bhilat Baba Fair, **Vol. 5**, 402
Bhilat Deo Fair, **Vol. 5**, 403
Bhim Ekadashi, **Vol. 5**, 106
Bhim Kund Fair, **Vol. 5**, 392
Bhimbathaka Fair, **Vol. 5**, 403
Bhimeshwara Temple Jatra, **Vol. 2**, 241
Bhimeswaraswamy Kalyanam, **Vol. 2**, 17
Bhingaram Dokra Fair, **Vol. 5**, 14
Bhoga Nanjundeshvara Jatra, **Vol. 2**, 241
Bhogi Pandigai Festival, **Vol. 3**, 306-07
Bhoj Fair, **Vol. 4**, 147
Bhoj Smriti Utsava, **Vol. 5**, 392
Bhojpur Jatra, **Vol. 5**, 394
Bhola Rameshvara Jatra, **Vol. 2**, 241
Bhoomi-Hunnime Festival, **Vol. 2**, 242
Bhopali Fair, **Vol. 5**, 403
Bhubaneshwar Fair, **Vol. 6**, 7 *See also* Jagannath Car Festival
Bhubaneshwar Jatra, **Vol. 6**, 84-93
Bhujariya Festival, **Vol. 5**, 403
Bhumeshwari Devi Fair, **Vol. 4**, 117
Bhunda Rohru, **Vol. 4**,149
Bhunda, **Vol. 4**, 148
Bhunjraru Chhinj, **Vol. 4**, 149
Bhupatamma's Temple Jatra, **Vol. 2**, 242
Bhur Singh Devta Fair, **Vol. 4**, 150
Bhura Baba Fair, **Vol. 4**, 457
Bibeksar, **Vol. 4**, 319
Bible Sunday, **Vol. 1**, 137, **Vol. 4**, 92

Bihar Sharif Jatra, **Vol. 6**, 7-8
Bihu Festival, **Vol. 6**, 300-304
Bija Pando, **Vol. 6**, 80
Bijbehara Fairs, **Vol. 4**, 279
Bijleshwari Devi Fair, **Vol. 4**, 458
Bilaimata Fair, **Vol. 5**, 14
Biligiri Rangasvami Temple Car Festival, **Vol. 2**, 243
Bilkharnath Fair, **Vol. 4**, 458
Binda Fair, **Vol. 6**, 41
Bir-Ner Devi Fair, **Vol. 4**, 458
Birshu-ki-Jatar, **Vol. 4**, 150
Bisalakashi Festival, **Vol. 6**, 177
Bisalakhi Fair, **Vol. 6**, 177
Bishtadevi Jatra, **Vol. 2**, 243
Bishu Fair, **Vol. 4**, 151, **Vol. 6**, 40
Bishu Festival, **Vol. 4**, 152-53, *See also* Bissu Fair/Festival
Bishwat Sankranti Fair, **Vol. 4**, 533
Bisri Thakurani Jatra, **Vol. 6**, 93
Bissu Fair, **Vol. 4**, 533, *See also* Bishu Fair
Bissu Festival, **Vol. 4**, 533, *See also* Bishu Festival
Bisucani Festival, **Vol. 6**, 45
Biswakarma Puja, **Vol. 6**, 94
Biyah Oja, **Vol. 6**, 304-305
Blessed Lady of Happy Voyage Feast, **Vol. 6**, 177
Blessed Lady of Rosary's Feast, **Vol. 6**, 178
Bo (Bodhi) Tree, **Vol. 6**, 27-28
Bodam Festival, **Vol. 6**, 94
Bodgeshwar Temple Fair, **Vol. 5**, 54
Bodh Gaya Temples **Vol. 6**, 24-27
Bohag Bihu Festival, **Vol. 6**, 305-309
Boi Sagu, **Vol. 6**, 309
Bomblya Vithoba Fair, **Vol. 5**, 244
Boori Boot Festival, **Vol. 6**, 26
Boramdeo Fair, **Vol. 5**, 404
Brahma Rathotsava, **Vol. 2**, 244
Brahmadatyar Fair, **Vol. 6**, 178
Brahmadeva Jatra, **Vol. 2**, 244
Brahmaramba-Melleswarswamy Temple, **Vol. 2**, 31
Brahmasthan Fair, **Vol. 6**, 9
Brahmaur Jatar, **Vol. 4**, 153
Brahmayoni Hill Jatra, **Vol. 6**, 9
Brahmeshwara Jatra and Chintamani Narasimha Jatra, **Vol. 2**, 245
Brahmi-Durga Parameshwari Temple Car Festival, **Vol. 2**, 245
Brahmotsavam, **Vol. 3**, 273, 276, 284-86
  – Annual, **Vol. 3**, 278, 288
Bramaramho Mallesacarswamy Temple, **Vol. 2**, 31
Brihaspati Kund Fair, **Vol. 5**, 403
Buchamma Tirunalu, **Vol. 2**, 23
Buddha Lord, **Vol. 6**, 22
Buddha Purnima, **Vol. 1**, 46-47, **Vol. 4**, 20, **Vol. 6**, 453
Buddhist Monasteries Ceremonies, **Vol. 4**, 250-51
Buddhist Religious Observances
  – Kinnaur and Lahul-Spiti, **Vol. 4**, 220
Bundu Fair, **Vol. 6**, 41
Buniyar Temple Jatra, **Vol. 4**, 280
Burha Babu Fair, **Vol. 4**, 458
Burhan Sahid's Urs, **Vol. 4**, 458
Burmese of Andaman, **Vol. 3**, 10
Buru Fair, **Vol. 6**, 40-41
Byangkandi Fair, **Vol. 6**, 178

C

C.S.I. Church Feast of St. Lukose, **Vol. 3**, 88
Camel Festival, **Vol. 4**, 385
Car Festival (Rath Yatra) Jagannath, **Vol. 6**, 92-93, 120, 147
Cattle Fair
  – Chanpatia, **Vol. 6**, 10
  – Karkatta, **Vol. 6**, 10
  – Neerathanullaur, **Vol. 3**, 341
  – Sonepur, **Vol. 6**, 34
Cauvery Festival, **Vol. 2**, 246
Chadak Fair / Festival, **Vol. 6**, 180
Chadia Fair, **Vol. 5**, 106
Chait Parab, **Vol. 6**, 94, 97
Chatti Badshahi, **Vol. 4**, 280
Chaiti Ghoda (Basai Puja), **Vol. 6**, 78-80
Chaiti Ghoda Nata Festival, **Vol. 6**, 94
Chaiti Mangalbara Osha, **Vol. 6**, 95
Chaitra Amavasya Fair, **Vol. 4**, 117
Chaitra Vishu Festival, **Vol. 3**, 308-311
Chaitra Sankranti Fair
  – Basantrai, **Vol. 6**, 41
  – Khairpal, **Vol. 6**, 41
Chaitra Pratipada Festival, **Vol. 5**, 245
Chaitrang Thasma, **Vol. 4**, 154
Chaitri Atham Fair, **Vol. 5**, 106
Chaitri Purnima Fair, **Vol. 5**, 112-17
Chaitri Punam Fair, **Vol. 5**, 117
Chakrana Fair, **Vol. 4**, 154
Chaliho, **Vol. 1**, 99, **Vol. 4**, 60
Chalukyan period, **Vol. 2**, 3

Chamar, **Vol. 5**, 22
Chamkanna Sahib Gurdwara, **Vol. 4**, 369-70
Champajhar Fair, **Vol. 5**, 5
Champakadhamaswamy Jatra, **Vol. 2**, 248
Champavati Fair, **Vol. 4**, 154
Chamunda Devi Fair, **Vol. 4**, 118
Chamunda Mata Fair, **Vol. 5**, 247, 405
Chamundesvari Ammana Rathothsavam, **Vol. 2**, 250
Chamundi Fair, **Vol. 2**, 251
Chandan Yatra, **Vol. 6**, 95, 97
Chandanakunda Mahotsavam, **Vol. 3**, 45
Chandanyi Festival, **Vol. 6**, 419
Chanded Karnali Fair, **Vol. 5**, 118
Chandeshvari Festival, **Vol. 2**, 257
Chandeshvari Jatra, **Vol. 2**, 257
Chandi Fair, **Vol. 4**, 154
Chandidas Fair, **Vol. 6**, 179
Chandidevi Fair, **Vol. 5**, 405
Chandod-Karnali Fair, **Vol. 5**, 118
Chandrabhaga Fair, **Vol. 6**, 95
Chandralamba Jatra, **Vol. 2**, 247
Chandranath Temple Fair, **Vol. 5**, 54
Chandrashekharaswamy Jatra, **Vol. 2**, 251
Changdeo Fair, **Vol. 5**, 246
Channabasavanna Temple Jatra, **Vol. 2**, 253
Channabasaveshvara Jatra, **Vol. 2**, 253
Channabasaveshwara Jatra, **Vol. 2**, 257
Channabasaveshwaraswami Jatra, **Vol. 2**, 255
Channakeshava Jatra, **Vol. 2**, 256
Channakeshava Temple Car Festival, **Vol. 2**, 256
Channakeshavaswamy Car Festival, **Vol. 2**, 254
Channakeshavaswamy Jatra, **Vol. 2**, 257
Channappaswami Matha Festival, **Vol. 2**, 256
Channarayaswamy Temple Festival, **Vol. 2**, 252
Channaveera Basaveshwar Fair, **Vol. 2**, 257
Chapchar Kut, **Vol. 6**, 400, 410
Char Dham Yatra, **Vol. 4**, 533
Charayoli Fair, **Vol. 4**, 155
Chathan Kandar Kavu, Utsavam, **Vol. 3**, 89
Chatti Badshahi, **Vol. 4**, 280
Chattibasaveswar Jatra, **Vol. 2**, 258
Chatur Masya, **Vol. 3**, 313
Chatushshringi Fair, **Vol. 5**, 247-48
Chaunra Fair, **Vol. 4**, 155
Chauntra Fair, **Vol. 4**, 156
Chaurasti Atari, **Vol. 4**, 318
Chavan Rishi Fair, **Vol. 4**, 119
Cheeren-di, **Vol. 4**, 156
Chehallum Hussain Tekri Fair, **Vol. 5**, 405
Cheiraoba Festival, **Vol. 6**, 338
Chemmanad Bhagavathy Temple Garudan Thookam, **Vol. 3**, 90
Chengalam Devaswam Meena Bharany Utsavam, **Vol. 3**, 91
Chennray Swamy Jatra, **Vol. 2**, 258
Cheraman Jama Masjid Festival, **Vol. 3**, 92
Chethanchara (circumcision) Perunal, **Vol. 3**, 47
Cheti Chand, **Vol. 1**, 99-100, **Vol. 4**, 59
Chhapar Fair, **Vol. 4**, 331-34
Chhapia Jatra, **Vol. 4**, 459
Chhariyon ka Mela, **Vol. 4**, 459
Chhariyun Fair, **Vol. 4**, 156
Chhata Festival, **Vol. 6**, 9, 179
Chhath Fair, **Vol. 6**, 10
Chhath Puru, **Vol. 6**, 10
Chhatiabata Jatra, **Vol. 6**, 97
Chhaya Bhagavathi Festival, **Vol. 2**, 258
Chheharta Fair, **Vol. 4**, 334
Chheshu, **Vol. 4**, 157
Chhokten, **Vol. 4**, 158
Chidambaram Temple Brahmotsavam, **Vol. 3**, 311
Children's Day, **Vol. 1**, 99, **Vol. 4**, 109
Children's Sunday, **Vol. 1**, 103, **Vol. 4**, 92
Chinakkathur Bhagavathy Temple Utsavam, **Vol. 3**, 93
Chindi Fair, **Vol. 4**, 158
Chintalamma Teertham, **Vol. 2**, 23
Chintamani Narasimha Jatra, **Vol. 2**, 245, 259
Chintamani Tirunal, **Vol. 3**, 374
Chintpurni Fair, **Vol. 4**, 159-60
Chirand Fair, **Vol. 6**, 10
Chirhnu, **Vol. 4**, 161
Chitalagi or Chitou Amavasya, **Vol. 6**, 96
Chitpavan Brahman, **Vol. 5**, 59
Chitou Amavasya, **Vol. 6**, 96
Chitrakoot Dham Jatra, **Vol. 4**, 460-61
Chitra-Pournami Festival, **Vol. 3**, 312
Chitra-Vichitra Fair, **Vol. 5**, 106-08
Chitrari Jatar, **Vol. 4**, 242
Chomanghan, **Vol. 6**, 310
Choorakkot Temple Utsavam, **Vol. 3**, 93
Choumukh Nat Fair, **Vol. 5**, 405
Chowdeswaridevi Jyothi Mahothsavam, **Vol. 2**, 24
Chowmoon Kando Poi Festival, **Vol. 6**, 282
Chowra pilgrimage, **Vol. 3**, 16
Chrari-Sharief, **Vol. 4**, 280

Christ King, **Vol. 1**, 132, **Vol. 4**, 91
Christian Festivals, **Vol. 1**, 131-138, **Vol. 4**, 85-93
Christmas, **Vol. 1**, 132-133, **Vol. 3**, 25, **Vol. 4**, 86-88
Chul Fair, **Vol. 5**, 119
Chumpha Festival, **Vol. 6**, 339
Chunanghi Bhagavathy Temple Pavakoothu, **Vol. 3**, 94
Chunchangiri Jatra, **Vol. 2**, 259
Chunehar Fair, **Vol. 4**, 161
Church of Our Lady of Health 'Saude' Feast, **Vol. 3**, 94
Church of Reis Mago's Feast, **Vol. 5**, 54
Coimbatore Cattle Fairs, **Vol. 3**, 313
Coonan Cross Shrine Feast, **Vol. 3**, 158

D

Dabbaguli Basaveshwara Temple Jatra, **Vol. 2**, 259
Dad Shisha Fair, **Vol. 6**, 11
Dadhi Kandotsava Festival, **Vol. 5**, 406
Dadhi Vamana Vishnu Temple Jatra Bhatli, **Vol. 6**, 101
Dadri Fair, **Vol. 4**, 461, **Vol. 6**, 11
Dadshisha Fair, **Vol. 6**, 11
Daivadrya Brahman / Shett, **Vol. 5**, 59
Dakhraini Festival, **Vol. 4**, 161-62
Dakke-Bali Festival, **Vol. 2**, 260, 263
Dakshineshwar Fair, **Vol. 6**, 180
Damdama Sahib Jatra, **Vol. 4**, 334
Damodar Kund, **Vol. 5**, 101
- Koliyak Fair, **Vol. 5**, 102

Dandanata Danda Jatra, **Vol. 6**, 98
Dandelappa Jatra, **Vol. 2**, 260
Dandi Marammana Jatra, **Vol. 2**, 260
Dangs Darbar, **Vol. 5**, 119
Darbharanyeshwarar Temple Festival, **Vol. 3**, 262
Dasain Festival, **Vol. 6**, 448
Dasara Festival-Mysore, **Vol. 2**, 261
Dashmi Fair, **Vol. 4**, 335
Dastgir's Urs, **Vol. 4**, 281
Dasthagiriswami Urs, **Vol. 2**, 24
Datta Janma Fair, **Vol. 5**, 249
Dattananda Maharaj Fair, **Vol. 2**, 262
Dattatraya Fair, **Vol. 5**, 406, **Vol. 6**, 11
Dattatraya Maharaj Jatra, **Vol. 2**, 262
Dattatreya Jayanthi, **Vol. 3**, 315
Dauji Fair, **Vol. 4**, 462
Death Anniversary of Sayyid Hussain Simnani, **Vol. 4**, 281
Dechang, **Vol. 4**, 162
Dedication Festival, **Vol. 3**, 186
Deepavali Pandigai Festival, **Vol. 3**, 314
Deewyali (Diwali), **Vol. 4**, 162
Dehra Jatar, **Vol. 4**, 162
Dehri Ghat Jatar, **Vol. 4**, 163
Deojhiri Fair, **Vol. 5**, 406
Deotari Fair, **Vol. 4**, 462
Deothi Dhar Fair, **Vol. 4**, 163
Dera Baba Jaimal Singh Congregation, **Vol. 4**, 336
Dera Baba Nanak Jatra, **Vol. 4**, 336
Deul Fair Hajo, **Vol. 6**, 311
Deul Festival, **Vol. 6**, 311
Deuri Bisu, **Vol. 6**, 312
Dev Bara Fair, **Vol. 4**, 164
Deva Prayag, **Vol. 4**, 534
Devasnana Purnima / Snana Yatra, **Vol. 6**, 98-100
Devshayanai Ekadashi Festival, **Vol. 1**, 47, **Vol. 5**, 123
Devazhiri Fair, **Vol. 5**, 406
Devi Dhar Fair, **Vol. 4**, 164
Devi Fair, **Vol. 4**, 462-63
Devi Jatra, **Vol. 2**, 262
Devi Ki Jat, **Vol. 4**, 165
Devi Navarathmulu, **Vol. 2**, 25
Devipatan Fair, **Vol. 4**, 464
Devlan Fair, **Vol. 5**, 123
Dev-Podhi Agiarash, **Vol. 5**, 123
Devshayami Ekadashi, **Vol. 5**, 123
Devuthani Giras Festival, **Vol. 4**, 119
Dewadas Baba Fair, **Vol. 5**, 406
Dhabaleswar Jatra, **Vol. 6**, 102
Dhada Bahnana Fair, **Vol. 4**, 165
Dhadi Ghunsa Jatar, **Vol. 4**, 165
Dhakke Bali Festival, **Vol. 2**, 263, *See also* Dakkes-Bali Festival
Dhaldighi Fair, **Vol. 6**, 181
Dham Sankranti Festival, **Vol. 6**, 100
Dhan Terash, **Vol. 1**, 49, **Vol. 4**, 20, 22
Dhangar Community, **Vol. 5**, 60
Dhanu Samkranti Festival, **Vol. 6**, 100
Dhanus Yajna Fair, **Vol. 4**, 464-65
Dhaoyali Fair, **Vol. 6**, 181
Dhara and Khoottudhara Festival, **Vol. 3**, 316
Dharanatha Jatra, **Vol. 2**, 263
Dhari Fair, **Vol. 4**, 165
Dharma Yatra Fair, **Vol. 6**, 41
Dharma Puja, **Vol. 6**, 41
Dharma Puja Festival, **Vol. 6**, 185
Dharmappa Rathothsavam, **Vol. 2**, 32

Dharmarajeshwar Mahadeva Fair, **Vol. 5**, 406
Dhauli Jatra, **Vol. 6**, 103-105
Di-Batai Festival, **Vol. 6**, 282
Dhodia Community, **Vol. 5**, 44
Dholbaha Jatra, **Vol. 4**, 337
Dhopap Ghat Fair, **Vol. 4**, 465
Dhuleti or Dhuli Padvo Dolotsav, **Vol. 5**, 124
Dhuredundeshwara Matha Car Festival, **Vol. 2**, 263
Dhuredundeshwara Jatra, **Vol. 2**, 264
Di-Batai Festival, **Vol. 6**, 282
Dnyaneshwar Fair, **Vol. 5**, 250
Digiali, **Vol. 4**, 166
Dimki Fair, **Vol. 4**, 166
Dindi Festival, **Vol. 5**, 54
Divaso Ashadh Vad 15 (Amas), **Vol. 5**, 124
Diwali, **Vol. 1**, 24, 47-52, 102, 108, **Vol. 4**, 15, 20-25, 62, 71, 162
Dol Festival of Makarchandi, **Vol. 6**, 185
Dol Jatra Festival, **Vol. 6**, 185-87
Dola Jatra, **Vol. 6**, 105-106
Dola Purnima (Holi), **Vol. 6**, 100-101
Doul Festival, **Vol. 6**, 312
Draupadi Amman Temple Festival, **Vol. 3**, 261
Dree Festival, **Vol. 6**, 262
Dronagiri Fair, **Vol. 5**, 407
Dubaraju Teertham, **Vol. 2**, 32
Dubla Community, **Vol. 5**, 44
Dudh Bahli Fair, **Vol. 4**, 166
Dudheswar Mahadev Fair, **Vol. 5**, 407
Dugri Shuri, **Vol. 4**, 281
Dukh Bhanjan Asthan, **Vol. 4**, 318
Dulas, **Vol. 4**, 76
Dumbaru or Tirthamukh Fair, **Vol. 6**, 457
Dumgyur-zalmo Fair, **Vol. 4**, 167
Durga Ashtami Fair, **Vol. 4**, 167
Durga Ashtami, **Vol. 3**, 142
Durga Devi Jatra, **Vol. 2**, 265
Durga Fair, **Vol. 6**, 188
Durga Mata Fair, **Vol. 5**, 251
Durga Puja Festival, **Vol. 6**, 101, 168, 188, 313, 340, 342, 452, *See also* Navaratri
Durga Temple Utsavam, **Vol. 3**, 95
Durgah Wale Miya's Urs, **Vol. 5**, 407
Durgambika Jatra, **Vol. 2**, 265
Durgamma Jatra, **Vol. 2**, 33, 265
Durgaparameshwari Jatra, **Vol. 2**, 265
Durgaparameshwari Temple Car Festival, **Vol. 2**, 266
Durgaparameshwari Temple Festival, **Vol. 2**, 266
Durgiana Mandir Fair, **Vol. 4**, 338
Dusain Festival, **Vol. 6**, 448
Dussehra, **Vol. 1**, 52-53, 102, **Vol. 4**, 21, 25-28, 62, **Vol. 5**, 4, 5, 94, 121, 248, 375
– in Bastar Region, **Vol. 5**, 5-14
– in Kullu (H.P.), **Vol. 4**, 168-74
– in Mysore, **Vol. 2**, 261 *See also* Vijaya Dashmi
Dutia Fair, **Vol. 6**, 12
Dwadesh-Parvi, **Vol. 1**, 115, **Vol. 4**, 72
Dwarka, **Vol. 5**, 138-41
Dyamavva Jatra, **Vol. 2**, 266

E

Easter Sunday, **Vol. 1**, 133-134, **Vol. 4**, 90
Ekadashi Fair, **Vol. 4**, 174
Ekadesi, **Vol. 3**, 42-43
Erathu Mukkalavattom Temple Sree Naryana Jayanthi, **Vol. 3**, 48
Eswaramma Aradhana, **Vol. 2**, 33

F

Fag Fair, **Vol. 4**, 175
Fagun Bazar Fair, **Vol. 5**, 407
Farah Fair, **Vol. 4**, 465
Fast of Ab, **Vol. 1**, 148, **Vol. 4**, 105
Fast of Esther, **Vol. 1**, 148-149, **Vol. 4**, 104
Fast of Gedaliah, **Vol. 1**, 148, **Vol. 4**, 101
Fast of Tammuz, **Vol. 1**, 151-152, **Vol. 4**, 105
Fast of Tebet, **Vol. 1**, 150, **Vol. 4**, 104
Fatehpur Sikri, **Vol. 4**, 514
Fathekhan Hajrath Urs, **Vol. 2**, 34
Feast of Christ the King, **Vol. 3**, 78, 160
Feast of the Confraternity of Our Lady of Mount Caramel, **Vol. 3**, 78
Feast of Hannuccah, **Vol. 1**, 149, **Vol. 4**, 103
Feast of Mary Immaculate, **Vol. 3**, 209
Feast of our Lady of Rosary, **Vol. 3**, 161, **Vol. 3**, 180
Feast of our Lady of Snows, **Vol. 3**, 78
Feast of Passover, **Vol. 1**, 150, **Vol. 4**, 104
Feast of Pentecost / Shabuoth, **Vol. 1**, 150-151, **Vol. 4**, 105
Feast of Purim, **Vol. 4**, 104
Feast of St. George, **Vol. 3**, 74
Feast of St. Joseph the Worker, **Vol. 3**, 77

Feast of St. Mary of Dolours, **Vol. 3**, 75
Feast of St. Sebastian, **Vol. 3**, 78, **Vol. 3**, 209
Feast of St. Xavier, **Vol. 3**, 79
Feast of Tabernacles, **Vol. 4**, 102
Fire Walking, **Vol. 4**, 77
First Navratra, **Vol. 4**, 281
Floating Festival, **Vol. 3**, 263
Forane Church Feast of St. George, **Vol. 3**, 96
Ful Dol Festival, **Vol. 5**, 407

G

Gabbar Hill Shrine—Ambaji, **Vol. 5**, 95
Gada Gusain Fair, **Vol. 4**, 176
Gadadam Venkataramanaswami Jatra, **Vol. 2**, 266
Gadda Fair, **Vol. 5**, 251-58
Gaddi-Khader Wali Urs, **Vol. 2**, 267
Gadge Maharaj Fair, **Vol. 5**, 258
Gahambars, **Vol. 1**, 140, **Vol. 4**, 98
Gahma Purnima (Rakhi Purnima) 106
Gajalingeshwara Jatra, **Vol. 2**, 267
Gajan Festival, **Vol. 6**, 189-93
– Bahulara, **Vol. 6**, 189
– Beliatore, **Vol. 6**, 191
– Dihar, **Vol. 6**, 191
– Ekteswar, **Vol. 6**, 192
– Ghaneswara, **Vol. 6**, 193
– Konarpur, **Vol. 6**, 193
– Panchal, **Vol. 6**, 193
– Shandeswar, **Vol. 6**, 193
Gajbar Sab Sabu Sayida and Khadirshah Urs, **Vol. 2**, 267
Gajbeej Festival, **Vol. 5**, 409
Gal Jatra, **Vol. 5**, 408
Galageshwara Temple Jatra, **Vol. 2**, 267
Gal-Devro Fair, **Vol. 5**, 125
Gana-Gour Festival, **Vol. 5**, 410
Ganapati Fair, **Vol. 5**, 259
Gandhiji's Birthday, **Vol. 1**, 155-156, **Vol. 4**, 108
Ganesh Chaturthi, **Vol. 1**, 53-55, **Vol. 4**, 26-28, **Vol. 5**, 260-63
Ganesh Choth, **Vol. 1**, 102, **Vol. 4**, 62
Ganesh Puja Fair, **Vol. 6**, 14
Ganeshotsav Fair, **Vol. 5**, 263
Ganga Devi Jatra, **Vol. 2**, 268
Ganga Dussehra, **Vol. 1**. 55-56
Ganga Fair, **Vol. 4**, 176, 466-67, **Vol. 6**, 194
Ganga Mata Fair, **Vol. 5**, 408
Gangasagar Fair, **Vol. 5**, 408, **Vol. 6**, 194
Gangadiya Puja Festival, **Vol. 6**, 194
Gangaur Festival, **Vol. 4**, 385-403
Ganges Story, **Vol. 4**, 535
Gangotri Temple, **Vol. 4**, 535
Gani Fair, **Vol. 4**, 176
Ganinath Fair, **Vol. 6**, 14
Gan-Ngai Festival, **Vol. 6**, 343-45
Garagalamma Teertham, **Vol. 2**, 34
Garbara Devi Fair, **Vol. 4**, 467
Garbaray, **Vol. 4**, 176
Gardeo Festival, **Vol. 5**, 417
Garhchandi Festival, **Vol. 6**, 194
Garibnath Baba Fair, **Vol. 5**, 412
Garudotsavam Festival, **Vol. 3**, 316
Gathas, **Vol. 1**, 140, **Vol. 4**, 99
Gaura Festival, **Vol. 5**, 412-16
Gauri Shankar Fair, **Vol. 5**, 417
Gauri Shankar Temple Fair, **Vol. 4**, 121, 467
Gauri Tij or Gauntri, **Vol. 4**, 176
Gaurikund, **Vol. 4**, 541
Gavi-Gangadhareshwara Jatra, **Vol. 2**, 268
Gavisiddheshwara Jatra, **Vol. 2**, 269
Gaya Jatra, **Vol. 6**, 12-13
Gayab Shah Vali Urs, **Vol. 2**, 35
Gay-Gohari Fair, **Vol. 5**, 125
Gayib Peer Shebah Urs, **Vol. 2**, 270
Genna Festival, **Vol. 6**, 383
Ghannai Fair, **Vol. 4**, 468
Ghanti Baba Fair, **Vol. 3**, 264
Ghatashi Mata Fair, **Vol. 4**, 176
Ghatku Deota Fair, **Vol. 4**, 543
Ghazi Mian Fair, **Vol. 4**, 468
Ghazi Peer Fair, **Vol. 4**, 469
Ghela Somnath Fair, **Vol. 5**, 125
Ghensio Fair, **Vol. 5**, 126
Ghiyasuddin Auliya Urs, **Vol. 6**, 317
Ghughutiya Festival, **Vol. 4**, 543
Ghuisernath Fair, **Vol. 4**, 469
Ghulam Ali Shah Badshah Shrine Jatra, **Vol. 4**, 282
Ghund Fair, **Vol. 4**, 176
Gija Festival, **Vol. 4**, 177
Girija-Kalyanotsava Festival, **Vol. 2**, 270
Gobardhana Puja Festival, **Vol. 1**, 56, **Vol. 6**, 195, *See also*, Govardhan
Godavari Pushkaram, **Vol. 2**, 35
Gogaji Fair, **Vol. 4**, 403-406

Gogga Pir Fair, **Vol. 4**, 469
Gokul, **Vol. 4**, 490
Gola Gokkarnath Jatra, **Vol. 4**, 469
Golden Car Feast of Our Lady of Snows, **Vol. 3**, 361
Golden Temple Festivals and Jatra, **Vol. 4**, 339
Golden Temple, **Vol. 4**, 317
Gol-gadhela Fair, **Vol. 5**, 126
Gollaleshvara Fair, **Vol. 2**, 271
Gommateshwara Mahamasthakabhishekka, **Vol. 2**, 271
Good Friday, **Vol. 1**, 134, **Vol. 4**, 90
Good Shepherd Church Feast, **Vol. 3**, 97
Gopalakrishna Jatra, **Vol. 2**, 272
Gopalakrishnaswami Rathotsavam, **Vol. 2**, 272, 274
Gopalaswami Fair, **Vol. 2**, 274
Gop-Ashtami, **Vol. 1**, 152, **Vol. 4**, 62
Gopastami Fair, **Vol. 6**, 15, 42
Gopinath Temple Mahotsava, **Vol. 6**, 195
Goryo / Gauri Vrata, **Vol. 5**, 126
Gosavi Community, **Vol. 5**, 61
Goshala Fair, **Vol. 6**, 42
Goshthashtami Fair, **Vol. 6**, 196-97
Got Mar Fair, **Vol. 5**, 416
Govardhan, **Vol. 1**, 56, **Vol. 4**, 490, *See also*, Gobardhan
Grand Festival of St. George, **Vol. 3**, 186
Great Andamanese tribes, **Vol. 3**, 4
Guddekal Siddheshwara Car Festival, **Vol. 2**, 274
Gugga Bhater Fair, **Vol. 4**, 177
Gugga Chamkyo Fair, **Vol. 4**, 178
Gugga Fair, **Vol. 4**, 178-82
Gugga Naumi/Navami, **Vol. 1**, 56-58, **Vol. 4**, 28-30, 120, 178, 182
Guggal Fair, **Vol. 4**, 543
Guma Fair, **Vol. 4**, 182
Gupt Kashi, **Vol. 4**, 536, **Vol. 4**, 541
Guru Angad Dev Fair, **Vol. 4**, 340
Guru Gobind Singh Fair, **Vol. 4**, 342
Guru Ka Bagh Fair, **Vol. 4**, 342
Guru Ka Mahal, **Vol. 4**, 318
Guru Nanak's Birthday, **Vol. 1**, 100-101, **Vol. 4**, 61
Guru Purnima, **Vol. 5**,127
Guru Ravi Das Fair, **Vol. 4**, 342
Guru Teg Bahadur Birthday, **Vol. 6**, 317
Gurudwara Akalgarh Fair, **Vol. 4**, 342
Gurudwara Ber Sahib Fair, **Vol. 4**, 342-43
Gurudwara Bhatta Sahib Fair, **Vol. 4**, 343
Gurudwara Dashmi and Naumi Padshahi, **Vol. 4**, 120
Gurudwara Garua Sahib Fair, **Vol. 4**, 343
Gurudwara Guru Hargobind Fair, **Vol. 4**, 343
Gurudwara Gurusar Fair, **Vol. 4**, 343
Gurudwara Hatt Sahib, **Vol. 4**, 344
Gurudwara Parivar Vichhora Sahib Fair, **Vol. 4**, 344
Gurudwara Sada Barat Festival, **Vol. 4**, 344
Gurudwara Sara Garhi, **Vol. 4**, 319
Gurudwara Shahid Ganj Baba Dip Singh, **Vol. 4**, 320
Gurudwara Sukh Chainan Sahib, **Vol. 4**, 345
Gurudwara Tahli Sahib Fair, **Vol. 4**, 345
Gurudwara Tami Sahib Fair, **Vol. 4**, 345
Gurudwara Tham Sahib Fair, **Vol. 4**, 345
Gurudwaras visited by Pilgrims, **Vol. 4**, 335, 337
Gurunathaswami Festival, **Vol. 3**, 317
Gurupurabs, **Vol. 1**, 58-59, **Vol. 4**, 9, 30
Guruvayur Temple Utsavam, **Vol. 3**, 97-99
Guthiamma Bhagavathy Temple Utsavam, **Vol. 3**, 82
Gyaneshwar Fair, **Vol. 4**, 470
Gyarwin, **Vol. 1**, 118-19, **Vol. 4**, 79

H

Hadaga Festival, **Vol. 5**, 265
Hadi Community, **Vol. 5**, 37
Hafiz Musa Sahib Urs, **Vol. 4**, 345
Hafiz Urs Fair, **Vol. 5**, 417
Hagaranada Habba Jatra, **Vol. 2**, 274
Haji Malang Fair, **Vol. 5**, 267-70
Haladamma Jatra, **Vol. 2**, 275
Halasiddhanatha Jatra, **Vol. 2**, 275
Haliyur Shri Anjaneyaswami Jatra, **Vol. 2**, 275
Halshasti Festival, **Vol. 5**, 418-24
Handeshwar Nath Mahadeo Fair, **Vol. 4**, 471
Hanriya, **Vol. 6**, 11
Hanuman Jayanti Utsav, **Vol. 6**, 15
Hanuman Fair, **Vol. 2**, 276
Hanuman Jatra, **Vol. 2**, 276
Hanuman Jayanti, **Vol. 1**, 59, 276, **Vol. 5**, 270
Hanuman Temple Fair, **Vol. 2**, 276, **Vol. 5**, 417
Hanumantha Car Festival, **Vol. 2**, 277
Harat Fair, **Vol. 4**, 182
Harela Festival, **Vol. 4**, 543
Hari Devi Fair, **Vol. 4**, 182
Hari Mallappa Temple Festival, **Vol. 2**, 277
Hari Talika Brat/Chiryun ka Brat, **Vol. 4**, 183
Hari Vallabh Sangeet Fair, **Vol. 4**, 345

Hariari Festival, **Vol. 6**, 48
Harihara Fair, **Vol. 2**, 277
Harishankar Jatra, **Vol. 6**, 128
Haritalika Vrata, **Vol. 5**, 270
Hariyali Amavas Festival, **Vol. 5**, 417
Harsiddhi Mahakali Fair, **Vol. 6**, 417
Harvest Festival Sunday, **Vol. 1**, 137, **Vol. 4**, 92
Haryana history, **Vol. 4**, 111-14
Hasanamba Temple Jatra, **Vol. 2**, 278
Hasim Data Fair, **Vol. 4**, 470
Hassan Peer Urs, **Vol. 2**, 278
Hastinapur Fair, **Vol. 4**, 470
Hatia Haran Fair, **Vol. 4**, 471
Hatkoti Dussehra, **Vol. 4**, 183
Haudeshwar Nath Mahadeo Fair, **Vol. 3**, 471
Hayagrira Festival, **Vol. 3**, 317
Hayyalappa Jatra, **Vol. 2**, 278
Hazarat Baba Hyderwali Urs, **Vol. 2**, 279
Hazarat Hameed Shah Quadri Urs, **Vol. 2**, 279
Hazarat Khader Vali Urs, **Vol. 2**, 37, 127
Hazarat Khaja Bunnabi Urs, **Vol. 2**, 279
Hazarat Lakhi Shah's Urs, **Vol. 4**, 120
Hazarat Lal Shahabaj Qalandar Urs, **Vol. 5**, 265
Hazarat Makhdum Faqih Ali Saheb Urs, **Vol. 5**, 266
Hazarat Niranjan Shah Vali Urs, **Vol. 2**, 37
Hazarat Shah Wali Urs, **Vol. 2**, 279
Hazarat Syed Bajith Shahid Aulia Urs, **Vol. 2**, 38
Hazarat Syed Basha Vali Urs, **Vol. 2**, 37, 128
Hazarat Syed Shah Jalaluddin Urs, **Vol. 2**, 38
Hazarat Syed Tajuddin Bagsawar Urs, **Vol. 2**, 279
Hazarat Tawakkal Mastan Shah Suhrawardi Urs, **Vol. 2**, 280
Hazrat Nizam-ud-din Auliya's Urs, **Vol. 4**, 9-11
Hazrat Sheikh Sadr-u-din Fair, **Vol. 4**, 353
Hazratbal, **Vol. 4**, 282
Heikru Hitongba Festival, **Vol. 6**, 345-47
Hindu Festival, **Vol. 1**, 39-98
Hemadramma Jatra, **Vol. 2**, 280
Hill Marias festivals, **Vol. 5**, 441
Hingula Yatra (Patua Yatra), **Vol. 6**, 106
Hira Bhumia Fair, **Vol. 5**, 424
Hobar Chhinj, **Vol. 4**, 184
Hola Fair, **Vol. 4**, 184
Hola Mohalla Fair
- Anandpur Sahib, **Vol. 4**, 346-51
- Dera Baba Gurbhag Singh, **Vol. 4**, 352-53

Hole-Lingeshwara Jatra, **Vol. 2**, 281
Holi, **Vol. 1**, 39-40, 60-61, 102, **Vol. 4**, 31, 62, **Vol. 5**, 94, 127, **Vol. 6**, 100-01, 362-67
Holi Spirit Church Fair, **Vol. 5**, 54
Holi, **Vol. 5**, 94
Holy Cross Church Feast, **Vol. 3**, 362
Holy Cross R.C. Church Feast, **Vol. 3**, 10
Holy Cross the Cruzmilagres Church Feast, **Vol. 3**, 99
Holy Spirit Church Fair, **Vol. 5**, 54
Holy week Festivals, **Vol. 1,** 135, **Vol. 4,** 89-92
Honnaralamma Jatra, **Vol. 2**, 281
Horo Mangalavara, **Vol. 2**, 282
Hospital Sunday, **Vol. 1**, 137
Household Celebrations (Manipur), **Vol. 6**, 342
Huchcharaya Swamy Jatra, **Vol. 2**, 282
Huliat Festival, **Vol. 4**, 543
Huligemma Temple Jatra, **Vol. 2**, 282
Huligere Dodda Matha Festival, **Vol. 2**, 282
Huma Jatra, **Vol. 6**, 107
Hunapongpi Festival, **Vol. 6**, 419
Hundan Fair, **Vol. 4**, 185
Hundelkoppa Mukappa Swamy Jatra, **Vol. 2**, 283
Hussain Vali Urs, **Vol. 2**, 38
Huttari Festival, **Vol. 2**, 283
Hut Ashani, **Vol. 5**, 127

I

Id-e-Milad, **Vol. 1**, 119-22, **Vol. 4**, 77
Id-ul-Fitr, **Vol. 1**, 121-22, **Vol. 4**, 81
Id-ul-Zuha, **Vol. 1**, 122-23, **Vol. 4**, 11, 82
Imam Jaffar Urs, **Vol. 2**, 283
Immaculate Conception Church Feast, **Vol. 3**, 101
Immaculate Conception's Feast, **Vol. 5**, 56
Immaculate of Merces's Feast, **Vol. 5**, 56
Inam Dattatreya Peetha Festival, **Vol. 2**, 284
Inda Festival, **Vol. 6**, 107
Independence Day, **Vol. 1**, 156-57, **Vol. 4**, 107
Indra Puja Fair/Festival, **Vol. 6**, 5, 15, 197
Infant Jesus Church Feast, **Vol. 3**, 101
Iralappa Festival, **Vol. 2**, 285
Irambamon Temple Utsavam, **Vol. 3**, 101
Iriangol Bhagavathy Temple Utsavam, **Vol. 4**, 102
Ishwara Temple Festival, **Vol. 2**, 285
Ismail Khadri Urs, **Vol. 2**, 286
Ismaili Khojas Festivals, **Vol. 1**, 128-29, **Vol. 4**, 84
Iwaan Jatar, **Vol. 4**, 185

J

Jagaddhatri Puja Festival, **Vol. 6**, 197
Jaganj Fair, **Vol. 4**, 185
Jagannath Maharaj Fair, **Vol. 2**, 286
Jagannath Car Festival/Rath Yatra, **Vol. 6**, 43, 109, 120-23
Jagannath Ji Ki Katha, **Vol. 5**, 424-28
Jagannath Temple Festival, **Vol. 6**, 108-11
Jagannath Temple Utsavam, **Vol. 3**, 102
Jagannatha Yatra, **Vol. 1**, 61-63
Jageshwar Mahadeo Jatra: Bandakpur, **Vol. 5**, 429
Jageshwari Devi Fair, **Vol. 5**, 429
Jagra, **Vol. 4**, 187, **Vol. 6**, 116
Jagra Festival, **Vol. 4**, 543
Jagra Jubbal, **Vol. 4**, 185
Jagra Rohru, **Vol. 4**, 186
Jagro, **Vol. 4**, 220
Jain Basadis Jatra, **Vol. 2**, 286, 287
Jain Fair, **Vol. 5**, 429
Jain Festivals, **Vol. 1**, 107-115, **Vol. 3**, 318, **Vol. 4**, 63-72
Jain Matha's Jatra, **Vol. 2**, 288
Jain Temple Pooja, **Vol. 3**, 103
Jains / Buddhists Religious Centre
- Rajgriha, **Vol. 6**, 29-30
- Bodhgaya, **Vol. 6**, 27

Jakh Fair, **Vol. 5**, 127-29
Jal Jholni Fair, **Vol. 4**, 122
Jal Vihar Fair, **Vol. 5**, 430
Jal-Jhilani Ekadashi Fair, **Vol. 5**, 129-36
Jalpa Kalpa Devi Fair, **Vol. 4**, 472
Jalpes Fair, **Vol. 6**, 198
Jalvihar Fair/Festival, **Vol. 4**, 471, 472, **Vol. 5**, 430
Jamal Vali Urs, **Vol. 2**, 39
Jambeshwar Fair, **Vol. 4**, 406-408
Jamdagni Kund Fair, **Vol. 4**, 472
Jamshedji Navroz, **Vol. 1**, 140-141, **Vol. 4**, 96
Janakesh Wara Mahadeva Fair, **Vol. 5**, 430
Janan Panchami, **Vol. 4**, 64
Janardhanaswamy Festival, **Vol. 2**, 288
Janardhanaswamy Temple Arat, **Vol. 3**, 103
Janardhanaswamy Temple Car Festival, **Vol. 2**, 288
Jand Sahib Fair, **Vol. 4**, 354
Janhi Osha, **Vol. 6**, 129
Janjgir (district) Chhattisgarh, **Vol. 5**, 2
Janki Niwas Fair, **Vol. 5**, 430
Janmashtami Fair/Festival, **Vol. 1**, 63-66, **Vol. 4**, 33-36, 62, 120, 180, **Vol. 5**, 137, 138-41, 170, 284-86, **Vol. 6**, 347
Jarajibli Fair, **Vol. 4**, 473
Jaram Nercha Festival, **Vol. 3**, 49
Jashans, **Vol. 1**, 141-143, **Vol. 4**, 97-98
Jashpur (district) Chhattisgarh, **Vol. 5**, 3
Jaswantri Devi Fair, **Vol. 4**, 473
Jateswar Mahadev Temple Fair, **Vol. 4**, 354
Jatra Fair, **Vol. 6**, 43
Jawala Devi Fair, **Vol. 4**, 122
Jawara Festival, **Vol. 5**, 430
Jaya Parvati Vrata, **Vol. 5**, 126
Jayadeva Fair, **Vol. 6**, 199
Jayanti Mata Fair, **Vol. 5**, 430
Jaychandi Fair, **Vol. 6**, 199
Jeelakarragatu Tirunala, **Vol. 2**, 39
Jeth-Sikar Festival, **Vol. 6**, 42
Jewish Festivals, **Vol. 1**, 147-53, **Vol. 4**, 99-106
Jhala Fair, **Vol. 5**, 141
Jhampan of Bak Devi, **Vol. 6**, 200
Jhampan of Bishahari Festival, **Vol. 6**, 201
Jhampan of Jagatgauri Festival, **Vol. 6**, 201
Jhamu Jatra, **Vol. 6**, 74, 129
Jhanda Fair, **Vol. 4**, 187-88
Jhanda Mela, **Vol. 4**, 544
Jhapan Festival, **Vol. 6**, 200-01, *See also* Jhampan
Jhoola Fair, **Vol. 5**, 16
Jhiri Fair, **Vol. 4**, 283
Jhirka Fair, **Vol. 4**, 122
Jhulan Jatra **Vol. 5**, 129
Jhusi Fair, **Vol. 4**, 473
Jitia Fair/Festival, **Vol. 6**, 16, 49
Jnan Panchami, **Vol. 1**, 108-09, **Vol. 4**, 64
Jog Tog Fair, **Vol. 4**, 202
Jogeshwar Jatra, **Vol. 4**, 544
Jogi Pir Fair, **Vol. 4**, 354
Joginathaswamy Uthsavam, **Vol. 2**, 41
Jogindarnagar Fair, **Vol. 4**, 189
Jokhya-Kushimig, **Vol. 4**, 189
Jor Fair, **Vol. 4**, 355
Joshimath, **Vol. 4**, 541
Journey of Christ to Calvary, **Vol. 6**, 202
Jugal Kishor Temple Fair, **Vol. 6**, 202
Jwaladevi Fair, **Vol. 4**, 544
Jwalamukhi Devi Fair, **Vol. 4**, 189, 283
Jwalamukhi Fair, **Vol. 4**, 473
Jwalatoranothsavam, **Vol. 2**, 41

Jyestha Yatra Fair
- Bhasko Harratoli, **Vol. 6**, 42
- Kisko, **Vol. 6**, 42
Jyothulu Festival, **Vol. 2**, 41
Jyotiba Fair, **Vol. 5**, 271

K

Kabirvad Tree (Banyan), **Vol. 5**, 211
Kadamuri Temple Utsavam, **Vol. 3**, 104
Kadappally Kumbhom Thira Festival, **Vol. 3**, 49-53
Kadasiddheswara and Maradi Matha Jatra, **Vol. 2**, 288
Kadaura Fair, **Vol. 4**, 474
Kadlota Festival, **Vol. 6**, 50
Kadlurayya Fair, **Vol. 2**, 289
Kadu Malleshwara Rathotsava, **Vol. 2**, 289
Kaggere Jatra, **Vol. 2**, 289
Kahar, **Vol. 5**, 23
Kaila Devi Fair, **Vol. 4**, 408-11
Kailas Zalmo, **Vol. 4**, 190
Kailash Fair, **Vol. 4**, 474
Kailash Temple Fair, **Vol. 4**, 475
Kajri Navmi, **Vol. 5**, 437-39
Kakatiyas, **Vol. 2**, 3
Kakkadu Sastha Temple Utsavam, **Vol. 3**, 105
Kakolat Fair, **Vol. 6**, 16
Kala Amb Holi Fair, **Vol. 4**, 190
Kalamma Temple Festival, **Vol. 2**, 290
Kalarickal Temple Utsavam, **Vol. 3**, 105
Kalaseshwara Temple, **Vol. 2**, 270
Kalbhairava Jatra, **Vol. 2**, 290, 291
Kaleshwara Jatra, **Vol. 2**, 291
Kalgudeshwara Temple Fair, **Vol. 2**, 292
Kali Chaudash, **Vol. 4**, 23
Kali Devi Fair : Tiun, **Vol. 4**, 190
Kali Devi Temple Fair, **Vol. 4**, 2
Kali Fair, **Vol. 4**, 190, **Vol. 5**, 439, **Vol. 6**, 203
- Jahartala, **Vol. 6**, 203
- Madhaipur, **Vol. 6**, 203
Kali Mai Fair, **Vol. 5**, 439
Kalighat Fair, **Vol. 6**, 203
Kalika Devi Fair, **Vol. 5**, 273
Kalikauu Utsavam, **Vol. 3**, 106
Kalikamaba Jatra, **Vol. 2**, 292
Kaliya Banba Fair, **Vol. 6**, 44
Kaliyattam, **Vol. 3**, 249
Kalashtami, **Vol. 3**, 318
Kalka Mata Fair, **Vol. 5**, 431
Kallercode Mahadeva Temple Utsavam, **Vol. 3**, 106
Kallisseri St Mary's Church Moom Nuymbu, **Vol. 3**, 107
Kalmeshwara Jatra, **Vol. 2**, 293
Kalpathi Theru, **Vol. 3**, 41, 45
Kalu Bai / Kalika Kaleshwari Goddess Fair, **Vol. 5**, 273-74
Kalubaba Fair, **Vol. 5**, 274
Kaluji Maharaj Fair, **Vol. 5**, 440
Kalyanaks, **Vol. 1**, 115, **Vol. 4**, 72
Kalyaneswar Siva Temple Fair, **Vol. 6**, 203
Kamahi Devi Fair, **Vol. 4**, 355
Kamakhya Temple, **Vol. 6**, 293
Kamakshi Temple Festival, **Vol. 5**, 54
Kaman Pandigal, **Vol. 3**, 324
Kambada Ugra Narasimha Jatra, **Vol. 2**, 293
Kamban Festival, **Vol. 3**, 324
Kamdi Shah's Urs, **Vol. 5**, 431
Kameli Baba Fair, **Vol. 2**, 42
Kampil Jatra, **Vol. 4**, 477
Kamru Nag Fair, **Vol. 4**, 190
Kana Baba Fair, **Vol. 5**, 440
Kanaka Chalpathi Temple Jatra, **Vol. 2**, 293
Kanakadurga Temple, **Vol. 2**, 29
Kanakalayeshwar Shivratri Fair, **Vol. 5**, 275
Kanakamoolam Fair, **Vol. 3**, 319
Kanakgiri Fair, **Vol. 2**, 294
Kanathua Kavu Utsavam, **Vol. 3**, 108
Kanathua Kavu Mahalingeswara Temple Utsavam, **Vol. 3**, 109
Kancheepuram Kamakshi Temple Brahmotsavam, **Vol. 3**, 319
Kandado Jatra, **Vol. 6**, 129
Kandamangalam Temple Koottakalam (Arattu Utsavam), **Vol. 3**, 108
Kandanyapur Fair, **Vol. 5**, 276
Kandoori Festival, **Vol. 3**, 263, 351
Kandul Jatra, **Vol. 6**, 130
Kang (Rath Yatra), **Vol. 6**, 355-57
Kangso, **Vol. 4**, 220
Kangyur Jalma, **Vol. 4**, 190
Kanifnath Fair, **Vol. 5**, 276
Kanji-Amla Osha, **Vol. 6**, 112
Kanker (district) Chhattisgarh, **Vol. 5**, 3
Kannamkulangara Devaswom Utsavam, **Vol. 3**, 109
Kanniyakumari Temple Festivals, **Vol. 3**, 363
Kans Fair, **Vol. 4**, 477

Kans Lila Fair, **Vol. 6**, 16
Kantabida Festival, **Vol. 6**, 130
Kapadia Community, **Vol. 5**, 23
Kapalmochan Fair/Festival, **Vol. 4**, 122, 283
Kapaleeswaras Temple Brahmotsavam, **Vol. 3**, 319
Kapil Muni Fair, **Vol. 4**, 411
Kapila Fair, **Vol. 5**, 431
Kapoteswaraswamy Festival, **Vol. 2**, 43
Karadayan Nombu, **Vol. 3**, 324
Karaikal Ammaiyar Temple Festival, **Vol. 3**, 265
Karalamma Temple Jatra, **Vol. 2**, 294
Karam Festival Puja, **Vol. 4**, 478, **Vol. 6**, 5, 50-53, 112, 130
Karanadighi Fair, **Vol. 6**, 204
Karchi Festival, **Vol. 6**, 458-60
Kardameshwarnath Fair, **Vol. 5**, 440
Karemma Jatra, **Vol. 2**, 294
Karen Tribe, **Vol. 3**, 11
Karhade Brahmin Community, **Vol. 5**, 63
Karhaiya Devi Fair, **Vol. 4**, 478
Karibasaveshvara and Venkamma Jatra, **Vol. 2**, 294
Karingachira Church Feast, **Vol. 3**, 110
Karkalaka Amavasya Festival, **Vol. 2**, 294
Karma Festival, **Vol. 6**, 39, 112
Karon Fair, **Vol. 4**, 478
Kartabhaja Festival, **Vol. 6**, 204
Karthigai Deepam Festival, **Vol. 3**, 273, 276, 322
Kartik Amavas, **Vol. 4**, 18
Kartik Cultural Festival, **Vol. 4**, 124
Kartik Puja, **Vol. 6**, 204
Kartik Purnima Cattle Fair, **Vol. 6**, 17
Kartik Purnima, **Vol. 1**, 109-10, **Vol. 4**, 65, **Vol. 6**, 113
Kartik Purnima Fair, **Vol. 4**, 478, **Vol. 5**, 142
– Babh Naul, **Vol. 6**, 16
– Jazira Raili, **Vol. 6**, 16-17
– Kita Chauhatlar, **Vol. 6**, 17
– Tilanthi, **Vol. 6**, 17
Kartika Deepotsava, **Vol. 2**, 295
Kartikotsava, **Vol. 2**, 295
Kartikotsava Festival, **Vol. 2**, 295
Karvi / Gabit Community, **Vol. 5**, 63
Karwa-Chouth, **Vol. 1**, 66-69, **Vol. 4**, 36-39
Kashi - Visveshvara Jatra, **Vol. 2**, 296
Kashi Ghats, **Vol. 4**, 523
Kashi Hindu Vishwa Vidyalaya, **Vol. 4**, 524
Kashi Vishwanath Temple, **Vol. 4**, 522
Kashtabhanjan Hanuman Fair, **Vol. 5**, 150
Kashtaharnath Fair, **Vol. 5**, 440
Kate Festival, **Vol. 6**, 420
Kathiawar people, **Vol. 5**, 82
Kathin Pio Festival, **Vol. 6**, 283
Kati Bihu Festival, **Vol. 6**, 318
Katte - Holeyamma Jatra, **Vol. 2**, 297
Kattimaramma Jatra, **Vol. 2**, 297
Katyayayani Devi Jatra, **Vol. 2**, 298
Kau Fair, **Vol. 4**, 191
Kaudanyapur Fair, **Vol. 5**, 276-79
Kauleshwarnath Fair, **Vol. 4**, 478
Kaulsar, **Vol. 4**, 319
Kaus Fair, **Vol. 4**, 477
Kaush Lila Fair, **Vol. 6**, 16
Kaushambi Jatra, **Vol. 4**, 478
Kavalelinga Jatra, **Vol. 2**, 298
Kedar Gowri Vratham, **Vol. 3**, 325
Kedareshvara Car Festival, **Vol. 2**, 298
Kedareshwar Fair, **Vol. 5**, 431
Kedarnath Temple, **Vol. 4**, 540
Kedu Festival, **Vol. 6**, 113
Kedu Jatra, **Vol. 6**, 130
Keechapallil Bhagavathy Temple, Thiruvathira Utsavam, **Vol. 3**, 53
Keehadamarus Festival, **Vol. 2**, 43
Keil Muhurta Festival, **Vol. 2**, 301
Kendadamonappaswamy Temple Jatra, **Vol. 2**, 301
Kendarchane, **Vol. 2**, 301
Kendarchane Festival, **Vol. 2**, 302
Ker Festival, **Vol. 6**, 458
Kerunnyi Festival, **Vol. 6**, 420
Kesaragutti Rameshvari Jatra, **Vol. 2**, 302
Keshava Deva Jatra, **Vol. 2**, 303
Keshava Navaratri Utsava, **Vol. 2**, 304
Keshavanarayana Jatra, **Vol. 2**, 303
Keshavrao Fair, **Vol. 5**, 279
Keteshvar Temple Festival, **Vol. 2**, 304
Kevda Trij Festival, **Vol. 5**, 153
Khaddi Festival, **Vol. 6**, 53-66
Khajiar Jatar, **Vol. 4**, 191
Khajuraho Festival, **Vol. 5**, 432-35
Khalari Devi Fair, **Vol. 5**, 5
Khanabarani Festival, **Vol. 4**, 283
Khandagiri Jatra, **Vol. 6**, 131-39
Khandoba Fair, **Vol. 5**, 280-84
Khanqah Sopore, **Vol. 4**, 283
Khardar Fair, **Vol. 4**, 191
Kharra Puja / Kharihani, **Vol. 6**, 66

Khatalsha Pir Fair, **Vol. 5**, 154
Khawakcha Festival, **Vol. 4**, 192
Khawangri Festival, **Vol. 4**, 192
Khaza Kabir Peer and Mahboob Subhami Urs, **Vol. 2**, 305
Khepa Fair, **Vol. 4**, 192
Kherai Puja, **Vol. 6**, 318-19
Khilla Hazarath Gale Shahid Urs, **Vol. 2**, 44
Khilunyie Festival, **Vol. 6**, 420
Khir Bhawani Fair, **Vol. 4**, 284
Khordad Sal, **Vol. 1**, 143-44, **Vol. 4**, 94
Khudawande Nunra Hussaini Urs, **Vol. 2**, 305
Khudurkuni Osa / Osha, **Vol. 6**, 114, 140
Khuthe Festival, **Vol. 6**, 420
Khuthei Festival, **Vol. 6**, 420
Khwaja Bande Nawaz Urs, **Vol. 2**, 305
Khwaja Chishti's Urs, **Vol. 4**, 479
Khwaja Habib Ullah Attar's Urs, **Vol. 4**, 284
Khwaja Habib Ullah Nowsheri Urs, **Vol. 4**, 284
Khwaja Karak's Urs, **Vol. 4**, 479
Khwaja Moinuddin Chishti Urs, **Vol. 4**, 415-21
Kidangamparampu Temple Mandapa Mahotsavam, **Vol. 3**, 111
Kikkeramma Festival, **Vol. 2**, 306
Kiliroor Kannummel Bhagavathi Temple Arat, **Vol. 3**, 111
Killikulangarh Bhagavathy Temple Utsavam, **Vol. 3**, 112
Kinnaur, **Vol. 4**, 227
Kinni Rathotsavam, **Vol. 3**, 264
Kirthal Jatra, **Vol. 4**, 480
Kiunr Jatar, **Vol. 4**, 192
Kochumandakat Ottahil Bhadrakali Temple Festival, **Vol. 3**, 53
Koda Festival, **Vol. 3**, 323
Kodandarama Temple Jatra, **Vol. 2**, 307
Kodungalloor Bhagavathy Temple Bharany Utsavam, **Vol. 3**, 112-16
Kojgari Purnima, **Vol. 5**, 284
Kokna Community, **Vol. 5**, 25
Kolau Gopalkrishana-Swamy Car Festival, **Vol. 2**, 307
Kolaramma Fair, **Vol. 2**, 308
Kole Anjaneya Festival, **Vol. 2**, 310
Kolloappa Jatra, **Vol. 2**, 292
Kollapura - Mahalakshmi Jatra, **Vol. 2**, 310
Kollapuramma Jatra, **Vol. 2**, 44
Komarpet Community, **Vol. 5**, 64
Kongappada Festival, **Vol. 3**, 114
Koodalmanickom Temple Utsavam, **Vol. 3**, 116
Koqsar Festival, **Vol. 5**, 440-43
Koriya (district) Chhattisgarh, **Vol. 5**, 1
Koshme, **Vol. 4**, 193
Kote-Anjaneya Festival, **Vol. 2**, 310
Koteshwar Mahadev Fair, **Vol. 5**, 154, 435
Kotha Sahib Fair, **Vol. 4**, 355
Koti Fair, **Vol. 4**, 193
Kottamala Temple Athapataharam, **Vol. 3**, 117
Kottuvallikavu Bhagavathy Temple Kumbha Bharany, **Vol. 3**, 117
Kovilakath Dharma Sabha Temple Thottotsavam, **Vol. 3**, 118
Koyithatta Temple Thirayattom, **Vol. 3**, 118
Krishna Janmashtami, **Vol. 5**, 284-86
Krishna Kund Fair, **Vol. 4**, 480
Krishna Pushkaram, **Vol. 2**, 45, 46
Krishna River Fair, **Vol. 5**, 286
Krishna Temple Festival, **Vol. 2**, 310
Krishnagiri Jatra, **Vol. 6**, 139
Krishnaswamy Temple Utsavam, **Vol. 3**, 54
Kshatriya Bhandari / Naik Community, **Vol. 5**, 65
Kshatriya Maratha, **Vol. 5**, 63
Kshetra Trimbakeshwar Fair, **Vol. 5**, 287-92
Kuber Nath Fair, **Vol. 4**, 481
Kuchu Fair, **Vol. 6**, 44
Kudachi's Urs, **Vol. 2**, 311
Kufri Fair, **Vol. 4**, 194
Kuka Fair, **Vol. 4**, 355
Kukkesubramanya Temple Car Festival, **Vol. 2**, 312
Kukkuteswaraswamy Teertham, **Vol. 2**, 48
Kulakumbi Jatra, **Vol. 2**, 312
Kulkula Asthan Fair, **Vol. 4**, 481
Kumar Purnima, **Vol. 6**, 115, 140
Kumaralingeshwara Temple Car Festival, **Vol. 2**, 313
Kumaranalloor Temple Thrikarthika Utsavam, **Vol. 3**, 118
Kumaraswami Temple Festival, **Vol. 2**, 313
Kumbh Fair, **Vol. 4**, 481-84, 544-47, **Vol. 5**, 364
Kumbha Sankramana Festival, **Vol. 2**, 314
Kumbhakudam, **Vol. 3**, 83
Kumbhar Community, **Vol. 5**, 39, **Vol. 5**, 65
Kumb-ka-mela, **Vol. 4**, 482
Kunbi Community, **Vol. 5**, 66
Kundalpur Jatra, **Vol. 5**, 436
Kundi Jatar, **Vol. 4**, 195
Kunnamkulam Simhasana Church Feast, **Vol. 3**, 119
Kunslaureau Festival, **Vol. 3**, 19
Kup Fair, **Vol. 4**, 355
Kurali Fair, **Vol. 4**, 356
Kurugadde Festival, **Vol. 2**, 314

Kuruthickal Devi Temple Makara Bharany, **Vol. 3**, 120
Kuruvadagadde Jatra, **Vol. 2**, 314
Kushan Gan Oja Pali, **Vol. 6**, 319
Kushinagar Jatra, **Vol. 4**, 484
Kushmanda Devi Temple Fair, **Vol. 4**, 484
Kuthah Fair, **Vol. 4**, 195
Kuthiyottam and Kettukazhcha in Chettikulangra Temple, **Vol. 3**, 54
Kuti Fair, **Vol. 4**, 356
Kutimt, **Vol. 4**, 220
Kuttadamma Fair, **Vol. 2**, 314
Kwakjatra, **Vol. 6**, 343

L

Labh Pancham Festival, **Vol. 4**, 21, **Vol. 5**, 154
Labrang Jalma, **Vol. 4**, 196
Lachandas Baba Fair, **Vol. 5**, 443
Ladakh Prominent Festivals, **Vol. 4**, 308-309
Ladle Moray Mushaik Urs, **Vol. 2**, 315
Lady Fatima Festival, **Vol. 2**, 49
Lahmocha Festival, **Vol. 4**, 196
Lahol Fair, **Vol. 5**, 197
Lai Haraoba Festival, **Vol. 6**, 347-50
Laila Fair, **Vol. 4**, 197
Lakh Data's Chhinj, **Vol. 4**, 198
Lakhi Jangal Fair, **Vol. 4**, 356
Lakhameshwar Fair, **Vol. 5**, 292
Laksha Deepotsava Festival, **Vol. 2**, 316
Laksha Grah Fair, **Vol. 4**, 547
Lakshmi Devi Mandita Festival, **Vol. 2**, 316
Lakshmi Keshva Car Festival, **Vol. 2**, 316
Lakshmi Narasimhaswamy Brahmothsavam, **Vol. 2**, 50
Lakshmi Narayan Jatra, **Vol. 2**, 315
Lakshmi Narayan Perantalamma Jatara, **Vol. 2**, 51
Lakshmi Puja (Manabasa Gurubara), **Vol. 6**, 117
Lakshmi Puja Festival, **Vol. 6**, 204
Lakshmi Temple Jatra, **Vol. 2**, 317, 318
Lakshmijanardhanaswamy Jatra, **Vol. 2**, 318
Lakshmikanta Car Festival, **Vol. 2**, 320
Lakshmikanta Temple Jatra, **Vol. 2**, 319
Lakshminarasimha Car Festival, **Vol. 2**, 320
Lakshminarasimha Jatra, **Vol. 2**, 321
Lakshminarasimhaswamy Car Festival, **Vol. 2**, 321
Lakshminarasimhaswamy Jatra, **Vol. 2**, 321
Lakshminarayan Fair, **Vol. 5**, 292
Lakshminarayana Deva Jatra, **Vol. 2**, 323
Lakshminarayana Jatra, **Vol. 2**, 322-23
Lakshmiranganatha Temple Jatara, **Vol. 2**, 323
Lal Pir's Urs, **Vol. 4**, 484
Lama Paza, **Vol. 4**, 220
Lamani Community, **Vol. 5**, 66
Lamat Fair, **Vol. 4**, 198
Lateef Shah Vali Alla Khadri Urs, **Vol. 2**, 51
Laul Fair, **Vol. 4**, 198-99
Laxmi Puja Festival, **Vol. 6**, 139
Lehri Shah Shiv Temple Fair, **Vol. 4**, 357
Lent, **Vol. 1**, 135, **Vol. 4**, 88
Lhabab Duchen Festival, **Vol. 6**, 420
Liekhwenyi Festival, **Vol. 6**, 420
Ligang, **Vol. 6**, 320
Lili Parikrama Fair, **Vol. 5**, 155-59
Lingaraja Lord Principal Festivals, **Vol. 6**, 91
Lingaraja Temple Festival Bhubaneshwar Jatra, **Vol. 6**, 140
Little Flower Church Cherupushpa Perunal, **Vol. 3**, 120
Little Flower Feast, **Vol. 3**, 120
Little Flower Mission Church Feast, **Vol. 3**, 121
Lohri, **Vol. 1**, 69, **Vol. 4**, 39
Lokanarkavu BhagavathyTemple Utsavam, **Vol. 3**, 122
Lokaparameshwara Temple Jatra, **Vol. 2**, 323
Lokmela Janmashtami Fair, **Vol. 5**, 159
Lom-Kivah Festival, **Vol. 6**, 350-51
Loni Fair *See* Sakharam Maharaj Fair
Lord Iggutappa Fair, **Vol. 2**, 324
Lord Madheshwar Nath Fair, **Vol. 6**, 17
Lord Rajarajeswaraswamy Kalyanothsavam, **Vol. 2**, 52
Lord Venkateswara Kalyanams, **Vol. 2**, 53
Losar Festival, **Vol. 4**, 199-200, 284
Lossar Festival, **Vol. 6**, 448
Luira Festival, **Vol. 6**, 352

M

M.P.S. Church Feast, **Vol. 3**, 124
Maadar / Jamuni Community (Goa), **Vol. 5**, 66
Machhayal Fair, **Vol. 4**, 200-201
Machhi Community, **Vol. 5**, 40
Madanagopalaswamy Festival, **Vol. 2**, 55
Madan-Kam Puja, **Vol. 6**, 295
Madar Shah's Urs, **Vol. 5**, 446
Madarsab Bavasab Urs, **Vol. 2**, 324
Madarasi (A & N), **Vol. 3**, 12

Madduramma Temple Jatra, **Vol. 2**, 324
Madeppa Swami Jatra, **Vol. 2**, 326
Madhavrai Fair, **Vol. 5**, 159-62
Madheshwaraswamy Jatra, **Vol. 2**, 326
Madhukeshwara Jatra, **Vol. 2**, 326
Madhuva Matha Festival, **Vol. 2**, 329
Madhva Jayanthi, **Vol. 3**, 336
Madhyamaheshwar Fair, **Vol. 4**, 548
Madre De Deus Church Festival, **Vol. 3**, 56
Madurai Cattle Fair, **Vol. 3**, 326
Magh Bihu / Maghar Domahi Festival, **Vol. 6**, 291, 321-22
Magh Fair/Festival, **Vol. 4** 357-358, 485, **Vol. 6**, 44
Magh Festival-Jaunsar, **Vol. 4**, 548
Magh Sainjra or Magh Bihu, **Vol. 6**, 322-23
Magha Parab, **Vol. 6**, 140
Maghar Jatra, **Vol. 4**, 485
Magha-Saptami, **Vol. 6**, 75
Maghe Parab, **Vol. 6**, 115
Maghe Sankranti, **Vol. 6**, 448
Maghi Purnima Fair
- Jazira Raili, **Vol. 6**, 18
- Siur, **Vol. 6**, 18

Maghothsavam Adhyanothsavam, **Vol. 2**, 55
Maha Basa, **Vol. 6**, 142
Mahalaxmi, **Vol. 1**, 101, **Vol. 4**, 61
Maha Magam, **Vol. 3**, 326
Maha Mritunjaya Fair, **Vol. 5**, 443
Maha Saptami Festival, **Vol. 3**, 326
Maha Shivaratri, **Vol. 3**, 41, 337, *See also* Shivratri
Mahabaleshwara Devara Jatra, **Vol. 2**, 330
Mahabiri Jhanda Fair, **Vol. 6**, 18
Mahabirji Fair, **Vol. 4**, 486
Mahabodhi Vihare, **Vol. 6**, 27-29
Mahadeo Puja Fair, **Vol. 6**, 44
Mahadev Fair, **Vol. 4**, 125
Mahadeva Fair/Jatra, **Vol. 2**, 332
Mahadeva Temple Jatra/Festival, **Vol. 2**, 333
Mahadeva Temple Utsavam, **Vol. 3**, 126-127
Mahadeva Temple Ashtami, **Vol. 3**, 124
Mahadevamangalam Temple Utsavam, **Vol. 3**, 127
Mahaganapati Car Festival, **Vol. 2**, 333
Mahaganapati Jatra, **Vol. 2**, 334
Mahaganapati Kartikotsava, **Vol. 2**, 334
Mahaganapati Rathotsava Festival, **Vol. 2**, 334
Mahakali Fair, **Vol. 4**, 548
Mahakali Festival, **Vol. 6**, 205
Mahakuteshwara Fair, **Vol. 2**, 335
Mahalakshmi Jatra, **Vol. 2**, 335
Mahalakshmi Temple Fair, **Vol. 5**, 56, 293-96
Mahalaya Pitra Amavasya, **Vol. 1**, 69, **Vol. 4**, 39
Mahalayam, **Vol. 3**, 338
Mahalingeshvara Fair, **Vol. 2**, 336
Mahalingeshvara Pooja, **Vol. 2**, 337
Mahalingeshvara Temple Rathotsava, **Vol. 2**, 337
Mahalingeshwara Fair, **Vol. 2**, 333
Mahamalleshappa Jatra, **Vol. 2**, 338
Mahamaya Jatra, **Vol. 2**, 338
Mahanataswani Fair, **Vol. 2**, 338
Mahang Sanga Festival, **Vol. 5**, 201
Mahar Community, **Vol. 5**, 67
Mahasiddha Baba Fair, **Vol. 5**, 298-99
Mahashivaratri, **Vol. 1**, 69-71, **Vol. 3**, 41, 337, **Vol. 4,** 3-41, **Vol. 5**, 296, *See also* Shivratri
- Bhilmaram, **Vol. 2**, 58
- Kaleshwar, **Vol. 2**, 59
- Khseerama Kshetram, **Vol. 2**, 60
- Kondakavur, **Vol. 2**, 60
- Kotipalli, **Vol. 2**, 62
- Pattaschala Kshetram, **Vol. 2**, 65
- Rajahmundry, **Vol. 2**, 67

Mahashivaratri (Jagara), **Vol. 6**, 116
Mahashivaratri Fair, **Vol. 2**, 338, **Vol. 5**, 55, 162, 297-99 *See also* Shivratri Fair
Mahasiddha Baba Fair, **Vol. 5**, 298
Mahasoba Fair, **Vol. 5**, 301
Mahasu Jatar, **Vol. 4**, 201
Mahaveera Festival-Kolankpaka, **Vol. 2**, 68
Mahavir Jayanti, **Vol. 1**, 110-11, **Vol. 4**, 67-68
Mahboob Subhami Baghdadi Urs, **Vol. 2**, 338, 339
Mahendragiri Jatra, **Vol. 6**, 140-42
Mahesh Pandit Fair, **Vol. 6**, 205
Maheshwar Jatra, **Vol. 5**, 447
Mahima Mala (Magha Sukla Chaturdasi), **Vol. 6**, 74
Mahishasuramardhani Teertham, **Vol. 2**, 70
Mahishasuramardhani Temple Festival, **Vol. 2**, 339
Mahu Nag Fair, **Vol. 4**, 201
Mahulgundi Festival, **Vol. 6**, 142
Mahuli Devi Jatra, **Vol. 2**, 339
Mahyavanshi Community, **Vol. 5**, 40
Mai Purnima, **Vol. 4**, 203
Maiku-Sum Phai Festival, **Vol. 6**, 283
Mailara Festival, **Vol. 2**, 340
Mailara Lingeswara Devara Jatra, **Vol. 2**, 341
Mailaralinga Jatra, **Vol. 2**, 340

Maintako Fair, **Vol. 4**, 202
Maisar Khana Fair, **Vol. 4**, 360
Makar Sankranti, **Vol. 1**, 71-72, **Vol. 4**, 41, **Vol. 6**, 75
Makar Sankranti Fair, **Vol. 6**, 17, 18
Makara Jatra, **Vol. 6**, 142
Makara Vilakku Festival, **Vol. 3**, 23-24
Makdum Sahib's Urs/Festival, **Vol. 4**, 285, 487
Maksi Jatra, **Vol. 5**, 447
Mal, **Vol. 4**, 203
Mal Purnima, **Vol. 4**, 203
Malang Shah Vali's Urs, **Vol. 2**, 341
Malappuram Nercha, **Vol. 3**, 129
Malayanath Fair, **Vol. 4**, 549
Malegaon Fair *See* Khandoba Fair
Mallaiah Jatra, **Vol. 2**, 341
Malleshvara Jatra, **Vol. 2**, 341
Malleswara Siva Fair, **Vol. 6**, 205
Malleswaraswamy Temple, **Vol. 2**, 28
Mallikarjuna Jatra, **Vol. 2**, 341, 342, 343
Mallikarjuna Matha/Temple Jatra, **Vol. 2**, 343
Mallikarjunaswamy Jatra, **Vol. 2**, 343, 344
Mallinath Fair, **Vol. 4**, 421
Malluramma Jatra, **Vol. 2**, 342
Malunda Jatar, **Vol. 4**, 203
Malur Fair, **Vol. 2**, 344
Mamankam, **Vol. 3**, 252
Mamita Festival, **Vol. 6**, 460-62
Mamu Bhaanza's Urs, **Vol. 4**, 125
Manabasa Gurubara (Lakshmi Puja), **Vol. 6**, 117, 142
Manader Jat Fair, **Vol. 6**, 205
Manakula Vinayakar Brahmothsavam, **Vol. 3**, 265
Manasa Puja, **Vol. 6**, 206-208, *See also* Mansa
Manavala Mamunigal Jayanthi, **Vol. 3**, 339
Mancompu Bhagavathy Temple Utsavam, **Vol. 3**, 130
Mandai Festival, **Vol. 5**, 447
Mandalampattu, **Vol. 3**, 88
Mandalvilakku, **Vol. 3**, 122
Mandarthi Duragaparmeshwari Temple Festival, **Vol. 2**, 344
Mandeswaraswamy Kalyanothsavam, **Vol. 2**, 70
Mandhata Fair, **Vol. 5**, 443-45
Manekthari Punam Fair/Festival, **Vol. 5**, 163-167
Mang Fair, **Vol. 4**, 203
Mangaldevi Temple Festival, **Vol. 2**, 344
Mangani Festival, **Vol. 3**, 266
Mangela Community, **Vol. 5**, 40
Mangesh Temple Festival, **Vol. 5**, 56
Mangkhap Festival, **Vol. 6**, 353
Mangla Fair, **Vol. 4**, 487
Mani Mahesh Fair, **Vol. 4**, 203
Manikprabhu Jayanti, **Vol. 2**, 345
Manikyagoda Dusahara, **Vol. 6**, 75
Maninath Math Festival, **Vol. 6**, 208
Manjhi Fair, **Vol. 6**, 18
Manju Matha Feast, **Vol. 3**, 57
Manjunatha Temple Festival, **Vol. 2**, 346
Mankeshwar Fair, **Vol. 5**, 299-301
Mankeshwar Mahadeo Fair, **Vol. 5**, 447
Mankuzhy Subramonia Temple Pooyam Utsavam, **Vol. 3**, 130
Mannarssala Kavu Utsavam, **Vol. 3**, 131
Mansa Devi Fair, **Vol. 4**, 126, *See also* Manasa
Mantralamma Jatara, **Vol. 2**, 71
Mar Elias, Patriarch Feast, **Vol. 3**, 58
Mar Thoma Pontifical Shrine Feast, **Vol. 4**, 131
Maradi Basaveshwar Jatra, **Vol. 2**, 346
Maradi Matha Jatra, **Vol. 2**, 228
Maramon Convention, **Vol. 3**, 58
Marari Thottam Temple Utsavam, **Vol. 3**, 132
Maratha, **Vol. 5**, 67
Mardan Ali Shah Saheb Urs, **Vol. 2**, 72
Maremma Jatra, **Vol. 2**, 347
Marg Sri Fair, **Vol. 4**, 488
Marh Koti Chhinj, **Vol. 4**, 204
Mari Jatra, **Vol. 2**, 347
Mariamman Festival, **Vol. 3**, 330
Marigudi Jatra, **Vol. 2**, 349
Marikamba Jatra, **Vol. 2**, 352
Marikamba Temple Jatra, **Vol. 2**, 353
Marikambadevi Jatra, **Vol. 2**, 350, 351
Mariyamman Temple Pongal, **Vol. 3**, 133
Markanda Fair, **Vol. 4**, 204
Markandeshvara Temple Jatra, **Vol. 2**, 353
Markandeshwaraswamy Jatra, **Vol. 2**, 354
Markandya Fair, **Vol. 4**, 126
Marle Jatra, **Vol. 2**, 354
Martand Cave Festival, **Vol. 4**, 286
Martyrs Day, **Vol. 1**, 157, **Vol. 4**, 107
Maruti Car Festival, **Vol. 2**, 355
Maruti Temple Fair, **Vol. 5**, 56
Masabti Urs, **Vol. 2**, 356
Masani / Sitla Mata Fair, **Vol. 4**, 127-30
Masi Magam, **Vol. 3**, 273
Masi Magha Festival, **Vol. 3**, 331

Masi Magham Festival, **Vol. 3**, 267
Mastan Vali Urs
- Guntur, **Vol. 2**, 73
- Kondur, **Vol. 2**, 74
- Kothacheruvu, **Vol. 2**, 74
Mata Jainti Devi Temple Fair, **Vol. 4**, 360
Math Ghoghra Fair, **Vol. 5**, 445
Math Kotal Fair, **Vol. 5**, 170-74
Matheni Devananda Satra, **Vol. 6**, 323
Mathura-Vrindavan Jatra, **Vol. 4**, 489-98
Mattu Pongal, Festival, **Vol. 3**, 276, 333
Matu Puja Festival, **Vol. 6**, 142
Maun Ekadashi, **Vol. 1**, 111, **Vol. 4**, 66
Maundy Thursday, **Vol. 1**, 112-13, **Vol. 4**, 89
Mauni Baba Temple Fair, **Vol. 4**, 498
Mauri Rajputs, **Vol. 5**, 23
Mayakka Jatra, **Vol. 2**, 357
Mayasha Kaliyan Urs, **Vol. 2**, 357
Mebi Sitang Festival, **Vol. 6**, 283
Mecheni Khela Festival, **Vol. 6**, 209
Me-Dam-Me Fie, **Vol. 6**, 324
Meenakshi Temple Brahmotsavam, **Vol. 3**, 335
Meenam Festival, **Vol. 3**, 123
Meeshah Saheb Festival, **Vol. 4**, 286
Mehla Jatar, **Vol. 4**, 206
Meiteis of Manipur, **Vol. 6**, 335-36
Mela Patt, **Vol. 4**, 286
Melai Chandi Fair, **Vol. 6**, 210-11
Meleingi Festival, **Vol. 6**, 420
Meos Ravan Fair, **Vol. 4**, 131
Meru Terash, **Vol. 1**, 114, **Vol. 4**, 72
Metmneo Festival, **Vol. 6**, 421
Mhasoba Fair, **Vol. 5**, 301-03
Mia Festival, **Vol. 6**, 421
Mian Mansabali Fair, **Vol. 4**, 498
Mim Kut Festival, **Vol. 6**, 400, 410, 421
Mindal Jatar, **Vol. 4**, 208
Minjar Fair, **Vol. 4**, 209
Miraculous Shrine of Kunnel Church Feast, **Vol. 3**, 133
Mirza Haleem Fair, **Vol. 6**, 19
Mirza Kamil Saheb: Srinagar, **Vol. 4**, 284
Mitha Community, **Vol. 5**, 41
Mithan Sar Fair, **Vol. 4**, 361
Mithgaudas, **Vol. 5**, 68
Mloko Festival, **Vol. 6**, 263-67
Mnyokum Festival, **Vol. 6**, 267-71
Moatsu Festival, **Vol. 6**, 421
Mohammad Shah Dulla Urs, **Vol. 5**, 447
Moharram, **Vol. 1**, 112-16, **Vol. 4**, 13, 73
Moharram Fair, **Vol. 4**, 498
Mohijuddin Sahed Urs, **Vol. 2**, 76
Moho-Ho, **Vol. 6**, 325-26
Molige Marayya Jatra, **Vol. 2**, 357
Momin Community, **Vol. 5**, 43
Mond Festival, **Vol. 4**, 549
Monyu Festival, **Vol. 6**, 422
Moola-Chalkanema Jatra, **Vol. 2**, 357
Moonnu Nompu, **Vol. 3**, 134
Mopin Festival, **Vol. 6**, 283-84
Morom Festival, **Vol. 6**, 271-76
Moti Baba Fair, **Vol. 5**, 448
Mount Caramel Church Feast, **Vol. 3**, 136
Mount Mary Fair, **Vol. 5**, 303
Mount Poinsur Feast (Fair), **Vol. 5**, 303-04
Mount Shatrunjaypalitana, **Vol. 5**, 171
Muda Ganapati Jatra, **Vol. 2**, 358
Mudhaneshwar Mahadev Fair, **Vol. 5**, 174-176
Muharram *see* Moharram
Mukkannur Kuthala Temple Utsavam, **Vol. 3**, 137
Mukta Devi Temple Fair, **Vol. 4**, 498
Muktabai Fair, **Vol. 5**, 304
Muktagiri Fair, **Vol. 5**, 445
Muktagiri Jatra, **Vol. 5**, 448
Mulamkadakom Temple Pathamudayam Festival, **Vol. 3**, 137
Mulasthaneswaraswamy Kalyanothsavan, **Vol. 2**, 77
Muleswaraswamy Kalyanam, **Vol. 2**, 77
Mullakal Devi Temple Utsavam, **Vol. 3**, 139
Mullappaswami Jatra, **Vol. 2**, 358
Mundar Fair, **Vol. 5**, 446
Mundeshwara Rathotsava Festival, **Vol. 2**, 359
Muneshwara Jatra, **Vol. 2**, 359
Muni Amawas Fair, **Vol. 6**, 18
Muntajabuddin Zar Zari Zar Buxsh Dulahen Urs, **Vol. 5**, 305
Murugimatha Festival, **Vol. 2**, 360
Murya Puno Fair, **Vol. 4**, 498
Musekhan Wali Fair, **Vol. 5**, 446
Music Festivals, **Vol. 3**, 340
Muslim Festivals, **Vol. 1**, 117-19, **Vol. 4**, 72-85
Muslim Pilgrim Centres (Kerala), **Vol. 3**, 25
Muthu Pallaku Festival, **Vol. 3**, 268, **Vol. 3**, 276
Muthuswamy Dhikshadar, **Vol. 3**, 340
Mutyalanmma Festival, **Vol. 2**, 78
Muthumariamman Temple Festival, **Vol. 3**, 268

N

Nabahi Fair, **Vol. 4**, 210
Nabanna Festival, **Vol. 6**, 117
Nadavali Festival, **Vol. 2**, 361
Nag Fair, **Vol. 4**, 210-11
Nag Madham Jatar, **Vol. 4**, 211
Nag Nona Fair, **Vol. 4**, 212
Nag Panchami, **Vol. 1**, 72-73, 103, **Vol. 4**, 42, 62, 212, **Vol. 5**, 176, 306
Nag Panchmi Fair, **Vol. 6**, 19
Naga Chauthi Osha Festival, **Vol. 6**, 117
Nagaji Fair, **Vol. 5**, 449
Naganatha Devara Jatra, **Vol. 2**, 362
Nageshwara Temple Jatra, **Vol. 2**, 363
Nageshwaraswamy Jatra, **Vol. 2**, 363
Nagnath Fair, **Vol. 4,** 499, **Vol. 5**, 307
– Aundha, **Vol. 5**, 307-08
– Mohol, **Vol. 5**, 308-11
– Wadwal, **Vol. 5**, 311-13
Nagoba Fair, **Vol. 5**, 313
Nagobha Jatra, **Vol. 2**, 78
Nagonath Fair, **Vol. 4**, 499
Naimisharanya Jatra, **Vol. 4**, 499
Naina Devi Fair, **Vol. 4**, 212
Najaf-i-Hind Fair, **Vol. 4**, 500
Naknya Lum Festival, **Vol. 6**, 422
Nalanda Jatra, **Vol. 6**, 19
Nalchha Mata Fair, **Vol. 5**, 448
Nalwar Fair, **Vol. 4**, 214
Namgan Ist or Chhota Namgan, **Vol. 4**, 215
Namgan 2nd or Bara Namgan, **Vol. 4**, 215
Namgan Chuan Festival, **Vol. 4**, 216
Namgang, **Vol. 4**, 220
Nanaji Maharaj Fair, **Vol. 5**, 314
Nanaksar Fair, **Vol. 4**, 361
Nancharamma Festival, **Vol. 2**, 80
Nancharamma Tirunali, **Vol. 2**, 80
Nancharammavari Jatara, **Vol. 2**, 79
Nanda Devi Fair, **Vol. 4**, 549
Nandashtami Fair, **Vol. 4**, 549
Nandi Basaveshwaraswamy Jatra, **Vol. 2**, 365
Nandishwara Jatra, **Vol. 2**, 365
Nanjundeshwara Fair, **Vol. 2**, 366
Nao Panao Fair, **Vol. 4**, 217
Naqshband Saheb Festival, **Vol. 4**, 287
Narada-Gadda Fair, **Vol. 2**, 368
Narali Purnima (Coconut Day), **Vol. 5**, 248
Narasimha Temple Fairs, **Vol. 4**, 287
Narasimha Car Festival, **Vol. 2**, 368
Narasimha Jatra, **Vol. 2**, 368, 370
Narasimhadeva Temple, **Vol. 4**, 542
Narasimhaswamy Car Festival, **Vol. 2**, 370
Narasimhaswamy Jatra, **Vol. 2**, 371, 372
Narayan Nagabali rite, **Vol. 5**, 291
Narayan Thal Temple Festival, **Vol. 4**, 289
Narayanamma Perantalu Uthsavam, **Vol. 2**, 81
Narayanaswami Jatra, **Vol. 2**, 372
Narayani Jatra, **Vol. 6**, 142
Narbod Festival, **Vol. 5**, 448
Narkanda Fair, **Vol. 4**, 217
Narkhan Fair, **Vol. 4**, 217
Narmada Pilgrim Centre, **Vol. 5**, 208
Narmadeswarswamy Brahmothsavam, **Vol. 2**, 81
Narsimha Fair, **Vol. 5**, 448
Narsingha Chaturdasi Festival, **Vol. 6**, 142
Narsinghnath Jatra, **Vol. 6**, 143-45
Nath Shashthi Fair, **Vol. 5**, 314-17
National Festivals, **Vol. 4**, 106-190
Nativity of the Blessed Virgin Mary Feast, Vechour, **Vol. 3**, 140
Naub, **Vol. 4**, 218
Nauchandi Fair, **Vol. 4**, 501
Nauleshwar Fair, **Vol. 4**, 550
Nauli, **Vol. 4**, 217
Nautha Fair, **Vol. 4**, 550
Nav Buddhist Festival, **Vol. 1**, 105, **Vol. 4**, 62-63
Nava Kalebare, **Vol. 6**, 118-19
Nava Tiruppathis Festival, **Vol. 3**, 341
Navaratra / Navaratri / Navarathri, **Vol. 1**, 73-74, **Vol. 3**, 23, 142, 269, 342, 345, **Vol. 4**, 21, 43, 218, 219, **Vol. 5**, 94, 112, 178-191
Navaratra Mahalakshmi Fair, **Vol. 5**, 317
Navaratri / Navarathri (Nine Sacred Days), **Vol. 3**, 23, 142, 269, 342, 345
Navdurga Pratipada Fair, **Vol. 4**, 502
Navle, **Vol. 4**, 218
Navdurga Temple Fair, **Vol. 5**, 56
Navratri *see* Navaratri
Navroz, **Vol. 4**, 94
Nawan Fair, **Vol. 6**, 19
Nawasang Sitang Festival, **Vol. 6**, 284
Nazhu Festival, **Vol. 6**, 423

Neelakanteswara Festival, **Vol. 2**, 82
Neelakantheshvara Jatra, **Vol. 2**, 373
Neelakantheshvara Pooja Festival, **Vol. 2**, 374
Neerathanullur Cattle Fair, **Vol. 3**,
Neerathanullur Festival, **Vol. 3**, 341
Negrito race, **Vol. 3**, 2, 8
Nellikulangara Bhagavathy Temple Vela, **Vol. 3**, 143
Nepali Festivals, **Vol. 6**, 211
Nerbudda Fair, **Vol. 5**, 449
Nercha Festival, **Vol. 3**, 145
New Sunday Festival, **Vol. 3**, 186
New Year, **Vol. 1**, 136, **Vol. 4**, 88, 94
New Year Day Festival, **Vol. 5**, 194-95
New Year Day of the Trees, **Vol. 1**, 152, **Vol. 4**, 104
New Year's Day, **Vol. 1**, 80, **Vol. 4**, 43
Ngadan Festival, **Vol. 6**, 423
Ngonyl Festival, **Vol. 6**, 423
Niku ka Jhal Fair, **Vol. 4**, 219
Nilkanth Fair, **Vol. 4**, 503
Nilkanth Mahadeo Fair, **Vol. 4**, 503
Nimai Tirtha Ghat Fairs, **Vol. 6**, 211
Ningol Chakkouba **Vol. 6**, 354-55
Nirathannadhatri Dokka Seethamma Vardhanti, **Vol. 2**, 82
Nirjala Ekadashi, **Vol. 1**, 80-82, **Vol. 4**, 44-45
Nirvanaswami Matha Jatra, **Vol. 2**, 375
Nirvaneshwara Jatra, **Vol. 2**, 375
Nishan Sahib, **Vol. 4**, 350
Nithyasahayamatha Titular Feast, **Vol. 3**, 145
Nitsokhu Festival, **Vol. 6**, 423
Nizakhu Festival, **Vol. 6**, 423
Nongkrem Dance Festival, **Vol. 6**, 384-86
Non Indian Devotees who are Remembered during Festival **Vol. 3**, 342
Nuakhai Festival, **Vol. 6**, 119, 145
Nukalamma Teertham, **Vol. 2**, 83
Nuliya Chandayya Jatra, **Vol. 2**, 376
Nunai Festival, **Vol. 4**, 550

O

Obaleshvara Jatra, **Vol. 2**, 376
Oee Nivu Festival, **Vol. 6**, 424
Oelsagam, **Vol. 3**, 40
Olarikkara Temple Utsavam, **Vol. 3**, 145
Oli, **Vol. 1**, 111-12, **Vol. 4**, 66
Omkareshwar Jatra, **Vol. 5**, 450-51
Onakkoor Bhagavathy Temple Utsavam, **Vol. 3**, 147
Onam, **Vol. 1**, 82-86, **Vol. 4**, 46-50
Ookayang Festival, **Vol. 4**, 219
Ossuary Feast, **Vol. 3**, 19
Ottam Festival, **Vol. 3**, 147
Our Lady Miracles Feast, **Vol. 5**, 56
Our Lady of Immaculate Conception's Feast, **Vol. 5**, 56
Our Lady of Lourdes Festival, **Vol. 3**, 269
Our Lady of Mevees's Feast, **Vol. 5**, 56

P

Pachpera Fair, **Vol. 4**, 503
Padmavati Utsava, **Vol. 2**, 376
Padmavatiamma Rathotsava, **Vol. 2**, 376
Pai-Leng Festival, **Vol. 6**, 284
Palara Fair, **Vol. 4**, 361
Palayur Church Feast and Fairs, **Vol. 3**, 60-61
Palkot Fair, **Vol. 6**, 45
Pallavas, **Vol. 2**, 2
Palli Festival, **Vol. 5**, 220-22
Pallipurathkavu Utsavam, **Vol. 3**, 148
Palm Sunday, **Vol. 1**, 136, **Vol. 4**, 89
Pamadevaru Car Festival, **Vol. 2**, 382
Pamalinga Temple Jatra, **Vol. 2**, 382
Pana (Festival), **Vol. 3**, 87
Pana Samkranti Festival, **Vol. 6**, 119
Pana Sankranti, **Vol. 6**, 145
Panch Kedar, **Vol. 4**, 541
Panch Pir's Urs, **Vol. 4**, 289
Pancha Giri Mahadeo Fair, **Vol. 4**, 504
Pancha Pandava group of temples, **Vol. 6**, 97
Panchalingeshwara Car festival, **Vol. 2**, 377
Panchamukhi Mahadeo Fair, **Vol. 5**, 318
Panchkroshi Jatra, **Vol. 5**, 451
Panchon Festival, **Vol. 4**, 550
Panchosiddh Jatra, **Vol. 4**, 505
Pandara Parambu Siva Temple Utsavam, **Vol. 3**, 150
Pandava Fair, **Vol. 5**, 452
Pandharpur Fair, **Vol. 5**, 318-19
Panduranga Fair, **Vol. 2**, 379
Pang-Lhabsol Festival, **Vol. 6**, 448
Panguni Uttiram Festival, **Vol. 3**, 343-44
Panj Pir Fair, **Vol. 4**, 361
Panjeli Fair, **Vol. 4**, 221
Papakshaya Ghat Jatra, **Vol. 6**, 145
Parabrahma Temple Kethukazhcha, **Vol. 3**, 150

Parappadom Bhadrakali Temple Bharany Utsavam, **Vol. 3**, 152
Parasavedeeswaraswamy Festival, **Vol. 2**, 84
Parasdoh Fair, **Vol. 5**, 452
Parasurama Kshetra and Jayanthi, **Vol. 3**, 347
Parbat Debata Puja Festival, **Vol. 6**, 145
Paresnath Jain Tirth, **Vol. 6**, 212
Pariyaram Vishnu Temple Utsavam, **Vol. 3**, 153
Parli Vaijnath Fair, **Vol. 5**, 325
Parshuram Fair, **Vol. 4**, 362
Parshuram Temple Festival, **Vol. 5**, 56
Parshvanatha Temple Fair, **Vol. 4**, 505
Parsi Festivals, **Vol. 1**, 139-45, **Vol. 4**, 93-99
Paryushana / Pajusan, **Vol. 1**, 112-14, **Vol. 4**, 69
Pasaka Fair, **Vol. 4**, 507
Pasati / Paseti, **Vol. 6**, 326
Patbhanga Festival, **Vol. 6**, 212
Pateti, **Vol. 1**, 144-45, **Vol. 4**, 94
Pathar-ka-khel, **Vol. 4**, 221
Pathar Chauth, **Vol. 4**, 221
Patratoli Fair, **Vol. 6**, 45
Patti Jubbar Fair, **Vol. 4**, 222
Patva Yatra, **Vol. 6**, 106
Paush Dashmi, **Vol. 1**, 115, **Vol. 4**, 72
Paush Shukla Panchmi Fair, **Vol. 6**, 20
Pavagadh Hills Festivals, **Vol. 5**, 111-12
Pawa Jatra, **Vol. 4**, 507
Pawapuri Jatra, **Vol. 6**, 20
Pawl Kut, **Vol. 6**, 400, 410
Peddamm Jatara, **Vol. 2**, 85
Peer Bhayanu Fair, **Vol. 4**, 222
Peer Budhan Fair, **Vol. 5**, 453
Peer Gaikwad Dargah Urs, **Vol. 5**, 327
Pehowa, **Vol. 4**, 131
Pendrawandrin Devi Fair, **Vol. 5**, 16
Pentecost, **Vol. 1**, 136-37, **Vol. 4**, 91
Perumankavu Bhagavathy Temple, **Vol. 3**, 153
Phagu Festival, **Vol. 6**, 44
Phagu Sendra Festival, **Vol. 6**, 47
Phagul Festival, **Vol. 4**, 222
Phalgu Fair, **Vol. 4**, 121
Pharas Fair, **Vol. 4**, 223
Pheri Fair, **Vol. 4**, 507
Phool Jatar, **Vol. 4**, 223
Phool-Walon-ki-Sair, **Vol. 4**, 13
Phul Dol Festival, **Vol. 6**, 213
Phulher Jatra, **Vol. 6**, 21
Phulwari Sharif Urs, **Vol. 6**, 20
Pindari Jatra, **Vol. 4**, 362
Pindori Mahantan, **Vol. 4**, 326
Pipli Saheb, **Vol. 4**, 318
Pir Banoi Fair, **Vol. 4**, 364
Pir Bhaiyabani Fair, **Vol. 4**, 508
Pir Dargar Fair, **Vol. 6**, 462
Pir Fair, **Vol. 4**, 131, 213-15
Pir Hazarat Ganje Gauhar Ali Shah Urs, **Vol. 2**, 379
Pir Hazarat Kaka Rafiq Ali-Ullah Urs, **Vol. 2**, 380
Pir Jumme Shah Fair, **Vol. 4**, 365
Pir Khan Fair, **Vol. 4**, 365
Pir Mahfil, **Vol. 6**, 215
Pir Mitha's Urs, **Vol. 4**, 290
Pir Roshan Shah Wali Urs, **Vol. 4**, 293
Pir Saheb Urs, **Vol. 6**, 216
Pir Sayed Ahmed Ali Shah Kadri Urs, **Vol. 5**, 327
Pir Shah Hussain Khufari Barijan Qadri Urs, **Vol. 2**, 380
Pir Shahansha Wali's Urs, **Vol. 4**, 295
Pir Syed Ahmad-Shah Qadri Urs, **Vol. 2**, 380
Pir Zahir Wali Shah's Urs, **Vol. 4**, 296
Piran Paronthas Urs, **Vol. 4**, 508
Piran Pir Fair, **Vol. 5**, 452
Piravom Old Church Feast, **Vol. 3**, 154
Pir-Mardon Tunga Baba Fair, **Vol. 5**, 453
Pishari Kavu Festival, **Vol. 3**, 66
Pitra Amavasya, **Vol. 4**, 39 *See also* Mahalaya
Pitri Paksha Fair, **Vol. 6**, 20
Podavadukkam Temple Pattu Utsavam, **Vol. 3**, 155
Pola or Vrishabhotsava, **Vol. 5**, 328
Pollaci, **Vol. 3**, 344-47
Pongal Festival, **Vol. 1**, 40, 86-87, **Vol. 3**, 345, **Vol. 4**, 15
Ponkili Sree Rama Temple Utsavam, **Vol. 3**, 156
Poora Mahotsavam, **Vol. 3**, 62
Poorada Dharman, **Vol. 3**, 63
Pooram, **Vol. 3**, 64
Poredam Mahadevan Temple Utsavam, **Vol. 3**, 64
Posh Parvan Festival, **Vol. 6**, 216
Prabhala Teertham, **Vol. 2**, 85
Prabodhani Ekadoshi Festival, **Vol. 1**, 87-88, **Vol. 5**, 193-97
Pradosha Vratham, **Vol. 3**, 348
Prasanna Someshwaraswami Jatra, **Vol. 2**, 381
Prasanna Subramanyaswamy Car Festival, **Vol. 2**, 381
Prasanna Venkataramaswami Jatra, **Vol. 2**, 382
Prasanna-Mallikarjuna Temple Jatra, **Vol. 2**, 381

Prathamastami, **Vol. 6**, 119
Pravara Sangam Fair, **Vol. 5**, 329
Puajiuntia and Bhaijiuntia Festival, **Vol. 6**, 146
Public Celebrations (Manipur), **Vol. 6**, 342
Puliyila Kochumandakat Bhgavathy Temple Utsavam, **Vol. 3**, 65
Punuamthottam Devi Temple Arat, **Vol. 3**, 66
Puram, **Vol. 3**, 23
Purandarsa Day, **Vol. 3**, 348
Puranmashi, **Vol. 1**, 88-89, **Vol. 4**, 50
Purification of the Blessed Virgin Mary Feast, **Vol. 3**, 157
Purmandal Fair, **Vol. 4**, 296
Purnima Fair, **Vol. 5**, 95, **Vol. 6**, 22
Pusha Punems Festival, **Vol. 6**, 119
Pushkar Fair, **Vol. 4**, 422-26
Pustipagiri Mallikarjunaswamy Car Festival, **Vol. 2**, 382
Puthiyakavu Temple Utsavam, **Vol. 3**, 157

Q

Qazi Alimuddin Khan Bahadur Urs, **Vol. 5**, 453

R

R.C. Church and the Coonam Cross Shrine Feast, **Vol. 3**, 158
Rabha Baikhu, **Vol. 6**, 327
Rafaleshwar Fair, **Vol. 5**, 197
Ragniya Bhagwati Fair, **Vol. 4**, 297
Rainka Fair, **Vol. 4**, 227-30
Raja Festival, **Vol. 6**, 146
Raja Parba, **Vol. 6**, 146
Raja Sankranti (Swing Festival), **Vol. 6**, 119-20
Rajapurmata Ji Fair, **Vol. 5**, 454
Rajarajeshwari Temple Car Festival, **Vol. 2**, 383
Rajashwala Sankranti Fair, **Vol. 6**, 45
Rajasthan Culture, **Vol. 4**, 379
Rajballabhi Devi Festival, **Vol. 6**, 216
Rajeswari Temple Fair, **Vol. 6**, 217
Rajgir Jatra, **Vol. 6**, 29
Rajim Fair, **Vol. 5**, 16
Rajni Devi Temple Fair, **Vol. 4**, 365
Rajrajesvara Temple Fair, **Vol. 6**, 217
Rajum Fair, **Vol. 5**, 16
Rakesh Puja, **Vol. 4**, 230
Raksha Bandhan, **Vol. 1**, 89-90, **Vol. 4**, 51, 69, 297
Rakshakali Puja Festival, **Vol. 6**, 218
Ram Tal Jatra, **Vol. 4**, 508
Ram Tirath Fair, **Vol. 4**, 365-67
Ramachandra Bharti Jatra, **Vol. 2**, 384
Ramalinga Car Festival, **Vol. 2**, 384
Ramalingeshwara Jatra, **Vol. 2**, 385
Ramalingeshwaraswami Jatra, **Vol. 2**, 386
Ramana Jayanthi, **Vol. 3**, 349
Ramdeora Fair, **Vol. 4**, 427-29
Ramdev Fair, **Vol. 4**, 131
Ramdev Pir Fair, **Vol. 4**, 426-27, **Vol. 5**, 197-98
Rameshvara Jatra, **Vol. 2**, 386, 387, 389
Rameshvara Puja Festival, **Vol. 2**, 389
Ramji Baba Fair, **Vol. 5**, 453
Ramkeli Fair, **Vol. 6**, 218
Ramlila Fair, **Vol. 5**, 454
Ramnavami and Rathotsava Fair, **Vol. 5**, 333-37
Ramnavami Cattle Fair, **Vol. 6**, 31
Ramnavami Fair/Festival, **Vol. 1**, 90-93, **Vol. 4**, 52, 62, 509, **Vol. 5**, 329-37, 433-35, **Vol. 6**, 29 *See also* Sri Ramnavami,
Rampari-ki-Jatar, **Vol. 4**, 230
Rampurpeth Jatra, **Vol. 2**, 389
Ramrekha Fair, **Vol. 6**, 46
Ramsar, **Vol. 4**, 319
Ramzan Id, **Vol. 1**, 121-22, **Vol. 4**, 81
Ranbireshwara Temple Fair, **Vol. 4**, 297
Randhan Chhath Festival, **Vol. 5**, 198
Rang Panchmi Festival, **Vol. 5**, 454
Rangada-Hobba Jatra, **Vol. 2**, 389
Rangamma Perantalu Jatra, **Vol. 2**, 85
Ranganathaswamy Brahmothsavam, **Vol. 2**, 86
Ranganathaswamy Fair, **Vol. 2**, 391, **Vol. 5**, 337-38
Ranganathaswamy Jatra, **Vol. 2**, 392
Ranganathaswamy Rathotsava, **Vol. 2**, 394
Rangjoon Festival, **Vol. 4**, 230
Rangnathswami Fair, **Vol. 2**, 391, **Vol. 5**, 337
Rani Sati Fair, **Vol. 4**, 429-33
Ras Festival, **Vol. 6**, 218-21, 424
Ras Leela, **Vol. 6**, 357-61
Ras Purnima Festival, **Vol. 6**, 146, 222
Rasa Festival, **Vol. 6**, 424
Rasa Mela Festival, **Vol. 6**, 327
Rasjatra Festival, **Vol. 6**, 221
Ras-Kayang, **Vol. 4**, 230
Rasotsava Festival, **Vol. 6**, 223
Rath Fair, **Vol. 4**, 231, 509

Rath Yatra (Car Festival), **Vol. 6**, 120-23
Rath Yatra (Kang), **Vol. 6**, 355-57
Rath Yatra Fair,
- Bhandari, **Vol. 6**, 45
- Bhanwar Pahari, **Vol. 6**, 45-46
- Jagarnathpur, **Vol. 6**, 46

Ratha Jatra, **Vol. 6**, 147
Ratha Jatra Festival, **Vol. 6**, 224-27
Ratha Jatra of Jagannath, **Vol. 6**, 227-30
Ratha Jatra of Radha Govinda, **Vol. 6**, 230
Rath-Rathani Fair, **Vol. 4**, 231
Ratnagiri Jatra, **Vol. 6**, 148-51
Ratneswar Siva Temple Fair, **Vol. 6**, 230
Ravalantha Temple Jatra, **Vol. 2**, 394
Ravanasidde Shvara Jatra, **Vol. 2**, 396
Ravi Das Jayanti, **Vol. 1**, 92-93, **Vol. 4**, 53
Razaqshah Vali Urs, **Vol. 2**, 395
Reh Festival, **Vol. 6**, 285
Rennuka Fair, **Vol. 4**, 509
Renukamba Car Festival, **Vol. 2**, 395
Renukamba Jatra, **Vol. 2**, 396
Republic Day, **Vol. 1**, 152-58, **Vol. 4**, 106
Revansiddha Fair, **Vol. 5**, 338
Ravanasiddheshvara Jatra, **Vol. 2**, 396
Revappayya Swami Jatra, **Vol. 2**, 396
Revelganj Fair, **Vol. 6**, 31
Ribba, **Vol. 4**, 153, **Vol. 4**, 225
Rihali Fair, **Vol. 4**, 232
Rishi Panchami Fair, **Vol. 4**, 233
Rishi Panchami, **Vol. 3**, 349
Rishi Pir Fair, **Vol. 4**, 298
Rishipanchami Fair, **Vol. 5**, 339
Rohru Fair, **Vol. 4**, 233-35
Rokfu Festival, **Vol. 4**, 235
Roman Catholic Church and the Coonan Cross Shrines Feast, **Vol. 3**, 158
Rosh Hashanah, **Vol. 1**, 152, **Vol. 4**, 100
Rudra Prayag, **Vol. 4**, 534
Rudramal / Rudramahalya ruins, **Vol. 5**, 145-47
Rukmangada Pandit Festival, **Vol. 2**, 396
Rupnath Fair, **Vol. 5**, 454
Rushkiling, **Vol. 4**, 226

S

S.S. Gervasis and Prothasis Church Feast, **Vol. 3**, 175
Saba Gachhi Fair, **Vol. 6**, 17
Sabarimala, **Vol. 3**, 67
Sacha Sauda Fair, **Vol. 4**, 132
Sacred Hearts Church Feast, **Vol. 3**, 160
Sadanandaswami Festival, **Vol. 2**, 397
Sadashiva Car Festival, **Vol. 2**, 398
Sadashivgad Pir Urs, **Vol. 2**, 398
Sadguru Festival, **Vol. 3**, 357
Safa Shahouri Masjid Festival, **Vol. 5**, 57
Sagadawa Festival, **Vol. 6**, 450
Sagar Community, **Vol. 5**, 41
Sahasralinga Jatra, **Vol. 2**, 398
Sahasralingeshwara Jatra, **Vol. 2**, 399
Saho Jatar, **Vol. 4**, 235
Sai Baba Abhishekam, **Vol. 2**, 87
Sai Baba Fair, **Vol. 5**, 340-42
Saint Goroba Fair, **Vol. 5**, 342
Saint Karimuddin Urs, **Vol. 2**, 399
Saint Monohar Das Mahotsava Festival, **Vol. 6**, 231
Saint Nath Fair, **Vol. 5**, 343-46
Saint Quadar Wali Urs, **Vol. 3**, 350
Saint Sakhi Sarwar Dargah Fair, **Vol. 4**, 371
Sair, **Vol. 4**, 235
Saiyad Baba Atalshah, **Vol. 5**, 454
Saiyed Ibrahim Urs, **Vol. 4**, 509
Saiyid Salar Masand Dargah Sharif Fair, **Vol. 4**, 509
Sakharam Maharaj Fair, **Vol. 5**, 331, 346
Sakleshwaraswamy Temple Jatra, **Vol. 2**, 400
Salat Community, **Vol. 5**, 41
Salbardi Fair, **Vol. 5**, 346-48, 454
Salem Cattle Fair, **Vol. 3**, 352
Salooni Jatar, **Vol. 4**, 236
Samalia Puja, **Vol. 6**, 151-53
Samanun Fair, **Vol. 4**, 236
Sam-Peyarchi Festival, **Vol. 3**, 271
Sandeswar Shiv Puja, **Vol. 6**, 232
Sangam Tirtha, **Vol. 5**, 224
Sangameshvara Fair, **Vol. 2**, 400
Sangameshvara Jatra, **Vol. 2**, 401, 402
Sangameshwara Car Festival, **Vol. 2**, 400
Sangameshwara Jatra, **Vol. 2**, 401
Sangameswaruni Brahmothsavam, **Vol. 2**, 91
Sangamnath Dev Jatra **Vol. 2**, 402
Sangharia Community, **Vol. 5**, 42
Sangken Festival, **Vol. 6**, 286
Sanh Sahib Fair, **Vol. 4**, 371
Sanjeevaraya Jatra, **Vol. 2**, 402
Sani-Peyarchi Festival, **Vol. 3**, 271

Sanjhi Festival, **Vol. 4**, 132
Sankar Math Festival and Fair—Ramrajatala, **Vol. 6**, 232
Sankardeva Festival, **Vol. 6**, 327
Sankat Mochan Mahabir Fair, **Vol. 4**, 509
Sankisa Jatra, **Vol. 4**, 510
Sankowan Fair, **Vol. 5**, 454
Sant Baba Dalip Singh Fair, **Vol. 4**, 371
Sant Deoji Fair, **Vol. 5**, 467
Sant Kaleranwale Fair, **Vol. 4**, 371
Santacruz Cathedral Feast, **Vol. 3**, 160
Santokhsar, **Vol. 4**, 319
Santoobai Jatra, **Vol. 2**, 402
Sappalam Jatra, **Vol. 2**, 403
Sappalamma Cattle Fair, **Vol. 3**, 352
Saptakoteshwar Temple Festival, **Vol. 5**, 57
Saptarishi Kund, **Vol. 4**, 535
Saptashringi Devi Fair, **Vol. 5**, 348
Saramukhi Kavu Utsavam, **Vol. 3**, 161
Saraugi Fair, **Vol. 4**, 510
Saraswat Brahman, **Vol. 5**, 69
Saraswati Puja Festival, **Vol. 6**, 361
Sarbamangala Temple Fair, **Vol. 6**, 233
Sare Sitang Festival, **Vol. 6**, 286
Sarekha Fair, **Vol. 5**, 455
Sarhul Festival, **Vol. 6**, 53-66, 153
Sarigiro Makkan Urs, **Vol. 2**, 403
Sarkara Bhagavathi Temple Kaliyoottu and Bharani, **Vol. 3**, 69
Sarnath Jatra, **Vol. 4**, 510-13
Sarnath, **Vol. 4**, 525
Saroga Chhinj, **Vol. 4**, 236
Sarravatsar Pratipada Festival, **Vol. 4**, 550
Sarthal Devi Temple Jatra, **Vol. 4**, 298
Sat Khumb Fair, **Vol. 4**, 132
Satbhaya Jatra, **Vol. 6**, 153-54
Sati Fair, **Vol. 4**, 236, **Vol. 6**, 32
Sati Malindi Devi Fair, **Vol. 4**, 513
Satighat Fair, **Vol. 6**, 32
Satyanarayan Puja, **Vol. 1**, 93-95, **Vol. 4**, 55-57
Satyanatheshwara Temple Jatra, **Vol. 2**, 403
Saumykeshava Temple Festival, **Vol. 2**, 403
Savitri Brata, **Vol. 6**, 123
Savitri Vrata, **Vol. 6**, 154
Sawan-ki-Saji, **Vol. 4**, 237
Sayed Ummer Quadri Urs, **Vol. 2**, 404
Sayyad Salar Masud Sahib Urs, **Vol. 2**, 404
Sazo Festival, **Vol. 4**, 237
Sedal Festival, **Vol. 3**, 271
Sehore Cattle Fair, **Vol. 5**, 455
Sekrenyi Festival, **Vol. 6**, 424
Sentinelese Tribe (A&N), **Vol. 3**, 15
Seoni Dussehra, **Vol. 4**, 238
Sha Ali Basha Urs, **Vol. 2**, 195
Shabadivanu Urs, **Vol. 2**, 92
Shab-e-Barat, **Vol. 1**, 127, **Vol. 4**, 81
Shab-e-Meraj, **Vol. 1**, 127, **Vol. 4**, 80
Shad Nongkrem Festival, **Vol. 6**, 385
Shah Abdul Quaddus's Urs, **Vol. 4**, 551
Shah Alam Urs, **Vol. 5**, 199
Shah Alauddin Sabir's Urs, **Vol. 4**, 551
Shah Arjan of Patna's Urs,.**Vol. 6**, 32
Shah Doula Rahiman Shah Gazi Urs, **Vol. 5**, 352-54
Shah Farid-ud-Din Sahib Fair, **Vol. 4**, 299
Shah Hamdani's Urs, **Vol. 4**, 300
Shah Jalal Tabrizi Fair, **Vol. 6**, 233
Shah Karim's Urs, **Vol. 4**, 513
Shah Khalid-Bin-Wala Dargah Fair, **Vol. 4**, 371
Shah Kumaish Fair, **Vol. 4**, 135
Shah Madar Fair, **Vol. 4**, 513
Shah Madari Dargah Jatra, **Vol. 6**, 32
Shah Nomani Asiri Urs, **Vol. 5**, 456-58
Shah Nur Jamal Fair, **Vol. 4**, 372
Shah Sadiq Qalander's Urs, **Vol. 4**, 300
Shah Turab-ul-Haq Urs, **Vol. 5**, 354
Shaheed Bunga Sahib Fair, **Vol. 4**, 372
Shaheedi Dihara Sardar Sewa Singh Fair, **Vol. 4**, 372
Shaheedi Mela, **Vol. 4**, 135
Shahidi Fair, **Vol. 4**, 372-73
– Hussainwala, **Vol. 4**, 369-70
Shahidi Jor Mela, **Vol. 4**, 367-69
Shaik Saheb Urs, Chintaki, **Vol. 2**, 404
Shaik Sufi Sarmast Saheb Urs, **Vol. 2**, 404
Shaikh Ahmed Khattu Ganj Bakhsh Urs Fair, **Vol. 5**, 202-205
Shaikh Salim Chishti's Urs, **Vol. 4**, 513
Shakatapura Samsthana Tengina Matha Festival, **Vol. 2**, 405
Shakhambari Devi Fair, **Vol. 2**, 404, **Vol. 4**, 516
Shakhambari Devi Jatra, **Vol. 2**, 404
Shakuna Ranganathaswami Jatra, **Vol. 2**, 405
Shalogra Fair, **Vol. 4**, 238
Sham Singh Atariwala Fair, **Vol. 4**, 373
Shamba Dasami, **Vol. 6**, 124-25, 154
Shambhulinga Temple Festival, **Vol. 2**, 406
Shambhulingeshwara Jatra, **Vol. 2**, 406

Shambu Mahadeo Fair, **Vol. 5**, 355
Shamlaji Fair, **Vol. 5**, 205
Shan Khodhar Fair, **Vol. 5**, 458
Shancha Fair, **Vol. 4**, 238
Shani Deva Jatra, **Vol. 2**, 407
Shani Maharaj Fair, **Vol. 5**, 357
Shanimahatmadevara Jatra, **Vol. 2**, 407
Shankara Narayana Car Festival, **Vol. 2**, 408
Shankaranarayanan Teertha Jatra, **Vol. 2**, 410
Shankareshwaraswami Jatra, **Vol. 2**, 410
Shankarlinga Jatra, **Vol. 2**, 408
Shankhodhar Fair, **Vol. 5**, 458
Shantadurga Temple Fair, **Vol. 5**, 57
Shanta-Rishyashringapura Jatra, **Vol. 2**, 410
Shanteri Jogavva Matha Festival, **Vol. 2**, 411
Shanth Festival, **Vol. 4**, 238
Shantigiri Jatra, **Vol. 2**, 411
Sharad Purnima Fair, **Vol. 4**, 239
Sharadamba Car Festival, **Vol. 2**, 412
Sharana Basaveshvara Fair, **Vol. 2**, 412
Sharannavavatryotsava Festival, **Vol. 2**, 413
Sharda Devi Fair, **Vol. 4**, 135
Sharif Sailani Shah Miya Urs, **Vol. 5**, 351
Sharif Sayed Mohamed Gouse Quadri Urs, **Vol. 2**, 413
Sharika Bhagwati Fair, **Vol. 4**, 300
Shatrunjay Hills Festivals, **Vol. 5**, 171-74
Shawal-ka-Bishu-Mithai ka Mela, **Vol. 4**, 239
Shawni Fair, **Vol. 4**, 239
Sheetla Ashtami, **Vol. 5**, 468-71
Sheetla Mata Fair, **Vol. 4**, 433-35
Sheikh Ahmad Mujaddid Alf-i-sani Fatehgarh Sahib Urs, **Vol. 2**, 377
Sheik Bahudin Jisdi Urs, **Vol. 2**, 413
Sheikh Misry Urs, **Vol. 5**, 357
Sheikh Sammaa Fair, **Vol. 4**, 516
Sheikh Zain-ud-Din's Urs, **Vol. 4**, 300
Shejjeshwara Jatra, **Vol. 2**, 413
Sherken Fair/Festival, **Vol. 4**, 239, 240
Shiah's Festivals, **Vol. 1**, 128
Shiami Kali Fair, **Vol. 4**, 240
Shians Festivals, **Vol. 4**, 83
Shibchaturdashi Fair, **Vol. 6**, 462
Shibrat, **Vol. 4**, 220
Shilgiri-ka-Bishu, **Vol. 4**, 241
Shimas Devi Fair, **Vol. 4**, 241
Shitla Devi Fair, **Vol. 4**, 241-42
Shitla Fair, **Vol. 4**, 242
Shitla Satam Festival, **Vol. 5**, 207
Shiv Chaturdashi Fair, **Vol. 6**, 47
Shiv Chautra, **Vol. 4**, 242
Shiv Shakti Fair (Chitrari Jatar), **Vol. 4**, 242
Shiva and Ayyapan temple Utsavam, **Vol. 3**, 167
Shiva Temple Fair, **Vol. 6**, 236
Shiva Temple Oottu-Eruvassi, **Vol. 3**, 163
Shiva Temple Utsavam
- Ettumanoor, **Vol. 3**, 163
- Kakkayur, **Vol. 3**, 166
- Thrikariyoor, **Vol. 3**, 166
- Kozhikode, **Vol. 3**, 166

Shivaganga Fair, **Vol. 4**, 551
Shivayoga Mandira Fair, **Vol. 2**, 413
Shivayogi Car Festival, **Vol. 2**, 414
Shivayogi Jatra, **Vol. 2**, 414
Shivratri / Sivarati Fair / Festival, **Vol. 2**, 97, **Vol. 3**, 23, **Vol. 4**, 135, 243-48, 374, **Vol. 5**, 218, 275, 458, 471, **Vol. 6**, 35, 162, 164, 237, 328, *See also* Maha Shivratri
Shivaratri Brahmolsavam, **Vol. 2**, 95
Shivaratri Utsavam, **Vol, 2**, 98, **Vol. 3**, 69
Shobhaparambu Bhagavathy Temple Nilankari Utsavam, **Vol. 3**, 162
Shogch Fair, **Vol. 4**, 248
Shonetang, **Vol. 4**, 220
Shonyachong Festival, **Vol. 4**, 248
Shrasti Fair, **Vol. 5**, 471
Shravani Fair, **Vol. 4**, 516
Shravanabelgola Jain Mahotsava, *See*, Jain Matha's Jatra, **Vol. 2**, 288
Shrawani Purnima Fair, **Vol. 6**, 35
Shree Jata Shankar Fair, **Vol. 5**, 459
Shri Baijnath Mahadeo Fair, **Vol. 5**, 459
Shri Datta Fair, **Vol. 5**, 358
Shri Jhadkhandi Vaijinatheswar Mahadeva Fair, **Vol. 5**, 460
Shri Mahavirji Fair, **Vol. 4**, 435-37
Shri Panchami (Vasant Panchmi), **Vol. 6**, 168
Shri Pishari Kavu Bhagavathy Temple Utsavam, **Vol. 3**, 174
Shri Rama Fair, **Vol. 5**, 359
Shri Ramdeo Jatra, **Vol. 5**, 460
Shrine of Our Lady of Vallarpadom Feast, **Vol. 3**, 162
Shripatananda Atmananda Swamiji Jatra, **Vol. 2**, 413
Shuklatirth Fair, **Vol. 5**, 208-11
Shuktok Festival, **Vol. 4**, 248
Shuzab Festival, **Vol. 4**, 248
Shyamsunder Puja Festival, **Vol. 6**, 234
Shymasunderji Puja Festival, **Vol. 6**, 234

Siddeshvaraswami Jatra, **Vol. 2**, 420
Siddeshwara Fair, **Vol. 2**, 415
Siddeshwara Festival, **Vol. 2**, 415
Siddeshwara Jatra, **Vol. 2**, 416
Siddeshwara Temple Car Festival, **Vol. 2**, 417
Siddeshwara Temple Jatra, **Vol. 2**, 418
Siddh Baba Temple Fair, **Vol. 4**, 516-18
Siddha Bhairava Temple Festival, **Vol. 6**, 154
Siddhaiahgiri Festival, **Vol. 2**, 92
Siddhalingeshwara Jatra, **Vol. 2**, 418
Siddhalingeshwaraswami Jatra, **Vol. 2**, 418
Siddhanath Fair, **Vol. 5**, 359-61, 362
Siddhappa Festival, **Vol. 2**, 94
Siddharameshwara Jatra, **Vol. 2**, 419
Siddharameshwari Belpatri Vahanan, **Vol. 2**, 419
Siddheshwar Fair, **Vol. 5**, 361, 363
Sidhasthan Fair, **Vol. 6**, 32
Sidheswar Fair, **Vol. 6**, 154
Sidhupur shrines , **Vol. 5**, 143-44
Si-Donyl Festival, **Vol. 6**, 276-78
Sigi Hunnive Festival, **Vol. 2**, 420
Simdega Fair, **Vol. 6**, 47
Simhastha Fair, **Vol. 5**, 460-65
Simhavahini Temple Fair, **Vol. 6**, 234
Sindhi festivals, **Vol. 4**, 58-62
Singaji Fair, **Vol. 5**, 456, 471-75
Singh Vahini Durga Fair, **Vol. 6**, 32
Singhaji Baba Fair, **Vol. 5**, 456, 471-75
Singheshwar Jatra, **Vol. 6**, 33
Singhpura Fair, **Vol. 4**, 375
Sinhastha Kumbha Fair, **Vol. 5**, 369
Sinvi Diwali Fair, **Vol. 4**, 249
Sipi Fair, **Vol. 4**, 249
Sirahatti Math Festival, **Vol. 2**, 420
Sitabari Fair, **Vol. 4**, 437-39
Sita-Dohar Fair, **Vol. 4**, 518
Sitakund Fair Jatra, **Vol. 5**, 16
Sital Sasthi Festival, **Vol. 6**, 154
Sital Shasthi, **Vol. 6**, 125
Sitala Devi Fair, **Vol. 4**, 518
Sitala Mata Fair, **Vol. 4**, 127-130
Sitala Sasthi, **Vol. 6**, 75
Siva Barat Fair, **Vol. 4**, 551
Siva Chaturddasi Fair, **Vol. 6**, 235
Sivarathri *see* Shivratri
Skanda Sashti Festival, **Vol. 3**, 352
Smasam Kali Puja Festival and Fair, **Vol. 6**, 232
Snanjatra of Jagannath, **Vol. 6**, 239
Snana Yatra, **Vol. 6**, 98-100
Sobu Tado, **Vol. 6**, 278-79
Sohorai/Sohrai Festival, **Vol. 6**, 39, 66-68, 164
Sokalpur Fair, **Vol. 5**, 475
Solan Fair, **Vol. 4**, 250
Solung Festival, **Vol. 6**, 279, 286
Somavar Observance, **Vol. 3**, 358
Somavati Amavas, **Vol. 1**, 42, **Vol. 4**, 17, 130
Somavati Amavas Fair, **Vol. 4**, 135
Someshwar Nath Jatra, **Vol. 4**, 518
Someshwar Mahadeva Fair, **Vol. 5**, 364-366, 465
Someshwara Car Festival, **Vol. 2**, 420
Someshwara Jatra, **Vol. 2**, 421, 422, 423, 424
Someshwaraswami Jatra, **Vol. 2**, 424
Someswara Festival, **Vol. 2**, 99
Somhardev Baba Fair, **Vol. 5**, 475
Somnath Patan, **Vol. 5**, 147-50
Sonabdeo Fair, **Vol. 5**, 476
Sonagir Jatra, **Vol. 5**, 466
Sonam Losoong Festival, **Vol. 6**, 450
Sonatopal Fair, **Vol. 6**, 240
Sonepur Cattle Fair, **Vol. 6**, 34
Sonepur Fair, **Vol. 6**, 34
Sontalaiya Fair, **Vol. 5**, 476
Sravana Sankranti Rihali, **Vol. 4**, 251
Sravasti Jatra, **Vol. 4**, 518
Sree Cherapuram Shiva Temple Utsavam, **Vol. 3**, 167
Sree Krishnaswamy Temple Arat, **Vol. 3**, 170
Sree Krishnaswamy Temple Utsavam, **Vol. 3**, 171
Sree Kurumba Temple Utsavam, **Vol. 3**, 172
Sree Marattil Kottaram Bhagavathy Devaswom Utsavam, **Vol. 3**, 70
Sree Narayana Jayanthi, **Vol. 3**, 49
Sree Padmanabhaswamy Temple Murajapam, **Vol. 3**, 71
Sree Padmanabhswamy Temple Utsavam, **Vol. 3**, 172
Sree Rakthakanta Swamy Temple Utsavam, **Vol. 3**, 146
Sree Subramonia Swamy Temple Utsavam, **Vol. 3**, 72
Sreekanteswaram Temple Utsavam, **Vol. 3**, 168
Sri Adikesavaswamy Brahmhothsavam, **Vol. 2**, 101
Shri Amaresmaraswamy Rathothsavam, **Vol. 2**, 101
Sree Sundareswara Temple Ustavam, **Vol. 3**, 175
Sree Vallabha Temple Uthraseeval, **Vol. 3**, 175
Sri Anjaneyaswamy Festival, **Vol. 2**, 104
Sri Atishayakshetra Jatra, **Vol. 2**, 425
Sri Augustine's Feast, **Vol. 6**, 244
Sri Balabrahmeswami Festival, **Vol. 2**, 105

Sri Beechupalleswamy Rathothsavam, **Vol. 2**, 110
Sri Beerappa Festival, **Vol. 2**, 111
Sri Bhavanarayanswamy Brahmothsavam, **Vol. 2**, 111
Sri Bhadrakalkamman Temple Bhrahmothsavam, **Vol. 3**, 271
Sri Bhavanarayanaswamy Festival, **Vol. 2**, 112
Sri Bhavanarayanaswamy Kalyanothsavam, **Vol. 3**, 113
Sri Bhimalingeswaraswamy Rathothsavam, **Vol. 2**, 115
Sri Bhoothappa Panduga Festival, **Vol. 2**, 118
Sri Brahmananda Eswaraswamy Festival, **Vol. 2**, 118
Sri Bugga Malleswaraswamy Aradhanothsavam, **Vol. 2**, 120
Sri Bugga Ramalingeswaraswamy Festival, **Vol. 2**, 119
Sri Bugga Venkateswaraswamy Festival, **Vol. 2**, 120
Sri Chaitanya Festival, **Vol. 6**, 241
Sri Chaitanya Rasa Festival, **Vol. 6**, 242
Sri Chennakesavaswamy Brahmothsavam, **Vol. 2**, 121
Sri Chennakesavaswamy Festival, **Vol. 2**, 123
Sri Chennakesavaswamy Rathothasavam, **Vol. 2**, 123
Sri Chikkanneswaraswamy Festival, **Vol. 2**, 122
Sri Chintalarayaswamy Festival, **Vol. 2**, 124
Sri Chithambaraswamy Car Festival, **Vol. 2**, 124
Sri Dharmarajaswamy Brahmothsavam, **Vol. 2**, 125
Sri Dona Thimmappa Festival, **Vol. 2**, 126
Sri Gajendramoksha Mahothsavam, **Vol. 2**, 126
Sri Gowthameswaraswamy Festival, **Vol. 2**, 127
Sri Gumani Saheb Urs, **Vol. 2**, 127
Sri Hazarat Khader Vali Urs-Kinakondla, **Vol. 2**, 37, 127
Sri Hazarat Syed Basha Vali Urs-Gooty, **Vol. 2**, 37, 128
Sri Honnurswamy Urs, **Vol. 2**, 127
Sri Jaganmohini Kesavaswamy Kalyanamahotsavam, **Vol. 2**, 128
Sri Jatayupureeswarar Temple Brahmothsavam, **Vol. 3**, 272
Sri Jwala Narasimhaswamy Jayanti, **Vol. 2**, 129
Sri Kalvagadda Anjaneyaswamy Rathothsavam, **Vol. 2**, 130
Sri Kanaka Mahalakshmamma Jatra, **Vol. 2**, 130
Sri Karibasavaswamy Car Festival, **Vol. 2**, 130
Sri Kati Koteswaraswamy Festival, **Vol. 2**, 135
Sri Kesavaswamy Kalyanamothsavam, **Vol. 2**, 135
Sri Khuntir Utsava, **Vol. 6**, 243
Sri Kodanda Ramaswamy Brahmothsavam, **Vol. 2**, 136
Sri Kodanda Ramaswamy Festival, **Vol. 2**, 137
Sri Kokilambal-Thirukameswarar Temple Festival, **Vol. 3**, 272
Sri Kona Ranganathaswamy Festival, **Vol. 2**, 138
Sri Korivi Veerabhadraswamy Festival, **Vol. 2**, 138
Sri Krishna Dharmaraja Brahmothsavam, **Vol. 2**, 139
Sri Krishna Jayanti, **Vol. 2**, 139
Sri Kshetra Baad Matha Festival, **Vol. 2**, 425
Sri Lakshmi Chennakesavaswamy Festival, **Vol. 2**, 140
Sri Lakshmi Narasimhaswamy Brahmothasavam
  – kadiri, **Vol. 2**, 140
  – Nalgonda, **Vol. 2**, 142
Sri Lakshmi Narasimhaswamy Kalyanomahothsavam
  – Antervedi, **Vol. 2**, 144
  – Karimnagar, **Vol. 2**, 146
  – Warangal, **Vol. 2**, 148
  – Vizianagaram, **Vol. 2**, 149
  – Nalgonda, **Vol. 2**, 150
Sri Lakshmi Vallabharayaswamy Brahmothsavam, **Vol. 2**, 151
Sri Lakshmipathiswamy Kalyanothsavam, **Vol. 2**, 150
Sri Maddanaswamy Chariot Festival, **Vol. 2**, 152
Sri Malleswaraswamy Brahmothsavam-Nellore, **Vol. 2**, 153
Sri Malleswaraswamy Rathothsavam, **Vol. 2**, 154
Sri Mallikarjunaswamy Festival,
  – Gorrekunta, **Vol. 2**, 154
  – Komarvelly, **Vol. 2**, 155
Sri Mallikarjunaswamy Kamakshikevi Brahmothsavam, **Vol. 2**, 156
Sri Manyamokonda Lakshmi Venkateswaraswamy Brahmothsavam, **Vol. 2**, 158
Sri Mohammad Shah Khader Vali Urs, **Vol. 2**, 160
Sri Mondi Bhirava Kondaiah Festival Bhairavaswamy, **Vol. 2**, 161
Sri Moolanadhar Temple Brahmothsavam, **Vol. 3**, 274
Sri Mulasthaneswaraswamy Brahmothsavam, **Vol. 2**, 161
Sri Mylareswaraswamy Aradhana, **Vol. 2**, 162
Sri Nageshwaraswamy Kalyanam, **Vol. 2**, 163
Sri Narasimhaswamy Brahmothsava, **Vol. 2**, 163
Sri Narasimhaswamy Festival, **Vol. 2**, 164, 165
Sri Narasimhaswamy Kalyanothsavam, **Vol. 2**, 166
Sri Narasimhaswamy Rathothasavam, **Vol. 2**, 166
Sri Nettekani Anjaneyaswamy Aradhana, **Vol. 2**, 168
Sri Panakala Lakshmi Narasimhaswamy Brahmothsavam, **Vol. 2**, 169
Sri Pandurangaswamy Kartika Uthsavams, **Vol. 2**, 171
Sri Papanaseswara Festival, **Vol. 2**, 174
Sri Pennsila Narasimhaswamy Festival, **Vol. 2**, 179
Sri Prasanna Venkateshwaraswamy Brahmottsavam, **Vol. 2**, 179
Sri Raghunayakaswamy Kalyanamahothsavam, **Vol. 2**, 181
Sri Rama Krishnaswamy Festival, **Vol. 2**, 182
Sri Rama Navami, **Vol. 2**, 191, **Vol. 3**, 355
Sri Rama Navami Festival, **Vol. 2**, 188, *See also* Ramnavami
Sri Ramachandra Kalyanothsavam, **Vol. 2**, 183
Sri Ramakoti Mahothsavam, **Vol. 2**, 184
Sri Ramakrishna Birthday Festival, **Vol. 6**, 243
Sri Ramalingeswaraswamy Festival, **Vol. 2**, 186, 187

Sri Ramalingeswaraswamy Lakshabilvardhana, **Vol. 2**, 187
Sri Ranganathaswamy Car Festival, **Vol. 2**, 192
Sri Ranganayakaswamy Festival, **Vol. 2**, 193
Sri Ranganadha Brahmothsavam, **Vol. 2**, 191
Sri Satyanarayana Vratham, **Vol. 2**, 193
Sri Sengazhuneeramman Temple Festivals, **Vol. 3**, 274
Sri Shah Masthan Vali Urs, **Vol. 2**, 195
Sri Shantika Parameshwari Devi Festival, **Vol. 2**, 426
Sringeri Matha Festivals, **Vol. 2**, 426
Sringirampur Jatra, **Vol. 4**, 518
Sripanchami (Basant Panchami), **Vol. 6**, 125
St. Andrew's Forance Church Feast of St. Sebastians, **Vol. 3**, 176
St. Antony Feast, **Vol. 3**, 355
St. Antony's Church Feast, **Vol. 3**, 178
St. Antony's Church Festival, **Vol. 3**, 72
St. Antony's Church Kamakinoda Festival, **Vol. 3**, 73
St. Agugustine's Feast, **Vol. 6**, 244
St. Augustine's Church Feast, **Vol. 3**, 179
St. Bonifice Church Feast, **Vol. 3**, 179
St. Days (list), **Vol. 4**, 92-93
St. Dominic Syrian Catholic Church Feast, **Vol. 3**, 180
St. Elias Day, **Vol. 3**, 186
St. Francis Church Feast, **Vol. 3**, 74
St. George' Church, **Vol. 3**, 182
St. George's Feast, **Vol. 3**, 181, 184-85
St. George's Church Festivals, **Vol. 3**, 74-76
St. George's Day, **Vol. 3**, 186
St. George's Jacobitesyrian Church Festival, **Vol. 3**, 186-187
St. George's Orthodox Syriyan Church Festival, **Vol. 3**, 76
St. Gregory Thoumathurgus Parish Church Feast, **Vol. 3**, 186
St. John the Baptist Church Feast, **Vol. 3**, 77
St. John's Church Feast, **Vol. 3**, 188
St. John's Feast, **Vol. 6**, 244
St. Jame's Church Vyttila Feast, **Vol. 3**, 187
St. John's Roman Catholic Church Feast, **Vol. 3**, 189
St. Joseph's Shrine Feast, **Vol. 3**, 190
St. Joseph's Cathedral Festival, **Vol. 3**, 77
St. Joseph's Church Feast, **Vol. 3**, 189, 190
St. Josephs Feast, **Vol. 2**, 429
St. Mary Magdalene's Church Titular Feast, **Vol. 3**, 203
St. Mary's Church Feast, **Vol. 3**, 192, 194-97, 199
St. Mary's Feast, **Vol. 2**, 429
St. Mary's Forane Church Feast, **Vol. 3**, 203
St. Mary's Forane Church Festival, **Vol. 3**, 78
St. Mary's Jacobite Syrian Church Feast, **Vol. 3**, 203
St. Mary's Orthodox Syrian Church Feast, **Vol. 3**, 204
St. Mary's Orthodox Syrian Church Festival, **Vol. 3**, 205
St. Michael's Church Feast of the Archangel, **Vol. 3**, 205
St. Orthodox Syrian Church Festival, **Vol. 3**, 76
St. Peter's Church Feast, **Vol. 3**, 206
St. Peter's ChurchFestival, **Vol. 3**, 207
St. Rita's Church Feast, **Vol. 3**, 208
St. Sebastian's Church Festival, **Vol. 3**, 78
St. Sabastian's Church Corpus Christi **Vol. 3**, 209
St. Sebastian's Feast, **Vol. 3**, 209, 211, 212, 213, 214, 215
St. Teresa of Avila Feast, **Vol. 3**, 276
St. Teresa's Church Vallam Feast, **Vol. 3**, 216
St. Thomas Catholic Church Feast, **Vol. 3**, 217
St. Thomas Church Feast, **Vol. 3**, 217
St. Thomas' Church Arrnoottimangalam Kurusumala Kayattom, **Vol. 3**, 218
St. Xavier's Cathedral Festival, **Vol. 3**, 363
St. Xavier's Church Feast, **Vol. 3**, 79
Sthanumalayaswami Temple Festivals, **Vol. 3**, 356
Suani Fair, **Vol. 6**, 164
Subodharanga Jatra, **Vol. 2**, 430
Subrahmanyeswaraswamy Brahmothsavam, **Vol. 2**, 99
Subramanya Fair, **Vol. 2**, 430
Subramanya Swamy Jatra, **Vol. 2**, 431
Subramonia Temple Utsavam, **Vol. 3**, 220-22
Sudasha Vrata, **Vol. 6**, 164
Sudh Mahadev Temple Festival, **Vol. 4**, 301
Sudhmahadev, **Vol. 4**, 302
Suggidevara Festival, **Vol. 2**, 431
Suggi-Kunita Festival, **Vol. 2**, 431
Sui Fair, **Vol. 4**, 251-253
Suknanni Oja Pali, **Vol. 6**, 328
Sultanpur Chhinj, **Vol. 4**, 253
Sume-Gelirak, **Vol. 6**, 126
Sun Temple Fairs, **Vol. 5**, 466
Sunabdeo Fair, **Vol. 5**, 476
Sundarer Utsavam, **Vol. 3**, 360
Sundla Chhinj, **Vol. 4**, 253
Suneya Feast of St. Mary, **Vol. 3**, 198
Sunia, **Vol. 6**, 164
Sunni Festivals, **Vol. 1**, 128, **Vol. 4**, 83
Sura Samharam, **Vol. 3**, 273
Suraj Kund Craft Mela, **Vol. 4**, 136
Suraj Kund Fair, **Vol. 4**, 136
Surpu Gompha Jhalma, **Vol. 4**, 253
Surya Grahana Fair, **Vol. 4**, 137
Suskar Festival, **Vol. 4**, 254-55

Swaminarayan Temple Festival, **Vol. 5**, 132-135, 151, 152
Swarnavalli Matha Festival, **Vol. 2**, 431
Swarnavalli Matha Jatra, **Vol. 2**, 432
Swing Festival (Raja Sankranti), **Vol. 6**, 119-20
Syed Abdul Khadar Shah Saheb Urs, **Vol. 2**, 100
Syed Baba Fakruddin Urs, **Vol. 2**, 432
Syed Hasan Shah Quadri Urs, **Vol. 2**, 432
Syed Hilal Naqishbandi Festival, **Vol. 4**, 303
Syed Jalaluddin Chanda Khadri Urs, **Vol. 2**, 432
Syed Janbaz Wali, **Vol. 4**, 303
Syed Jatmalin Baba Urs, **Vol. 2**, 432
Syed Mohammad Shariful Madani Urs, **Vol. 2**, 433
Syed Qamar Saheb's Urs, **Vol. 4**, 303
Syed Salar Makhdum Husain Urs, **Vol. 2**, 433
Syed Shams Alam Hussainali Urs, **Vol. 2**, 433
Syed Sheik Mir Hazarat Urs, **Vol. 2**, 433
Syed Sultan Ali Shah Urs, **Vol. 2**, 100
Synod Church of Dyampar Feast, **Vol. 3**, 222
Syrian Church Feast, **Vol. 3**, 222

T

Tai Pusam Festival, **Vol. 3**, 364
Taj Fair, **Vol. 5**, 476
Talappoli, **Vol. 3**, 252
Talwandi Sabo, **Vol. 4**, 325
Tanakeshwara Mahadeva Fair, **Vol. 5**, 477
Tap-Keshwar Mahadeo Fair, **Vol. 4**, 551
Tapti Fair, **Vol. 5**, 477
Tara Tarini Jatra, **Vol. 6**, 155
Taradevi Chaturdasi Fair, **Vol. 6**, 244
Taradevi Fair, **Vol. 4**, 256
Taraknath Temple Festival, **Vol. 6**, 245
Taranpurthi Jains Teerth Jatra, **Vol. 5**, 477
Teej, **Vol. 1**, 95-96, **Vol. 4**, 57, 257
Tegh Bahadur Martyrdom, **Vol. 4**, 315
Tejaji Cattle Fair, **Vol. 4**, 439-42
Tejaji Fair, **Vol. 5**, 480-82
Temple Celebrations (Manipur), **Vol. 6**, 42
Teppotsava Festival, **Vol. 2**, 433
Teppotsavam, **Vol. 3**, 287
Terhunyi Festival, **Vol. 6**, 425
Teru-Malleshwara Jatra, **Vol. 2**, 434
Thadari, **Vol. 1**, 101, **Vol. 4**, 60
Thaikkatt Amma's Feast, **Vol. 3**, 222
Thakurani Jatra, **Vol. 6**, 75, 155-57
Thara Sahib, **Vol. 4**, 318
Tharola Fair, **Vol. 4**, 257
Thavanurakavu Siva Temple Utsavam, **Vol. 3**, 223
Thayumanavar Festival, **Vol. 3**, 372
Thekenyi Festival, **Vol. 6**, 426
Theppotsavam Festival, **Vol. 3**, 366
Theppotsavam Festival, **Vol. 3**, 366
Therine Festival, **Vol. 6**, 426
Therukkoothu, **Vol. 3**, 375 ·
Thethavavu Matha Festival, **Vol. 3**, 278
Theyuukhupfu Festival, **Vol. 6**, 426
Thimmarayaswamy Jatra, **Vol. 2**, 434
Thirukkalyanam Festival, **Vol. 3**, 367
Thirukkarthigai Festival, **Vol. 3**, 367
Thirumala Devaswom Utsavam, **Vol. 3**, 223
Thirumala Venkataramana Temple Rathotsava, **Vol. 2**, 434
Thirunakkara Mahadeva Temple Utsavam, **Vol. 3**, 224
Thiruvaiyaru Temple Brahmotsavam, **Vol. 3**, 367
Thiruvakkandam Trikkoikal Temple Festivals, **Vol. 3**, 228
Thiruval Amthuruthy Bhagavathy Temple Gramotsavam, **Vol. 3**, 228
Thiruvananthapuram, **Vol. 3**, 23
Thiruvarathu Kavu Bhagavathi Temple Kodiyettu Utsavam, **Vol. 3**, 228
Thiruvathira Utsavam, **Vol. 3**, 53
Thiruvevankavu Devi Temple Utsavam, **Vol. 3**, 229
Thiruvottiyur Temple Brahmotasavam, **Vol. 3**, 368
Thrikkara, **Vol. 3**, 29
Thrikkodithanam Temple Utsavam, **Vol. 3**, 231
Thrippokudam Siva Temple Arat Utsavam, **Vol. 3**, 229
Thula Vishu, **Vol. 3**, 373
Thyagaraja Aaradhana, **Vol. 3**, 368
Tibangma, **Vol. 4**, 221
Tibba Devl Jatra, **Vol. 2**, 434
Tihar Festival, **Vol. 6**, 450
Tikari Chhinj, **Vol. 4**, 257
Tijri, **Vol. 1**, 101-02, **Vol. 4**, 60
Tilbhandareshwar Mahadev Fair, **Vol. 5**, 479
Tilokpur Fair, **Vol. 4**, 257
Tipperudraswamy Car Festival, **Vol. 2**, 435
Tirmuri, **Vol. 1**, 103, **Vol. 4**, 62
Tirthankara Ajitnatha Fair, **Vol. 5**, 479
Tiruchendur Temple Brahmotsavam, **Vol. 3**, 370
Tirugnana Sambandar Jayanti, **Vol. 3**, 374
Tirunavai, **Vol. 3**, 24
Tirunelveli Cattle Fair, **Vol. 3**, 370
Tirupathi Temple, **Vol. 2**, 4
Tiruvannamalai Cattle Fair, **Vol. 3**, 370

Tiruvalluvar Tirunal and Chintamani Tirunal, **Vol. 3**, 374
Tiruvatira, **Vol. 3**, 23, 233-37
Tiruvatirakali, **Vol. 3**, 235
Tiruvisanallur Lyerval, **Vol. 3**, 374
Tisagarh Jatar, **Vol. 4**, 258
Tistamai Fair, **Vol. 6**, 246
Tiwa Jon-Bil Fair, **Vol. 6**, 329
Tohar, **Vol. 4**, 258
Tokhu Emong Festival, **Vol. 6**, 426
Tora, **Vol. 4**, 221
Torgya Festival, **Vol. 6**, 281
Torgya, **Vol. 4**, 221
Tori Fair, **Vol. 4**, 519
Tramat Fair, **Vol. 4**, 259
Tribeni Fair, **Vol. 4**, 259
Tribeni Fairs and Festivals, **Vol. 6**, 246
Tribeni Jatra, **Vol. 6**, 157, 158
Tribhoni Fair, **Vol. 4**, 259
Triekranyl Festival, **Vol. 6**, 427
Trikaviyoor Temple Utsavam, **Vol. 3**, 237
Trimbakeshwar
- Fair, **Vol. 5**, 286
- Temples, **Vol. 5**, 288
- Tirthas, **Vol. 5**, 289-92

Trinath Fair, **Vol. 6**, 157
Trinatha Mela, **Vol. 6**, 157
Trinetreshwar Mahadev Fair, **Vol. 5**, 211
Tripurari / Trupuri Purnima, **Vol. 5**, 212
Triveni Fair, **Vol. 5**, 480, *See also* Tribeni Fair
Trivikramraiji Fair, **Vol. 5**, 213-14
Triyugi Narayana, **Vol. 4**, 537
Tryamboli Fair, **Vol. 5**, 367
Tsatekhu Festival, **Vol. 6**, 427
Tsechu Fair, **Vol. 4**, 259
Tsokum Festival, **Vol. 6**, 427
Tsungrem Mong Festival, **Vol. 6**, 427
Tsunyi Festival, **Vol. 6**, 428
Tukaram Maharaj Fair, **Vol. 5**, 367-70
Tulasi Kshetra Temple Festival, **Vol. 6**, 158
Tuljabhavani Fair, **Vol. 5**, 370-71
Tulsi Fair, **Vol. 4**, 519
Tuluni Festival, **Vol. 6**, 428
Tusu Puja, **Vol. 6**, 330
Twaritapuri Devi Fair, **Vol. 5**, 373
Twashta Kasar, **Vol. 5**, 69
Tyagaraja Utsavam, **Vol. 3**, 376

U

Uchchangi Amma Temple Dasara Festival, **Vol. 2**, 435
Uda Parab, **Vol. 6**, 111
– Keonjhar, **Vol. 6**, 97
Udaneyang Festival, **Vol. 4**, 261
Udayanapuram Temple Utsavam, **Vol. 3**, 238
Udayeshwara Temple Fair, **Vol. 5**, 482
Udham Singh Shaheedi Fair, **Vol. 4**, 376
Udumaradi Ranganatha Car Festival, **Vol. 2**, 435
Udusalamma Jatra, **Vol. 2**, 435
Ujjain Temples, **Vol. 5**, 461-65
Ukhang, **Vol. 4**, 262
Ulaichandi Festival, **Vol. 6**, 248
Ulto-Ratho Festival, **Vol. 6**, 249
Uma Maheshwara Vratham, **Vol. 3**, 378
Umarali Urs, **Vol. 2**, 436
Un Jatra, **Vol. 5**, 483-87
Unai Mata Fair, **Vol. 5**, 215-17
Unao Fair, **Vol. 5**, 481-82
Unakuti Fair, **Vol. 6**, 463
Upakarmam Festival, **Vol. 3**, 376
Urla Fair, **Vol. 4**, 262
Urs Sheikh Ahmad Mujaddid Alf-i-Sani Fatehgarh Sahib, **Vol. 4**, 377
Uthrattathi, **Vol. 3**, 239
Utkanteshwar Mahadev Fair, **Vol. 5**, 217
Uttaravahini Festivals, **Vol. 6**, 251
Uttarayan Fair, **Vol. 6**, 249-50
Uttarayini Fair, **Vol. 4**, 551

V

Vadakkekara Madappalpali Kavu Utsavam, **Vol. 3**, 241
Vadakkekavu Utsavam, **Vol. 3**, 242
Vadakkumnathan Temple Pooram, **Vol. 3**, 242
Vadayattukotta Sree Krishnaswamy Temple Astami Rohini Festival, **Vol. 3**, 244
Vadiraja Jatra, **Vol. 2**, 436
Vagh Barash, **Vol. 4**, 21-22
Vaikasi Visaka Festival, **Vol. 3**, 379
Vaikkathashtami, **Vol. 3**, 388
Vaikunta Ekadasi Festival, **Vol. 3**, 380
Vairamudi Festival, **Vol. 2**, 436
Vaisali Jatra, **Vol. 6**, 35
Vaishakh Purnima, **Vol. 1**, 105, **Vol. 4**, 63

Vaishno Devi Jatra, **Vol. 4**, 303-307
Vakulamma Teertham, **Vol. 2**, 196
Vallalar Vizha, **Vol. 3**, 388
Valmiki Jayanti, **Vol. 1**, 106-07, **Vol. 4**, 58
Vankhandeshwar Fair, **Vol. 4**, 137
Vantha Fair, **Vol. 5**, 223, **Vol. 5**, 226
Varadarajaswami Temple Brahmotsavam, **Vol. 3**, 383
Varahi Devi Fair, **Vol. 4**, 551-52
Varahi Fair, **Vol. 4**, 519
Vara-Lakshmi Vratha, **Vol. 3**, 382
Vara-Lakshmi Worship, **Vol. 3**, 389
Varanapally Siva Temple Makara Sankrama Utsavam, **Vol. 3**, 245
Varanasi Jatra, **Vol. 4**, 519-522
Vardayini Mata Palli Fair, **Vol. 5**, 218-19
Varshikotsava Festival, **Vol. 2**, 437
Vasant / Sri Panchmi, **Vol. 6**, 168, **Vol. 6**, 453
Vasanta Navarathri, **Vol. 3**, 385
Vasanta-Parameshvari Temple Jatra, **Vol. 2**, 438
Vasantha Uthsavam, **Vol. 3**, 279
Vasantotsavam Festival, **Vol. 3**, 384
Vasuki Fairs, **Vol. 4**, 307
Vat Savitri Purnima Festival, **Vol. 1**, 107-08, **Vol. 5**, 222
Vat Savitri Vrata, **Vol. 5**, 374
Vate Festival, **Vol. 6**, 428
Vautha Fair, **Vol. 5**, 223-26
Vayanakavu Utsavam, **Vol. 3**, 245
Vayunathaseva Festival, **Vol. 2**, 438
Vedakkekara Madappalli Kavu Utsavam, **Vol. 3**, 241
Vedanta Desikar Jayanthi, **Vol. 3**, 389
Vedavyasa Jatra, **Vol. 6**, 158
Veera Shaiva Matha Festival, **Vol. 2**, 442
Veera Shaiva Sharana Dohara Kakkayya Jatra, **Vol. 2**, 443
Veerabhadra Jatra, **Vol. 2**, 439, 440, 441
Veerabhadra Temple Car Festival, **Vol. 2**, 441
Veerabhadra Virupaksha Jatra, **Vol. 2**, 441
Veerabhadraswamy Agnigunda Mahothsavam, **Vol. 2**, 196
Veerabhadraswamy Festival, **Vol. 2**, 197
Veerabhadraswamy Kalyanothsavam, **Vol. 2**, 197
Veerabhadreshvara Fair, **Vol. 2**, 442
Veerabhadreshvara Jatra, **Vol. 2**, 442
Veeramma Perantalu Tirunala, **Vol. 2**, 198
Vehicle Festival, **Vol. 3**, 279
Vela, **Vol. 3**, 249
Velip Community, **Vol. 5**, 70
Vengamamba, Tirunala, **Vol. 2**, 199
Venkataramana Car Festival, **Vol. 2**, 443
Venkataramana Devara Jatra, **Vol. 2**, 443
Venkataramana Jatra, **Vol. 2**, 444, 445
Venkataramana Temple Festival, **Vol. 2**, 445
Venkataramana Temple Laksha Deepotsava, **Vol. 2**, 446
Venkataramanaswami Car Festival, **Vol. 2**, 446
Venkataramanaswami Temple Jatra, **Vol. 2**, 446
Venkateshwara Car Festival, **Vol. 2**, 447
Venkateshwara Jatra, **Vol. 2**, 447
Venkateswaraswamy Festival, **Vol. 2**, 199, 201
Vennimala Eravipurath Perumal Devasmom Utsavam, **Vol. 3**, 246
Venugopalaswamy Brahmothsavam, **Vol. 2**, 202
Venugopolaswamy Temple Jatra, **Vol. 2**, 447
Vettakkorumakan Pattu, **Vol. 3**, 246-50
Vijai Dashmi / Vijaya Desami / Vijayadashmi, **Vol. 3**, 142, **Vol. 4**, 262, **Vol. 5**, 375-76, *See also* Dussehra
Vijayanagar Kingdom, **Vol. 2**, 3
Vijayeswara Temple, **Vol. 2**, 27
Vikhukephm Festival, **Vol. 6**, 428
Vinayaka Chathurthi, **Vol. 3**, 385
Vindeshwari Devi Fair, **Vol.4**, 526
Vindhyachal Devi Fair, **Vol. 4**, 526
Viraja Temple Festival, **Vol. 6**, 159-62
Virgin Mary's Day, **Vol. 3**, 186
Viroba Fair, **Vol. 5**, 376
Virudhunagar Cattle Fair, **Vol. 3**, 384
Virupakshaswamy Jatra, **Vol. 2**, 448
Vishnu *avatars* and Manifestations, **Vol. 3**, 293
Vishnu Prayag, **Vol. 4**, 534
Vishnu, **Vol. 3**, 248
Vishwator Fair, **Vol. 4**, 263
Visuva Samkranti, **Vol. 6**, 127
Visweswaraswamy Temple Kalyanothsavam, **Vol. 2**, 202
Vithoba Fair, **Vol. 5**, 377-81
Vithoba Jatra, **Vol. 2**, 448
Vivah Panchmi Fair, **Vol. 6**, 36
Vrichika Ravi, **Vol. 3**, 386
Vyas Sarobara Mela, **Vol. 6**, 75
Vyasa Puja Festival, **Vol. 3**, 371

W

Wainyee Festival, **Vol. 6**, 280
Wan Lu Poi Festival, **Vol. 6**, 288

Wangala Festival, **Vol. 6**, 386-87
Warla, **Vol. 5**, 486
Wa-Ok Sitang Festival, **Vol. 6**, 288
Week of witness, **Vol. 1**, 137-38, **Vol. 4**, 92
Weekly Sunday, **Vol. 1**, 137, **Vol. 4**, 91

Y

Yag Samagam, **Vol. 4**, 263
Yagnavalkya Jayanthi, **Vol. 3**, 390
Yagyo Paveet, **Vol. 4**, 218
Yallammadevi Fair, **Vol. 5**, 381
Yamdvitya Fair, **Vol. 4**, 526
Yamunotri, **Vol. 4**, 534
Yaosang (Holi), **Vol. 6**, 362-67
Yarra Festival, **Vol. 6**, 367
Yatra Fair, **Vol. 6**, 47
Yedeshwar Devi Fair, **Vol. 5**, 389
– Shrine, **Vol. 5**, 383
Yellamma Devi Jatra, **Vol. 2**, 448
Yellamma Jatra, **Vol. 2**, 206, 449, 450
Yellamma Temple Jatra, **Vol. 2**, 450
Yellinga Maharaja Math, **Vol. 2**, 451
Yoganarasimhaswamy Jatra, **Vol. 2**, 451
Yom Kippur, **Vol. 1**, 147, **Vol. 4**, 101
Youth Sunday, **Vol. 1**, 137, **Vol. 4**, 92
Yungnas, **Vol. 4**, 263

Z

Zahiruddin Shah Urs, **Vol. 2**, 451
Zarthost-no-Diso, **Vol. 1**, 145, **Vol. 4**, 96
Ziarat-Budaun, **Vol. 4**, 527
Zikkar, **Vol. 3**, 256
Zinda Shah Madar Urs, **Vol. 2**, 451
Zinshok, **Vol. 4**, 221
Zoroastrian Festivals, **Vol. 1**, 139-45